Ali Riaz is Professor and Chair of the Department of Politics and Government at Illinois State University, USA. He has previously taught at Dhaka University, Bangladesh, the University of Lincoln, UK and Claflin University, South Carolina, USA, and worked as a broadcast journalist at the BBC World Service in London, England. He holds a PhD in Political Science from the University of Hawai'i.

BANGLADESH

A Political History since Independence

ALI RIAZ

I.B.TAURIS

LONDON · NEW YORK

Published in 2016 by
I.B.Tauris & Co. Ltd
London • New York
www.ibtauris.com

International Library of Twentieth Century History 72

ISBN: 978 1 78076 741 3
eISBN: 978 1 78672 075 7
ePDF: 978 1 78673 075 6

A full CIP record for this book is available from the British Library
A full CIP record is available from the Library of Congress

Library of Congress Catalog Card Number: available

Typeset in Garamond Three by OKS Prepress Services, Chennai, India
Printed and bound by CPI Group (UK) Ltd, Croydon, CR0 4YY

Dedicated to those Bangladeshis who are fighting to uphold the founding principles of the state: human dignity, equality, and social justice.

CONTENTS

List of Tables   viii
List of Figures and Maps   ix
List of Appendices   x
Abbreviations and Acronyms   xi
Acknowledgements   xv

Introduction   1

1. Making of the Nation, Making of the State:
    Nationalism and Mobilization   9
2. The Rise and the Demise of Authoritarianism (1972–90)   38
3. From Optimism to Retreat of Democracy (1991–2015)   76
4. Democracy: Aspiration, Nature and Quality   109
5. Political Parties, Elections and Party System   151
6. Quest for a National Identity: Multiple Contestations   185
7. Unpacking the Paradox of Development   219

Conclusion   Looking Back, Looking Ahead   231

Appendices   237
Notes   250
Bibliography   289
Index   305

LIST OF TABLES

Table 4.1. Attributes of Democracy: Bangladesh and South Asia   117

Table 4.2. Nature and Duration of the Different Forms
of Government   128

Table 4.3. National Elections – Fairness Index   130

Table 4.4. Subcategories of Political Rights and Civil Liberties   138

Table 5.1. Ideological Orientations of Political Parties   153

Table 5.2. Taxonomy of Islamist Political Parties   167

LIST OF FIGURES AND MAPS

Figures

Figure 5.1. Bangladesh Awami League Fragmentation   170

Figure 5.2. Bangladesh Nationalist Party Fragmentation   171

Maps

Map 1. Political Map of South Asia   xvii

Map 2. Administrative Map of Bangladesh   xviii

LIST OF APPENDICES

Appendix 1. Bangladesh Voter Turnout: 1973–2008   237

Appendix 2. Election Results: 1973   238

Appendix 3. Elections Results: 1979–88   239

Appendix 4. Elections Results: 1991–2001   241

Appendix 5. Election Results: 2008   243

Appendix 6. Election Results: 2014   244

Appendix 7. Islamists' Share of Votes: 1991–2001   245

Appendix 8. Islamists' Share of Popular Votes: 2008   246

Appendix 9. Jatiya Party Fragmentation   247

Appendix 10. Jatiya Samajtantrik Dal (JSD) Fragmentation   248

Appendix 11. Communist Party of Bangladesh (CPB)
Fragmentation   249

ABBREVIATIONS AND ACRONYMS

ABT	Ansarullah Bangla Team
ACC	Anti-Corruption Commission
AI	Amnesty International
AL	Awami League
APAC	All-Party Action Committee
APO	Acting President's Order
ASK	Ain o Salish Kendra
BDR	Bangladesh Rifles
BEC	Bangladesh Election Commission
BGB	Border Guard Bangladesh
BJL	Bangladesh Jatiya League
BJP	Bharatiya Janata Party
BKSAL	Bangladesh Krishak Sramik Awami League
BLF	Bangladesh Liberation Force, later renamed Mujib Bahini
BLP	Bangladesh Labour Party
BNP	Bangladesh Nationalist Party
BPL	Bangladesh People's League
BRAC	Bangladesh Rural Advancement Committee
BSCF	Bangladesh Scheduled Caste Federation
BSS	Biplobi Sainik Sangstha
BTI	Bertelsmann Transformation Index
BYS	Bangladesh Youth Survey

C-in-C	Commander-in-Chief
CAS	Country Assistance Strategy
CDL	Community Development Library
CEC	Chief Election Commissioner
CGS	Chief of General Staff
CID	Combined Index of Democracy
CMLA	Chief Martial Law Administrator
COP	Combined Opposition Parties
COP (Pakistan)	Combined Opposition Party
CPB	Communist Party of Bangladesh
CPI	Corruption Perceptions Index
CPR	Contraceptive Prevalence Rate
CSP	Civil Service of Pakistan
CTG	Caretaker Government
DAC	Democratic Action Committee
DDP	Director Defense Purchase
DFI	Defense Forces Intelligence
DGFI	Directorate General of Forces Intelligence
DL	Democratic League
EBR	East Bengal Regiment
EC	Election Commission
EC	Executive Committee
EIU	Economist Intelligence Unit
EPCS	East Pakistan Civil Service
EPIDC	East Pakistan Industrial Development Corporation
EPR	East Pakistan Rifles
EU	European Union
FDI	Foreign Direct Investment
FPTP	First-past-the-post system
FSSAP	Female Secondary School Assistance Program
GAL	Gano Azadi League
GBS 2010	Governance Barometer Survey Bangladesh 2010
GD	Gonotontri Dal
GDP	Gross Domestic Product
GMP	Ganatantric Majdoor Party
GNP	Gross National Product
GOJ	Gono Oikya Jote
GP	Gonotontri Party

HI	Hefazat-e-Islam
HRW	Human Rights Watch
HUJIB	Harkat-ul-Jihad al-Islami Bangladesh
ICT	International Crimeş Tribunal
IDA	International Development Association
IDBP	Industrial Development Bank of Pakistan
IDL	Islamic Democratic League
IFES	International Foundation for Election Systems
IOJ	Islami Oikya Jote
IRI	International Republican Institute
JAGPA	Jatiya Ganatantrik Party
JAL	Japan Air Line
JF	Jatiyatabadi Front
JI	Jamaat-e-Islami
JJP	Jatiya Janata Party
JMB	Jamaat-ul-Mujahideen Bangladesh
JMJB	Jagrata Muslim Janata Bangladesh
JP	Jatiya Party
JRB	Jatiya Rakkhi Bahini
JSD	Jatiyo Samajtantrik Dal
KPP	Krishak Praja Party
KSP	Krishak Sramik Party
LDCs	Least Developed Countries
LDP	Liberal Democratic Party
MDG	Millennium Development Goals
MENA	Middle East and North Africa
ML	Muslim League
MP	Member of Parliament
NAP	National Awami Party
NC	National Committee
NDF	National Democratic Front
NDI	National Democratic Institute
NER	Net Enrolment Rate
NF	Nationalist Front
NGOs	Non-Government Organizations
NHRC	National Human Rights Council
NI	Nizam-e-Islam Party
NUF	National United Front

ODA	Official Development Assistance
OIC	Organization of Islamic Cooperation
PDM	Pakistan Democratic Movement
PICIC	Pakistan Industrial Credit and Investment Corporation
PM	Prime Minister
PML	Pakistan Muslim League
PPP	Pakistan People's Party
PPR	Political Parties Regulations
PRIO	Peace Research Institute Oslo
PRCGS	Pew Research Center Global Survey
RAB	Rapid Action Battalion
RAW	Research and Analysis Wing
RMG	Ready-Made Garments
RTI	Right to Information
SCF	Sector Commanders Forum
SDSA	State of Democracy in South Asia
SKSD	Sramik Krishak Samajbadi Dal
SP	Sarbahara Party
TFR	Total Fertility Rate
TI	Transparency International
TIB	Transparency International Bangladesh
UN	United Nations
UNDP	United Nations Development Program
UNROB	United Nations Relief Organization in Bangladesh
UPP	United People's Party
USAID	United States Agency for International Development
USSD	United States' State Department
VI	Vanhanen Index
WB	World Bank
WP	Workers Party
WSAG	Washington Special Actions Group
WVS	World Values Survey

ACKNOWLEDGEMENTS

I am deeply indebted to a number of individuals and institutions for their support throughout the period of writing this book. Thanks to Woodrow Wilson International Center for Scholars at Washington DC for hosting me in the autumn of 2013 as a Public Policy Scholar, which allowed me to concentrate on the book. I am particularly thankful to Bob Hathaway, then Director of the Asia Program of the Center, and Ambassador William B. Milam, a Senior Public Policy Scholar at the Center, for their encouragement and support. The principal librarian of the Center, Janet Spikes, was immensely helpful in gathering various resources. Heartfelt appreciations to Janet and her colleagues.

My engagement with the Wilson Center would not have been possible without the sabbatical leave from Illinois State University. I thank the University for approving the leave; Professor Greg Simpson, Dean of the College of Arts and Sciences, for supporting the request; and my colleague Professor T. Y. Wang for shouldering the department chair's responsibility during my absence.

Alex Beck of the University of Wisconsin-Madison, and Breanna Sherlock and Fahmida Zaman of Illinois State University worked as my assistants at the Wilson Center and ISU, respectively. I truly appreciate their help. They had to bear with my requests to get things done at short notice. Thanks to Mohammad Sajjadur Rahman, a friend. Although he was extremely busy with his teaching assignments at Chittagong University, Bangladesh at the time of writing the book, he enthusiastically read drafts of several chapters. His comments and suggestions helped to clarify some ideas. His constant enquiry was a source of inspiration. A very special thanks to my friend Dr Marina Carter. Despite her busy schedule and own research, she read the manuscript more than once, and made valuable suggestions. Comments of two anonymous reviewers were extremely helpful in redrafting some parts of the book, exploring some new resources, and bring clarity to some issues discussed in the book. I cannot thank them enough for their attention to the details, incisive comments and helpful suggestions.

It is customary to thank the commissioning editor for the book, but my gratitude to Azmina Siddique at I.B.Tauris is far from routine. I truly owe a great deal of debt to her. Azmina Siddique's interest, enthusiasm and encouragement began at the very early stage of the project and continued throughout, despite my tardiness. Her enquiry of the progress of the manuscript was, in fact, more of a motivation than a reminder of the deadlines. This book would not have been completed if she was not so persistent from our very first email communication. Thanks also to Dan Shutt, production editor at I.B.Tauris, for his help and patience through the last stage of the book.

Finally, I thank my wife Shagufta Jabeen and our daughter Ila Sruti for being patient and supportive.

Acknowledging the help of all these people and institutions does not imply that they are in any way responsible for the content of this book; errors and omissions are mine and mine alone.

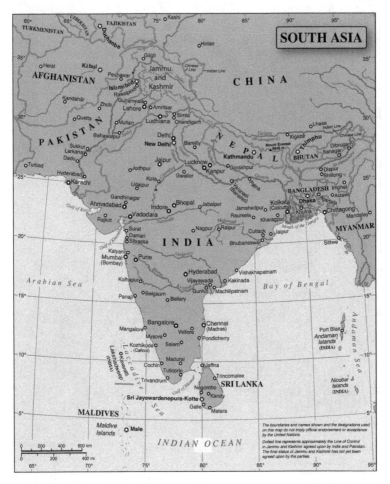

Map 1 Political Map of South Asia. Source: Map No. 4140 Rev. 4, United Nations, December 2011. Available at: http://www.un.org/Depts/ Cartographic/map/profile/Souteast-Asia.pdf

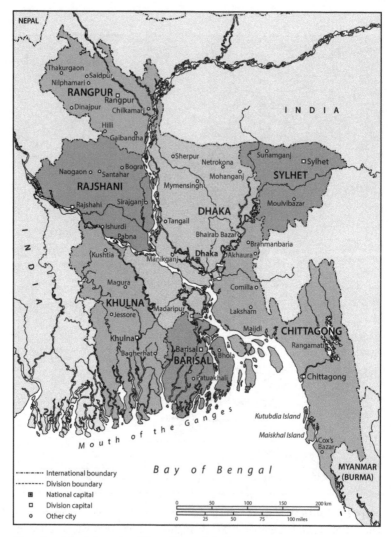

NEPAL

INDIA

Thakurgaon
Saidpur
Nilphamari
RANGPUR
Rangpur
Dinajpur
Chilkamari

Hilli
Gaibandha

Sherpur
Netrokona
Sunamganj
Sylhet
Mohanganj
SYLHET

Naogaon
Santahar
Bogra
Mymensingh

RAJSHANI
Sirajganj
Moulvibazar

Rajshahi
DHAKA

Ishurdi
Tangail

Pabna
Bhairab Bazar
Brahmanbaria

Kushtia
Manikganj
Dhaka
Akhaura

Magura
Comilla

KHULNA
Madaripur
Laksham

Jessore

Majdi
CHITTAGONG

Khulna
Rangamati

Bagherhat
Barisal
Bhola

BARISAL
Chittagong

Patuakhali

Mouth of the Ganges
Kutubdia Island

Maiskhal Island
Cox's Bazar

Bay of Bengal
MYANMAR (BURMA)

---·-·-·-· International boundary
- - - - - - - Division boundary
▣ National capital
□ Division capital
○ Other city

0   50   100   150   200 km
0   25   50   75   100 miles

Map 2   Administrative Map of Bangladesh

INTRODUCTION

Bangladesh, the eighth most populous country in the world, is also the youngest nation-state in South Asia. It emerged as an independent country in 1971 after experiencing a genocide that cost millions of lives.[1] The nine-month long war devastated the country, thousands of women were raped, and millions were either internally displaced or took refuge in neighboring India. The birth of the country was soaked in blood and, to borrow the characterization of the events of 1971 by a US diplomat, was 'cruel'.[2] Indeed, it was the 'transformation of [a] seemingly forlorn Dream into a bright shining Reality'.[3] But since then the country has seen tumultuous times; hopes and despair mark the past 45 years of its existence. To say that the political history of Bangladesh is mercurial and eventful is an understatement. Over the past four decades the country has been ruled by military and pseudo-military regimes for more than 15 years. Governance by the elected civilian political regimes has been marred by corruption and instability. Democracy has remained only an aspiration, although the people of the country have shed blood many times since independence hoping each time that a change will arrive. Bangladesh has undergone a variety of systems of governance – from a Westminster-style parliamentary government to one-party presidential rule to a multi-party presidential system. The country returned to the parliamentary system of government in 1991 after waltzing with the presidential system for the preceding 15 years. Bangladesh also invented a unique system of its own called the Caretaker Government (CTG) and then discarded it in a contentious manner. These systems of governance have made indelible marks on the political landscape of the country, shaped the contours of Bangladeshi politics in many ways, and influenced the political culture.

The proclamation of independence in 1971 pledged a country which will deliver equality, human dignity and justice, but soon these foundations were forgotten by the political class. The country, in its first constitution, promised to practise democracy at all levels of governance, which was first flouted by the framers of the constitution and then by the military regimes. The record of elected civilian regimes since 1991 is no different in this regard. The constitution promised to circumvent the explosive mix of religion and politics, a central feature of Pakistani politics from which the independent nation was expected to make a break. Hope of a secular state soon faded as Islam emerged as a political ideology, found a place in the constitution, was named state religion, and assumed a perceptible role in the public sphere. Those who were in power and those who wanted to be in power, including parties which once championed the separation between state and religion, adopted the religious rhetoric. Islamist militancy found its way to the country which used to take pride in its syncretic tradition. The volatile political environment, violence, and breakdown of governing institutions have frequently drawn the attention of the world's media to Bangladesh.

But the country has also produced a development success story: 'Bangladesh is 1 of only 18 developing countries with an annual growth rate that has never fallen below 2 per cent.'[4] Notwithstanding the economic growth, annually over 6 per cent in the past decade and the reduction in the incidence of poverty from an estimated 70 per cent in 1971[5] to 31.5 per cent in 2010[6], the country 'has achieved rapid and spectacular improvements in many social development indicators during the last two decades or so'.[7] The decline achieved in maternal mortality (from 574 per 100,000 in 1990, to 194 per 100,000 in 2010, to 170 per 100,000 in 2014),[8] in infant mortality (from 100 per thousand in 1990 to 38 per thousand in 2012),[9] children under five years mortality rates (from 144 per thousand in 1990 to 31 per thousand in 2015),[10] and in increasing equitable access in education (Net Enrolment Rate: 98.7 per cent; girls: 99.4 per cent, boys: 97.2 per cent), are noteworthy. According to the 2013 Human Development Report of the UNDP, between 1980 and 2012, Bangladesh's life expectancy at birth increased 14 years, a notable achievement indeed. These seemingly conflicting trends have given rise to phrases such as the 'Bangladesh Paradox', 'Bangladesh Conundrum' and 'Development Puzzle'.

The 'Paradox', however, is not only that the country achieved a remarkable economic progress despite the absence of good governance and political stability, but also that a huge incongruity exists between the popular aspiration and the reality, between hope and despair which arrived in quick succession. This book is an effort to look at both paradoxes. My objective is to offer a critical examination of Bangladeshi politics since 1971. Unlike previous political histories of Bangladesh, this book examines the political processes, institutions and actors in an attempt to unravel the problems and prospects of this young nation. Conventional accounts of the country's politics tend to take regime histories not only as their point of departure but also as the central focus. Taking a break from this mold this book examines the political challenges and outcomes of the past 45 years. The regime-centric history or chronological narratives tend to overlook long-term changes and assign particular regimes pivotal roles, at times unduly. This book is instead organized around three crucial themes of Bangladeshi politics: democracy, identity, and development, and scrutinizes the achievements and failures from a long-term perspective. Understanding the institutional, behavioral and cultural changes that have shaped the polity over the past 45 years is the focus of this endeavour.

However, a critical thematic presentation of the political history requires that we familiarize ourselves with the events that led to the founding of Bangladesh in 1971 and the defining features of governance since then. Three chapters of this book provide the narrative of the political events between the 1960s and 2015. They serve as background to the succeeding thematic chapters but also demonstrate how one can break away from the conventional periodization of Bangladeshi political history. Chapter 1 looks at the formation of the Bengali nation as a political entity in the twentieth century as opposed to Bengali as an ethnic identity, which existed for centuries. The chapter also examines the processes of the formation of the Bangladeshi state, which on the one hand built upon the Pakistani state edifice, while growing out of unresolved contestations among various political forces on the other. Construction of a nation is a conscious process, and a political project of a social force; but it does not follow a linear path and instead twists and turns to shape the contours of the imagined community. Neither the forces which engage in this project nor those who oppose the construction determine the pathway. A nation, in the words of Ernest Renan,

> is a soul, a spiritual principle. Two things, which in truth are but one, constitute this soul or spiritual principle. One lies in the past, one in the present. One is the possession in common of a rich legacy of memories; the other is present-day consent, the desire to live together, the will to perpetuate the value of the heritage that one has received in an undivided form.[11]

The process of nation-making is, therefore, rediscovering past events and contextualizing them within the present. Cultural artefacts, rituals, history and prospect coalesce in the new configuration of nation. The making of the Bengali nation follows the same trajectory. Highlighting the political processes between 1947 and 1971, when the land was the eastern wing of Pakistan, I demonstrate that although various imaginations of nationhood were engaged in contestation, some of which underscored religion, some the social classes, the 'Bengali' nationhood which subsumed religion and class issues became dominant.

The construction of the new nation was followed by the formation of the state, which is discussed in the second part of the chapter. The election of 1970 not only provided constitutional legitimacy to the Bengali leadership but also made them the representative of the majority of the Pakistani citizens. The unwillingness of the Pakistani military bureaucratic elite to accept the results of the elections paved the way for the emergence of a new state. Beginning with the non-cooperation movement in early March, a parallel state emerged in the eastern part of Pakistan. But it was the genocide unleashed on the night of 25 March 1971 which put the last nail on the coffin of a United Pakistan: by the next morning Pakistan, as it was created in 1947, was dead. Various trends and tendencies appear within the resistance group and the Bangladesh government-in-exile. But the leadership withstood the adverse environment and led the nation to a victory, becoming the first secessionist movement to earn the distinction since World War II. These tendencies, in some way, became the precursor of the political forces after 1971.

The political events since 1972 can be divided into four epochs according to governance characteristics: the era of the rise and demise of authoritarianism (1972–90); the era of hope and despair (1991–2006);

the era of democracy deficit (2007–08); and the era of polarization and democracy's retreat (2009–15). How each era has fared compared to the others and how the elusive quest for democracy remains the central question of Bangladeshi politics are the foci of Chapters 2 and 3. Discussions on the first era presented in Chapter 2 highlight both the populist authoritarian phase (1972–75) and military dictatorship (1975–90). The chapter is not intended to obliterate the difference between civilian and military rule but underscores that in both instances the country witnessed and experienced consolidation of power in one office. Notwithstanding the differences between the leaderships in the first two decades, the governance reflected a sharp departure from the pronounced objectives of the nation and the state principles articulated in the constitution. Volatility, assassinations, coups and counters coups represent one part of the story while the transformation of Bangladesh – from a state which promised egalitarianism to a capitalist state, from an aspiring secular state to a state with 'state religion' – tells the other side. Inclusive democracy remained a dream. The emergence and legitimation of religio-political forces is as important a development as the cooptation of their agenda by the secularists for reasons of expediency. Chapter 2 chronicles these events, trends and actors. In one way, violence marks the entire period and wrong turns at critical junctures seem to be the fate of the nation. But a popular uprising in 1990 brings an end to this phase of the nation's journey as hope triumphs over pessimism.

The period between the optimistic new beginning in 1991 and the flawed election in 2014, the third and fourth decades of the country, represents not only another phase in the tumultuous journey of Bangladeshi politics but also a period of lost opportunity. Save the interregnum of two years, 2007–08, popularly elected regimes ruled the country; yet the period lacks a consensus among the political class and the citizens at large as to how democracy can be institutionalized. Power alternated between two parties, but a small party emerged as the kingmaker. The arrival of clandestine religion-driven militancy and the continuation of mainstream acrimonious politics, both made their presence felt. Chapter 3 shows how the nation became polarized and began to take a course away from inclusive democracy.

Three issues can be gleaned from the historical account; that the Bangladeshi state was founded on the basis of democratic aspiration which was articulated in the constitution as one of the four state principles; that democracy has remained under stress and took a reverse course in many instances; and that even after renewed democratization efforts since 1991 faced serious challenges. Chapter 4 addresses the issue of democracy and democratization in Bangladesh since its founding in 1971. Indications abound as to the desire of Bangladeshis to establish a democratic system of governance. But it is important to ask what Bangladeshis consider democracy, what characteristics do they associate with the term 'democracy' and how governance fared vis-à-vis these expectations. Democracy is not conceptualized in similar manner universally, and perceptions and expectations do not remain static among citizens of any country. They shift based on a variety of factors, time being one of them, the political situation being the other. Therefore, one must listen to the popular voice over time and under different circumstances. In view of these factors, 13 surveys conducted between 1996 and 2012 were consulted for understanding the popular perceptions and attributes attached to democracy; extent of the support; attitudes towards politics, elections and parties; and popular expectations of leadership. These surveys demonstrate the wide and unwavering support for democracy, but also show there is no consensus as to what Bangladeshis view as the central tenets of democracy and/or democratic governance. However, protecting individuals' rights and freedoms and ensuring equality of all citizens remained the fundamental reasons they support democracy. These surveys also show that Bangladeshis identify elections as a central element of democracy. Interestingly, surveys, particularly a 2004–05 survey, revealed that the Bangladeshi population has a proclivity towards 'strong leaders without democratic restraints'. One can easily identify a paradox here: on the one hand the centrality of elections and a high degree of participation, while on the other hand the acceptability of strong leadership without restraints.

However, democracy is not only about aspirations and elections; it is also about governance. Ten elections were held in four decades, between 1973 and 2014. What kind of democracy, in terms of nature and quality, has these elections and governance produced in Bangladesh? The second part of the chapter explores the answer to this question. Our assessment of the nature and quality of democracy concludes that the country has displayed the symptoms of a 'hybrid regime', a regime 'characterized by a mixture of institutional features which are typical of a democracy with other institutions typical of an autocracy'.[12] Six indicators in regard to the nature of democracy – competitive elections, corruption, democratic quality (checks and balances), press freedom, civil liberties, and the rule of law – were considered in assessing the nature of democracy. The only positive indicator, until the end of 2013, was holding successive free and fair elections, but the 2014 election marks a serious departure from this tradition and rings an alarm bell.

Political parties are important elements of a political system; they are essential to a democratic system. This makes it imperative that we take a closer look at the party system in Bangladesh. It became more important because various surveys revealed that Bangladeshi citizens do not have a positive view about political parties nor are they satisfied with the party processes. This can be traced to various factors such as the absence of intra-party democracy and 'dynastic' succession of party leadership, to name a few. However, despite such displeasure citizens have shaped a *de facto* two-party system through elections since 1991. Chapter 5 documents the salient features of the party system and the changes it has undergone since independence, particularly since 1976. Concomitant to the hybrid regime, there have been attempts to create a dominant party system; to date, all of these efforts have failed. But, I also argue that the system reached a crossroads, thanks to the polarization in the past decade and the 2014 election. These changes in the Bangladeshi party system include the shift of the political landscape rightward and the creation of space for conservative rightwing parties to emerge and influence the political discourse and agenda. Two conflicting trends have also emerged: fragmentation of parties and forging alliances with other parties. All but two major parties have experienced fragmentation, yet appeal of the major parties and their leadership has not weakened. The inclination for building alliances neither indicates a growing importance of smaller parties, nor an increasing ideological affinity among parties; instead the tendency is driven by expediency and to dissuade parties to rally around the rival.

Chapter 6 deals with the issue of national identity which has bedeviled the country almost since its founding. The dominant narrative suggests that there is a clear binary opposition between the secular identity and the Muslim identity. It is often argued that the founding of Bangladesh was a rejection of a religiously informed national identity. But the Bangladeshi population has long embraced multiple identities and religiosity should not be viewed as antagonistic to secularism. The support for the founding of Pakistan in 1947 by East Bengal Muslims does not constitute an unambiguous assertion of Muslim identity akin to north Indian Muslims; in a similar vein, the salience of Bengali identity in critical junctures of history does not necessarily mean a specific understanding of secularism was embraced uncritically. The salience of Muslim identity in post-1975 Bangladesh is a result of, on the one hand an imposition from above through state patronage and changes in the global arena, while on the other hand, reassertion of an identity from below. The debate over identity, I argue, is not a simple contestation between secularism and Muslim identity; instead multiple contestations are present within the debate. Variations within Islamic ideas and constructions of Muslimness are one part of it. The other part is the variations within the proponents of 'secularism'.

Despite contestations over identity, poor governance, repeated retreat from the path of democracy, and natural disasters, the country has made remarkable economic progress, especially since 1991. The economic growth is matched by development in social indicators. I have referred to some of these accomplishments at the beginning of this introduction, commonly described as the 'Bangladesh paradox.' They warrant an explanation; specifically we need to understand what prompted these successes and who should be credited for these achievements. In Chapter 7, we delve into the causes of and conditions for these anomalous successes. Two significant aspects are highlighted: regime changes have had little effect on macro-economic policies since 1991 and political commitment to social development remained consistent across regimes; and the poorer productive sections of the society – farmers and workers, particularly women – are the foundation of the economic success. Positive social developments are the result of concerted efforts of public sector and non-governmental organizations. That being said, we must be cognizant of the fact that as the nation achieved the economic growth income inequality had increased and that those who serve as the backbone of these achievements receive far less than their fair shares.

A question Bangladeshis and observers of Bangladeshi politics have asked many times in the past four decades is what does the future hold for the nation? The recurrence of this question suggests that the nation is not yet on a stable course. One can extrapolate from the past and paint a pessimistic picture in response to this question, but no nation's journey is ever linear. The concluding chapter identifies the challenges the nation and its citizens face and discusses what needs to be done to move the nation forward.

CHAPTER 1

MAKING OF THE NATION, MAKING OF THE STATE: NATIONALISM AND MOBILIZATION

It was a winter Thursday morning in Dhaka, a besieged city. The morning of 16 December 1971 was tense, uncertain and frightening. Would the city become the last battle ground? Would blood flow through the city streets? Would millions, unable to flee, become casualties in the ensuing battles? It was not a question as to who would lose the battle, for it was a foregone conclusion, but how long would it take to defeat the occupiers and at what cost? Almost nine months had elapsed since the genocide was started by the Pakistani army against unarmed Bengalis in this city on 26 March, a guerilla war having been waged since then by freedom fighters throughout the country, and 13 days earlier India had joined the war. Cities throughout the country had fallen, one after another in the days leading up to 16 December, according to international media and the clandestine radio station of the freedom fighters. Despite Pakistani propaganda of an imminent victory on both the Western and the Eastern fronts, none of the residents of Dhaka believed that the occupation could last much longer. After relentless attacks, the Indian air campaign was halted during the fifteenth morning: a sign of optimism that the occupiers were tamed and a cause of anguish that a ground offensive was imminent. An offer to surrender had been made to Pakistani generals in Dhaka on 14 December by the Indian command, according to the media. Before the midday of Thursday, rumours began to spread that the surrender was in the making. Although a curfew was in force, some residents ventured into the city streets in the morning – in some areas no Pakistani soldiers to be found, at others people were shot at. By noon, the streets were filling up with pedestrians; no private cars were seen but already Indian army vehicles had been spotted close to the Dhaka Cantonment, a few helicopters marked with Indian air force insignia were seen flying over the city, and Indian radio announced that the Pakistani forces had agreed to surrender. People began to converge at the Race Course, the smell of victory was in the air. A small makeshift 'stage' – that is a small table with two chairs, was assembled by the Indian army officers. Hundreds of Pakistani soldiers in their vehicles reached the Race Course, stood in columns, guarded by members of the Indian Army. The Commander-in-Chief of the Eastern Command of Indian Forces Lieutenant General Jagjit Singh Aurora arrived. Soon after came a jeep with Lieutenant General Amir Abdullah Khan Niazi, Commander of the Eastern Command of the Pakistan Army. A short typed document called the 'Instrument of Surrender,' which had been agreed upon by the Indian and the Pakistani military commanders about two and a half hours before at the Pakistan Army's Eastern GHQ, which stipulated that Pakistani forces would surrender to the General Officer Commanding-in-Chief of the Indian and Bangladesh forces, was placed on the table before them. General Niazi signed the document, followed by General Aurora. It was 5:01 pm. The crowd burst into thunderous cheers, 'Joy Bangla.' At the very place where Sheikh Mujibur Rahman had called for a non-cooperation movement and declared the struggle for independence of the Bengalis, a new nation-state, Bangladesh, a nation-state of the Bengali nation, was born.

Nations are not natural entities, they are constructed; they are 'imagined communities' as Benedict Anderson has convincingly argued.[1] Bengali nationhood is no exception. The emergence of Bangladesh in 1971 as a nation-state of the ethnic Bengali community in the eastern part of Bengal cannot be understood without examining how the 'Bengali nation' was imagined and constructed, at what juncture of history was the construction made and by whom. The making of the Bengali nation and the utilization of Bengali nationalism as a tool of mobilization influenced the subsequent political developments of the country. Discussion of the making of a nation begs the question whether a nation is a political entity or a cultural entity. Bengal as a land and Bengali as an ethnic group, with all their cultural distinctiveness, have existed for centuries. It can be said with some degree of certainty that although Bengali as a cultural entity has been around for quite some time, ethnic Bengalis did not become a 'nation' and utilize ethnic identity and 'nationhood' as their primary marker of political identity until the twentieth century.

Making of the Nation

The debate over whether a nation is a political entity or a cultural entity is yet to be resolved. Ethnicity is a cultural marker; nation is a marker of political identity. Often they merge in the making of a national identity. Those who argue that nation is a political entity, for example Anderson, who insists 'it is an imagined political community', stress that nationalism provides legitimation to the state apparatuses, therefore within this frame of reference nations are intrinsically the political expression of a community. Those who insist on the cultural dimension of nationalism, for example Smith,[2] highlight the solidarity of a community based on emotional attachments; therefore in their view nations are primarily a cultural construct. The difference is rooted in the primacy of culture or politics in the making of the nation. The epistemological root of this dichotomy can be traced back to Emmanuel Kant and Johann Gottfried von Herder,[3] but the dichotomy remains strong in discussion as to how nations have emerged. The historical narratives of the emergence of nations in the West, particularly in Europe, are of little help in identifying the process outside Europe, particularly in postcolonial societies.

The argument that Western education in the colonies played a part in creating cultural consciousness towards imagining nationhood is well known and is a recurrent theme in both colonial and postcolonial historiographies;[4] but we are also aware that in non-Western contexts, contesting imaginations of nation emerged. If one imagination of nation emerged as a result of colonial education and as a mirror image of colonial discourse, what Partha Chatterjee[5] described as 'derivative discourse', other imaginations have appeared in opposition to Western education and as counter-images.[6] In both instances, education remained a cultural artefact and a part of a wide variety of other cultural endeavours for increasing awareness about the distinctiveness of the colonized, and to create a collective consciousness. Creating a collectiveness is the primary act towards constructing a nation. Mirolav Hroch[7] insists on both 'objective relationship' and 'subjective reflection in collective consciousness' as crucial to identification as a nation. Hroch goes on to say that there are three keys to creating a nation: a 'memory' of a common past, treated as a 'destiny' of the group; a density of linguistic or cultural ties enabling a higher degree of social communication within the group or beyond it; and a conception of the equality of all members of the group organized as a civil society.

Although the idioms, icons, and symbols of Bengali nationalist ideology began to occupy relatively more space in the political discourse in the then-East Pakistan and the idea of a 'Bengali nation' was being talked about as a 'fact of life' from the mid-1960s, the cultural consciousness or 'a narrative of nation' (to borrow from Homi Bhaba[8]) was in the making at various stages over a long period of time. This was created by insisting on two aspects: the memory (i.e. the past), and linguistic and cultural ties. The linguistic and cultural ties among the community as opposed to the newly founded Pakistan came to the fore when the Pakistani government declined to recognize Bengali as a state language. Instead Pakistani leaders opted for Urdu as the *lingua franca* as early as 1948. Culture and cultural consciousness is a necessary, but not sufficient, element to create a nation. These are not divorced from the material dimensions of politics and economics. In the case of the emergence of Bengali nationhood both these dimensions had to come together to form the nation.

The Bengali identity of the population was not new, nor was the idea of a nationalist ideology. In the early nineteenth century, the middle class, educated, urban population of Calcutta adopted an ideological position in order to seek their 'legitimate share' from the colonial state. The political objective of the so-called 'Bengal Renaissance' of the nineteenth century, led and eulogized by the *bhadrolok* (gentlemen) middle class, was to achieve greater participation in the colonial administration. While this strand of nationalism sought to collaborate with the colonial state, yet create a sub-hegemonic structure to subsume other subordinate classes, the subordinate classes created their own brand of nationalist ideology which altogether rejected colonial domination and resisted the colonial state and its functionaries on many occasions.

The *bhadrolok* strand of nationalism, until recently considered to be the only nationalist movement by the elite historians, had a number of limitations in terms of the social origin and the space within which it operated. First, it was confined to the educated middle classes. Secondly, it was a Hindu middle class phenomenon; the Muslim middle classes were yet to be incorporated into the power bloc that performed the role of functionaries of the colonial state. Thirdly, the entire movement was limited spatially within urban Calcutta. Although there were some variations within the *bhadrolok* class, overall they shared common characteristics. Broomfield wrote that 'education is the hallmark of *Bhadrolok* status – both as defining and excluding factor.'[9] The genesis of the class is intrinsically linked to the educational policy of the British colonial administration as laid out in the oft-quoted lines in the 'Minute in Indian Education' of 1835 by Thomas Babington Macaulay:

> We must at present do our best to form a class who may be interpreters between us and the millions whom we govern; a class of persons, Indian in blood and colour, but English in taste, in opinions, in morals, and in intellect. To that class we may leave it to refine the vernacular dialects of the country, to enrich those dialects with terms of science borrowed from the Western nomenclature, and to render them by degrees fit vehicles for conveying knowledge to the great mass of the population.[10]

Broomfield adds that the class became distinguishable by 'many aspects of behavior – the deportment, their style of speech, their occupations, and their associations – and quite as fundamentally, by their cultural and sense of social propriety'.[11]

Joya Chatterji, in her seminal work on the partition of Bengal, writes, 'The Bengali bhadralok were essentially products of the system of property relations created by the Permanent Settlement. They were typically a rentier class who enjoyed intermediary tenurial rights to rent from the land [...] The bhadralok gentleman was the antithesis of the horny-handed son of the soil.'[12] As for the religious nature of the renaissance, Chatterji writes, 'notwithstanding the fact it was led by the avowedly 'modern', progressive and anglicised, *bhadrolok* nationalism drew inspiration, to quite a remarkable extent, from Hindu 'revivalist' ideologies. Contrary to this elite imagination of the nation existed a subordinate class's strand of nationalism, reflected in the peasant uprisings of Bengal, such as the Indigo Cultivators Strike in 1860, and the Peasant Movement in Pabna in 1872–3, to name but two. This strand was militant and deeply rooted in the class struggle of the subordinate classes. Given the social structure of Eastern Bengal, subordinate class's nationalism was relatively more powerful than the elite strand of nationalism. None of these imaginations, however, found a common geographical space or imagined geography.

Although the imagination of a nation based on ethnicity was not on the horizon, religion-based solidarity had already found a home in various parts of East Bengal. The Islamic revivalist Faraizi movement and Tariqah-i-Muhammadiya offered one variation of the imagination. The Faraizi movement, founded by Hazi Shariatullah (1781–1840), spread through a large part of eastern Bengal in the early part of nineteenth century. After Shariatullah's death, his son Dudu Miyan (1819–62) succeeded to the leadership. The Tariqah-i-Muhammadiya, which originated in northern India, reached Bengal during the 1820s and 1830s and was led by a peasant leader, Sayyid Nisar Ali, alias Titu Mir (discussed in detail in Chapter 6). Neither of these movements was nationalist in the typical sense of the term, but both in some ways provided a point of solidarity, based on religion and imagined a nation that would strive for political rights/justice.

The partition of Bengal in 1905, which was annulled after six years in the face of intense opposition from the population of West Bengal, provided the missing element of nationhood (that is, the geographical space) on the one hand, while it revealed a cleavage within the ethnic Bengali community. This cleavage is described along religious lines – Hindu-majority West Bengal versus Muslim-majority East Bengal, as well as along class lines – representatives of the land-owning class versus the peasants. Neither of them exclusively explains the reactions – resistance to, and support for, partition; instead a combination needs to be considered. But the deep division within the community limited the imagination on the one hand, and opened up the possibility of a different imagination on the other. What is worth noting is that since then political expressions of Bengal were different from other parts of India, and there was also a difference between eastern and western parts of Bengal. The rise of the Swaraj Party under the leadership of C. R. Das in the 1920s, and the Krishak Praja Party under the leadership of A. K. Fazlul Huq in the 1930s are constant reminders of this difference. The imagination of a Bengali nation and a state based on ethnicity resurfaced in April 1947 as a last-ditch effort to avoid the partition of Bengal. The effort was short-lived but the significance was not minor in any way; a link between the nation and the state was, for the first time, established.

After the partition of 1947, the Bengali nationalist ideology, which prompted the united Bengal as an independent nation for obvious reasons, lost ground, while within the subaltern class militant nationalist ideology prevailed in a dormant form. Given the setback of the Communist Party in East Pakistan, the militant nationalist movement of the subaltern classes could not be transformed into a radical resistance against the newly emergent Pakistani state. But sporadic resistance in different parts of East Pakistan continued in the early phase of the Pakistan-era. A severe food crisis in the early 1950s and reduction in jute prices, matched with the exploitation of *jotedars*, gave impetus to the subaltern classes to confront the state. It was in this context that the language movement of 1952 erupted. Although the question of language was of little significance for the illiterate subaltern classes, they joined the urban middle classes to pressure the colonial state. This was again possible because the ruling political party (i.e. Muslim League) emerged from within the landed class in Bangladesh. As such, the resistance against Muslim League rule and alien colonial rule were one and the same to the poor peasants of East Bengal. This led to the historic defeat of the Muslim League in the 1954 Provincial Legislative Assembly against the United Front, the coalition of four parties – the Awami League, the Krishak Praja Party, the Ganatantri Dal (Democratic Party) and Nizam-e-Islam Party led by A. K. Fazlul Huq, Huseyn Shaheed Suhrawardy and Maulana Bhashani.

By the time of the promulgation of the first martial law in Pakistan by General Ayub Khan in 1958, Pakistan had not only experienced abundant political instability, a few governments in quick succession since 1954 and a short-lived constitution, but had also seen Islam elevated to the pedestal of 'national identity' by the ruling regimes primarily to contend with the assertion of regional and linguistic ethnic identities by Bengalis, Sindhis, Pathans, and Baluchs. What should have been an open discourse on national identity, and an effort to accommodate the regionally differentiated, economically disparate, and culturally different nations was wrecked by the Punjabi-dominated state machinery's insistence that 'Islam' was the *raison d'être* of Pakistan. It was the Muslim minority in Bengal who had voted for Pakistan, yet their patriotism was questioned almost every day, and their discourses of difference were perceived as a lack of loyalty to a national identity. It was increasingly evident to the Bengali population that their political disenfranchisement was an integral feature of the emerging Pakistani polity. The Muslim League no longer represented the Bengalis. The emergence of the Awami Muslim League in 1948 under the leadership of Huseyn Shaheed Suhrawardy, its division leading to the founding of the National Awami Party in 1957 under the leadership of Maulana Bhashani, and the Ganatantri Dal led by Haji Danesh founded in 1952 made it abundantly clear that new parties had emerged to represent the population of the eastern part of Pakistan, and their priorities were different from the pan-Pakistani imagination of nation and polity.

The fanfare associated with the celebration of the Ayub regime's decade in power in 1968, styled as the 'Decade of Development', could not mask the fact that the Bengali community saw their experience from a different perspective. A tightly controlled system of representation invented by the military regime, named 'Basic Democracy', was ineffective from the day of its inception as it was neither representative nor democratic. The economic disparity between the two wings of Pakistan, the rejection of the regional autonomy issue by Pakistani ruling elites in the 1956 constitution, and the short stint of the AL in central government in 1956 provided enough motivation to the Bengali political forces to emphasize the demand for equity in a forceful manner. The demand that brought disparate parties to form the United Front in 1954 was reshaped as the 'Six Point Demand' in 1966 by the AL, led by Sheikh Mujibur Rahman (Mujib).

The Six Point Demand may be summarized as follows:

1. A Federation of Pakistan based on the Lahore Resolution of 1940, with a parliamentary form of government based on the supremacy of a directly elected legislature and representation on the basis of population.
2. The federal government to be responsible only for defence and foreign affairs.
3. A federal reserve system designed to prevent the flight of capital from one region to the other.

4. Taxation to be the responsibility of each federating unit, with necessary provisions for funding the federal government.
5. Each unit to retain its own foreign exchange earnings as well as the power to negotiate foreign trade and aid.
6. Each unit to maintain its own paramilitary forces.

The extent of the disparity became public knowledge as more and more information became available in the late 1960s and in 1970, thanks to a new generation of Bengali economists. This is akin to what Miroslav Hroch described as the first phase of the construction of a national identity where activists strive to lay the foundation for a national identity. An official report of the panel of economists published in 1970 by the Government of Pakistan vividly documented this disparity; East Pakistan received less than half of the revenue and development expenditure West Pakistan received between FY1950/51 and FY1969/70.[13] Almost 32 years later a Pakistani journalist recalled:

> In the tumultuous March of 1970 the Planning Commission convened an advisory panel of economists from East and West Pakistan to provide input to the outline of the Fourth Five-Year Plan. The panel consisted of 12 economists, six from each wing, and held six meetings in three different cities. The panel could not come to an agreement regarding important questions of growing regional disparities in Pakistan, and as a result split into two different groups. The economists from East Pakistan went off in a group led by Mazharul Haq who was the chairman of the panel, while their West Pakistani colleagues worked separately to produce their own report. As a result, two separate reports were submitted to the government from the same panel.[14]

Information regarding economic disparity revealed the material ground of the nationhood: the sense of deprivation was not an abstract perception but a real political–economic concern. The monopolistic grip of the West Pakistani elites over the civil and military bureaucracy was evident. As of 1968, East Pakistan's representation in the civil service was only 36 per cent. In the central services, the share of East Pakistan was about 27 per cent in 1970; at the higher levels of administration it was even less: 13 per cent; Only 3 per cent of grade I officers in the Cabinet Division were Bengali. In 1969, the Planning Ministry had the highest share of Bengalis: 28 per cent. In 1956, in the Army, 14 out of 908 officers, in the Navy 7 out of 600 officers, and in the Air Force 40 out of 680, came from East Pakistan.[15] In mid-1955, East Pakistan made up only 1.5 per cent of army officers, while the corresponding percentage for the Navy and Air Force was 1.1 and 9.3 respectively.[16] In 1964, the last year of the data available in this format, the share of East Pakistanis in the officer ranks of defence forces was 5 per cent in the Army, 10 per cent in the Navy, and 16 per cent in the Air Force. It was in this context of economic deprivation, political exclusion and neglect by the central government during the war between Pakistan and India in 1965 that the 'Six Point Demand' was formulated.[17] The intellectual basis of the Six Point Programme was the theory of 'two economies' propounded by Bengali economists. The origin of the 'two economics thesis' can be traced back to the works of a group of economists in mid-1950s. Nurul Islam, who became the Deputy Head of the Bangladesh Planning Commission in 1972, and was a junior member of the group recalls:

The idea that Pakistan consisted of not one but two economies was advanced for the first time in 1956 as the basis for the formulation of development plans for Pakistan at the Special Conference of Economists of East Pakistan on the draft first Five Year Plan of Pakistan (1956–1960). This conference was held at Dhaka at the end of August 1956. The main idea of the concept was elaborated in the Report of the Special Conference of Economists of East Pakistan on the Draft Five Year Plan which was submitted to the Pakistan Planning Commission on September 1, 1956. The following quotations from the report are self-explanatory: 'For purposes of development planning, particularly for the creation of employment opportunities, Pakistan should be conceived of as consisting of two economic units.' 'The problem of planning in Pakistan is best approached by considering the basic characteristics of the two wings, particularly the heavy pressure of population in East Pakistan, the comparative lack of employment opportunities and the high degree of immobility of labour between the two wings.' 'The primary requisite of planning in our opinion is a complete zonal breakdown of statistics, namely national income, balance of payments and financial resources – internal and external.' This was prepared and signed by ten economists and approved by the conference.[18]

The idea and the imagination of a nation must have a cultural element to it; politics alone cannot create an imagined community. While political marginalization and economic deprivation affected the Bengalis, it was the sense of an attack on the cultural distinctiveness of the Bengalis that increasingly alienated them from the idea of the Pakistani nation. The most significant issue in this regard was the treatment of Rabindranath Tagore (1861–1941) the only Bengali Nobel laureate until that time. First, the government attempted to prevent the celebration of his birth centenary, which was being commemorated worldwide and then, the state-controlled radio station excluded Tagore songs from being broadcast in 1965 during the war between Pakistan and India. The final blow came in June 1967, when the minister for broadcasting informed the national parliament that the state-controlled electronic media had been directed to stop broadcasting any Tagore song that was opposed to the ideals of Pakistan and to gradually decrease broadcasting other Tagore songs as well.[19] Perhaps no other cultural issue had made such a big impact on the Bengali middle class psyche since the language movement in 1952. The attempt to introduce the Arabic script in 1950 and to ban Tagore's songs in the state-controlled media reflected deliberate attempts of the state to crush the cultural heritage of the Bengali people and, thus, render them subordinate to the alien culture patronized by the state apparatus. It is important to note that these issues were part and parcel of the middle class culture of the Bengali population. By 1969, when a popular uprising engulfed both wings of Pakistan against the military ruler General Ayub Khan and finally toppled him, the Awami League and its charismatic leader Sheikh Mujibur Rahman had become the voice of East Pakistan, a geographical space and the Bengalis, a nation.

What warrants further explanation is how the middle class imagination of a nation was subscribed to by other segments of the society or in other words why the 'nation' rallied around the AL, particularly Sheikh Mujibur Rahman, and what were the defining characteristics of Bengali nationalism. There is no denying that the essence of the Six Point Demand was regional autonomy for the province under federal parliamentary government with total control over revenue earnings and foreign trade by the federating states. It was a charter for the rising Bengali bourgeoisie and the middle class.[20]

Despite internal colonialism and blatant regional disparity, since the mid-1960s a small group of wealthy Bengalis had emerged in East Pakistan. Ahmed and Sobhan record:

> The last two years of united Pakistan witnessed the apotheosis of the Bengali upper bourgeoisie. During the phase, the development allocations to the eastern region accelerated. In 1968–69 the East Wing received a record allocation of development funds of Rs. 2881 million, which was 55.45 per cent of total public sector development of Pakistan. This trend was accompanied by a record net inflow of external resources into the regions of Rs. 1454 million and by accelerated financial allocations to the private sector in East Pakistan through the public financial institutions. Of the loans approved by PICIC [Pakistan Industrial Credit and Investment Corporation] and IDBP [Industrial Development Bank of Pakistan] up to the end of 1971, 46.2 per cent was approved between the period 1969 [and] 71.[21]

According to another account, actual public sector investments in East Pakistan doubled between 1960 and 1965.[22] By the late 1960s, with the help of the East Pakistan Industrial Development Corporation (EPIDC), 36 Bengali-controlled enterprises were created in jute, 25 in textiles, and one in sugar. Additionally, at least 16 large firms were involved in jute exports, 12 in the inland water transport sector; 12 insurance companies and one Bengali-owned bank were also in operation. In the import business, 39 Bengalis were listed among those with import entitlements above Rs. one million. The Six Point Demand represented the articulation of their grievances and was reflective of their aspirations. To the aspirant political leaders of Bangladesh, the post-1948 experience showed how meagre their access was to state power; to merchants it was obvious that non-Bengalis were taking advantage of the opportunities arising from their closer relations with the bureaucracy, while to the urban salaried class it represented clear domination by non-Bengalis. The goal of the middle class and its political representative the AL was to exert tightly controlled and well-orchestrated extra-legal pressure on the colonial state in order to open avenues of negotiations.

The Six Point Demand initially failed to appeal to the population particularly the subordinate classes. It remained silent about the problems of sharecroppers, small peasants, *kulees* working in tea plantations, and industrial workers. Ethnic minorities, such as the tribal population in Chittagong Hill Tracts, Santhals and Garos were not even featured in the demands. However, by the late-1960s, the objective conditions for unrest among the poorer sections, such as decline in real wages of workers and per capita income of peasants, brought them closer to the AL and its Six Point Demand. It is, indeed, true that the convergence was able to take place primarily because there was an absence of class consciousness among the working class and peasantry or, in other words, absence of a process that could transform the 'class-in-itself' to a 'class-for-itself.' But, additionally, three significant factors contributed to the convergence of interests between the middle and working classes, making the AL the representative of demands that cut across class boundaries: the first was the failure of the left forces to present an alternative to the Six Point Programme of the AL; second was the success of the middle class in appropriating and incorporating the concerns of the poor; and third was the Pakistani regime's suppression of the AL and its leaders, particularly Sheikh Mujibur Rahman.

Since the inception of Pakistan, the Communist Party had been officially outlawed, but remained active. However, the communists failed to pursue a consistent line of action. In 1953, the Party was split on the question of whether members should work inside a progressive, lawful, petty-bourgeois party or not. In the mid-1960s, the umbrella organization of the left, the National Awami Party (NAP), also faced a rift as a consequence of the division in the international communist movement. The pro-Peking leftist organization experienced further disintegration when the Ayub regime established good relations with China. Maulana Bhashani, a staunch critic of the military-bureaucratic oligarchy and a supporter of regional autonomy, extended his tacit support to the Ayub regime. The pro-Moscow groups favoured a close relationship with the AL in realizing 'national demands' as they considered the national contradiction to be the prime one. The radical, underground, leftist organizations overemphasized the class aspect of

Pakistani colonial rule and overlooked the national question altogether. These weaknesses together made the leftist organizations a non-viable alternative.

In the face of the gradual rise in support for the Six Point Demand, and the mass upsurge of 1966 in which the working class actively participated, the AL leaders started to highlight the issues of peasants, workers, and the rural population and interpreted the Six Point Demand for regional autonomy as the panacea. Their ability to link the marginalization of poor to the political process rather than the structural elements of the economy was the key to the success of the AL's emergence as the representative of the entire nation.

Through the decade of military rule, particularly in the second half, the Ayub regime was instrumental in creating a small comprador bourgeois class in Bangladesh 'who would have no doubts as to the source of their advancement and would thus promote and fund Ayub's political hegemony in East Pakistan'.[23] But it also employed coercive measures against the AL. Sheikh Mujib was repeatedly incarcerated. The most glaring example of the coercive strategy was the case, *State vs Sheikh Mujibur Rahman and others* (popularly known as the *Agartala Conspiracy Case*), initiated in 1968 against Sheikh Mujib and others for an alleged conspiracy to separate the East Wing by violent means, in collusion with India. Thirty-five individuals, including three high-ranking members of the civil service, one naval officer, a few non-commissioned officers and seamen, were charged. Although Mujib had been in prison for most of the period during which the alleged conspiracy was being hatched and the initial list of accused did not include him, when the trial started it became clear that its primary goal was to undermine Mujib's credibility and demonstrate that the Six Point Programme was merely a façade for a secessionist movement.[24] The machination backfired. The case galvanized East Pakistan. The trial became the target of a mass movement opposing the Ayub regime and demanding autonomy for East Pakistan. This led to an upsurge in the popularity of the AL in general and Sheikh Mujib in particular making him the symbol of resistance to colonial exploitation. The mass upsurge of 1969, though initiated by the leftist student organizations and based upon an 11-point demand – which included calls for the nationalization of banks, insurance companies, and all big business; reduction of the rates of taxes and revenues on peasants; fair wages and bonuses for workers; and quitting various military alliances – eventually led to a movement popularizing the AL. The leadership of the movement rested primarily with the student leaders, but was steered by Maulana Bhashani, who earned the infamous title the 'Prophet of Violence'.[25] The mass upsurge in Bangladesh matched the mass agitation in West Pakistan and gradually turned into a violent anti-systemic upheaval. However, it was contained through removal of the Ayub regime and the promulgation of martial law bringing Yahya Khan to power. The 'conspiracy case' was withdrawn on 22 February 1969 before the downfall of the Ayub regime, and Sheikh Mujibur Rahman was vested with the appellation of 'Bangabandhu' (Friend of Bengal) by the student leaders in a mammoth public gathering in Dhaka.

What were the defining characteristics of the nationalism propounded by the AL? Or, in other words, whose imagination became the hegemonic notion of the Bengali nation? The Bengali nationalism in question emphasized 'Sonar Bangla', a golden Bengal, a pre-colonial retreat of classlessness. As Anthony Smith has reminded us, central to the understanding of nationalism is the role of the past. He goes on to say that for nationalists, 'the role of the past is clear and unproblematic. The nation was always there, indeed it is part of the natural order, even when it was submerged in the hearts of its members. The task of the nationalist is simply to remind his or her compatriots of their glorious past, so that they can recreate and relive those glories.'[26] The term 'people of Bengal' was used as frequently as possible, as if the people of Bangladesh were an undifferentiated mass and all of them would equally benefit from the cancellation of the colonial state. Under its rubric, the proponents, 'sought to forge a unity between the alienated urban elite groups and rural masses'.[27] They transposed class conflict onto the inter-nation level identifying the whole of Bangladesh as 'oppressed' and West Pakistan as an 'oppressor' and 'capitalist;' and, hence, the prime task was to eliminate the colonial presence that caused oppression and underdevelopment.[28] The process of the making of the nation also brought various expectations, ideas and struggles together; they coalesced and created a broad movement which was seen by almost all segments of the Bengali society as their own struggle. In the words of Rehman Sobhan, struggles for democracy, regional autonomy, social justice and secularism coalesced within the broader struggle for self-rule for East Pakistan. (While there is little debate whether the first three were at the heart of the nationalist movement, long after the independence of Bangladesh, in the 2010s, some questioned whether, secularism was a component of the movement.

By 1969, the middle class imagination of the Bengali nation articulated by the AL had become the dominant notion of nation. The Bengali nation as a political entity came into being. What was left was the juridico-legal recognition of the nation and the constitutional legitimacy of its political representatives. That took place in the general election in 1970.

The election of 1970 was the first ever held in Pakistan with universal adult franchise. It was organized by the military regime of Yahya Khan, who usurped state power from Ayub Khan in the wake of the popular movement in 1969 and promised to establish a constitutional government. In the run up to the elections, a natural disaster of epic proportions, a tropical cyclone, devastated the coastal areas of Bangladesh and cost approximately 500,000 lives. Opposition leaders in East Pakistan accused the government of gross negligence and utter indifference and alleged that the military had not acted swiftly in saving lives and in organizing relief operations. This added to growing disgruntlement with the Pakistani ruling elites. The election delivered the AL a landslide victory. It obtained 167 seats out of 169 seats allotted to East Pakistan in the National Assembly, 288 out of 300 seats in the provincial Assembly of East Pakistan, and gained 72.6 per cent of the votes cast. The victory, according to some analysts, was unanticipated even by the AL.[29] Pakistani political elites had expected that the East Pakistani voters would vote for several parties and this would preclude the emergence of a single party with a mandate. But the results provided a clear majority to the AL, which used the Six Point Demand as an election promise/manifesto. According to the international press, 'A new order in Pakistan', emerged. A day after the election, a reporter for the *Guardian* wrote from Karachi:

> Pakistan has the new democratic leader she expected – Sheikh Mujibur Rahman – but also a new political situation beyond any expectation. Sheikh Mujibur's victory is fitting compensation for East Pakistan's horrific cyclone disaster. It focused attention on West Pakistan's neglect for the East, and may well have increased the size of the Sheikh's victory.[30]

Making of the State

The election results posed a challenge to the Pakistani state and an impasse regarding the transfer of power to the elected representatives emerged. The election was projected by the AL as a referendum on its Six Point Programme, thus for the party leaders these demands were inviolable and not on the agenda for discussion. The programme, which essentially called for the weakening of the centralized bureaucracy and removal of the mechanism which allows the bureaucrats to extract the surplus, was unacceptable to the military-bureaucratic oligarchy. This is because without that mechanism, it was impossible to support, 'the coercive and administrative organizations [which] are the basis of the state power'.[31] Under such circumstances, a conflict between the Pakistani state and the elected majority representatives of (East) Pakistan became inevitable. Zulfiqar Ali Bhutto, whose Pakistan People's Party (PPP) secured a victory in the Western wing of Pakistan with 83 seats, was as unwilling to compromise as was Mujibur Rahman. Z. A. Bhutto, a Western-educated lawyer from a privileged family of Sindh who served in the cabinets of both military rulers of Pakistan, was in no mood to be an opposition leader in the parliament. Framing a new constitution and reshaping the nature of the Pakistani state was at stake. Protracted negotiations between the military-bureaucratic oligarchy and the elected representatives of Pakistan ensued. But the negotiations made little headway because of Bhutto's insistence on having an equal say in the framing of the constitution and his argument that the 'majority alone does not count in national politics'.

When the parliament session, scheduled on 3 March 1971, was cancelled by President Yahya Khan two days before the session without any consultation with the majority party or its leader Mujib, ostensibly due to the threat of Bhutto to boycott the session, a spontaneous uprising in East Pakistan started. Within days, the radical faction of the party, particularly the student activists, hoisted what they claimed to be the flag of independent Bangladesh, and read out a manifesto for independence at a public meeting in the presence of Mujib outlining the principles of an independent Bangladesh which included a 'socialist economy and a government of peasants and workers', and 'full-fledged democracy including freedom of individuals, freedom of speech and freedom of the press'. A song written by Rabindranath Tagore was declared to be the national anthem, and Sheikh Mujib was proclaimed as the Commander-in-Chief.

The AL called for a non-cooperation movement and the entire province complied. The radical faction of the party began putting pressure on Mujib to declare the independence of Bangladesh. The radical elements within the party had been clandestinely organized since 1962 as the Bengal Liberation Force. Since then they had gained power within the AL. They were a product of the increasing radicalization of the body politic. The mass upsurges of 1966 and 1969, and the failure of leftist political parties to bring the youth under their umbrella made it possible for the AL to attract these young radicals. Within a brief period, they acquired so much clout that they forced the leadership to incorporate a pledge to establish socialism in the election manifesto of 1970. They played a significant role in the landslide victory of the AL in the elections of 1970 and therefore Mujib to some extent was indebted to them.

In the face of the Pakistani military elite's insistence on a compromise between Bhutto and Mujib before commencing the parliament session, Bhutto's fervent opposition to the issues of immediate withdrawal of martial law and the inclusion of regional autonomy in the new constitution, and the growing demands from the streets to declare independence, Mujib called for continuation of the non-cooperation movement. He, however, repeatedly insisted that he was for a negotiated settlement. This is reflected in his historic speech of 7 March 1971 where, on the one hand, he made the declaration, 'This struggle is for emancipation! This struggle is for independence!', while on the other hand laying out four conditions for negotiations and attending the newly scheduled parliament session on 25 March:[32]

His rousing speech had a double meaning. It evoked two meanings of independence by promoting constitutionalism and a freedom struggle. Despite its ambiguity, however, this landmark speech inspired a popular revolution, whose force and organisation came from outside the halls of constitutional politics and quickly commandeered East Pakistan state institutions, as it generated numerous unambiguous declarations of national sovereignty, composed and endorsed by major public figures.[33]

By the middle of the month, as more clashes between civilians and the Pakistani army were taking place it became evident that the civilian administration loyal to Pakistan had completely collapsed. The Volunteer corps of the AL and other political parties were engaged in maintaining law and order; overall the situation was peaceful but incidents of violence against non-Bengalis were on the rise. The most important element of state formation took place on 11 March: 'Bengali associations of the East Pakistan Civil Service and Civil Service of Pakistan declared loyalty to Sheikh Mujib.'[34] These developments indicate that a parallel administration had emerged; a rudimentary form of the Bangladeshi state was in the making. Mujib and the AL leadership were not yet ready to declare 'independence' or form a 'government' for 'Bangladesh' although many political figures, from both East and West Pakistan, were urging Mujib to do so.

The possibility of separation between the two wings of Pakistan, in fact, began to emerge soon after the election. Bhutto, in a public meeting at Karachi on 20 December 1970, within two weeks of the election, declared that he wanted to be the 'Prime Minister of West Pakistan' and that his party could not wait for five years to be in power. Declassified US documents reveal the US administration's opinion that partition was on the cards. The President's Assistant for National Security Affairs, Henry Kissinger, wrote a note to President Nixon on 22 February opining that if Mujib's pursuit for autonomy was foiled he was likely to declare East Pakistan's independence. A memorandum from Harold Saunders and Samuel Hoskinson of the US National Security Council Staff to Kissinger on 1 March 1971 stated, 'Events in Pakistan today took a major step toward a possible early move by East Pakistan for independence.'[35] Mujib, in his speech at the public gathering on 3 March, told the West Pakistani politicians, particularly Bhutto, 'If you don't want to frame one constitution, let us frame our constitution and you frame your own. Then let us see if we can live together as brothers.' Bhutto, on 14 March at a public rally, echoed a similar sentiment when he called for transfer of power to PPP in West Pakistan and AL in East Pakistan. Bhutto's statement came after his meeting with the president who was on his way to negotiate with the AL leaders in Dhaka. After intense negotiations between 15 and 24 March, the final proposal laid out by the AL leaders, to be approved by Yahya Khan, was almost identical to that of Mujib on 3 March with one significant change: the

AL was proposing 'a confederation' rather than a 'Federation' of Pakistan. Bhutto, who joined the negotiations on 21 March, had objected to the idea of transfer of power to the provinces until broad issues related to the constitution of Pakistan had been thrashed out.

Until the middle of the night of 25 March, Mujib and his team of experts on constitutional and economic affairs were waiting for a call from President Yahya in regard to the proclamation of the withdrawal of martial law;[36] but unknown to them the president had already left Dhaka that evening giving the final approval to execute a military plan to crush the uprising.[37] Throughout the negotiations, a Pakistani military buildup was underway while the AL leaders were hoping that a constitutional solution could be found. The negotiations broke down.

On the night of 25 March the Pakistani military began its crackdown, named 'Operation Searchlight'. Yahya Khan addressed the nation on the following evening describing Sheikh Mujibur Rahman's action as 'an act of treason', and announcing, 'The man and his party are enemies of Pakistan and they want East Pakistan to break away completely from the country.' Khan banned the AL as a political party and praised the army for showing 'tremendous restraint'. But between launching the military operation on the night of 25 March and the presidential speech on the evening a tectonic shift had taken place in the history of the region: the independence of Bangladesh was proclaimed. There are conflicting narratives as to who declared independence, but two points are beyond doubt: that it was 26 March when the declaration was made, and that it was broadcast over a clandestine radio station from the southeastern port city of Chittagong.

The chain of events surrounding the formal declaration of independence has become an issue of contention and division in Bangladeshi politics, particularly since the 1980s. The dominant narrative, backed up by the organizers of the clandestine radio from where the declaration was first made, suggests that Sheikh Mujibur Rahman declared independence in the early hours of 26 March before surrendering to the Pakistani Army while key leaders of the AL fled Dhaka and crossed the border to India. The text of Sheikh Mujib's declaration of independence, is the following: 'This may be my last message, from today Bangladesh is independent. I call upon the people of Bangladesh wherever you might be and with whatever you have, to resist the army of occupation to the last. Your fight must go on until the last soldier of the Pakistan occupation army is expelled from the soil of Bangladesh and final victory is achieved.'[38] According to one account' Mujib communicated the instruction through a wireless communication via the East Pakistan Rifles (EPR) to the entire nation, another claims that it was communicated to an AL leader in Chittagong and a third that special transmission equipment was used from a public park in Dhaka to send the message.[39] The authenticity of the claim that Mujib declared independence has been questioned by his detractors and A. K. Khondker, the Deputy Chief of Staff of the Bangladesh Armed Forces during the liberation war.[40] The principal argument is that the East Pakistan Rifles radio channel through which Mujib was claimed to have sent the message to the port city of Chittagong was already knocked out by the Pakistan Army and that with so many foreign reporters in Dhaka it is preposterous to suggest that Mujib would have resorted to a clandestine channel.

Tajuddin Ahmed and other AL leaders who were with Mujib until 8 pm of that fateful night were not told of the decision. Various accounts suggest that Tajuddin Ahmed brought a draft announcement which Mujib refused to sign or to make an audio recording of his own voice. Two reporters, Simon Dring of the *Daily Telegraph* (London) and Howard Whitten of AAP-Reuters, who were in Dhaka at the time of the crackdown and were expelled by Pakistan along with 33 other reporters after the genocide began on 25 March, reported that a call was made to Sheikh Mujibur Rahman's residence shortly before 1:00 am of 26 March. But no one reported receiving information from Mujib's residence that he had proclaimed independence.[41] Robert Payne's book *Massacre*, which vividly documents the atrocities, states, 'Sheikh Mujib was calmly waiting to be arrested.'[42]

According to a report of Sydney Schanberg based on an exclusive interview with Sheikh Mujib on 16 January 1972, 'at 10:30 PM [25 March] he [Mujib] called a clandestine headquarters in Chittagong, the southeastern port city, and dictated a last message to his people, which was recorded and later broadcast by a secret transmitter.'[43] Newspapers around the world, beginning 27 March 1971, reported that Mujib had declared independence. The *New York Times* published an Associated Press report dateline New Delhi, 27 March, which states 'The Pakistan radio announced today that Sheik Mujibur Rahman, the nationalist leader of East Pakistan, had been arrested only hours after he had proclaimed his region independent and after open rebellion was reported in several cities in the East.[44] An editorial in *The Age* of Melbourne, in the same issue that it published Whitten's report, wrote, 'The Sheik retaliated [the military crackdown and proscription of the AL] by proclaiming, for a clandestine radio, the independence of his besieged province.'[45] The *Los Angeles Times* wrote on 27 March:

> Sheikh Mujibur Rahman declared independence for East Pakistan Friday as the long smoldering feud between the two wings of the Islamic nation flamed into open civil war. A clandestine radio broadcast monitored here from a station identifying itself as 'The Voice of Independent Bangla Desh (Bengali homeland),' said, 'The sheik has declared the 75 million people of East Pakistan as citizens of the sovereign independent Bangla Desh.'[46]

The headline of the report of *The Times* (London) on 27 March which quotes the Press Trust of India (PTI) as the source, read, 'Heavy Fighting as Shaikh Mujibur Declares E Pakistan Independent.'

A declassified US government document is perhaps the most reliable document in support of the narrative that Mujib declared independence on 26 March. The Defense Intelligence Agency's Operational Intelligence Division's Spot Report prepared for the White House Situation Room on 26 March at 2:30 pm Eastern Standard Time (Bangladesh Time 27 March 2:30 am) states, 'Pakistan was thrust into civil war today when Sheikh Mujibur Rahman proclaimed the east-wing of the two-part country to be the "the sovereign independent People's republic of Bangladesh".'[47]

Those who claim that Ziaur Rahman (Zia), a major stationed in Chittagong, declared independence believe he rebelled on the night of 25 March, killed his commanding officer and on 26 March was asked by the organizers of the radio station to make an announcement. In this version Zia, on 26 March, made a declaration in the evening.[48] The 'Official history of the 1971 India–Pakistan War' of the Indian Defense Ministry written in 1992 described this announcement of Zia in following manner:

> The beginning of the history of an independent and sovereign Bangladesh was made when Major Ziaur Rahman, an officer of the

8th Battalion of the EBR [East Bengal Regiment] at Chittagong, on 26 March, shortly after the military crack-down, made an electrifying broadcast on Swadhin Bangla Betar Kendra (Free Bangla radio) announcing the establishment of an independent Bangladesh.[49]

The announcement Zia made was:

> This is Swadhin Bangla Betar Kendro. I, Major Ziaur Rahman, at the direction of Bangabandhu Sheikh Mujibur Rahman, hereby declare that the independent People's Republic of Bangladesh has been established. At his direction, I have taken command as the temporary Head of the Republic. In the name of Sheikh Mujibur Rahman, I call upon all Bengalis to rise against the attack by the West Pakistani Army. We shall fight to the last to free our Motherland. By the grace of Allah, victory is ours. Joy Bangla.

Similarly, Jyoti Sen Gupta in a book published in 1974 insisted that Zia made the declaration. According to him Zia's announcement was 'picked up by a Japanese ship anchored mid-stream in Chittagong harbour. When the news of the declaration was broadcast by Radio Australia, the rest of the world came to know of it.'[50] Memoirs of Pakistani military officials who served in East Pakistan in 1971 also describe the announcement. For example Brigadier Zahir Alam Khan who arrested Sheikh Mujib on the early hours of 26 March writes:

> While having our evening meal we turned on the radio and heard an Indian radio station, probably All India Radio, Calcutta, announce that Sheikh Mujib had safely crossed over to India. We also heard Major Zia ur Rehman, the second in command of 8 East Bengal Regiment, broadcast declaring the independence of Bangladesh and proclaiming himself the commander-in-chief of the Bangladesh army.[51]

In support of this narrative, an array of newspaper reports published during the week in various international newspapers are cited. For example, Howard Whitten's report in the *Sydney Morning Herald* on 29 March refers to the announcement of Ziaur Rahman:

One clandestine broadcast claimed a provisional government had been set up in East Pakistan and had appealed for recognition from other countries. The broadcast, monitored by Indian sources, said a Major Zia Khan had been appointed temporary head of the new Government of Bangladesh (Bengali Nation), 'under the leadership of Sheik Mujibur Rehman.' The radio gave no explanation why neither Major Zia nor the Sheik had been appointed the de facto leader of the new Government.[52]

However, the editorial entitled 'Plunge into Chaos' of the same newspaper informs that after breakdown of the talks Mujib called for independence. The Reuters report from New Delhi filed on 28 March and published in the *Baltimore Sun* on 29 March highlights Zia's announcement (although with the inaccurate name: Zia Khan).

It is well to bear in mind that the following day, Ziaur Rahman made a new plea 'on behalf of the supreme leader Bangobandhu Sheikh Mujibur Rahman' identifying him as the provisional Commander-in-Chief of Bangladeshi forces, announced that a 'sovereign legal government has been framed under Sheikh Mujibur Rahman', and called upon 'all democratic nations of the world' to recognize the Bangladesh government. This was recognized by the government in exile as the first announcement of the formation of the Bangladesh government. Tajuddin Ahmed, the PM of the government in exile, in his first speech to the nation on 10 April 1971, described how various commands of Army put up resistance to the Pakistani forces, and mentions the announcement of Ziaur Rahman. Ahmed says, 'immediately after the primary victory [in Chittagong] Major Ziaur Rahman founded a command center. From here you have heard the first voice of the independent Bangladesh. This is where the first announcement of the formation of the independent Bangladesh Government was made.'[53] The debate as to who proclaimed the independence remains contentious.[54]

Expected or not, by 26 March a new independent state called Bangladesh had been born and a war to provide a geographical space with defined boundaries for the new state had started. On 17 April, in a small mango grove located in Meherpur (later named Mujib Nagar), leaders of the AL read out the formal proclamation of independence (adopted on 10 April) in a ceremony which included the oath of a civilian government with Mujib as the President, Tajuddin Ahmed as the Prime Minister and Colonel M. A. G. Osmani as the Commander-in-Chief. In the absence of Mujib, Nazrul Islam, the Vice President, was designated the Acting President. A few members of the Pakistan Civil Service were also present. The proclamation within the boundaries of Bangladesh, establishing a structure of government, a command structure of the resistance force and the involvement of civilian bureaucrats completed the fundamental elements of the state-making process. Bangladesh was no longer an idea but a state with a juridico-legal entity. The proclamation also laid out the basis of the new state and its fundamental principles. It states in unequivocal terms that independence is being proclaimed 'in order to ensure for the people of Bangladesh equality, human dignity and social justice'.

A state, even in its strongest articulation, is not a monolithic, homogenous entity. Conflicting tendencies try to pull the state in different directions, and constitutive groups tend to engage in contestations to shape the state according to their own ideologies and interests. These contestations are fierce, often violent and occasionally become detrimental to achieving the ultimate goal when a state is in its formative stage, engaged in a war and facing an existential threat, Nationalist movements, which struggled to establish independent countries, have faced internecine squabbles. State formation in Bangladesh was no exception; there were divisions among both political and military leaders on vital issues such as who should be Prime Minister[55] and whether or not the government in exile should respond to the United States' initiative for a solution within the framework of the existing Pakistani state.[56] Military leaders jockeyed for leadership and disagreed on strategies of war.

As the AL, from its inception, had attempted to represent a broad range of classes, cleavages within the organization always existed. Events prior to, and during, the liberation struggle accentuated divisions within the party. In 1971, there were at least three factions within the AL: first, the radical elements; second, the liberals; and third, the conservatives. Leaders of the radical faction came to prominence after 1969 and had spearheaded street agitations from 1 March 1971. They transformed the AL from a constitutional movement for self-rule to a popular uprising for establishment of an independent country. The second strand, comprised of liberal elements, was more pragmatic. The prime minister of the government in exile, Tajuddin Ahmed, belonged to this faction. In spite of pressure from both the radical and the conservative sections, and severe resource constraints, the leaders of the liberal wing of the AL played a prominent role in coordinating the activities of the government in exile. The third faction of the party, the conservatives, strove throughout the war to seize power from the liberals. A number of attempts were made to remove Tajuddin Ahmed from the position of PM. Interestingly, on several occasions this section worked closely with the radicals who also attempted to remove Tajuddin.

Infighting within the AL began as early as April, 1971.[57] Tajuddin Ahmed who crossed the border into India in late March and sought help from the Indian authorities to continue the resistance against Pakistani forces, decided to form the government as a pragmatic step but without any consultations with the AL leadership. Tajuddin's aides insisted that he should shoulder the responsibility of the prime ministership. Tajuddin, with great difficulty, assembled the leaders in Calcutta, the capital of the Indian state of West Bengal on 9 April, held a meeting of the elected representatives next day where the proclamation of independence was adopted and broadcast a speech over a clandestine radio network in which he proclaimed himself prime minister of the government of Bangladesh. Khondoker Mushtaq Ahmed, a senior leader, joined the other AL leaders, but expressed discontent that Tajuddin had become PM. He argued that as the senior member of the team he should have taken the top job. He also expressed his desire to leave the country and go to Mecca for the rest of his life.

With the formal declaration of independence and the formation of a cabinet on 17 April, the conflict subsided but did not end. The dissension resurfaced when the AL members of the National and Provincial Assemblies met in Shiliguri (Agaratala district of India) on 5–6 July 1971. By then Sheikh Moni along with three other youth leaders, Tofail Ahmed, Abdur Razzak, and Serajul Alam Khan, had organized a separate armed group – the 'Bangladesh Liberation Force' (BLF, later renamed Mujib Bahini). Significantly, this force was organized with the active help of an Indian counter-insurgency agency, the Research and Analysis Wing (RAW). An Indian Major General, Uban, was in charge of the training and supply of this group. The structure, leadership, training, and operation patterns of this force were deliberately concealed from the Bangladesh government in exile. The BLF was operating on its own. The Mustaque faction of the party, following an abortive attempt to conduct negotiations with the Pakistani regime, moved to oust Tajuddin Ahmed from power. On 12 September, 40 elected representatives of the Southern administrative zone belonging to the Mustaque and Sheikh Moni groups, met and adopted a resolution calling on the AL high command to force Tajuddin's resignation from both the general secretary position of the party and cabinet membership. In September, another faction led by two prominent AL leaders, Kamruzzaman and Yusuf Ali, attempted to increase their influence over the freedom fighters in the northern part of the country. They even contacted some pro-China, leftist political parties operating out of Calcutta.

The East Bengal Regiment of the Army, the EPR and the Police were the first targets of the military onslaught on the night of 25 March and subsequent days. Most of the members of these forces were either disarmed or killed. The EPR and the Police bore the brunt of the first attack by the Pakistan Army and lost a large number of their members within the first two days.[58] Yet, this numerically insignificant force compared to Pakistani forces of about 30,000 mounted the first resistance against the military operation practically without direction or leadership from the leading political parties. After initial sporadic resistance, military units decided to coordinate their efforts. They met on 4 April at the operational headquarters of the East Bengal Regiment. In their first meeting, strategies were drawn up and a hierarchy of leadership was established.[59] M. A. G. Osmani, a retired colonel of the Pakistani Army, who is credited with founding the East Bengal Regiment (EBR), was chosen to be the Commander-in-Chief, subject to approval by the future Bangladesh government, of what was described as the Mukti Bahini (The Liberation Force). Major Ziaur Rahman who declared himself the provisional C-in-C in his 27 March address expected that this meeting would validate that announcement. But both Major Khaled Musharraf and Major Shafiullah repudiated his action.[60] Osmani was the consensus choice. It provided a temporary relief to a simmering tension among the military leadership.

Personal rivalries resurfaced among the trio – Ziaur Rahman, Khaled Musharraf and Shafiullah – in July 1971. Colonel Osmani decided to raise a brigade comprised of three battalions (1 East Bengal, 3 East Bengal, 8 East Bengal). Major Ziaur Rahman was appointed at the head of the brigade, which was named 'Z' force in his honour. Soon after the decision was taken, Khaled and Shafiullah pressured the central command for two more brigades named in their honour. Despite the lack of trained manpower (especially officers) and ammunition, within two months two further brigades had been raised: 'K' force and 'S' force.[61] A latent tension between political and military leaderships surfaced in the first formal meeting between the military commanders and the government-in-exile on 10–15 July. Ziaur Rahman and seven other commanders proposed to set up a 'war council' led by military officials to coordinate the war. The proposal was opposed by a section of military officials and rejected by the government.[62]

There were differences among the military leadership on how the war should be conducted. Colonel Osmani was initially in favour of raising a regular force and conducting a conventional war. He was never enthusiastic about guerilla warfare. Ziaur Rahman, in contrast, was more interested in dividing the regular army battalions into small companies and conducting commando-style activities along with the guerrillas. Both of them, however, were chiefly concerned with equipping the regular army. Shafiullah and Khaled preferred a coordination of activities between the guerrillas and the conventional forces, with the latter in command. What was common among them was their interest in raising the army to a preeminent position in the war. In October, when the sector commanders met in Calcutta, Lieutenant Colonel Abu Taher and Lieutenant Colonel Ziauddin, both of whom joined the war effort after fleeing Pakistan, raised serious objections to this line of thinking. They suggested that instead of increasing the number of regular forces, they should strengthen the guerrilla brigades involving both the regular army and peasants to fight a long-term war. They strongly opposed the dependence on Indian forces for the supply of arms and ammunition. They recommended that the forces' headquarters be moved to a position inside Bangladesh. Most significant was their plan for the future Bangladesh Army. They maintained that if guerrilla brigades could be raised, they would act as the core of the production-oriented army in independent Bangladesh. Ziaur Rahman also supported this idea.[63]

While different trends and tendencies surfaced within the emergent state, the political leadership remained focused on the objective of winning the war. The process finally saw the light of day on 16 December 1971 when Pakistani forces surrendered to a joint military command of Indian and Bangladesh forces.[64] By then, millions had died,

India had given shelter to ten million refugees, provided all-out support and sanctuary to the Bangladesh forces, and engaged in a 13-day war with Pakistan. US President Richard Nixon had helped the Pakistani government violate the US laws, the US had tried to dissipate the movement in at least three different ways, and two superpowers – the United States and the Soviet Union–came close to a clash in the Bay of Bengal. Both global and regional dynamics changed as the process of the formation and emergence of the Bangladeshi state came to fruition. The imagined community – the Bengali nation – had found a geographical space. The Bangladesh government-in-exile returned to Dhaka on 22 December 1971, Sheikh Mujibur Rahman was released from a Pakistani prison on 8 January 1972 and made a triumphant return to Bangladesh on 10 January 1972 via London.

CHAPTER 2

THE RISE AND THE DEMISE OF AUTHORITARIANISM (1972–90)

Nowadays 6 December is not accorded any particular significance in Bangladeshi media; the year 1990 seems a distant memory and the past seems to be another country. Yet, one can hardly write off the day and its significance. The date had been in the making since 10 October. The opposition parties, who were assembled into three alliances and an Islamist party, were in a deep quandary as to what could they do to unseat the military regime after two failed popular uprisings, in 1983 and 1987. The situation took a dramatic turn on 10 October. The almost routine demonstration programme of the opposition was dealt with heavy handedness by the police on the morning, which soon spread through the capital as street battles between police and activists. Little did the autocratic regime know that it had signed its own death warrant; that tricks which helped it survived previously would not work this time around and that the unfolding events would take the country along a different route to that taken since the founding of the nation. The student leaders emerged as the standard bearers, created their own alliance overlooking their political differences, defied the national leaders, and promised to one of their fallen fellow activists that they would not go home without a victory against the regime. National political leaders joined them. An upheaval had begun. On 27 November, a state of emergency was declared, but only to be defied by people of all walks of life as by then the protest had turned into a mass uprising.

Seven days later, on the night of 4 December, President General Hussain Muhammad Ershad offered his resignation, and after a day of hectic parley among the opposition alliances, Chief Justice of the Supreme Court Shahabuddin Ahmed was chosen by the opposition parties to head a caretaker regime. On 6 December 1990, at 2:48 pm, Chief Justice Ahmed was sworn in as the Vice President, and soon afterwards Ershad handed over his resignation to him. Fifty-six days of street agitation, innumerable deaths, and an autocrat's failure to divide had not only brought about the demise of an autocrat, but had given the nation a new sense of optimism. The country embarked on a journey away from authoritarianism, civil or military.

Populist Authoritarianism (1972–75)

The promise of an inclusive democracy and a just society marked the beginning of the regime of Sheikh Mujibur Rahman (Mujib). Policies such as nationalization and pledges of land reforms were matched with socialist and egalitarian rhetoric, demonstrating the populist agenda of the regime. Populist politics requires a charismatic leader with appeal cutting across class, gender and other social boundaries. Sheikh Mujibur Rahman was an embodiment of the populist leader on many counts including mesmerizing oratory, simple lifestyle, and dedication to the cause.

At the beginning the regime faced three sets of problems: administrative, economic and political. A report of the World Bank prepared in August 1972 summarized these challenges as follows:

> First of all the refugees had to be returned and resettled, with appropriate relief provided them to get them through until the first harvest. Secondly, law and order had to be re-established – the euphoria resulting from the independence was threatening to veer into anarchy especially given the ample supply of weapons left over from the war period. Thirdly, adequate supplies of food had to be obtained and distributed through the damaged transport system, to avert the threat of famine. Fourthly, the political and administrative structure had to be reconstituted and new institutions created to fill the gap left by the former Central

administration. Fifthly, the task of reconstruction had to be commenced and the economy restored to the ante bellum status quo as quickly as possible. Furthermore, these tasks had to be achieved with what was previously a provincial administration with a notably poor record in implementation.[1]

Central to the administrative challenge was not only the weakness of the civilian administration inherited from Pakistani rule but also the factionalism that emerged due to the war. The war of liberation was not initiated to overthrow the colonial state structure or to bring about a radical change in the social order, therefore during and after the war there was no plan or effort to undermine the extant civilian administration. The government-in-exile, in its first proclamation, accepted the continuance of the structures it inherited and at no time attempted to build a parallel administration. Even before the war was over the cabinet took the decision to rely on the 'civil administration' for the restoration of law and order. In a cabinet meeting held on 22 November 1971, the issue of 'civil administration set up in liberated Bangladesh' was discussed. The cabinet was of the opinion that, 'A large purge of the Government employees may create an administrative vacuum', and formed a subcommittee of the secretaries 'to examine the serious facets of the problem of setting up civil administration'.[2] The subcommittee was comprised of the Secretaries of Defence, Home, Cabinet, Finance, and General Administration.[3] Additionally, on 16 December, after the liberation of Bangladesh, a memo from the Establishment Secretary was sent to the deputy commissioners of the different districts to take control of the civilian administration. The memo also stated, 'The magistracy and the police have to be put back in their proper position as the lawful authority for maintenance of law and order.'[4] A number of factors contributed to the government's reliance on the existing civil administration for restoring law and order. First, there was no single command of the freedom fighters that could be mobilized for this purpose, because in addition to those freedom fighters trained by the government in exile, there were a number of groups operating autonomously from within the country. Second, as mentioned earlier, no alternative structure had been put in place to take over. Third, the ruling party was not a monolithic organization, nor was it ready to shoulder total responsibility.

As with the ruling party, rifts beleaguered the bureaucracy.[5] In the early days of independence (i.e., December 1971–December 1972), the higher public service officials could be divided into three categories: (1) officials who went into hiding inside Bangladesh, (2) those who joined the exiled government, and (3) those who were attending to their duties and willingly or unwillingly, cooperating with the military regime.[6] In addition, there was another source of schism: those who had served the central government of Pakistan (i.e., Civil Service of Pakistan CSP) and those who were under the provincial government (i.e., East Pakistan Civil Service EPCS). These groups engaged in a bitter feud regarding their positions in the emerging state apparatus. Factionalism was aggravated by the decision of the government to put all those who had worked in Mujibnagar at the forefront, brushing aside established rules and procedures.

It was not only the civilian administration which was internally fractured; so was the nascent military establishment. The infighting that intermittently surfaced within the military leadership during the war reappeared upon its conclusion. The rapid developments of early December 1971, leading to full-scale war and direct Indian involvement in the liberation of Bangladesh, were so overwhelming that these conflicts within the Bangladesh army could not easily be resolved. The cleavages within the military were along various lines. The primary division was, of course, along the line of involvement in the liberation war. According to Azad, the Bangladesh armed forces were comprised of five types of erstwhile Pakistan Army personnel:

1. those who actively participated in the liberation war by joining the Mukti Bahini officially;
2. those who helped organize the resistance movement in their homes and villages;
3. those who left the Pakistan Army and did not participate further;
4. those who were arrested and remained in Army custody until liberation;
5. those who served the occupation army.[7]

The members of the military were also divided ideologically. The fundamental point of contention was whether or not the military should be reorganized according to the existing colonial structure. While the larger section was in favour of maintaining the status quo, a small segment was pushing for a thorough restructuring and organization of a 'people's army'.

The administrative challenge was accentuated by the lack of physical infrastructure, which also posed a major economic challenge to the government. According to the United Nations estimate the war caused a loss of about $938 million[8] and reconstruction required 15 per cent of the GDP annually for at least three years. Nevertheless, the United Nations Relief Organization in Bangladesh (UNROB) and other affiliated organizations helped the regime deal with the situation. The initial performance of the regime in terms of reconstruction of infrastructure was commendable. The largest sea port of the country (Chittagong) was cleared, all damaged bridges, with the exception of one, were repaired, and industrial production began to make a recovery.

The most daunting challenge of the regime was to deal with the issue of the easy availability of firearms and the large number of people trained to use them. During the nine-month long war, resistance forces evolved spontaneously all over the country. Most of them were neither organized hierarchically nor had any command structure. As a result, no one was sure about the total number of freedom fighters and the quantity of firearms under their control. Furthermore, during the war a number of armed paramilitary forces (e.g., Razakars, totalling about 10,000) were organized by the Pakistani occupation forces. The occupation forces also supplied arms to members of the right-wing political party, Jamaat-e-Islami, which organized at least two politically motivated forces – Al-Shams and Al-Badr. The latter were the most ruthless and killed at least 50 intellectuals in planned attacks during the last three days of the war (i.e., 14–16 December 1971). While hundreds and thousands of people possessed all sorts of firearms – unlisted, unregistered, unknown, and unaccountable – the law enforcement agencies such as the Police and the Bangladesh Rifles were in complete disarray. The situation was complicated because of the government's unwillingness to involve freedom fighters in post-independence reconstruction measures. In the adverse political situation a number of the freedom fighters became involved in antisocial activities. The armed members of underground, leftist political parties, though small in number, also became a threat to the restoration of peace. In the initial stages the government achieved commendable success in establishing control. Although large numbers of firearms remained in the hands of people with contending ideological convictions, or people with no political convictions at all, the government restored control over all parts of the country. The presence of the Indian defence forces – until 17 March 1972 – helped them a great deal, but it was the ruling party and the feeble civil service who ran the day-to-day administration. The government, in the short term, had succeeded in containing any possibility of civil war but the weapons did not vanish. The ceremonial surrender of weapons by the freedom fighters to Sheikh Mujib, held on 30 January 1972, was chiefly of symbolic value.

The economic challenge to the government, as the WB report had underscored, was no less pressing and formidable than the law and order situation. Ten million refugees who fled to neighbouring India began to return after the war was over. The regime was faced with urgent tasks such as providing immediate relief to the returning refugees, reconstructing the economic infrastructure, and ensuring the future development of the country. The massive flow of aid into the country in the early days of independence helped the regime avert an imminent famine and mass starvation, even though the level of consumption went down considerably. The food situation did not improve much in the following year because of a shortage in agricultural production caused by drought. In addition to the massive relief operation carried on by the United Nations Relief Operations in Bangladesh (UNROB) until 31 December 1973, there were a number of countries that came forward to help Bangladesh avert a famine and begin reconstruction. For example, the United States, which had supported and aided the Pakistani regime in 1971, committed $287 million of reconstruction and relief aid in the first year.[9] In the first six months after independence, a total of $612 million was committed to Bangladesh followed by a commitment of another $886 million in 1972–73.[10]

The political problem faced by the regime, which worsened in subsequent years, had its roots in the pre-independence years' factionalism within the party. The unsettled battle between the radicals, liberals and conservatives took a new and more ideological shape that Kamal Hossain, a close confidant of Sheikh Mujibur Rahman and the first Law minister of the country in 1972, acknowledged 42 years later:

The latent tensions in the nationalist movement, which had begun to manifest themselves during the nine months of the liberation war, were reflected in the contending factions and pressure groups that emerged at the end of the liberation war. Thus, there were younger militants ranged against the older moderates, and there were radical students and workers, who felt that a social revolution could be launched immediately, pitted against those who counselled restraint. Among the latter were property owners who wanted to preserve as much of their interests as they could. But there were others, committed to basic social and economic transformation, who also urged caution as they felt that in absence of effective instruments such as political cadres and well-motivated party organization, to embark on a full-scale social revolution, in particular in the countryside, was a prescription for anarchy and chaos.[11]

It was against this background that the new government formulated its policies, took political steps, and shaped the nature of governance. Beyond the political ideology of socialism, that is to confer on the state a central role in economic activities, two factors affected the policies of the regime: economic crisis and political opposition.

The ruling party's proclivity to expand the role of the state and secure a predominant position for the state in the economy came through its decision to pursue the policy of nationalization as early as January 1972. The government's actions toward industrial enterprises, which later served as the genesis of the nationalization program, brought a dramatic change in the political economy of the country. A large number of businesses (including industrial enterprises) belonged to Pakistani entrepreneurs who had left the country, abandoning their properties.[12] The government promulgated a law on 3 January 1972 (*Acting President's Order No. 1*, 1972), enabling it to take control of the properties and organize their management. While the APO 1 of 1972 vested the right of control and management in the government, the Bangladesh Abandoned Property (Control, Management, and Disposal) Order 1972 (i.e., PO 16 of 1972) promulgated on 28 February 1972, transferred the abandoned properties to the government. Simultaneously, the Planning Commission outlined a policy for massive nationalization. In early February, the Commission submitted a paper to the Cabinet on policy options and recommendations for the nationalization of industries (Bangladesh Planning Commission 1972).[13] It was recommended by the Commission that all enterprises in jute, textile, and sugar industries with fixed assets of over Tk. 1.5 million be nationalized. Accordingly, the PM, in a policy statement on 26 March 1972, announced that all large industries and financial institutions with assets over Tk. 1.5 million were henceforth nationalized and would be managed by the state. It was also announced that compensation would be paid for the nationalized enterprises owned by Bangladeshi citizens. This announcement changed the nature of the Bangladesh economy overnight. According to Sobhan and Ahmad, 'On the 27th of March, 1972 Bangladesh was faced with a situation where under law public ownership and control over the economy had increased from 10 per cent of GDP to 16 per cent. In the sphere of industries public ownership of fixed assets increased from 34 per cent to 92 per cent of modern industry and the number of enterprises under public management from 53 to 392.'[14]

There are two lines of explanation as to why the government adopted the policy of nationalization – pragmatist and ideological.[15] According to the former, it was circumstantial necessity that compelled the regime to follow a policy of nationalization. First, the large number of enterprises (including banks and insurance companies) abandoned by Pakistani owners needed to be restored. Second, the entrepreneurial class of Bangladesh was relatively small and ill equipped in both capital and management skills and, hence, could not be entrusted with the responsibility. As such, the government had very little choice but to take control of the abandoned units. Although there is no doubt that this situation played a vital role in the formulation and implementation of nationalization policies, it was not the driving force behind the sweeping measures. If such had been the case, the industrial units owned by Bangladeshi nationals would have been spared. In the jute and textile industries, for example, the proportion of total assets owned by Bangladeshi nationals was 34 and 53 respectively.

The ideological explanation, on the other hand, contends that the AL regime was committed to the cause of socialism, which motivated them to nationalize industries. This explanation is extremely problematic, because the beneficiary of nationalization was mostly the middle class, not the working class. Secondly, the policy of nationalization alone cannot create a socialist society, especially where agriculture constitutes the core of the economy. The nationalization policy of the government left foreign interests completely untouched.[16] It is, however, true that the government adopted a socialist posture and made this the driving force behind nationalization policies. In order to broaden the base of the party and contain the radical elements both within and outside the party, the AL made electoral pledges in 1970 that the banking and insurance sectors would be nationalized. They also promised that if they were voted to power, they would work to eliminate exploitation and establish a just and egalitarian society. Following the liberation struggle, these commitments were interpreted as a promise for a socialist transformation of the society. Nationalization became the 'first step' toward achieving this socialist goal. In addition to the rhetoric of the AL leaders, a number of government documents emphasized similar points.

The justifications for the nationalization of industries in 1972, therefore, were based on circumstantial necessity and the regime's desire to prove its socialist credentials. However, the most significant impact of the policy was that the state was conferred a pre-eminent position in the economic and social arena. In addition to its heightened command over resources, the state became the chief source of patronage. The other feature that stands out is the class character of the beneficiaries of the nationalization policy. It was the interests of the urban intermediate classes connected to the ruling regime that were promoted. One can argue whether the pre-eminence of the state in the economy contributed to the economic crisis, but it is beyond doubt that it did not help the government address the economic crisis that began to unfold.

Despite early successes in averting famine and reconstructing the infrastructure, the economic situation began to take a turn for the worse by the end of 1972. The cost of living jumped from Tk. 208 in January to Tk. 297 in October, nearly 50 per cent. According to one account, the cost of living index of an industrial worker rose to 200.31 from the base of 100 in 1969–70.[17] In the first year of the Five Year Plan, the total output in the industrial sector was 25 per cent lower and in the agricultural sector 12–13 per cent lower than in 1969–70.[18] Food grain production although was below the target (12.5 million tons), surpassed the 1969–70 level (11.8 million tons compared to 11.2 million). The balance of payments surpassed the projected deficit by 23 per cent. The import bill was higher than the projected estimate by Tk. 635 million ($79 million) and export receipts fell short of the projection by Tk.

220 million ($27 million). The inflow of foreign aid fell from the projected amount of Tk. 3700 million to Tk. 3070 million ($463 million to $348 million) resulting in short-term borrowing and drawing from the resources approximately $217 million. Exports of raw jute and jute goods, the principal foreign exchange earning commodities, were far below targeted levels: 2.7 million bales compared to the target of 3.6 million bales.[19] The production level of the nationalized sector was decreasing, causing a huge loss. The total money supply almost doubled (from Tk. 387 crore to 696 crore), causing massive inflation. The prices of essential consumer goods rose by about 40 per cent. Large scale smuggling from Bangladesh to India played a key role in driving up the prices of essential consumer goods. The economic crises faced by the regime were aggravated by global economic events, both manmade and systemic.

Concurrent to the economic crisis was the growing political opposition to the regime and increasing violence. The first challenge came from within the ruling party. The radical wing of the party, which had been at the forefront of the movement prior to the war and wrestled to get an upper hand during the war, confronted the leadership on the issue of socialism. The Awami League declared that the objective of the regime was to establish an exploitation-free, just society and, hence, socialism was being considered as one of the principles to be included in the constitution. It was presented as an element of a new ideology called 'Mujibism', after Mujib. But the AL leadership's concept of socialism was challenged by the radical elements of the party as well as by small leftist parties. The radical fraction of the AL, mostly students and youths, contended that the liberation struggle was an unfinished revolution and called for the establishment of 'scientific socialism'.[20] Disenchanted with Sheikh Mujib and the party, the radical members of the AL left in April 1972. The student leaders initiated the split and their lead was soon followed by the peasants' wing (May 1972) and the workers' wing (June 1972). Finally, these splinter groups launched their own party – the Jatiyo Samajtantrik Dal (JSD, National Socialist Party) in October 1972.

Within a brief period of time, the JSD captured the attention of the public becoming so popular that its leaders were compared with Sheikh Mujib who was still called *Bangabandhu* (the friend of Bengal). Significantly, these leaders took a position that was ideologically opposed to that of the ruling class. They insisted that the socialist transformation of society could be achieved only through a revolution of the proletariat class. Furthermore, they maintained that the (nascent) bourgeoisie of Bangladesh had captured state power and were perpetuating the exploitative social structure; they also maintained that a revolutionary uprising of the proletariat was the only way to make independence meaningful to the oppressed classes. In spite of incoherence and inconsistencies in their ideological positions, they demonstrated that the principal contradiction in independent Bangladesh was between social classes and that one's identity stemmed from one's class affiliation.

Around the same time, another clandestine radical left political group, the Sarbahara Party (SP, Proletariat Party), under the leadership of Siraj Sikdar, gained considerable support in rural areas. The SP, as articulated in their party manifesto, considered the AL regime 'a puppet of Soviet social imperialist and Indian expansionists'. The Sarbahara Party engaged in armed conflict with the police and other paramilitary forces and began to annihilate 'enemies of the revolution' – the rich farmers.

Other leftist forces also began to gain support from the public and by the end of the year a seven-party electoral alliance (All-Party Action Committee, APAC) was formed under the leadership of Moulana Bhashani, a populist octogenarian leader and the President of the National Awami Party, to contest the upcoming parliamentary elections (see details in Chapter 5). On 1 January 1973, two student supporters of the National Awami Party (NAP, led by Muzaffar Ahmed, a pro-Moscow leftist political party and a close ally of the ruling AL) were shot and killed by police during a procession against the Vietnam War and US aggression. Initially, the NAP and the Communist Party of Bangladesh (CPB, the pro-Moscow communist party and close ally of the AL) took a stand against the ruling party and a wave of demonstrations including a spontaneous successful general strike rocked the cities.

On most matters, these political parties and alliances were pursuing different paths. But their rise clearly indicated that the ruling classes' hegemony over the subaltern classes was ruptured. The ruling classes, operating a 'politics of consensus' did not fully dictate or control the political discourse. The politics of 'class conflict' gradually occupied centre stage.[21] Many of those who opposed the independence of Bangladesh joined the newly emerged parties, both legitimate and clandestine. For them creating an ungovernable situation was the primary objective, and to a great extent they succeeded.

Law and order began to deteriorate in an unprecedented manner. According to figures presented by the Home Minister to the parliament on 6 July 1973, in the first 16 months (i.e., January 1972–April 1973) 4,925 persons were killed by miscreants, 2,035 secret killings of a political nature took place, 337 women were kidnapped and 190 were raped. According to a report published in the *Morning News* on 3 August 1973, 23 police stations and outposts had been attacked by 'anti-state elements' between January 1972 and July 1973. The number of attacks on police stations increased substantially over subsequent months. In October 1973 alone, the *Daily Ittefaq* reported that 11 police stations and sub-stations were attacked and looted. The incidence of political murders also increased significantly. The *Daily Ittefaq* reported on 2 March 1973 that 20 AL workers were killed in February. On 5 November 1973, the *Morning News* reported that in the first 20 months after independence more than 6,000 political murders had been committed. The AL claimed that five of its Parliament Members (MPs) and 20,000 supporters were killed by 'extremists'. Sheikh Mujib, in a televised speech to the nation on the eve of the Victory Day of 1974, admitted that four of his MPs and 3,000 AL supporters had been killed.[22] The opposition claimed that 60,000 activists had been murdered in the previous two years. There is no way to evaluate the charges and counter-charges of the AL and the opposition as to who was responsible for the violence. While the government-controlled mass media carried accounts of opposition violence and killings of AL supporters, the only opposition daily and almost all the weeklies were full of reports of violence perpetrated by the government and the members of the ruling party.

One of the major accomplishments of the AL regime in the early days of independence was the framing of a constitution in less than seven months: the constitution was adopted by the Constituent Assembly on 4 November 1972 and came into effect on 16 December 1972. The constitution encapsulated the four fundamental principles of the state: democracy, secularism, nationalism, and socialism. The salient features of the constitution included the introduction of a Westminster-type parliamentary system, providing the Parliament with supreme authority on important issues like declaration of, or participation in, war and imposing and collecting taxes. Additionally, the constitution made provisions which appeared to amount to 'guaranteeing' the fundamental rights of the people and 'ensured' the separation of the judiciary from the executive organ of the state. But it was less democratic than it appeared at first sight; alongside these provisions there remained others that could enable the government to 'legitimately' act to the contrary.[23] Despite some limitations, the constitution provided the legal basis for governance.

Problems such as the failure to deliver economic success, to check the deterioration of law and order, to address rampant corruption, and to deal with the excesses of party members, decreased the popular appeal of the regime within a very short time. In the face of growing economic and political crises, especially the growth of the opposition and the waning of ideological hegemony, the regime drifted toward coercive measures rather than making efforts to co-opt the opposition and combat the underlying reasons for the crises.

The coercive drift of the regime was first reflected in its decision to establish a paramilitary force, called the Jatiya Rakkhi Bahini (JRB, the National Defence Force).[24] There are three explanations for the establishment of the JRB: administrative, political and realistic imperatives. The administrative explanation underscores the lack of a strong law enforcement agency. Immediately after independence, the government began to reorganize law enforcement agencies such as the police, the Bangladesh Rifles, and the army. The regime was well aware of the need for a strong law enforcement agency in a post war situation where firearms were in the hands of many different factions. The political explanation emphasizes that anticipating violent political opposition the regime felt that an organized legitimate force under the control of the party and its leaders would be a better solution. The ground reality made it imperative that a new force incorporating the freedom fighters had to be set up; the third line of argument suggests:

> Initially, it was decided to absorb several thousand young freedom fighters into the BDR [Bangladesh Rifles, the border guards] to add to its strength. It is not widely known that this was prevented by the determined refusal of the BDR to allow those who they

regarded as young boys to be inducted into the BDR, to the extent of threatening to resist such induction by force. To normalise the situation, it required Sheikh Mujib, along with other leaders, to go to the BDR Headquarters, listen to their appeal, and subsequently accept their appeals. This led to the decision to form a separate force called the *Rakkhi Bahini*.[25]

Whatever explanation one subscribes to one cannot escape the fact that questions pertaining to the aim and purpose of the force, as well as control over the JRB, were kept vague leaving ample space for manoeuvering. The Order was devoid of any specifics about the organization, its methods of operation, its powers and authorities, and its accountability as a law enforcement agency. In terms of the objects and purposes of the JRB, Article 8 of the Order stated that it would be employed for the purpose of assisting the civil authority in the maintenance of internal security when required and it would perform such functions as the government would direct. In terms of the rules of its functioning, the Order only stated that the Government would make rules and regulations for functioning, including the conduct of its members and their powers and functions (Article 17). An organized force of 20,000 members equipped with sophisticated weapons was created, but it was not accountable to any specific institution of government. No one can doubt that this ambiguity was the result of a deliberate strategy of the ruling party to accord enormous power to the Rakkhi Bahini and its members.

Reports from different parts of the country revealed the excesses committed by members of the Rakkhi Bahini. They had to deal with 'anti social elements' such as smugglers, black-marketeers, hoarders, and *dacoits* (armed robbers), but the political dissidents became their prime targets. A critic of the JRB described it as 'a storm-trooper, a crack-force for a lightening strike'.[26] The criticisms from various shades of political opinion led to the amendment of the JRB Ordinance.[27] But the amendment legalized all acts committed by the JRB in the past or in the future by including the provision that no suit, prosecution, or other legal proceedings could be brought against any member of the JRB who had acted in good faith (Article 16A). The amendment also provided the JRB with the power and authority to search any place and arrest anyone without warrant (Article 8A). These provisions effectively authorized the JRB to operate beyond the reach of the law. The officers of Rakkhi Bahini admitted in court that the JRB had no rules or procedures or codes of conduct.[28] A JRB officer acknowledged they 'do not have to maintain any paper or document or record of their activities or conduct in the operations they used to undertake. There was no record of any arrest or search, or seizure they made.' In response to a question as to how they worked, a senior deputy leader told the court, 'We work the way we decide.'[29] The numerical strength of the JRB reached 29,000 in subsequent years. A plan to raise the number to about 130,000 by the year 1980 was drawn up by the government.

The first parliamentary elections were held on 7 March 1973. The ruling party secured a landslide victory (292 of 300 seats, 72.4 per cent of votes cast). But the elections were marred by intimidation of political opponents, and abuse of government power to sway the votes in favour of the AL. It was a foregone conclusion even before the election that the ruling party would secure a respectable majority despite growing discontent. The disunity of the opposition as well as the charisma of Mujib worked heavily in favour of the ruling party, but not to the extent represented by the election results. Barua maintains that 'a reasonably free and fair election would have returned to the first Parliament about 50 to 60 opposition members, and these would have included 15 to 20 major opposition party leaders.'[30] One day after the election the president and general secretary of the National Awami Party, Muzaffar Ahmed and Pankaj Bhattacharya, alleged that the government had forcibly defeated opposition candidates. They claimed that if the government had not resorted to rigging the election at least 70 opposition candidates would have won.[31] This statement carries some weight, coming from a party that has maintained an excellent relationship with the AL. The disunity among opposition political parties and their failure to present any pragmatic alternative programme to that of the AL weakened the opposition's appeal to the voters. The ruling party utilized the state-controlled mass media, including radio and television, as a virtual 'party-spokesman'. Interestingly, Sheikh Mujibur Rahman still enjoyed the enormous confidence of the people.

The democratic spirit of the constitution was delivered a serious blow on 22 September 1973, as the ruling party amended the constitution and incorporated provisions relating to preventive detention and proclamation of a state of emergency (Part IXA). One of the significant features of this amendment was that the government could now detain anyone for an initial period of six months in order to prevent that person from engaging in any action, which, in the opinion of the government, constituted a threat to public safety and the sovereignty of the state. With the incorporation of Part IXA in the Constitution, provisions were made that the president could issue a proclamation of emergency, make laws inconsistent with the fundamental rights enshrined in the constitution, and suspend the court's authority to enforce such fundamental rights during the period of emergency. The shift towards authoritarianism was becoming obvious. The constitutional change was preceded by the *Printing Presses and Publication (Registration and Declaration) Ordinance, 1973* (Presidential decree on 28 August and approved by the parliament on 19 September 1973), and followed by the *Special Powers Act 1974* (passed in parliament on 5 February 1974). The former replaced the colonial-era restriction on media imposed by a 1960 law, but only in name. It provided enough power to the government to clamp down on any press or editor, at will.

The latter contained provisions for preventive detention. According to the *Special Powers Act*, a person could be detained if the government was satisfied that it was necessary to do so with a view to preventing him from committing any 'prejudicial act' (section 3). The Act also dealt with sabotage (section 15) and the prohibition of prejudicial acts including the publication of any prejudicial report (section 16). The Act curtailed the freedom of association and authorized the government to impose control over such associations that would 'act in a manner or to be used for the purpose prejudicial to the maintenance of public order'; it also gave the government necessary power to 'direct the association to suspend its activities for such period not exceeding six months' (section 19 and section 20). The Act laid down that the persons engaged in hoarding, black marketing, sabotage, printing, possessing, or distributing any 'prejudicial report' shall be tried by a Special Tribunal created under the Act (sections 26–29). Anyone accused or convicted of an offence punishable under the Act could not be released on bail (section 32). Furthermore, in the original Act, an appeal from the judgment of the Special Tribunal lay with the High Court Division, but, through an amendment on 23 July 1974, the jurisdiction was taken away. The amendment also contained a provision for 'firing squads' for the execution of persons found guilty by the Special Tribunals.

The political and economic situation continued to worsen in mid-1974 as an opposition party, the JSD, adopted a drastic programme of mass upsurge beginning with *gheraos*[32] of several important government offices. On 17 March the programme to *gherao* the home minister's official residence ended in the deaths of six protestors, and arrests of the top-ranking JSD leaders including its president and general secretary. Subsequently an offensive by the ruling party and law enforcing agencies was launched against the JSD workers all over the country. The entire organizational network of the JSD was shattered and they were driven underground. Consequently, the JSD changed its strategy and decided to launch an armed struggle against the regime. They raised their own armed group Gonobahini (People's Force) within a short time.

In the economic arena, GDP registered a growth of 2 per cent while the population grew by nearly 3 per cent resulting in a negative per capita growth rate. The total production of food grains was 12.6 per cent less than the targeted amount and lower than previous year. Production in the jute sector declined by 8 per cent.[33] The balance of payments situation worsened rapidly. The economic crisis reached its apogee in the middle of 1974 when the country faced a devastating flood in July–August, considered to be the worst in the history of the region. The government acknowledged the death of 27,500[34] while researchers have put the number at no less than 100,000.[35] The government's effort to combat starvation by opening a 'gruel kitchen' saved many lives but was inadequate. By the end of the year these kitchens were closed and the food situation improved. While the flood wiped out a considerable quantity of food grains, many have argued that global politics played a part in failing to provide relief to the affected people (see Chapter 7 for details).

In late 1974, the regime officially resorted to emergency rule. The proclamation of the emergency, on 28 December 1974, was both *de facto* and *de jure* recognition that the regime was in crisis and the extant laws were not helping the ruling party address the situation. Within less than a month of the promulgation of emergency rule, the parliament hurriedly passed a constitutional amendment without any discussion or debate that essentially brought an end to parliamentary rule in Bangladesh. *The Constitution (Fourth Amendment) Act (Act No. II of 1975)* passed on 25 January 1975, made sweeping changes. The country entered into a new constitutional arrangement where only one political party could exist and the executive branch with the president at its apex assumed supremacy over the legislative and judicial organs of the state. Additionally, by the amendment itself, Mujib was made president for the next five years and with an opportunity to hold the office for an unlimited number of terms.

Contrary to the earlier constitutional provision that the president would be elected by the parliament, the new system provided that the president would be elected by the people in a direct election (Article 48) and the executive authority of the republic would be vested in him (Article 56). The amendment made it more difficult to impeach the president by increasing the number of members required to sign a notice of motion to initiate impeachment proceedings (a minimum of two-thirds as opposed to the previous one-third) and the number of votes required to pass the resolution (three-fourths as opposed to two-thirds). The 'Council of Ministers' was made responsible to the president, not to the parliament as under the original constitution. The ministers, including the prime minister, were to be appointed by the president and would hold office at his pleasure.

One of the principal features of the original constitution was the sovereignty of parliament, which had supreme power and authority in law-making. Any bill passed by parliament would become law and the president had no power of veto. But under the new system the president could withhold assent to any bill passed by the parliament.

In Part II of the original constitution, where the fundamental principles of state policies were laid down, Article 11 contemplated that people would effectively participate through their elected representatives in the administration at all levels in order to ensure a democratic system. Accordingly, Chapter III of Part IV of the original constitution provided for local government at every administrative unit of the republic composed of elected persons. The fourth amendment omitted the provisions and, thus, made it possible for the president to appoint local governments.

The separation of the judiciary and the executive is considered to be one of the basic conditions, as well as the strength, of the democratic process. The primary function of the judiciary in a democratic society is to oversee the executive branch, strike a balance between the law and its application and administer justice. That is why any democratic constitution strictly prohibits interference by the executive in the functioning of the judiciary. But the fourth amendment severed the very root of the independence of the judiciary and made it subservient to the executive branch. As opposed to the original constitutional provision that 'the Chief Justice of the Supreme Court shall be appointed by the President, and other judges shall be appointed by the President after consultation with the Chief Justice' (Article 95(1)), the new amendment empowered the president to appoint all judges without any consultation with the chief justice. In terms of the tenure of the office of judges, the president assumed total power as opposed to the previous stipulation 'a resolution of Parliament supported by a majority of not less than two-thirds of the total number of members of the Parliament' would be required (Article 96(2)). Under the new condition, the president could remove a judge including the chief justice simply by an order on the grounds of misbehavior or incapacity. The president also assumed the authority to appoint additional judges to the Supreme Court without any consultation with the chief justice.

The power and authority of the Supreme Court was severely curtailed. The authority of the Supreme Court in matters of appointments to, and control and discipline of, subordinate courts was withdrawn and vested in the president (Article 115 and Article 116). The power of the High Court Division in respect of the enforcement of fundamental rights and to issue certain orders and direction was circumscribed.

While the fourth amendment established the supremacy of the executive over the legislative and judicial organs of the state and, thus, left no room for opposition to the concentration of power, it also barred dissidents from entering into the political arena through the introduction of a one-party system (Article 117A (1)).

In pursuance of the new constitutional stipulation, Sheikh Mujib in his farewell speech to the parliament on the day of the passing of the fourth amendment declared the beginning of a 'Second Revolution', followed by the formation of the 'national party', Bangladesh Krishak Sramik Awami League (BKSAL), on 24 February 1975. The organizational structure of the party was announced on 6 June 1975. The government promulgated the *Newspapers (Annulment of Declaration) Ordinance 1975* on 16 June by which it allowed only four daily newspapers to continue publication and banned the rest. *Dainik Bangla, Bangladesh Observer, The Daily Ittefaq* and *Bangladesh Times* were taken under the control and management of the government.

Although a complete agenda for reform was never documented and made public, three speeches made by Mujib shed some light on the principal features of his 'second revolution'. These speeches were delivered on 26 March in a public gathering in Dhaka, on 19 June at the first meeting of the BKSAL central committee, and on 21 July to the newly appointed district governors. These important speeches were unwritten and often lacked consistency. However, a broad outline of the changes Mujib envisaged can be gleaned from them.

The salient features were the formation of compulsory, multipurpose cooperatives in every village; revamping the local-level administration; abolishing the highly powerful secretary position; and establishing tribunals or courts at a thana (i.e., lowest tier of administrative unit) level. According to Mujib, compulsory, multipurpose cooperatives would be formed in all 65,000 villages over the following five years, in phases. Each cooperative would be comprised of 500–1,000 families and would bring together all the able-bodied persons of the villages, whether they were landowners or landless. The ownership of the land would remain with the current owners, but the produce would be divided into three parts: one to the owner, one to the local co-operative members, and the other to the government.

In terms of revamping the local-level administration, the prevalent structures of thana and district administration would be dismantled. The responsibility of the thana and district administrations would be assigned to a thana and district administrative council respectively. In contrast to the prevailing structure, where the civil servants enjoyed the supreme authority, these administrative units would be headed by the chairman and the governor, respectively. They would be appointed by the central government and the only required qualification would be party membership. Thus, anyone, including a government official, could be appointed to that position because government officials were also given the opportunity to be members of the 'national party'. The District Administrative Council was vested with immense authority with regard to planning and implementation of development projects. The district commissioner, the highest-ranking civil administrator, would be the secretary of the Council and work under the direction of the governor. The governor would control all government departments at the district level including the paramilitary forces.[36]

Mujib's speeches repeatedly mentioned abolishing the highly powerful secretary position and the establishment of tribunals or courts at the thana level without any indication of what he was really intending to do. Mujib promised to abolish the secretariat, removing bureaucratic bottlenecks called red-tapism and establishing a people-oriented system. He never mentioned how and when these would be done. The fourth amendment conferred powers on the president to establish a court or tribunals at the thana level and Mujib frequently mentioned that he would exercise this power.

No reference was made as to how the economy would be disciplined, how the ills of corruption and inefficiency in the nationalized sector would be fought, or the proper functioning of the economic system ensured. One further point involving the composition of the new national party should be mentioned here. In spite of his call for national unity, Mujib failed to attract much support from outside his own party. The old allies of the AL, the CPB and NAP (M), enthusiastically joined the bandwagon. But they were not included in the policy-making bodies of the BKSAL. The 15-member Executive Committee, the highest policy-making body of the organization, had no members from outside the former AL. The former AL stalwarts dominated the 115-member Central Committee. Of the 28 members who came from outside the AL, 21 were senior bureaucrats.

Despite some elements of egalitarianism, the programme of the so-called 'second revolution' fell far short of a programme for the socialist transformation of the society as its proponents insisted. Ironically, it was not a radical programme of capitalist development either. Some analysts argue that the government was compelled to implement a programme of radical reform due to 'the awesome constraints which a war-ravaged country and a political scene riddled with diverse and conflicting social groups imposed on Mujib and the Awami League government',[37] while others have argued that the move was designed to establish unbridled control over power of the party and Mujib.

When the era of populist authoritarianism came to an end, the nation paid a high price. On the morning of 15 August 1975, Mujib, 21 members of his extended family (except his two daughters, Sheikh Hasina and Sheikh Rehana, who were on a trip abroad) and his close associates were brutally murdered in a military coup, and a prolonged era of military dominated regimes began in Bangladesh.

Military Dictatorship (1975–90)

During the 15 years of *de facto* military dictatorship, two strong men – Ziaur Rahman (1975–81) and Hossain Muhammad Ershad (1982–90) – dominated the political scene of Bangladesh, but the nature and course of politics under their rule was virtually identical. These regimes faced similar crises, and adopted similar policies to earn legitimacy and sustain themselves in power. While there were attempts to civilianize the regimes, and one brief interregnum (June 1981–March 1982), both regimes were characterized by repression, curtailment of democratic rights, and the manipulation of constitutional processes, and brought religion into the political arena.

The pre-dawn *coup de main* of 15 August 1975 was engineered by a small number of junior officers, numbering about 30. Of them, six majors were in command. According to the available accounts and documents the key planners of the coup were: Syed Farook Rahman, Khondoker Abdur Rashid, Abdul Aziz Pasha, Sharful Islam Dalim, Bazlul Huda, and Shamsul Islam Nur. Captains Khairuzzaman and Abdul Majed and Lieutenants Muslehuddin, Kismet Hashem, and Nazmul Ansar also played prominent roles.[38] Not all coup leaders were in service at the time of the coup. Some of them were retired, some had lost their jobs on charges of corruption, and some had been discharged on disciplinary grounds.[39]

The putsch came as a surprise to senior military officers. But, it had been in the making for quite some time as resentments were rife within the Army or at least within a segment of it. A range of issues had alienated various sections of the Army. These included the treatment of the army as an institution, decrease in resource allocation, personal rivalry, and tensions between those who participated in the independence war and those who were repatriated from Pakistan after 1973. A large section of the army felt that the regime founded the Rakhhi Bahini to weaken the Army and that it had created a parallel organization to the detriment of the institutional interests of the army. The allocation of $28 million for defence in 1973, half that of the previous year, was viewed by some as an outcome of a policy decision rather than a consequence of the resource constraints faced by the government. Some viewed this as an Indian plan to keep the country under its wing. The appointment of Major General Shafiullah as the first Chief of Army Staff

(CAS) was not well received by Ziaur Rahman (the Deputy CAS) or Khaled Mosharraf (the Chief of General Staff). Their long-standing differences contributed to the simmering tension. Added to these was the return of 28,000 military personnel, particularly 1,100 officers from Pakistan in 1973. These members of the army were in what was then West Pakistan at the beginning of the war and became stranded. Most of them were interned in 1971, although a handful of officers worked with the Pakistani Army. Upon return they were absorbed into the Army without any screening. The freedom fighters were apprehensive of these personnel, particularly of the officers, while those who were repatriated found that junior officers had received promotion due to their participation in the independence war.

There were indications that a coup was not entirely an impossible scenario, although the government seems to have not taken them seriously. According to a declassified telegram from the US Embassy in Dhaka to the State Department on 15 May 1974, 'in the past two years [. . .] reports of army dissatisfaction and talk of coups have reached [the] Embassy'.[40] Lieutenant-Colonel Abu Taher mentioned the plot in his resignation letter in September 1972. Taher, a war hero who lost a leg in battle with the Pakistani Army during the war, was initially appointed adjutant general, but was shuffled around to various positions including brigade commander and finally consigned to a desk job. Taher, who insisted on a building the army as a 'People's Army' instead of following a conventional structure, had differences with the higher military echelon and political leadership, which led to his resignation in 22 September 1972. In his resignation letter he mentioned that he had identified a coup plan to remove Mujib from power and reported to the CAS accordingly. His letter to the Prime Minister states:

I came to know that some officers of the army along with a member of the cabinet was [sic] trying to stage a coup d'etat taking the opportunity of the absence of the Prime Minister from the country (The Chief of the Army Staff has appraised the Prime Minister already about the conspiracy). Far from taking any action against the conspirators, the Chief of the Army Staff [Major-General KM Shafiullah] has told me to relinquish the command of 44th brigade and take the responsibility of

D.D.P. [Director Defense Purchase] instead. I feel that the conspiracy is still going on and many others are associated with that.[41]

According to another declassified telegram of the US State Department, Major Rashid and Major Farooq made an unscheduled visit to the Economic and Commercial Section of the US Embassy in Dhaka on 11 July 1973 requesting information on availabilities and prices of weapons including spare parts purportedly on behalf of the Armament's Procurement Committee headed by then DCAS Brigadier Ziaur Rahman. The telegram informs that Major Farooq had visited the embassy in 1972 with similar requests. The unusual nature of the request was noted in the cable, '[It is] somewhat irregular for military officers to appear [at the] embassy without appointment requesting such information.'[42] Major Farook made another approach to the US government in 1974. The earlier mentioned declassified telegram of May 1974 reports that he called in 'unannounced at the home' of US Embassy official William F. Gresham. Farook informed Gresham that the Army was very dissatisfied with the Bangladesh government and that he had come 'at the instance of the highest ranking Bangladesh Army Officer' to ascertain what the attitude of the US government would be toward any takeover of the Bangladesh government. Farook also inquired whether the US government would be able to see to it that there would be no foreign interference following the takeover.[43]

One concrete piece of evidence suggests that Mujib was informed of the likelihood of an imminent coup. The minutes of the US Secretary of State's Staff Meeting of 15 August 1975 recorded the following conversation between Henry Kissinger, North East Asia Under Secretary Atherton, and Bureau of Intelligence Research (INR) representative Hyland:

SECRETARY KISSINGER: Let's talk about Bangladesh.

MR. ATHERTON: Well, it was a remarkably well-planned and executed coup for Bangladesh.

SECRETARY KISSINGER: What does that mean? Is Mujibur alive or dead?

MR. ATHERTON: Mujibur is dead; his immediate clique, which was largely family, nephews, brothers.

SECRETARY KISSINGER: I get good advice from INR.

MR. HYLAND: He wasn't dead when I talked to you.

SECRETARY KISSINGER: Really? Did they kill him after some period?

MR. ATHERTON: As far as we know — I can't say we have got all the details. But the indications are that the plan was to kill him. And they simply surrounded his palace and went in and killed him. That is as far as we know now.

SECRETARY KISSINGER: Didn't we tell him that last year?

MR. ATHERTON: In March we had lots of indications —

SECRETARY KISSINGER: Didn't we tell him about it?

MR. ATHERTON: We told him at the time.

SECRETARY KISSINGER: Didn't we tell him who it was going to be, roughly?

MR. ATHERTON: I will have to check whether we gave him the names.

MR. HYLAND: We were a little imprecise on that.

MR. ATHERTON: He brushed it off, scoffed at it, said nobody would do a thing like that to him.[44]

Either as a continuation of earlier efforts (i.e. 1972–74) or as a new move to stage a coup, planning began in March 1975. Farook Rahman, one of the key planners, met the then Deputy Chief of Army Staff, General Ziaur Rahman on 20 March 1975 and hinted at their intention to make 'some changes necessary for the betterment of the country'. Zia declined to be involved with anything like this, but said 'if you want to do something, the junior officers should do it themselves'.[45] Zia neither reported it to the president, nor attempted to stop them from getting involved in such activities. The coup-makers' repeated claim that Zia was aware, if not well-informed, about the coup has been contradicted by Zia supporters. Zia, however, maintained a dubious silence regarding such allegations during his entire lifetime.[46] The plotters, according to a number of sources, contacted a section of discontented AL leaders sometime in April. Most prominent among them was Khondoker Mushtaq Ahmed, then foreign trade minister of the cabinet. Khondoker Abdur Rashid, who happened to be a nephew of Mushtaq, played the key role in making the arrangements for a meeting between the coup-planners and Mushtaq in the first week of August. Subsequently, three meetings took place — on 12, 13 and 14 August. Contacts were also made with another prominent AL leader, Taheruddin Thakur, then-information minister; and a prominent former Foreign Service official – Mahbubul Alam Chasi.[47] Whatever the real truth, on the morning of 15 August 1975, a group of Army officers took power and killed Mujibur Rahman and his family. Following the coup, Khondoker Mushtaq Ahmed was installed as president and a cabinet was hastily organized. The cabinet consisted entirely of AL leaders. In fact, 11 of the 19 ministers and eight of the nine ministers of state of the Mujibur Rahman cabinet joined the government. No military officer was included, but the real power remained with the coup-makers, especially the six majors commanding the armoured and infantry regiments.

Clearly, three centres of power emerged out of the coup: constitutionally, the president and the civilian cabinet remained the supreme authority (even though they had very little control over the situation); the army, as a whole, remained under the command of its regular senior officers, who were caught off guard by the coup; and the third source of authority was the putsch-makers themselves, hiding in the safety of the presidential palace (Bongobhavan) with loyal soldiers. They instructed the president on all matters. Soon after the coup, junior officers were asked by army command to return to their normal duties. They declined to do so because they feared a court martial for breaking the chain of command.

After the takeover, the majors declared Bangladesh an Islamic state. Khondoker Mustaq himself, however, did not mention anything of that sort. Despite the involvement of the officers who had actively participated in the liberation war, it was known that the coup leaders held conservative views. While confusion, chaos, and tension were running high in the cantonment and in the presidential palace, the Mushtaq government made some important decisions: it repealed a part of the constitution that was related to the formation and functioning of the BKSAL (the presidential form of government, however, was kept intact); it rescinded the scheme to make changes in local government (i.e., to divide Bangladesh into 61 districts and run by district governors); it annulled the Presidential Order no. 9 of 1972 (which enabled the government to dismiss any government officer without assigning any reason); it merged the Rakkhi Bahini with the Army; and it withdrew the ban on some of the newspapers imposed under the fourth amendment of the constitution. Within days, a major shake-up in the military and civil bureaucracy took place. The Chief of Army Staff, Major General Safiullah, was replaced by Major General Ziaur Rahman. The Chief of the Air Force, A.K. Khondoker, was replaced by Air Vice Marshal M. G. Tawab. A. B. S. Safdar was appointed Director General of Defense Forces Intelligence (DFI). Mahbub Alam Chasi was appointed Principal Secretary to the President, and General (Rtd.) Osmani was appointed defence advisor to the president, a post created to handle the internal feuds of the army.[48] The only freedom fighter that benefited from these changes was Brigadier Khaled Musharraf. He was elevated to the position of Chief of General Staff (CGS). Hossain Mohammed Ershad (who was in India for military training at that time) and Kazi Golam Dostagir were also elevated in the ranks, and Ershad became the Deputy Chief of Staff. Both of them, we must recall, were repatriated to Bangladesh from Pakistan after the liberation war. Immediately tensions at two levels emerged, on the one hand, between the junior officers who staged the coup and the senior officers who were in command, and on the other hand, between the former freedom fighters and the repatriates.

Over subsequent days, it became evident that nobody was in control of the country. Mushtaq, in collusion with the bureaucrats, was trying to establish his authority; the majors, especially Rashid and Farook, were trying to exert their power; and senior army officers were annoyed by Mushtaq's 'mistreatment' and attempted division among them. To preclude any potential resistance from the AL loyalists, some 35 prominent AL leaders including acting president of the government in exile, Nazrul Islam, PM of the government in exile, Tajuddin Ahmed, PM of the ousted Mujib regime, Mansoor Ali, a minister in the ousted government, Kamruzzaman, and the political secretary of Sheikh Mujib, Tofail Ahmed, were all taken into custody. Mushtaq issued an ordinance on 26 September 1975 to indemnify himself and his associates against possible future punishments for their crimes, which included the killing of Mujib and his family members.[49] Mushtaq, in a nationally televised speech on 3 October, promised that the restrictions on political activity would be lifted on 15 August 1976, and that parliamentary elections would be held on 28 February 1977. His characterization of the coup-makers in his speech as 'the valiant sons of the soil' was viewed as approval of the arrogance of the majors and drew the ire of senior military officers. Interestingly, parliament survived through this chaotic condition and Mushtaq attempted to gain the approval of the parliament in a meeting on 16 October held inside the presidential residence. But the meeting ended in pandemonium before proceedings had properly begun.

In early November, led by Brigadier Khaled Mosharraf and Colonel Safaet Jamil, a group of Army officers supportive of restoring the chain of command, hastily drew up a plan for takeover. The plan went into effect after midnight on 2 November. Ziaur Rahman, the CAS, was put under house arrest and armoured regiments moved to take control of Bangabhavan from the majors.[50] Although the majors initially declined, they changed their minds the next morning and negotiated a compromise that would allow them to leave the country. The coup was ill-planned, hastily organized, and was strictly limited in its objective – bringing down the arrogant majors. It was after the majors' expulsion that the coup-makers begin to think about the changes necessary to establish their total control over the army. In this anarchic situation, as various groups were wrestling for power, four prominent AL leaders, Nazrul Islam, Tajuddin Ahmed, Monsoor Ali, and Kamruzzman were brutally murdered by some army men in the early hours of 3 November inside the Dhaka jail at the instruction of the August coup-makers with the approval of President Mushtaq. A section of coup leaders angrily reacted to the news of the killings of the AL leaders and forced Mushtaq to resign. He was replaced by Chief Justice of the Supreme Court, Abu Sadat Mohammad Sayem. Rumours spread that a section of pro-AL army men in collusion with India had taken over and an Indian intervention was imminent. Whether or not these rumours were deliberately created is difficult to determine. But the consequence was evident: a complete rejection of the coup. Nationalistic feelings ran high and everyone began to talk about a possible retaliation by freedom fighters in the Army. The question of national sovereignty and independence acquired a new dimension and the fear of Indian hegemony loomed large.[51]

The radical forces that had been waiting in the wings for months for an opportune moment to strike and bring down the entire 'exploitative social system' decided the time to act was at hand. Zia reached out to Taher, his wartime colleague, who had developed a clandestine political network within the army named the Biplobi Sainik Sangstha (BSS, Revolutionary Soldiers Union), to save his life. On 5 November the BSS, an organization of non-commissioned soldiers supported by the JSD and led by Taher, called upon the soldiers to revolt against the army officers who had been exploiting them for their own selfish and ambitious reasons, staging one putsch after another.[52] The soldiers were moved by the call. On the night of 6 November they began to rise with a force that would eventually shake the state of Bangladesh; it was the first soldiers' mutiny on such a scale since that of 1857 against the British in colonial India. At least 33 other officers, some of their families, and nearly 100 enlisted men including Khaled Musharraf and Lieutenant-Colonel A. T. M. Haider, both valiant freedom fighters, were killed.[53] Ziaur Rahman was freed by the Sepoys.

On the morning of 7 November, troops from Dhaka cantonment poured into the city and paraded through the streets shouting slogans and firing their weapons into the air. An unprecedented situation emerged as civilians and soldiers participated together in processions. There were, however, two different political strands involved: one that was in favour of the unity among the soldiers and the people, and another in support of Mushtaq and purported to be against India.

Ziaur Rahman was freed from captivity by members of the Biplobi Sainik Sangstha (Revolutionary Soldiers Union). Zia reluctantly agreed to sign a copy of the 12 point demand as a gesture of his commitment, but did not refer to it in his speeches on that day and increasingly demonstrated his discomfort with the BSS leadership. In one of his speeches Zia declared himself the chief martial law administrator (CMLA). Within hours, it became evident to the organizers of the uprising that Ziaur Rahman, 'an ambitious and seemingly non-political man who lacked a progressive personality but had popularity among the soldiers as a patriot and war hero',[54] was no longer their front man. Instead he had his own agenda to pursue. The conventional army command and key figures such as General Osmani, General Khalil, Air Vice Marshal M. G. Tawab, M. H. Khan, and Mahbub Alam Chasi, had become his source of counsel. It was on their advice that Zia had reluctantly accepted the idea of Sayem continuing to be the president and the CMLA. Zia was asked to be one of the three DCMLAs. Once again, as on 26 March 1971, Zia had to retract his announcement to be the head of the state. Although Zia and his new advisors agreed to release 'all political prisoners', which met one of the 12 demands, they categorically declined to talk about the 12 point demand as such. The decision to release some political prisoners was extremely beneficial to the JSD, for all its key leaders were in jail at the time of the coup. But after this meeting, it became clear Zia had taken advantage of the situation and began to shake off the coup-makers. A day that began with extreme hope for the revolutionaries ended with utter defeat. The only achievement was the release of its party leaders (A. S. M. Abdur Rab and Major M. A. Jalil) from jail. Upon their release, the JSD leaders denounced Zia and asked the Sepoys not to surrender their arms until their demands were met, while Zia conversely ordered the soldiers to return to barracks, surrender weapons looted from the armouries, and refrain from attacking officers. On 15 November 1975, a martial law regulation was promulgated, evidently aimed at JSD activists, instituting a death sentence against anyone encouraging mutinous actions. Eight days later, JSD leaders were again arrested on charges of sedition. Colonel Taher and a large number of JSD activists were arrested on 24 November on charges of mutiny and treason as reportedly Taher was hatching another coup. Thus, the 'revolution' ended.

Eighty-four days of chaos and confusion, coups and counter-coups, killings and counter-killings, conspiracy, and uprising finally paved the way for the rise of Ziaur Rahman as the strong man.[55] A man who neither took the risk of engineering a coup nor participated in one became the ultimate beneficiary of all the changes. Contending groups within the army fought each other only to hire a 'front man', Zia, who cleverly took advantage of the situation. In the process, they exposed and exhausted themselves. The rise of Zia quite appropriately reminds us of the situation in France between 1848 and 1851 leading to the emergence of Louis Bonaparte (Napoleon III as he is more commonly known); 'All fell on their knees, equally mute and equally impotent, before the rifle butt',[56] and all that once seemed achievements 'vanished like a series of optical illusions before the spell of a man whom even his enemies do not claim to be a magician'.[57] However, there is another explanation for the meteoric rise of Ziaur Rahman: 'Zia's success, it appears, was due mainly to the fact that, despite his pre-eminent stature in the military elite, until the decisive final stages of the power struggle – in which he was, of course, a key participant – he remained without firm ideological or personal commitments.'[58]

In his first speech after the 7 November uprising, President Sayem dissolved the parliament and suspended the constitution. The president was nominally in charge; the core of the central authority was composed of military officials, particularly army officers. A council of advisors, primarily comprised of civilian and military bureaucrats, was created. The dominance of bureaucrats in governance and policy-making continued throughout the Zia regime. For example, in 1981 – the year Zia was assassinated in an abortive coup – there were 24 cabinet ministers and of them, six were military bureaucrats, five were civil servants, six were technocrats, four were businessmen, one was a landlord, and two were lawyers.

In a sharp departure from the policies of the earlier regime, the defence budget was increased significantly. The original allocation – left over from the Mujib regime for 1975–76 – was raised from 7 per cent (Tk. 750 million) to 20 per cent of the national budget (Tk. 1109.34 million).[59] Similar increases were made for police and other law enforcement apparatuses. According to Vivekananda,[60] in 1977 the regime was spending $1,606 per soldier. In 1979, this went up to $1,697. We should recall here that the per capita annual income in Bangladesh at that time was less than $100. Available statistics show that during the period of 1976–80 Bangladesh annually spent about $593 per person in the military.[61] Following the coups and counter-coups of 1975, the numerical strength of the defence forces and members of law enforcement agencies increased at a spectacular rate. The total defence force personnel (including the Air Force and Navy) was about 26,500 in 1974, which grew to 63,000 in 1976; by 1982, the number had reached 80,000. The Army expanded from five divisions in 1975 to eight divisions in 1981. Within the first three years of the military takeover, a new army division was created. Paramilitary forces grew from 29,000 to about 46,000. The strength of the police force increased from about 40,000 to about 70,000, with a combat-ready special police force of 12,500 men.[62]

The military government embarked on a series of policies, which were diametrically opposed to those of the Mujib regime, and consequently changed not only the system of governance and the composition of the ruling elite, but also the nature of the Bangladeshi state. On the economic front, these steps included disinvestment/denationalization[63] of state-owned enterprises; raising and subsequently abolishing the ceiling on private investment; withdrawal of restrictions on private foreign investment; and providing credit to private entrepreneurs.

Some policy measures, for example the revised investment policy, were declared as early as December, even before the country had recuperated from the spiral of coups. The policy of privatization was pursued with utmost urgency. By the end of 1977, 21 industrial units had been disinvested and handed over to the new owners; 15 units were disinvested but not handed over; and 33 units were in the process of disinvestment.[64] The process intensified after 1977. By March 1982, a total of 236 industrial units had been disinvested/denationalized. Between 1982 and 1989, another 156 units were disinvested. Some small-sized enterprises were privatized during the Mujib regime (i.e. industrial enterprises having fixed assets up to Tk. 2.5 million). During the military regimes medium and large industrial units (for example, in the 1982–83 fiscal year the average sale price of an industrial unit was about Tk. 32.65 million) were being transferred to private entrepreneurs. It is worth noting that these figures do not include commercial and trading entities, and in many cases, units were sold without any public bidding primarily to those who could establish close contacts with the regime.

Although Ziaur Rahman did not assume the presidency until 1977, he emerged as the *de facto* ruler of the country from 7 November 1975. Until 1978, the regime faced periodic rebellion within the army organized by a radical left political party – the Jatiya Samajtantrik Dal (JSD, National Socialist Party), particularly the Biplobi Sainik Sangstha (BSS, Revolutionary Soldiers Union).

Following the arrest of Taher and the JSD leaders in 1975, serious troubles began to erupt in several cantonments. Hundreds of soldiers were arrested and, allegedly, summarily executed. In December 1975 'disturbances' were reported from Chittagong naval base and in March, 1976, an Army unit in Chittagong was reported to have mutinied. Although it was not clear whether Biplobi Sainik Sangstha was involved, three officers were killed. Zia personally intervened to bring an end to the trouble. In April, Air Vice Marshal M. G. Towab, one of the DCMLAs, attempted to takeover through a right-wing coup d'etat. The exiled majors were brought in by Towab and one of them joined a tank regiment stationed in Bogra to begin the assault. This short-lived coup attempt, staged on 30 April 1976, cost Towab his job. He was thrown out of the country. Farook Rahman, who managed to reach his loyalists in Bogra, was convinced by his parents and sister to give in. He was then sent out of the country again. Two months after the coup attempt, the tank regiment that rallied with Farook was disbanded and about 250 of its members were charged under the Service Act.

Seven months after the arrests in November 1975, 33 persons including Colonel Taher and the JSD leaders were charged with treason. Twenty-two of them were members of the defence services, the remaining 11 were prominent JSD leaders. In a trial held in camera Colonel Taher was sentenced to death, Jalil and Rab to life imprisonment and 14 others were sentenced to imprisonment for various terms. On 21 July 1976 Taher was hanged at dawn in Dhaka Central Jail.

Bogra, hometown of Ziaur Rahman, ironically became a citadel of anti-Zia military activists. On 17 July 1976, a day-long rebellion caused considerable problems for the regime. Rapid actions contained the rebels. But another rebellion began to stir. One year later, on 29–30 September 1977, an uprising of soldiers took place in Bogra. The members of Biplobi Sainik Sangstha reportedly took over Bogra city and marched through the streets carrying their weapons and shouting slogans against the regime. Some members of the rebel group were involved in looting as well. Mutineers alleged that the government had 'sold out' the country to foreign powers. The next day, they freed some political prisoners and exchanged fire with local police. According to the official account, the mutineers were dealt with without much trouble. Only one officer was killed. The police, with the help of local people, apprehended five of the runaway 'miscreants'. But insiders insist hundreds of soldiers were either killed or later executed.

Even before Bogra was brought under the control of government forces, Dhaka was shaken by another attempt to unseat the regime. In the early hours of 2 October, a full-fledged soldiers' uprising took place, presumably organized by Biplobi Sainik Sangstha. According to one account, the Bogra and Dhaka uprisings were not isolated events but rather part of a grand design; the proximity of these two events gives credence to the claim, but substantial evidence has not been found to back such an assertion. Nevertheless, the Dhaka uprising was well organized and more powerful than the Bogra attempt. The rebel soldiers – claiming to be members of Gonobahini – took control of the radio station for about three hours and announced that an armed revolution was taking place led by the armed forces, students, peasants, and workers. In the early hours of the day, in addition to the radio station, rebels captured some vital points of the cantonments and Dhaka city, advanced toward the president's residence, and attacked the airport where Air Force Chief A. G. Mahmood and some senior military officers were engaged in negotiations with international skyjackers (Japanese Red Army) of a JAL airliner. A large section of army and air force personnel participated in the coup and it almost toppled the government. This was the bloodiest coup attempt since the 7 November 1975 uprising. Eleven senior air force officers, 10 army officers, and an estimated 200 soldiers were killed in the battle between the rebels and the pro-government forces at the airport.

The failed attempt was followed by brutal executions. Martial law tribunals set up by the government hurriedly prosecuted the soldiers and airmen. According to the government account, within 25 days of the incident 92 persons had been sentenced to death, 34 persons received imprisonment for life, and 18 others received various terms of rigorous imprisonment. Ziaur Rahman himself confided to a reporter of the *New York Times* that 460 officers and soldiers were tried for their involvement in the 2 October coup attempt. Only 63 of them were acquitted.[65] *The Times* of London reported on 5 March 1978, on the basis of conversations with senior army officers, that more than 800 servicemen had been convicted by military tribunals. Mascarenhas reckoned that 1,143 men were hanged in the two months following October 1977. According to one account at least 1,100 military personnel were executed after an abortive coup in 1977 within months of the coup.[66] The regime faced more than three well-organized coup attempts and dozens of sporadic rebellions.

In the face of violent opposition from within the military Zia sought both political and constitutional legitimacy to his rule. To gain political legitimacy he amended the fundamental principles of the constitution and charted a new course for the country. These amendments, proclaimed through an executive order (*Second Proclamation Order no. 1*, 23 April 1977), included redefining the state principles, and identifying the citizens as 'Bangladeshi' as opposed to Bangalee (Bengali). The most important element of these changes was Islamization of the constitution and the polity. The word 'secularism', appearing in the preamble and Article 8 as one of the four fundamental principles, was substituted with 'absolute trust and faith in the Almighty Allah'; and a new clause (1A) was inserted to emphasize that 'absolute trust and faith in almighty Allah' should be 'the basis of all actions.' Additionally, the words *Bismillah-ar-Rahman-ar-Rahim* (In the name of Allah, the Beneficent, the Merciful) were inserted above the preamble.

Along with the process of ideological legitimation, concrete steps to gain constitutional legitimacy were initiated by the Zia regime. A referendum on his presidency in 1977, a presidential election in 1978 and the organization of a political party in 1978 were intended to provide the regime with a semblance of legitimacy. But the elections were blatantly rigged, to say the least and thus did not bolster the image of the regime.

The executive orders, issued between 1976 and 1979, removed the ban on forming political parties based on religious ideology and allowed individuals who had collaborated with the Pakistani army in 1971 to participate in politics. One of the key steps was the promulgation of the Political Parties Regulations (PPR) Act in July 1976 which required all political parties to register with the government, and restricted their functioning (e.g., regulating scale and location of meetings). Scores of new parties emerged. The Islamists, especially those who were members of parties like the Jamaat-e-Islami (JI) prior to independence, rallied under the banner of a newly formed party, the Islamic Democratic League (IDL). The IDL became the fountainhead of a new Islamist movement in Bangladesh.

The newly founded political party under the auspices of the government – the Bangladesh Nationalist Party (BNP) – brought together an array of anti-AL political forces ranging from radical leftists to defectors from other parties to those who opposed the war of liberation and others who had close connections with religious organizations. Indeed this combination carved out a space in the political landscape of the country and cultivated a support-base within the populace, but the landslide victory of the BNP in the 1979 parliamentary election (207 out of 300 seats) was far greater than the support-base could have delivered without the direct assistance of the administration. Nevertheless, the fifth amendment to the constitution passed by parliament in 1979 provided constitutional legitimacy to the regime and incorporated the Islamization provisions into the constitution. However, these steps did not bring an end to the coup efforts against Ziaur Rahman. On 17 June 1980, there was another abortive attempt to overthrow the regime and assassinate the president. This time it was a combination of the August 1975 coup-makers and a small group of political activists previously connected to the JSD and some other leftist organizations. The attempt failed, but Zia was assassinated within less than a year, in May 1981 in an abortive military coup. A state of emergency was declared as the country teetered on the brink of another military takeover. As a mark of constitutional continuity, Vice President Abdus Sattar succeeded Zia, initially as interim president and in November as an elected president. Sattar's lack of charisma and his inability to provide leadership mask the fact that he was the first (and to date, the only) directly elected civilian president of the country. While he faced no contestation within the party for his nomination for the presidency, his grip over the party was tenuous at best. Soon it became evident that the country was once again facing a crisis of governance.

Internal squabbles and the presence of an ambitious general at the helm of the Army, sealed the fate of the Sattar presidency. Within ten months of Zia's assassination and four months of the election, the then Army Chief General Hussain Muhammad Ershad usurped power through a coup. He too faced a legitimacy crisis similar to that of the Zia regime of 1975. Ershad diligently tried to tread Zia's path – formation of a party (1984), and holding of a referendum (1985), parliamentary elections (1986, 1988), and a presidential election (1986) in quick succession are testimony to that effort. But unlike Zia he faced intense challenges from the political parties, who formed two alliances – one centred on the AL and the other centred on the BNP. The Islamists, particularly the Jamaat-e-Islami (JI), distanced themselves from the military ruler in a bid to gain public acceptance by participating in the pro-democracy movement, in spite of the fact that to prove his Islamist credentials General Ershad made another amendment to the constitution in mid-1988 which declared Islam the state religion.

The Third Parliament, elected in 1986, passed the sixth amendment of the constitution approving the actions of the regime since its takeover and therefore rendering it a legal authority from the constitutional point of view. But public discontent continued to grow and the repressive measures of the regime further alienated the ruling party. The initial opposition to Ershad came from the students in 1983, but it took almost three years to become a grassroots popular movement headed by the

AL and the BNP. The regime's shrewd move to divide the opposition worked on several occasions, for example the 1986 parliamentary election, held in May, was boycotted by the BNP and an alliance of left parties while the AL and the JI participated. Taking advantage of the situation the regime held the presidential election in October 1986 hoping to further the schism within the opposition, but all parties boycotted the election. These moves breathed new life into the regime, but did not prevent continuing street agitation against the regime.

The year 1987 witnessed particularly widespread protests, organized jointly by almost all the opposition parties. In November a state of emergency was declared and the parliament was dissolved in December. With the arrests of opposition leaders, imposing strict control over the media and adopting repressive measures, the regime survived the most serious challenge. During the upheaval of 1986, the idea of holding elections under a neutral caretaker regime had been floated by the Jamaat-e-Islami (JI) and later subscribed to by all opposition parties. The general election was held in March 1988, but the opposition boycott was highly successful, producing a political stalemate. The state of emergency was withdrawn in April. But as the elections, boycotted by the opposition parties (e.g. 1986, 1987, 1988) failed to garner enough public support for the ruling Jatiya Party (JP, established in 1984), the regime began to unravel in October 1990. Demonstrations against the regime began on 10 October and by mid-November galvanized the entire country with one single demand: that the president resign immediately. Despite the closing of the universities the student movement emerged as the driving force of protest, forcing the divided opposition parties to act in unison against Ershad. A state of emergency, declared on 27 November, backfired; as the *New York Times* reported, never had martial law been so little respected.[67] With scores of deaths, the opposition received support from all walks of life: teachers, journalists, doctors and public servants resigned or went on strike. The president retracted his earlier announcement that he would seek re-election in 1991 and offered a peace plan on 3 December, which was immediately rejected by the opposition. Sensing victory, the protestors redoubled their efforts. With growing dissent within the army,[68] and the military's refusal to comply with the order[69] Ershad's fate was sealed. The regime practically collapsed on 4 December 1990.

As the popular uprising gained momentum and the days of the regime were numbered, constitutional questions such as how to transfer power from the pseudo-military regime to popular political parties, and to whom, came to the fore. A unique transitional arrangement was devised by the opposition alliances as a constitutional way out from the military regime of General Ershad. As described at the beginning of this chapter, on 5 December the opposition alliances agreed on a formula that would enable Ershad to hand power to an interim government headed by the chief justice of the Supreme Court. Consequently on 6 December the interim government was formed with the chief justice as the head and a council of advisors comprised of eminent citizens. However, by then deep-seated changes in Bangladeshi society, politics and the economy had taken place. The most conspicuous were the heightened role of religion, to be precise Islam, in politics, and the adoption of the capitalist path to development. In these respects, similarities between the Zia and Ershad regimes were striking. These similarities are not limited to the path they took in legitimizing their rule, but were also ideological in many respects. These regimes' success in bringing Islam into the political discourse facilitated the the Islamists gaining legitimacy – both constitutionally and politically, which delivered a serious blow to the secular ideal. Yet, as the nation embarked on its third decade, it was a moment of renewed hope. For understandable reasons, the degree of optimism was not the same as in 1971 although many euphorically described this as the second liberation, but in some ways it was a new beginning. Indeed, it brought an end to the authoritarianism, both civilian and military, that had plagued the nation since its inception in 1971.

CHAPTER 3

FROM OPTIMISM TO RETREAT
OF DEMOCRACY (1991–2015)

In the early days of 1991, with the parliamentary election approaching on 27 February, the first to be held without an incumbent and under a caretaker government, political parties were busy drawing up candidate lists, and drafting election manifestos. There was unprecedented enthusiasm among voters and political activists. The media were ecstatic to have the opportunity to cover the forthcoming campaign without any fear of intimidation. Yet a cloud remained hanging over the heads of all concerned: the parliament had very little power under the extant constitution. The country was still under a presidential system of governance, introduced through the fourth amendment of the constitution in 1975. Much had changed since then, but the presidential system had not. Almost all political parties, except the BNP, were committed to the parliamentary system and demanded its reintroduction during the pro-democracy movement. The popular expectation was that the country would return to the parliamentary system. The eyes were mostly on the two major political parties, the Bangladesh Awami League (BAL) and the Bangladesh Nationalist Party (BNP). What would they offer, what promises would they make to the electorate? Although it was the AL which switched to the presidential system, the BNP was the principal beneficiary of it. The Jatiya Party (JP), led by former dictator H M Ershad, had never operated under a parliamentary system. On 28 January, the BNP announced the election manifesto with no reference to the system of governance. When asked by a reporter, Khaleda Zia responded, the decision about the system of government will be made in the parliament. Many analysts pondered, did she skirt the hard question or leave open the option of changing her party's position in future? Eight days later, on 6 February, the BAL issued its manifesto; no surprise there – it laid out its plan to revert to the pre-fourth amendment system: a parliamentary system of government. The election delivered a victory to the BNP, a result one could describe as popular support for the presidential system. But the BAL continued to press for the reintroduction of the parliamentary system. Sheikh Hasina, in a public meeting on 7 March reiterated the demand. Members of the civil society, preferring a more accountable system of governance, urged the BNP to reconsider. On 1 July 1991, then Prime Minister Khaleda Zia, in a nationally televised speech announced that her party had decided to reintroduce the parliamentary system. Next day, the BNP introduced the twelfth amendment of the constitution. A month and three days later, after much debate and discussions, late at night, two amendments were passed by the parliament – the eleventh and the twelfth amendments of the constitution. The former ratified, confirmed and validated all powers and actions of the interim government headed by Justice Shahabuddin Ahmed, and the latter reintroduced the parliamentary system (subject to ratification through a referendum). This was a unique night in the parliamentary history of the nation – the only two amendments ever to be passed by a Bangladesh parliament with the support of both ruling and opposition members. In some measure, this reflects the optimism that emerged after the downfall of authoritarianism.

The Era of Hope and Despair (1991–2006)

The third decade of the nation's political history began when a civilian government headed by Khaleda Zia took power through a free and fair election from another civilian regime, and an era of representative democracy was ushered in. The reintroduction of the parliamentary system is one of the high marks of this era which lasted until 2006. But there were also positive features such as holding of elections at regular intervals, and institutionalization of the caretaker government. But the period saw a number of negative developments: incessant squabbling between the two major political parties (BAL and BNP) with ever-increasing belligerent posturing on both sides, the rise of Islamist militancy as a serious threat to peace and order, and the gradual assault on the democratic future of the country. Four parliamentary elections were held between 1991 and 2006. Of these three were held on time and were remarkably fair; while one was entirely the opposite. The 1991 election brought the BNP to power with the tacit support of the Jamaat-e-Islami (JI). Khaleda Zia became the first woman prime minister in the history of Bangladesh. The honeymoon between the BNP and the JI did not last long. The JI later joined the AL-led opposition in 1994, organized street agitation against the BNP government and its elected representatives resigned from the parliament in concert with all other opposition members forcing the untimely demise of the Fifth Parliament. The AL was demanding an amendment to the constitution to make the neutral caretaker government during the election a permanent provision.

By 1995, the demand for a caretaker government became the battle cry of the AL, reflecting the suspicion that the ruling party would not be able to hold elections peacefully, fairly, and impartially. This came after a by-election of a parliamentary seat was blatantly rigged by the ruling party to ensure the victory of its candidate. The BNP underestimated the tenacity of the AL and refused to bring any constitutional amendments for more than a year. But the resignation of the opposition parliament members − 147 out of a total of 300 − made the parliament ineffective. As the street agitation began gaining momentum, the parliament was dissolved in November 1995, ahead of schedule. This required holding an election within 90 days. Consequently an election was held on 15 February 1996. The election, boycotted by the opposition parties, was rejected by a majority of the electorate as only 20 per cent turned out to vote. Blatantly manipulated by the state machinery the election gave the BNP a two-thirds majority in parliament. This was followed by massive popular unrest and an indefinite non-cooperation movement. The BNP finally succumbed. The 6th parliament was dissolved in March 1996. But in a marathon session before the dissolution, parliament amended the constitution and made the caretaker government (CTG) a part of the constitution through the thirteenth amendment of the constitution.[1]

One cannot but agree with the Bangladeshi analysts who stressed that the system of caretaker government 'does not provide credit to the uprightness of politicians or of the government. It manifests one simple fact: that the politicians have no trust in each other. It palpably implies the absence of a healthy political system in the country.'[2] The thirteenth amendment stipulated that upon dissolution of the parliament at the end of its five-year term, an 11-member non-party caretaker government (CTG) headed by the chief adviser would function as an interim government for 90 days. The amendment provided that the immediate past chief justice would be the head of the caretaker government. (The constitution stipulated four other options for appointing the chief advisor if the immediate past chief justice was unavailable or unwilling to take up the job. If all other options proved unworkable, the president could head the caretaker government in addition to his presidential duties.) The caretaker government would be dissolved on the date that a new prime minister assumed office. The constitution also stipulated that during the term of the interim government, the defence ministry would be under the president's control, who otherwise does not have this power and only serves as the ceremonial head of the state.

The inclusion of the caretaker government in the constitution was regarded by almost all political parties as a panacea. But later, on more than one occasion, it became evident that the amendment had opened the door for the politicization of the judiciary, impacted upon the presidency (as the outgoing ruling party feel that the president is the best man to represent their interests), and made the Army dependent on partisan politicians (as it remains under a partisan political appointee whereas the state apparatuses are run by non-partisan individuals). Since political expediency was the driving force behind introducing the system, the long-term consequences were scarcely contemplated. Many important details such as the modus operandi of selecting the members of the CTG (described as advisors), the relationship between the Election Commission and the CTG, and the relationship between the Army and the CTG, to mention a few, remained unexplained. These came to haunt the nation in 2007.

In June 1996, fresh elections were held under the CTG headed by the immediate past chief justice. The caretaker government experienced a jolt in late May when the army chief General Abu Saleh Muhammad Nasim allegedly tried to stage a coup, a charge Nasim denied. According to various sources[3] the events began to unfold when the Directorate General of Forces Intelligence (DGFI) tapped telephone conversations of two senior officers who allegedly had been conspiring with retired officers to stage a coup since March. On 18 May, on advice of the DGFI, the president decided to send these officers to early retirement. The army chief was informed of this decision and was asked to issue formal orders, which he declined. On the contrary, he demoted four officers including the director general of the DGFI. By 20 May, General Nasim had asked commanding officers of four cantonments to move their forces towards Dhaka. Two complied and ordered their forces to march to the capital. The DGFI also claim that they tapped Nasim's telephone conversations with a retired army captain with links to the AL where he described his plan to 'force the President to resign on health grounds.' the president consulted both civilian and military officials, and the chief advisor. After a tense day that involved efforts on the part of Nasim to capture the radio and television stations and the deployment of soldiers loyal to the president, General Nasim was sacked by the president. Altogether 15 high-ranking officers were relieved from their duties: eight were dismissed and seven were sent to forced retirement. Uncertainty gripped the country until it became evident that the army chief had been removed. The nation awaited the return of military rule with some trepidation.

Despite this incident the election was held relatively peacefully. The AL emerged as the largest single party in the seventh parliament, although it fell short of the majority required to form the government. The unconditional support of the Jatiya Party of General Ershad ensured the return of the AL to power after 21 years. Sheikh Hasina became the prime minister. But, 'just as the AL refused to accept its defeat in the 1991 elections, the BNP refused to accept defeat in 1996'.[4]

The bitter rivalry continued throughout the five years of AL rule. But the Hasina regime completed its term in 2001, the first government in the history of Bangladesh to do so. Power was handed over to the CTG on 15 July and the election to the eighth parliament was held on 1 October 2001. Unlike the previous pre-election situation when there were deep concerns whether a peaceful transfer of power would take place, the CTG took over without any incident. By then, the JP had split and the party had officially withdrawn its support from the government, and joined hands with the BNP and the JI to form an alliance against the ruling AL. The Islami Oikya Jote (IOJ), a conglomeration of seven radical Islamist parties, also became a partner of the alliance. A centre-right four-party coalition was formed in late 1998. The alliance contested the election and secured a landslide victory with a two-thirds majority. Within a week a new cabinet was installed with two members from the Jamaat-e-Islami. It was an ironic moment for a nation that had emerged in 1971 on the basis of secular-socialistic principles, and whose first constitution imposed an embargo on the use of religion in politics. Thirty years later an election had brought a coalition to power with two Islamist parties as partners. The more prominent of the two, the Jamaat-i-Islami (JI), openly professes 'Islamic revolution' and calls for the establishment of an 'Islamic state' in Bangladesh. The other, smaller, partner was even more radical. Some of the leaders of the Islami Oikya Jote (IOJ) had previously expressed solidarity with the Taliban regime in Afghanistan. The AL, faced with a crushing defeat in the election, alleged that the president, the advisors of the caretaker government, and the Election Commission had manipulated the results in favour of the four-party combine. Following the election, even before power was handed over to the BNP–JI coalition, party activists launched a series of attacks on religious minorities, particularly Hindus throughout the country.[5]

The most worrying development of this era was the rise of Islamist militant groups, such as the Harkat-ul-Jihad al-Islami Bangladesh (HUJIB) and the Jamaat-ul-Mujahideen Bangladesh (JMB, the Assembly of Holy Warriors), in various parts of the country. Although some of these organizations were clandestinely organizing during the last days of the AL regime (1996–2001), they found a hospitable environment under the four-party rule and began to engage in violent activities. In the summer of 2004 a militant group named Jagrata Muslim Janata Bangladesh (JMJB, The Awakened Muslim Masses of Bangladesh) under the leadership of Siddiqur Rahman (alias Bangla Bhai) unleashed a reign of terror in the northwestern district of Rajshahi. Despite global media coverage, the government initially refused to acknowledge the existence of this organization but finally proscribed the JMB and the JMJB. But the first show of the strength and reach of the militant group was on display when an assassination attempt was made on the leader of the opposition on 21 August 2004. The grenade attack on a public meeting addressed by Hasina left 24 dead and Hasina injured. The reaction from the government was appalling as it tried to portray the attack as an inside job. Eventually, the government made a day labourer with no connection to militancy a scapegoat. The AL insisted that the attack took place with the blessings of the government, especially Khaleda Zia's son Tareq Rahman.

A year later, in August 2005, the situation in regard to militancy took a turn for the worse, as the JMB and the HUJIB put up an unprecedented show of force. On 17 August within less than an hour 450 homemade bombs exploded all over the country. These events were followed by four incidents of suicide attacks over the next several months, killing at least 30 people and wounding 150 more. The victims included judges, lawyers, policemen and journalists. Under intense international pressure the government in October 2005 banned the HUJIB, the Pakistan-based militant organization and fountainhead of all militant groups in Bangladesh. By March 2006, seven key leaders and hundreds of members of the militant network had been arrested, and by September 2006 the death sentences of seven militant leaders were confirmed by the Supreme Court.

As the term of the BNP-led coalition government was nearing an end in 2006, the country gradually crept toward a political crisis. The conflict between the ruling coalition and the opposition parties under the leadership of the AL began in the summer of 2006, and centred on four major issues: the head of the caretaker government; the composition of the EC, particularly the chief election commissioner (CEC); the voters list; and the politicization of the civil administration.

Opposition political parties insisted that they would not accept the immediate past Chief Justice K. M. Hasan as head of the CTG on the grounds that he had previously held a position in the BNP hierarchy and that the retirement age of the Supreme Court judges had been extended to make him eligible for the position. They demanded the removal of the CEC, Justice M. A. Aziz, who had been appointed for his loyalty towards the ruling party. The opposition alleged that the EC officials including the field level officials were partisans. The appointment of hundreds of party activists as field level officers of the Election Commission gave credence to their allegations. The law required that the voter's list drawn up in 2000 be updated before the election, but the CEC unilaterally decided to draw up a new list. In so doing he flouted the High Court's instructions and then lost an appeal in the Supreme Court. The list contained 91.31 million voters while thousands complained of having been left out, and the demographers' projections showed no more than 76.68 million people eligible to be voters. Even after the EC claimed that the errors had been corrected through a month-long drive in October–November 2006, the National Democratic Institute (NDI) of the United States found 15.5 per cent errors in the voter list.

Politicization of the administration is nothing new in Bangladesh. All ruling parties have tried to sway the administration in their favour by appointing their own henchmen, but beginning in early 2006, the coalition began to appoint men with the upcoming election in mind. Both at the central and local level, loyal officials were placed. The police administration was particularly swollen with party activists.

The ruling party not only disregarded the opposition's demands but also continued with their contemptuous acts. The appointment of two party loyalists to the EC in early 2006 is a case in point. The opposition parties organized street agitation, sit-ins, general strikes and blockades. These programmes resulted in clashes between party activists and the law enforcement forces, police excesses, and deaths of civilians. Repeated calls from civil society and the business community for negotiations were ignored by both political camps. In early October both parties agreed to meet at the secretary general level, but they chose to do so outside the parliamentary forum and remained intransigent on their positions.

On 28 October 2006 the low-scale violence and conflict erupted into full-blown street battles between government forces and government supporters on the one side and opposition activists on the other bringing about a collapse of law and order in the capital, Dhaka. The country descended into chaos, with general strikes, and transport blockades disrupting public life, causing damage to public property and enormous economic losses and above all, the deaths of innocent people in clashes between law enforcement officers and political activists.

The opposition, by then a cohesive alliance of 14 parties, drew support from various segments of society, and vowed to resist an interim government headed by Justice K. M. Hasan. Although Justice Hasan finally declined the position, violence continued, taking 12 lives in a single day. The situation took a turn for the worse when President Iajuddin Ahmed assumed the position of head of the CGT (in addition to his responsibilities as the president) and appointed a ten-member council. While his move followed the letter of the constitution, it was inconsistent with the spirit of the 'neutral caretaker government' and therefore added to an already volatile situation. The president's subsequent actions such as a refusal to negotiate with the Grand Alliance of the opposition parties (comprised of the AL and 14 of its allies, the JP led by General Ershad, the newly formed Liberal Democratic Party – a breakaway faction of the BNP), rejection of an agreement with the political parties negotiated by some members of the advisory council, the appointment of two BNP loyalists as new Election Commissioners, and the deployment of the army without consulting the members of the Council, to name but a few, demonstrated that the president was acting at the behest of the BNP. This led to the resignation of four members of the advisory council. The lack of neutrality of the president was bitterly criticized by members of the civil society and diplomatic corps. During this period opposition continued, with street agitations, and organized blockades and general strikes in major cities.

Hectic parleys by the diplomatic corps led by the US and UK envoys persuaded the opposition to join the poll, and subsequently the Grand Alliance submitted their nomination papers. But the EC's decision to disqualify General Ershad from becoming a candidate was the straw that broke the camel's back. The opposition withdrew their nominations on 3 January 2007 and all-out violence leading up to the election was on the horizon. Clashes between the police and opposition activists became a regular event and economic activities practically ground to a halt. Despite mounting domestic unrest and international concerns, the Election Commission, the CTG, and the BNP and the Jamaat-e-Islami were bent on completing the unilateral polling exercise. The government, particularly the president, rejected a call to defer the election date on the pretext that a 90-day limit was set by the constitution.

The Era of Democratic Deficit (2007–08)

It was against the backdrop of increasing violence, an obdurate president acting on behalf of the previous regime, and strident opposition that the international community moved in a concerted way on 11 January 2007 to put pressure on President Iajuddin Ahmed and the CTG to back down from the controversial plan to hold elections on 22 January.[6] The United Nations (UN) Secretary-General Ban Ki-moon stated that the political crisis in Bangladesh had 'severely jeopardized the legitimacy' of the polls, the European Commission warned that it would reassess its trade relations and cooperation with Bangladesh if the government went ahead with the election, and the UN, European Union (EU) and the Commonwealth announced that they were suspending their election observation missions with immediate effect. Additionally, in a press statement, UN Resident Coordinator in Bangladesh Renata Lok Dessallien stated that the deployment of the armed forces in support of the election process in Bangladesh would raise questions if the 22 January elections proceeded without the participation of all major political parties. The UN executive said, 'This may have implications for Bangladesh's future role in UN Peacekeeping Operations.'[7] These moves resulted in the declaration of a state of emergency with the support of the armed forces, the resignation of Iazuddin Ahmed as the chief of the CTG, dismissal of the cabinet he appointed and cancellation of the elections scheduled for 11 days later.[8] On the following day, an 11-member military-backed technocratic interim government, headed by the former chief of the central bank, was installed.

Thus large-scale bloodshed was avoided, but the nation paid a very high price − the loss of elected governance. The 15-year democratic phase of Bangladeshi politics came to an unceremonial end. The installation of the military backed CTG added a new phrase called 1/11 in Bangladeshi political lexicon. This step could have been taken by the military because of the unique situation, which Jalal Alamgir described as 'constitutional limbo':

> The constitution allows a state of emergency under exceptional circumstances, and it also requires a neutral caretaker administration to organize national elections. The two, however, had never coexisted.[9]

Ironically, the political change, despite the suppression of fundamental rights, received public approval. The administration was viewed by the mass of the people as neutral and capable of making necessary political and institutional changes for effective democracy.

As the military-backed caretaker government took power concerns were voiced over the likely consequences of the military's political intervention. Many analysts expressed apprehension that this may be the beginning of a long 'military rule' akin to the 1975–90 period. It was feared that in the long term, the intervention of the military in politics might prove terminal for Bangladeshi democracy. *The Economist*, for example, speculated that either the army might remain in politics by forming its own party, or worse, it might 'not bother with such niceties and declare outright martial law'.[10] On the other hand, the caretaker government's promises of sweeping reforms to the political system and building institutions necessary for sustainable democracy were welcomed by a large segment of the country's citizens. The vast scale of the corruption that has plagued Bangladeshi politics over the past decade and a half, the acrimonious relationship between the two political parties which made the parliament dysfunctional, the proliferation of Islamist militancy that shook the nation in August 2005, and the violence that preceded the declaration of emergency made citizens worried about the future direction of the country. Indeed, the attitude of many was captured by *The Economist*, which described developments as 'not uniformly bad' and praised the army for having intervened 'sensibly' in a 'failing democracy'.[11] But there is no doubt that none of this can pass the test of democracy.

After assuming power, the government launched a campaign against corruption. Hundreds of prominent political leaders of the BNP and the AL were arrested. The arrested leaders included, among others, a son of the former PM, close associates of the latter, and former ministers of Khaleda Zia's cabinet on the one hand, and leaders of the AL and advisors and aides of Sheikh Hasina, on the other. Extensive changes in laws related to detention, confiscation of property, bail, and trial were made providing the caretaker administration with enormous powers. Cases were filed against some of the arrested persons, but many were detained without any specific charges.

The interim government pledged to push through a string of reforms to put democracy back on track before holding elections by the end of 2008. The goals were to reshape the political parties, change the political culture and free institutions like the EC and Anti-Corruption Commission (ACC) from partisan influences. Critics, such as Alamgir, accept the premises of such reform measures but insist that the CTG misdiagnosed the problem. He writes:

> The caretaker government was right to maintain that governance
> in Bangladesh had been reduced to a shambles, and that

fundamental reforms were in order. It was also able to prosecute, to widespread public approval, many political figures who had been accustomed to misbehaving with impunity, including Tarique Rahman and other members of his Hawa Bhaban clique. But the administration misdiagnosed the root problem by blaming the democratic system as a whole. The ills that tore at the country's political life sprang from semiauthoritarianism and electoral manipulation specifically in the mid 1990s and after 2001. The problem was not democracy, but rather its subversion.[12]

By mid-2008, it was evident that many aspects of the political reforms necessary for sustainable democracy could not be achieved for an array of reasons including the nature of the government (i.e. not having the popular mandate) and resistance from entrenched political interests (including, but not limited to, the major political parties). In some cases the time was too short to bring about change, in other cases the CTG lacked prudence. The effort to exile the two leaders, Sheikh Hasina of the AL and Khaleda Zia of the BNP, commonly referred to as 'Minus Two Formula', not only failed but also caused a backlash.

By the end of 2008, a few of the achievements that remained were the compilation of a new error-free voters list with pictures of the voters, appointment of an independent Election Commission, and the separation of judiciary from executive. The electoral laws were changed to address the lack of democracy within political parties, a major problem for institutionalizing democracy, but it was clear that as soon as a political party came to power it would be able to flout them at will. The institutional autonomy of the ACC, created during the caretaker regime, was weak and was destined to become ineffective without the political will and support of the government.

Thus, at the end of the two years, the great expectations of the Bangladeshis (and observers of Bangladeshi politics) who saw this as an unprecedented opportunity to bring about qualitative changes in Bangladeshi politics remained unfulfilled. But even the staunch critics of the caretaker government acknowledged, 'although its goal of reforming politics remained unmet, the caretaker government delivered credible elections and a peaceful transfer of power'. The interregnum was over.

Polarization and Democracy's Retreat (2009–15)

The election held in December 2008 constituted a milestone in the history of the nation – on many counts, from the high turnout of voters to the unprecedented result. The AL-led alliance secured a landslide victory (four-fifths of parliament seats), the BNP and its allies recorded its worst ever electoral defeat, the Jatiya Party (JP) headed by General H. M. Ershad regained its position as a key player in Bangladeshi politics and the Islamists, particularly the Bangladesh Jamaat-e-Islami (BJI), experienced a setback. However, the 2008 elections will be remembered for reasons beyond these results: the campaign was violence-free, candidates of all parties by and large adhered to strict electoral rules, participation of the voters was higher than ever before, the election-day atmosphere was festive, and the elections were free, fair and credible. Successful completion of two key conditions for democratic transition, an election participated in by all parties and the peaceful transfer of power, once again raised hopes that Bangladesh may have turned the page of its bitter past and proceed towards strengthening democracy.

But the regime faced a serious challenge within a month of assuming power; a large-scale mutiny by the paramilitary Bangladesh Rifles (BDR), responsible for patrolling the borders, tested the regime. According to official sources, 74 people including the 57 military officers seconded from the army, were killed. The government showed restraint and brought the rebellion to an end through negotiations; but it caused resentment among a section of the army. Initial investigations revealed that the primary causes of the violent incident were low levels of pay and poor conditions, combined with resentment of the privileges of the officers, most of whom were seconded from the regular army. Some senior military officers were strongly critical of the government's approach, and alleged that the choice of negotiation with the mutineers over force may have contributed to the deaths of army officers. Subsequently, a number of army officers were dismissed or forcibly retired. In the months following the mutiny numerous arrests were made and trials involving several thousand alleged insurgents began in November. There were accusations that many of the detainees were severely mistreated; at least 39 detainees suffered 'unnatural' deaths while in custody. In July 2010 the Council of Ministers approved a draft law that provided for the introduction of the death penalty in cases of mutiny. In January 2011 the BDR were restructured and renamed the Border Guard of Bangladesh. In October 2012, the BDR mutiny trials concluded. In 57 cases 5,926 members of the erstwhile BDR were convicted in 11 special courts during the 27-month trial period. A total of 115 were acquitted and five individuals were dropped from the mutiny charges. A specially appointed civilian court, established under the Bangladesh Criminal Procedure Code, heard a case against 847 people – 824 soldiers and 23 civilians, including former BNP lawmaker Nasiruddin Ahmed Pintu and local AL leader Torab Ali, accused of serious criminal conduct such as rape, murder, arson, looting and conspiracy. In November 2013 the court sentenced 152 people to death; a further 161 defendants were sentenced to life imprisonment, 256 received prison terms of between three and ten years, and 277 were acquitted.[13] These trials generated some criticisms, for example, when a military court sentenced 611 BDR members in June 2012, the US-based organization Human Rights Watch (HRW) condemned 'the mass trials', claiming they did not meet international standards and violated the country's constitution. Later HRW called for the trials to be suspended and for the establishment of an independent task force with sufficient authority to investigate rigorously and, where appropriate, prosecute all allegations of unlawful deaths, torture, and mistreatment of suspects.

A series of court decisions in 2010 and 2011 made a significant impact on Bangladeshi politics and governance. These verdicts will reverberate through the next decades. In July 2010 the Appellate Division of the Supreme Court upheld the 2005 verdict of the High Court annulling the fifth amendment of the constitution.[14] The amendment had provided legitimacy to the three regimes that held power between 15 August 1975 and February 1979, headed by Khandakar Mushtaq Ahmed, Abu Sadat Mohammad Sayem and General Ziaur Rahman (General Zia). Although the court expressed its support for the various administrative works carried out during 1975–79 that had not infringed on citizens' rights, it declared martial law to have been illegal. In a similar vein, in August 2010 the High Court annulled the seventh amendment of the constitution, which had provided constitutional legitimacy to the Ershad regime; the verdict was upheld by the Supreme Court in May 2011.[15] In March 2011, delivering a judgment on four separate writ petitions submitted by members of the family of the late Lieutenant-Colonel (retd) Abu Taher, the High Court declared the trial and subsequent execution of Taher to have been illegal and unconstitutional. The judgment asserted that his execution had been cold-blooded murder 'masterminded by the then chief martial law administrator, Gen. Ziaur Rahman'.[16] It was followed by the annulment of the thirteenth amendment of the constitution, which had been introduced in 1996 and had allowed for the creation of a non-party caretaker government system, by the Supreme Court in May 2011.[17] The Court also made two pertinent observations that the next two parliamentary elections could be held under the caretaker system, and that parliament could amend the charter by deleting the provisions requiring the former chief justices or the judges of the Appellate Division to head the caretaker government. Most of the eight amicus curiae of the thirteenth amendment case and representatives of the civil society organizations, underscored the need to heed the Supreme Court's suggestion.[18]

The full text of the verdict, issued more than a year after the summary (known as the short order) was issued, revealed that there was no consensus among the justices as to whether the thirteenth amendment was unconstitutional. Of the seven judges of the apex court, four were in favour of declaring the caretaker provision unconstitutional; two dissented; and one opined that the matter should be left to parliament. But there was unanimity on two issues. Firstly, that the system should be kept for two more elections. Secondly, in their joint observation, the judges concurred with the concerns of the amicus curiae that an election under a party government is a recipe for disaster. The judges observed: 'The senior lawyers of the country expressed apprehension that there would be anarchy if the ensuing election is held under party government. And we cannot ignore their view.'

The short order of the court verdict provided the legal cover to the ruling party to bring drastic changes to the CTG system, already being planned after the annulment of the fifth amendment by the court. The parliamentary committee, in which the BNP decided not to participate, was appointed to recommend the changes. (See Chapter 4 for deliberations of the committee.)

In the midst of these controversies, the *Fifteenth Amendment Bill* (confirming the annulment of the thirteenth amendment) was passed by parliament on 30 June 2011. With the assent of the president, on 2 July 2011 the amendment became law. In addition to the annulment of the CTG, the fifteenth amendment added two provisos to the constitution: Articles 7A and 7B. Article 7A made any attempt to abrogate or suspend the constitution an act of sedition, punishable by death. Article 7B prohibited any further amendments to 55 clauses of the constitution describing these as the 'basic structure of the constitution'. The fifteenth amendment also created an unprecedented option of holding the parliamentary election without the dissolution of the existing parliament. Article 123 (3) states, 'a general election of the members of parliament shall be held (a) in the case of a dissolution by reason of the expiration of the term within the 90 days preceding such dissolution'. As such, the elections will be held at a time when an elected parliament will remain effective. This is inconsistent with the Westminster-style parliamentary system (e.g. in Britain, Australia, Canada and New Zealand) where parliament is dissolved first before the new parliamentary election. The BNP immediately declared its intention to boycott any national election unless the CTG was reinstated.

The issue of the caretaker government came to prominence at a time when another issue was brewing: trying those who committed war crimes during the independence war in 1971. The AL, in line with its election promise, established the International Crimes Tribunal (ICT) in 2010 under the *ICT Act 1973* as amended in 2009.

During the war of liberation the Pakistani military committed genocide, and a small number of political parties, particularly the Jamaat-e-Islami (JI) and the Muslim League (ML), colluded with the Pakistani forces, and members of these political parties became members of paramilitary forces which perpetrated various crimes. Soon after independence, on 24 January 1972, the government promulgated the *Bangladesh Collaborators (Special Tribunals) Order* by a presidential decree which provided for the prosecution of 'collaborators' before 'special tribunals'. Upon return from his captivity, Sheikh Mujib repeatedly promised to try those who had committed war crimes. The government identified 1,100, later scaled down to 195, of 93,000 Pakistani prisoners of war[19] suspected of committing war crimes.[20] Bangladesh expressed its desire to try them. But it came under pressure from various countries, especially Muslim majority countries in the Middle East who were yet to recognize the country, not to conduct the trial. The fate of about 400,000 Bangladeshis stranded in Pakistan hung in the balance as Pakistani President (later PM) Zulfiqar Ali Bhutto threatened to try many of them, particularly those who were working for the Pakistani government at the time of the war.[21] At least 203 Bengali officials were arrested in 1973, and Bhutto told Indian PM's special envoy P. N. Haksar that 'if Bangladesh did proceed with the trials, he would be forced to charge 203 Bengali civilian officials in Pakistan with espionage and high treason'.[22] Previously Bhutto had indicated that Pakistan would not hesitate to use its close relationship with China to block Bangladesh's entry to the United Nations; this come to pass when China vetoed in August 1972.[23] China argued that it exercised its veto because, 'the new country has failed to observe UN resolution calling for prisoner repatriation'[24] clearly a reference to Bangladesh's efforts to hold the trials.

While the trial of alleged Pakistani war criminals became an issue at the global stage, the *International Crimes (Tribunals) Act 1973* (Act No. XIX of 1973) was passed by the parliament on 20 July 1973, and was incorporated into the constitution. The *ICT Act* was considered groundbreaking as it was considered to be consistent with the international norms and practices at that time. As the government was trying to remain committed to the trials, it faced practical problems and domestic criticism for using the *Collaborators Act* expansively. This led to a clemency and a general amnesty, on 16 May 1973 and 30 November 1973, respectively. The general amnesty, however, was not granted to those accused of murder, rape, arson, or genocide.

Under the *Collaborators Act*, between 1972 and 1974, some 37,471 people were arrested. Altogether 73 tribunals were established to try these cases. Over the course of these trials 22 people were sentenced to death, 68 to life imprisonment and 752 to imprisonment for various terms. After the clemency and general amnesty most of the arrested were freed, and cases against about 11,000 people were filed. These include senior leaders of the proscribed political parties, such as Khan Abdus Sabur, Fazlul Qauder Chowdhury of the Mulism League and Shah Azizur Rahman of the Pakistan Democratic Party, and Abbas Ali Khan of the JI.

The war crimes trials, especially of Pakistani military personnel, took a dramatic turn on 9 April 1974 as the tripartite agreement between Bangladesh, Pakistan and India was signed. The treaty acknowledged that 'there was universal consensus that persons charged with such crimes as the 195 Pakistani prisoners of war should be held to account and subjected to the dues process of Law' but 'having regard to the appeal of the Prime Minister of Pakistan to the people of Bangladesh to forgive and forget the mistakes of the past, the Foreign Minister of Bangladesh stated that the Government of Bangladesh has decided not to proceed with the trials as an act of clemency'.[25] What prompted this u-turn of the Bangladesh government in regard to the trial of the alleged war criminals? According to Raghavan:

> The Indians suggested to their Bangladeshi counterparts that the trials be postponed to facilitate the resolution of the other issues. By this time, the problem of international recognition, especially entry to the United Nations, was weighing heavily on Mujib's mind, and the possibility of reprisal trials by Pakistan was equally troubling.[26]

According to another account the war crimes trial issue was dropped by Mujib in exchange for Pakistan's formal recognition in February 1974. A delegation team of Islamic Summit Conference,[27] comprising Hasan-ul-Tohmay (Secretary General) and representatives of Kuwait, Somalia, Lebanon, Algeria and Senegal visited Dhaka on 20 February to persuade Mujib to attend the summit at Lahore beginning on 22 February. He agreed to join only after the formal recognition of Bangladesh by Pakistan was announced. But, he also agreed that the war crimes trial would not be pursued further.[28]

Whatever narrative one subscribes to, what should not be ignored is that for Mujib it was a bitter pill to swallow. His reactions after the signing of the tripartite treaty described by Kamal Hossain, then foreign minister and a signatory of the treaty, testifies to his sense of despair:

> I recall my first meeting with Bangabandhu after signing of the agreement. He was deeply pensive and brooding. Looking up, he said, 'Bengalis have demonstrated their generosity to the world. We have made the maximum contribution to opening a new chapter in the region.' But, he added, 'For me, I am borne down by the thought that this is the first time in my life that I have not been able to fulfill a public commitment. I had told our people

that the war criminals shall be tried on the soil of Bangladesh.
I have not been able to keep my word [. . .] Let us hope that this act
will bring some good to our people'.[29]

Therefore, despite making promises and initiating the processes, the
trials never took place and 195 alleged war criminals were repatriated to
Pakistan along with the POWs.

As for the trials of the collaborators, the process continued until the
law was repealed in December 1975, a few months after the coup that
deposed the Mujib regime.[30] Military rulers and political parties who
came to power later avoided the uncomfortable truth as almost all of
them befriended those who were suspected criminals. In February 1992,
Jahanara Imam, mother of a martyr, initiated a civil society movement
demanding justice. The National Coordinating Committee for the
Realization of Bangladesh Liberation War Ideals and Trials of War
Criminals of 1971 (commonly known as the Nirmul Committee)
comprising eminent members of the civil society was founded with the
support of an array of social, cultural, political and women's
organizations and trade unions. The Committee appointed an enquiry
committee to look into a number of alleged war criminals, most of
whom were the leaders of the JI. Based on the report of the enquiry
committee, a public tribunal (akin to the International War Crimes
Tribunal founded by Bertrand Russell in 1966 regarding the Vietnam
War) was held in 1992. This was followed up by another enquiry
committee and another public tribunal in 1993. Public support for the
symbolic trials was immense, while the government cracked down on
the organizers. The civil society movement continued, albeit weakly.
The issue gained attention in 2007 as a forum of former commanders of
the liberation war started a public campaign. Throughout the tenure
of the caretaker government between 2007 and 2008, the Sector
Commanders Forum (SCF) organized public consultation meetings
while all political activities were banned. While the SCF was
campaigning demanding the trials, the JI Secretary General Ali Ahsan
Mojahid asserted that there were no war criminals in Bangladesh.[31] The
statement infuriated many and added impetus to the SCF's demand.

The AL incorporated the demands as one of the chief objectives in its
2008 election manifesto, made some changes in the *ICT Act* in 2009, and
set up the tribunal in 2010 (a second tribunal was appointed in March

2012 and scrapped three years later). With the arrest of Delwar Hossain Sayeedi in October 2011, the process commenced. The BJI, which had always insisted that none of its leaders had participated in crimes against humanity, contested that the ICT was politically motivated and demanded that it be scrapped, appealing for demonstrations and general strikes to be staged in support of this on several occasions. In late 2012 the party intensified its pressure on the government to this end, staging increasingly violent demonstrations, to which the government responded in a heavy-handed manner. The BNP, until early 2013, maintained an ambivalent position towards the process, offering support in principle but at the same time arguing that the current tribunal lacked transparency and that the process was inconsistent with international standards.

While there is considerable support among Bangladeshis for the trial of the perpetrators of crimes against humanity in 1971, the trial process continues to attract criticism.[32] There are some apprehensions about the fairness of the trial process among the Bangladeshi population, but also from outside the country. The US Ambassador-at-Large for War Crimes Issues, Stephen J Rapp, has visited Dhaka on four occasions including a trip in May 2013 and expressed reservations about the process. In May 2011 HRW called upon Sheikh Hasina to amend the *International Crimes (Tribunals) Act 1973* to ensure a credible and fair tribunal; a number of amendments regarding rules of procedure were accordingly effected in June 2011. However, these amendments failed to win over the critics. In November 2012 the UN Working Group on Arbitrary Detention upheld complaints issued by some of the tribunal's defendants and requested that the government take steps to conform to the International Covenant on Civil and Political Rights and the Universal Declaration of Human Rights.

A controversy added to the concerns about the process. The controversy ensued in December 2012 when a national daily newspaper, *Amar Desh*, allied to the opposition party and a fierce critic of the Tribunal, published transcripts of internet telephone conversations and e-mails between ICT-1 Chairman Justice Md Nizamul Huq and Ahmed Ziauddin, an expatriate Bangladeshi expert in international law. Shortly before the newspaper began publishing the transcripts, the ICT announced that Justice Huq's computer, along with his e-mail and internet accounts, had been hacked. *Amar Desh*, claiming that it had collected the records from a foreign source, published the conversations in their entirety. However, on 13 December the ICT issued an injunction prohibiting the national media from publishing the leaked correspondence. On the same day Fazle Kabir (hitherto head of the ICT-2) was appointed ICT-1 Chairman, following Justice Huq's resignation on 11 December. Meanwhile, a British magazine, *The Economist*, also acquired possession of the correspondence between Justice Huq and Ziauddin. *The Economist* published a report on 15 December in which it concluded that the correspondence 'raise(s) profound questions about the trial' and 'suggests the government tried to put pressure on Mr Nizamul, albeit he seems to have resisted it'. The leaks also raised 'questions about conflicts of interest', as Ziauddin appeared also to have advised members of the prosecution team at the ICT.

By the beginning of 2013, two issues dominated the political scene: the now defunct caretaker government system, and the war crimes trials. While the AL was opposed to the reintroduction of the CTG system, the demand for CTG had overwhelming public support.[33] On the other hand while the JI (and BNP, to a great extent) were opposed to or critical of the war crimes trial, the trials had the backing of the overwhelming majority of Bangladeshi citizens.

The tribunal began delivering its verdicts in early 2013. The sentencing of the BJI leader Abdul Quader Mollah to life imprisonment in early February unleashed a series of events with serious consequences. After the verdict discontented youths began a demonstration at Shahbagh public square near Dhaka University, alleging that the court had shown leniency to the accused as part of a secret deal between the BJI and the government. The demonstrators, mostly online bloggers, spearheaded a movement demanding that those convicted of war crimes be awarded the death penalty. Their demands also included the outlawing of the BJI and the arrest of *Amar Desh*'s editor for the publication's portrayal of the uprising as fascist in nature. The demonstration quickly became the rallying point of secularists and drew unprecedented spontaneous participation from women of all walks of life. Protests in solidarity with those at Shahbagh spread across the country and further afield, fuelled by social media. The government moved quickly to co-opt the grassroots movement, with Sheikh Hasina extending support to the participants. Confronted by growing demands that the government appeal against the sentence awarded to Abdul Quader Mollah, three amendments to the

International Crimes (Tribunals) Act 1973 were approved by parliament in mid-February 2013 (with retrospective effect from 14 July 2009) The amendments enabled the ICT to charge and place on trial organizations for their role in the 1971 war of liberation, allowed the government, a complainant, or informant to appeal an order of acquittal or order of sentencing, and imposed a statutory obligation on the Appellate Division of the Supreme Court to dispose of any appeal filed before it within 60 days.

As the Shahbagh movement gained momentum, the BNP vacillated on the question of how to react; with the government continuing to steer the movement, the BJI was at risk of being outmanoeuvred; meanwhile, other Islamist organizations began to mobilize. Following the brutal murder of a prominent political blogger in mid-February, Islamist activists alleged that he had previously made blasphemous statements in his writing. Islamists condemned the uprising and its organizers as anti-Islamic and branded the government as atheist owing to its support for the movement. A number of media organizations associated with the BJI and the BNP, particularly *Amar Desh*, highlighted these allegations and helped to promote an emerging Islamist alliance. Although the allegation of being atheist was previously brought against individuals, especially secularist and feminist authors, the issue was never at the centre of political debate in Bangladesh until late 2013. The Shahbagh demonstrators (popularly known as Gonojagoron Mancha), on the other hand, often labelled its critics 'opponents of the spirit of liberation war', thus questioning their loyalty to the nation.

In this contentious political environment, a new Islamist organization, Hefazat-e-Islam (HI – Protector of Islam), emerged. An umbrella organization of smaller Islamist organizations, and Islamic scholars associated with privately operated traditional *qawmi madrassas* (Islamic seminaries), was resuscitated under the leadership of Mufti Ahmed Shah Shafi at a conference in March 2013. The sudden emergence of the HI was intriguing. Two interpretations are available with regard to its emergence and prominence: firstly, the Islamists sensed an existential threat and acted accordingly; second, the organization was propped up with tacit support as an antidote to the JI, to demonstrate that the JI is not the only Islamist force in the country. The organization demanded that the government immediately dismantle the Shahbagh

movement and arrest the activists, and declared that a protest march to
Dhaka would begin in April. After negotiations between the HI and the
government, it was allowed to stage a mass gathering in the capital.
While the ruling party and its allies declared to disrupt the gathering of
the HI, the BNP extended its support to the HI campaign and its local
activists provided assistance; General Ershad's Jatiya Party, a member of
the ruling coalition, also extended its support. Despite various
impediments, almost 500,000 HI activists, mostly *madrassa* students,
staged a peaceful rally. They issued a 13-point list of demands, and
pledged to blockade the capital if their demands were not met by 5 May.
The demands included the introduction of an anti-blasphemy law
carrying the death penalty for anyone found to have insulted Islam and
the Prophet Muhammad; an end to the pro-women development policy;
a ban on men and women mixing in public; an end to 'shameless'
behaviour and attire; and an appeal for the controversial reformist
Ahmadiyya sect to be declared non-Muslim. After initial mixed
messages in regard to the demands, the PM rejected the HI's demand for
an anti-blasphemy law, but stated that the government would consider
the organization's other demands. The editor of *Amar Desh*, a key backer
of the HI, was arrested on 11 April 2013.

A month after its first Dhaka gathering, on 5 May, HI activists from
all over the country staged a major rally in Dhaka and imposed a
blockade of the capital. While the rally itself remained peaceful, violence
broke out nearby as HI activists, allegedly with BJI involvement, set fire
to various buildings including banks, shops, government offices and the
Communist Party of Bangladesh headquarters, and attacked security
personnel. At least 13 people, including a police officer, died in clashes
during the day. As the HI leaders resolved to continue their rally
throughout the night (defying an earlier agreement with the
authorities), and Khaleda Zia urged Dhaka residents to join the HI
protest, a team of 10,000 police officers, members of the Rapid Action
Battalion (RAB – an élite police force) and the BGB launched a late-
night operation, forcing the demonstrators from the square within an
hour. Prior to initiating the operation, police cut the power supply in the
city's commercial area and closed down pro-opposition television
stations, although a small number of reporters were allowed to
accompany the security personnel. The government claimed that no one
was killed during the dispersal of the protesters, but the BNP and HI

leaders claimed that thousands had lost their lives, with police having taken away many bodies, and that thousands more were injured. The number of deaths could not be verified independently but *The Economist*, quoting European diplomats in Dhaka, put the number at 50.

Through the Summer and Fall of 2013, five sets of events continued to play out in parallel; they were at one level interrelated, while autonomous on the other. The ICT continued to deliver verdicts; BNP and its allies including the BJI stepped up violent street agitations in support of the demand for the caretaker government; the BJI continued to unleash a reign of terror after each of the verdicts against its leaders were issued; the Shahbagh movement, although beginning to lose its appeal, pressed on for death penalties for all war criminals and proscription of the BJI; and the ruling party and its allies began preparing for an election even if the opposition should boycott it. In the midst of these events, in August, the High Court declared the BJI's registration with the Election Commission void due to the conflict between the national constitution and the party charter. The court verdict came in response to a writ petition filed by a little-known religion-based political party, the Tariqat Federation, an ally of the ruling AL in early 2009.

As for the verdicts of the tribunals as of February 2016: BJI leader Abdul Quder Mollah was sentenced to life imprisonment on 5 February 2013 (which was converted to the death sentence on 17 September 2013 by the Supreme Court, on appeal from the government. He was executed on 12 December after his appeal was rejected); Delwar Hossain Sayeedi was sentenced to death on 28 February 2013 (his sentence was reduced to 'imprisonment till death' by the Supreme Court on 17 September 2014); Kamaruazzaman was sentenced to death on 9 May 2013 (and executed on 11 April 2015); Ghulam Azam was sentenced to 90 years imprisonment on 15 July 2013 (and died of natural causes on 23 October 2014); Ali Ahsan Mojaheed was sentenced to death on 17 July 2013 (and executed on 22 November 2015); Salahuddin Quader Chowdhury – then a BNP MP – was sentenced to death on 1 October 2013 (and executed on 22 November 2015); Abdul Alim was sentenced to life imprisonment on 9 October 2013 (and died of cancer on 30 August 2014); Choudhury Mueenuddin and Ashrafuzzaman Khan were sentenced to death *in absentia* on 3 November 2013; Matiur Rahman Nizami was sentenced to death on 29 October 2014.

Several rounds of violence shook the country in 2013. The first outburst took place between 28 February and 4 March in the wake of the conviction by the ICT of Delwar Hossain Sayeedi. The ensuing clashes between BJI activists and security officers were described by the British Broadcasting Corporation as the worst day of political violence in Bangladesh's history and claimed the lives of at least 40 people on a single day. Activists attacked police stations, vandalized local government offices, set ablaze railways carriages, dismantled railway lines, and torched a power sub-station. Concurrently, Hindu temples and houses of minorities were attacked, looted and vandalized. General strikes called by the BNP and the BJI in subsequent days resulted in further loss of life and damage to properties. More than 80 people were reported to have been killed in five days of unrest. The second major outbreak of violence ensued on 5 May, the day on which the HI imposed a blockade of Dhaka. At least 13 people died in clashes between police and HI supporters during the day, and a further 50 were reported to have been killed during a police operation to disperse HI protesters. On the following day at least 27 people, including three security officers, died in clashes between the authorities and HI activists in various parts of the country. On 7 May UN Secretary-General Ban Ki-moon expressed concern and appealed for calm.

The country witnessed a third spate of violence in September when Quader Mollah's appeal process ended with a death sentence verdict. Scores died over a three-day period of general strikes called by the BJI. The fourth major outbreak began as soon as the election schedule was announced on November 25. According to press reports and ASK, 75 people died between 25 November and 15 December in general strikes and blockades imposed by the opposition. These deaths are attributed to police atrocities and violence perpetrated by opposition political activists. The violence continued until the election day and the death toll continued to rise. While the general strikes were on going, the execution of Quader Mollah on 12 December added another strand of violence. At least 30 people died over a few days of clashes throughout the country.

The efforts to reconcile the positions of the ruling and opposition parties about the nature of the government to oversee the election, by the members of Bangladeshi civil society and the international community, failed due to intransigence of both parties. Three trips by UN Assistant

Secretary for Political Affairs Oscar Fernandez-Taranco, including one in December 2013, and various proposals from the members of the civil society including one from Transparency International Bangladesh (TIB) bore no results. Requests from the European Union and the US Secretary of State also fell on deaf ears. Fernandez-Taranco's request during his last trip (6–9 December) to defer the election to allow the opposition to reconsider its decision to boycott was not entertained by the government and the PM cancelled the second meeting with him. The government insisted that the election must be held for the sake of constitutional continuity even if it was boycotted by the opposition. Hasina offered a slight compromise in November proposing an 'all party' cabinet during the election and inviting the BNP to join, but the BNP declined. On 18 November as the 'all party cabinet' took oath, it became obvious that only AL allies who had been part of the cabinet for the past five years had agreed to join it. All other opposition parties rejected the ruling party's offer. Seven days later the Election Commission announced the election schedule with the poll date on 5 January 2014.

The government proceeded with the election. The 'March for Democracy' called by the BNP-led opposition on 29 December 2013 was foiled by the government using a heavy-handed approach. Khaleda Zia was put under virtual house arrest. The opposition, on the other hand, failed to mobilize its activists, let alone the public at large. Opposition's adoption of violence as a tactic in the previous weeks alienated it from the public although the one-sided election was unacceptable to the citizens. This may well be a reflection of the reservation of the public about the alliance with the BJI, once an asset for the BNP in electoral politics.

The victory of the ruling alliance led by the AL was a foregone conclusion, given the opposition boycott. Only 12 of 40 parties registered with the Election Commission participated, the lowest tally in the history of the country. Some of these parties had only a handful of candidates. After the deadline for the withdrawal of nominations passed, it became known that more than half of the members of the parliament, 153 out of 300, were elected unopposed. The voter turnout was remarkably low. Official sources, including the EC, claimed that the turnout was 39 per cent. But this figure is contested by the local and international press, with estimates varying from 10 to 22 per cent at best. In about 50 of the 18,200 polling places (at least

120 of which had been burned on the day and evening before the election), no votes at all were cast. The election results showed that the AL alone secured 233 seats. Twenty members of the JP, including Rowshan Ershad, were elected unopposed, while 14 including General Ershad were elected in the poll. The JP emerged as the second largest party in the tenth parliament. International media described the election a 'farce'[34] and the victory of the AL became, even in the eyes of sympathizers, 'hollow.'[35]

The results of the election positioned the JP led by General Ershad as the parliamentary opposition. But a series of events before and after the election show that the JP was handpicked perhaps coerced, into joining the election. Although the JP was a member of the AL-led grand coalition which ruled the country, General Ershad announced in early November that his party would boycott the election unless other opposition parties joined. Subsequently, he announced his departure from the coalition on 18 November, only to join the 'all-party government' on the same day and participate in the election. A few days later, on 3 December, he changed his mind again, deciding to boycott the election and asked his colleagues in the cabinet to resign. As a large number of the JP withdrew their nominations, a small group under the leadership of his wife Rowshan Ershad remained in the race. Several meetings between the PM and Rowshan Ershad took place. Ershad's request for withdrawal of his candidature was denied by the EC. Finally, on 12 December, he was picked up by the RAB from his home and admitted to a military hospital. He remained incommunicado while some members of his party went on participating in the election. Ershad himself was elected from one constituency. Soon after the election, the Parliament Secretariat announced that the Rowshan Ershad led JP was the parliamentary opposition. Three members from the party were inducted into the new cabinet which was sworn in on 12 January 2014; General Ersahd was named special envoy of the prime minister. The inclusion of the JP in the cabinet essentially turned the tenth parliament into one without any opposition party.

After a relatively calm year, the country descended into a spiral of violence in early 2015. In January the BNP called for demonstrations to mark the anniversary of the controversial election and pressed for the election to be held under a neutral government. The BNP-led alliance was prohibited from organizing a public rally and the

BNP leader Khaleda Zia was confined at the party office. The BNP launched general strikes and imposed a countrywide blockade which unleashed violence. Incidents of throwing homemade petrol bombs and burning public transport, especially public buses with passengers inside, took place in great numbers. The government blamed the BNP for orchestrating these incidents while the BNP alleged that they were carried out by ruling party activists to defame the opposition movement. Although arrests of some ruling party activists with homemade bombs similar to those being used for arson attacks gave some credence to the BNP's allegation, there was very little doubt that attacks were being perpetrated by BNP supporters and activists of the BJI. In the initial days of the movement the regime and the ruling party showed nervousness. But the inability of the BNP to lead public mobilization (such as rallies, and demonstrations) gradually weakened its claim to enjoy public support. Their tactics, if not the demand, lost appeal. The conspicuous absence of the BNP leaders on the political scene raised scepticism about the goal while Khaleda Zia and her confidants continue to claim success. Over time, the party seemed to lose grip of the movement which appeared to be a series of sporadic violent activities. The popular perception that the actions were conducted under the instructions of Tareq Rahman, son of Khaleda Zia with a chequered past who is in self-exile in London, did not help the party.

Law enforcement agencies were given a free hand in dealing with opposition activists. Overall, 138 people died in the violence that gripped the country for 91 days. Of these 74 died in incidents of bomb attacks or incidents of burning vehicles, 10 died in clashes with either law enforcement agencies (such as the police, the RAB, and the Bangladesh Border Guards) or between supporters of the government and the opposition. At least 37 people were killed in 'crossfire'/'encounters' – official descriptions used to justify extra-judicial killings by the law enforcement agencies (for extrajudicial killings and abductions since 2004, see Chapter 4). The government's decision to resort to harsh tactics including arresting opposition leaders and the killing of activists by law enforcement forces, exacerbated the situation. According to human rights groups at least 18,000 people, mostly opposition activists, were arrested and many were detained without charge. Deaths from the political violence, clashes between the members of the law enforcing agencies and opposition activists, and extra judicial killings perpetrated by the law enforcing agencies continue to mount. Repeated calls from the international community and members of the civil society within Bangladesh for a dialogue to address the political impasse were rejected by the ruling party. The opposition also declined to scale down its agitation. By the time the three-month long agitation and violence came to an end, the country had already suffered heavy losses – in terms of the economy $2.2 billion, almost 1 per cent of its GDP growth; public examinations for students had to be postponed several times; while educational institutions lost school days, creating disarray in the academic calendar.

The 91 days of violence and political turmoil came to a temporary halt as the date of elections for two city corporations in Dhaka and Chittagong were announced. Like elections to other local government bodies, these are non-partisan, but only on paper. After some wavering the BNP decided to join the poll, despite the fact that one of its mayoral candidates in Dhaka and many ward level candidates were unable to campaign due to a number of pending cases and rejection of the bail petition. But the glimmer of hope faded as the Election Commission was either unwilling or unable to create a level playing field, and the day of election – 28 April 2015 – was marked by widespread irregularities. The BNP withdrew its candidates in the middle of the election day itself. The ruling party candidates won handsomely. Thus, by the middle of the year the political situation was once again characterized by a forceful government, a weakened opposition, and prevalent political uncertainty.

Political events since 2013 have been marked by two ominous developments: brutal killings of the self-proclaimed atheist bloggers and widespread use of a law limiting criticism both of the government and of religious sentiments. These two developments, coming from two conflicting sources, placed serious strain on the freedom of speech. The former has been attributed to militant Islamist groups while the latter is state-sponsored. In the words of an analyst, freedom of speech, is 'caught between machete and magistrate.'[36]

Alleging that bloggers and secular online activists are demeaning Islam and the Prophet, Islamists began demanding anti-blasphemy laws and severe punishments for those writers, while the state continue to make use of the *Information and Communication Act*, particularly Article 57, to silence its critics. In the context of the growing demands of the Islamists and deepening religiosity among the population, radical Islamists threatened to kill anyone who they deemed critical of Islam. Fringe militant groups acted on this threat. On the evening of 15 February, Ahmed Rajib Haider was hacked to death near his home in Dhaka. The brutal murder of Rajib, an organizer of the Shahbagh movement which was at its height at the time of his killing in terms of popular support and media attention, shocked the nation. This was a chilling reminder of another attack nine years earlier when an author Humayun Azad was attacked outside the national book fair. Azad was known to be an atheist and anti-Islamist. Azad survived the assassination attempt but died a few months later in Munich during a research assignment.

A previously unknown group, Ansarullah Bangla Team (ABT), claimed responsibility for the killing of Rajib Haider. The killing generated intense debate, especially because soon afterwards his writings in various blogs and social media became known to a wider audience, thanks to the pro-BNP daily, *Amar Desh*. These writings were reprinted with great enthusiasm to suggest that they were demeaning to Islam and the Prophet. These comments were considered blasphemous by some, while others felt that the comments were within his right of freedom of expression. The HI and even pro-BAL *ulema* groups (for example the Bangladesh Ahle Sunnat wal Jamaat, the Bangladesh Ulema League) demanded that the government crack down on the anti-Islamic blogs.

Four other bloggers and a publisher of a book by one of the slain bloggers were murdered in 2015. The bloggers are Avijit Roy (a US-based Bangladeshi-American blogger, killed on 26 February); Washiqur Rahman Babu (hacked to death by three men in Dhaka on 30 March); Ananta Bijoy Das (killed in Sylhet while on his way to work in on 12 May); and Niloy Chatterjee Niloy (hacked to death at his home in Dhaka on 6 August). Faisal Arefin Dipon, publisher of books by Avijit Roy, was hacked to death inside his office on 31 October. The ABT (occasionally referred to as Ansar al Islam, self-claimed representative of the AQIS) claimed responsibility for these killings. These murders have sent a chilling message to those who want to speak without fear of the restrictions imposed by religious dictats. The extent of the fear has become palpable by late 2015, as many bloggers have imposed self-censorship, and others have fled the country.[37]

Three concerns have emerged: first, that these murders are not sporadic but planned as these victims are drawn from a publicly available list of 'atheist' bloggers (see below); secondly, that there is a deep division within society as to whether their works constitute blasphemy; thirdly, the government has gradually began to shun the bloggers instead of providing adequate protection.

The press have reported a list of 84 bloggers who are described as atheist by Islamists.[38] The issue of the list first came to be known in early 2013. In the wake of the emergence of the HI, the government began conversations with various religious groups. The government appointed a nine-member committee to gather information and identify the blogs and bloggers. One Islamist group provided a list of nine blogs and 56 bloggers whom it considered anti-Islamic.[39] With suggestions from others, the committee compiled a list of 84 bloggers. The committee blocked a number of pro-Islamist blogs and arrested four 'atheist bloggers'.[40] (The bloggers were arrested under the *Information and Communication Act*, an issue which we will discuss shortly.) Arrested bloggers were released on bail after some months in detention, but the cases are still pending. But the list soon began to circulate in the media, including being posted on a pro-BJI Facebook page. Those who were murdered featured in the list.

Each of these killings has generated debate in mainstream media, online and in the public sphere on whether the bloggers' opinions are blasphemous, whether killing for blasphemy is justified, and whether there should be a limit on freedom of expression. While one can say that such debate helps create consensus, the content of these debates has revealed a deep division within the society on the issue of religious sensibilities. Over time, it has become apparent that heightened 'religious sensitivity' is not restricted to Islamists or a small group of people.

An unfortunate development in this regard is the shift in the attitude of the ruling party. It was not hesitant in embracing the bloggers in early 2013, but by late 2015 it had become critical of them. In 2013 the prime minister visited the parents of Rajib Haider and described him as a 'martyr',[41] but she only made a call to the father of Avijit Roy in 2015 and it was not made public. In May 2015, the prime minister's son and her information and communication technology affairs adviser Sajib Wazed said that 'the political situation in Bangladesh is too volatile for her [the Prime Minister] to comment publicly [on Avijit's killing]'.[42] Two days after the murder of Niladry Niloy, the inspector general of police advised the bloggers not to write blogs that may hurt religious sentiments.[43] The home minister stated that 'actions as per the existing law of the country will be taken against those who will write anything on blogs or any other media hurting religious sentiment'.[44] The prime minister essentially echoed the position when she said that, the government 'won't allow anybody to hurt religious sentiments'.[45] Additionally, the Bangladesh Ulema League, a wing of the BAL, demanded capital punishment for hurting religious sentiment.[46] These developments have not only frustrated the 'secular' bloggers but frightened them as well.[47]

The fear, which a blogger described as a 'threat from the state,' emanates from Article 57 of the *Information and Communication Act*, which deals with the penalty for 'hurting' religious sentiment. As mentioned previously, four bloggers were arrested in 2013 under this Act. The Act was formulated in 2006 and was not applied until 2008. There was an amendment made in 2009 but the most significant and far-reaching changes were brought about in 2013. The amended law not only provides the power to the law enforcement agencies to arrest someone without a warrant but also to detain him/her for an indefinite period. Article 57 states,

> If any person deliberately publishes or transmits or causes to be published or transmitted in a website or in any other electronic form any material which is false and obscene and if anyone sees, hears or reads it having regard to all relevant circumstances, its effect is such as to influence the reader to become dishonest or corrupt, or causes to deteriorate or creates possibility to deteriorate law and order, prejudice the image of the State or person or causes to hurt or may hurt religious belief or instigate any person or organization, then this activity will be regarded as an offence.

The penalty for the violation is 14 years' imprisonment and a fine of a *crore taka* ($125,000). The Act, since 2013, has become a tool for curtailing freedom of speech, for allegedly hurting religious sentiment, and criticizing the government. The law has been used against a newspaper editor (Mahmudur Rahman of the *Amar Desh*), two human rights activists (Adilur Rahman and Nasiruddin Elan of the Odhikar), and a newspaper (the *Inquilab*) for expressing dissent. The Editors Council criticized the abuse of the law, particularly Article 57 and demanded the repeal of this clause.[48] A prominent lawyer pointed out that 'the offense in the ICT Act is vague and unspecific, practically anyone dissenting can be framed under this law'.[49] As of September 2015, 12 cases have been disposed of by the cyber crimes tribunal. Among these, accused persons in seven cases were convicted and sentenced to jail for different terms, while five have been acquitted. In 2014 the number of cases filed was 33, while as of September 2015, the number was 37. At least 115 cases were pending at that time. The Act has had two effects – shielding the government from criticism and preventing any discussions on religion. The latter usage of the Act has turned this into a *de facto* anti-blasphemy law.

Therefore, the phase of Bangladesh history which began with high optimism for a democratic transformation with the removal of the military from power in 1991, after several ups and downs, almost a quarter century later reached a point which definitely cannot be claimed to have achieved the goal of institutionalization of democracy and establishment of an inclusive system. The initial successes in this regard appear to be lost and democracy has started on a reverse course.

CHAPTER 4

DEMOCRACY: ASPIRATION, NATURE AND QUALITY

Noor Hossain is a very common name in Bangladesh. But very few Noor Hossains are part of the history of the nation's quest for democracy. One Noor Hossain, a 26-year-old who had only attended school up to eighth grade, and had just learnt to drive, took his place in the nation's history on 10 November 1987. It was a day when the opposition parties called the 'Dhaka Blockade', demanding the resignation of the military ruler General H. M. Ershad. As the morning progressed, millions thronged the roads of the capital. Among them was Noor Hossain, son of Mujibur Rahman and Marium Bibi, a member of the local chapter of the youth wing of the AL. He had no shirt on; instead two slogans were written across his bare chest and back, 'down with autocracy' and 'let democracy be freed'. Marked with bold white letters, chanting slogans fearlessly, he was easily spotted by photographers. But soon after his picture was taken he was shot and killed by the police near the centre of the capital. In that moment he was immortalized and the pictures, depicting the rallying cry of the nation, 'let democracy be freed', became the public symbol of the struggle. If there is any single picture that epitomizes the aspiration of the Bangladeshi population for democracy, it is the picture of Noor Hossain.

The periodic popular uprisings, such as the one in which Noor Hossain and many like him made the supreme sacrifice, are an indicator of this aspiration. So too are the presence of the plethora of parties, and widespread participation in national elections. While these indicators show the popular aspirations for democracy, they do not reveal the perception of democracy and its attributes as seen by Bangladeshis: what do they mean by democracy and what do they want democracy to deliver?

Democracy Defined

There is no universally accepted definition of 'democracy', although some argue that it is a universal value.[1] It is one of the most used and contested terms in political science and is capable of generating passionate debates and discussions among political scientists and policy-makers alike. Schumpeter defined democracy as an 'institutional arrangement for arriving at political decisions in which individuals acquire the power to decide by means of a competitive struggle for the people's vote'.[2] In the view of Samuel Huntington democracy is 'a political system in which the most powerful collective decision makers are selected through fair, honest, and periodic elections in which candidates freely compete for votes and in which virtually all the adult population is eligible to vote';[3] and Przeworski et al. claimed that 'democracy is a system in which parties lose elections', and that it is hence characterized by (1) *ex ante* uncertainty; (2) *ex post* irreversibility; and (3) repeatability.[4] Available studies on democracy are both normative and empirical in nature; i.e. explaining how it ought to be and what democracy looks like on the ground. Generally speaking, these studies are also guided by an underlying difference; while some view democracy as a system of governance others insist that it is essentially a set of values.

The elusive nature of the definition of democracy stems from the fact that there cannot be one kind of democracy; it varies both temporally and spatially. In plain and simple terms: no two democracies are alike. However, normatively speaking, there are certain attributes which should be integral to the political and social system to be identified as democratic. Drawing on the rich tradition of studies within the discipline of political science I maintain that three attributes are essential to democracy: (1) universal suffrage; (2) regular, free, competitive, multiparty elections for legislative and chief executive offices; (3) respect for civil and political rights including freedom of expression, assembly and association as well as a rule of law under which all citizens and agents of the state have true and legal equality. These attributes comprise the minimalist definition of democracy and should be considered as a package instead of mutually exclusive indicators. That means, to be called a democratic country, one must meet all three criteria. Additionally, they should not be considered the end of the process but the first step towards establishing a sustainable democratic system of governance. Their presence alone does not ensure that a society has achieved a democratic polity. The minimalist definition of democracy, as O'Donnell[5] has correctly pointed out, is not entirely 'minimalist' as there are some intrinsic conditions; take for example the definitions provided by Schumpeter and Huntington, both require a few other elements to work. Schumpeter has underscored free competition, free votes and a number of other conditions as essential for democracy to work; Huntington too insisted that elections should take place in a broader context that allows for free competition, a fair and honest electoral process, and alternation in power.

The working definition of democracy laid out here, as a precursor to assess the nature and quality of democracy in Bangladesh, is not free from limitations. Its bias towards procedural aspects cannot be ignored. However, in going forward I also keep in mind Dahl's preconditions for 'polyarchy' as essential elements of democracy.[6] According to Dahl, there are seven pre-requisites for a system to be considered 'democratic': elected officials, free and fair elections, universal suffrage, the right to run for office, freedom of expression, alternative sources of information, and freedom of association. Dahl insists that democracy requires 'not only free, fair, and competitive elections, but also the freedoms that make them truly meaningful (such as freedom of organization and freedom of expression), alternative sources of information, and institutions to ensure that government policies depend on the votes and preferences of citizens'.[7]

A combination of the procedural aspect and elements beyond it warrants us to differentiate between formal and substantive democracy. Formal democracy is a system where all the democratic institutions exist, but they are either abused or managed by a small group of elites for narrow interests and personal gains. The system may allow regular elections, methods of apparent political participations, and some semblance of the rule of law; but in essence functions as an oligarchy of some kind. Substantive democracy, on the other hand, evinces the spirit of democracy; that is the empowerment of people to pursue their interests autonomously from the entrenched structures and dominance of privileged segments of the society.

We need to be cognizant of the various dimensions of democracy as we proceed to gauge the support of democracy among Bangladeshis and its various manifestations in Bangladeshi politics.

Overabundance of Political Parties

Political parties play a pivotal role in democracy. Strong democracy requires the existence of well-functioning political parties. In the words of Max Weber, political parties are 'the children of democracy'. Weber writes:

> The most modern forms of party organizations stand in sharp contrast to this idyllic state in which circles of notables and, above all, members of parliament rule. These modern forms are the children of democracy, of mass franchise, of the necessity to woo and organize the masses, and develop the utmost unity of direction and the strictest discipline.[8]

Similarly, Seymour Lipset has described political parties as indispensable for democracy.[9] Another way of characterizing the relationship between democracy and political parties is to say that they are related symbiotically: one cannot exist without the other. A political party is, according to one account, 'an organized association of people working together to compete for political office and promote agreed-upon policies'.[10] We must take note that it is not only the competition for power that makes an association a political party, but also promotion of policies based on their ideological orientations.

By this measure, the Bangladeshi political landscape is vivacious. A total of 41 parties are now registered with the Bangladesh Election Commission. Although not all parties have equal strengths and equal reach to the populace, they represent a wide variety of political orientations. On the other hand, the list is not complete in the sense that there are parties which are not registered with the BEC. There are parties which sought but were not granted registration (for discussion on parties and party system, see Chapter 5). One of the key features of Bangladeshi political parties is that they are national in scope, as opposed to regional parties, a phenomenon common in other South Asian nations.

Vox Populi/People's Voice

The support for democracy is not only reflected in the presence of a plethora of political parties, but is also voiced in various opinion polls conducted since 1996.[11] These surveys reveal that while there is almost unanimous support for government run by democratically elected representatives in Bangladesh, there is no consensus as to what Bangladeshis view as the central tenets of democracy and/or democratic governance.

In the two rounds of the World Values Surveys carried out in Bangladesh, Bangladeshis have expressed unequivocal backing for the idea of democracy.[12] In 1996 almost 98 per cent said that 'having a democratic political system' is a very good and a fairly good idea. The support remained at a similar level in the 2002 survey. In a survey conducted by the United States Agency for International Development (USAID) in late 2003, Bangladeshis expressed their explicit support for democracy.[13] The survey report states, 'Overall, [...] there was fairly strong support for democracy among the public, and the public's associations with the term "democracy" were largely positive.' For example, on a favourability scale of 0–100,[14] 'democracy' received a fairly positive average score of 64. Younger adults aged 18 to 29 expressed a somewhat more favourable view of democracy, giving it an average score of 66, compared to an average of 62 among those aged 30 to 44 and an average of 61 among those aged 45 and over.[15] It was also revealed that nearly two-thirds of the respondents (62 per cent) chose a 'government ruled by democratically elected representatives' as the preferred system of governance. As for other choices, a 'government ruled by Islamic law, with respected religious figures as leaders' was favoured by 21 per cent, followed by 'a government ruled by a military leader who got things done' at 11 per cent and 'a non-elected government ruled by specialists, experts, and business leaders who know what it takes to develop a country' at 3 per cent.[16] In the *Daily Star* survey, conducted in 2008, over 81 per cent said they want a democratic parliamentary system. 7 per cent respondents said they want the country to be governed by Islamic laws. 6 per cent favoured a caretaker system, while martial law and a presidential system of government were favoured by 3 per cent each.[17]

Similarly, the regional survey conducted in five countries (e.g. Nepal, Pakistan, India, Bangladesh, and Sri Lanka) in 2004–05 demonstrated that democracy is associated with positive terms by 98 per cent of Bangladeshi respondents. Democracy is not only seen in a positive light but also as the preferred option by the Bangladeshis. The 'State of Democracy in South Asia' study (SDSA),[18] shows that 41 per cent of Bangladeshi respondents preferred democracy while only 4 per cent preferred dictatorship; 15 per cent of respondents opined that it makes no difference. 40 per cent of respondents expressed 'no opinion' on the question.[19] Among those who have responded 69 per cent preferred democracy, 6 per cent preferred dictatorship and 25 per cent said that it does not matter.[20] The survey results published by the Pew Research Center in 2013, show that 70 per cent of Bangladeshis prefer democracy as opposed to 27 per cent who prefer a 'strong leader'.[21]

What does it mean to support the idea of 'democracy'? The question was asked by the SDSA team in regard to the region in general and the answer is worth recalling:

When people say that they desire or prefer democracy, are they saying anything significant? Or are they just paying lip service to a universal norm, to what is seen as the only legitimate model for governing a country? The evidence presented thus far permits a limited conclusion: 'Democracy' has become an object of desire – something that is viewed positively, is considered suitable, and is generally preferred over its opposite.[22]

What prompts such overwhelming support for democracy? Respondents of the USAID survey gave democracy strong marks for being the best system for protecting individuals' rights and freedoms (79 per cent), ensuring equality of all citizens (69 per cent), providing order and security (69 per cent), keeping the country united (68 per cent), and solving community problems, because it gives everyone the chance to speak about their concerns and interests (59 per cent). 84 per cent of the respondents also agreed with the statement that 'Democracy may have problems, but it is better than any form of government.' The same question in the WVS 1996 survey generated 97.50 per cent agreement;

in the WVS 2002, 98.20 per cent. While the 1996 and 2002 figures are close, the late 2003 figures in the SDSA survey shown a drop of 14 per cent. The respondents of the WVS surveys were also asked how much they agree with the statement that democracies are indecisive and involve too much squabbling. In 1996, 30 per cent agreed, but the percentage went down to 13.20 per cent in 2002. These numbers reveal that Bangladeshis are getting used to the workings of democracy.

There is a long-standing debate whether democracy is compatible with non-Western cultures, particularly with Muslim majority societies. Arguments have been made for and against these positions. Two key elements of the arguments have been that democracy is a Western construct; therefore it does not sit well within non-Western social milieu and that Islamic theology is contrary to the basic tenets of representative democracy. The Global Survey conducted by the Pew Research Center in 2002 (PRCGS) showed that 57 per cent of Bangladeshis are of the opinion that 'western style democracy can work' in their country, while 12 per cent described it as incompatible.[23] In 2004, the USAID survey noted that there is a strong division within the Bangladeshis on the suitability of democracy. The strongest division was found on the statement, 'Democracy is a Western idea and is not compatible with our culture and values.' The survey report states, 'A plurality (42 per cent) disagreed that democracy is incompatible, but about one third (31 per cent) agreed with this statement. Another 28 per cent said they "do not know." More educated individuals were slightly more likely to agree with the notion that democracy is incompatible.' According to the SDSA survey conducted in 2004, 59 per cent have either said that democracy is very suitable or suitable (20 per cent and 39 per cent, respectively) to Bangladesh, only 4 per cent described it as not suitable. 37 per cent had no opinion.[24]

Despite such overwhelming affinity with democracy, there is a lack of clear understanding, perhaps awareness, among Bangladeshis as to what democracy means. In the open-ended question in the USAID survey as to what is their understanding of democracy, close to 30 per cent of respondents (29 per cent) did not offer a definition of democracy. 15 per cent did not identify democracy when asked to rank it on the 0–100 favourability scale, and 12 per cent said 'do not know' when asked whether they felt democracy was an important issue facing the country. Respondents in the Governance Barometer Survey Bangladesh 2010

(GBS 2010),[25] provided 56 distinct responses to the question of what democracy means. The responses include 'could not express understanding' (46 per cent), 'freedom of movement' (12 per cent), 'freedom to express own opinion' (10 per cent), 'right to vote' (5–6 per cent), 'equal right to all people' (5–6 per cent), 'right to oneself' (5–6 per cent), 'government elected by people' (5–6 per cent), 'meeting the basic demand' (3 per cent), 'judiciary and justice' (3 per cent), 'equal rights for all' (1 per cent), 'meeting basic demands' (1 per cent), 'working together' (1 per cent), and 'work for the country' (1 per cent). Other surveys, such as the SDSA poll, also reflect the unclear and greatly varied general sense of democracy. In response to the open-ended question in the USAID survey, 'What do you understand as democracy?' the leading response (32 per cent) was the 'right to vote and choose leaders in elections', followed by 'do not know' (29 per cent). Freedom of speech and opinion came in third (22 per cent), followed by respect for human rights (12 per cent). Though open-ended survey questions fail to map the understanding of democracy among the respondents, polls have often adopted two ways to gather the perception. One is to offer distinct narrowed options to the question; the other is to ask for specific attributes of democracy as seen by the respondents.

Distinct, narrowed options of 'what democracy means' often revealed the understanding. For example, weighted narrowed responses of the GBS 2010 reveal that 80 per cent of respondents felt elections were the critical ideal of democracy, above free public debate (71 per cent), rule of consent (60 per cent), ability to participate in decision making (50 per cent), and ability to access information on government activities (40 per cent).[26] It is worth noting here that, in both the USAID Survey and the GBS 2010, there is an overwhelming emphasis on elections and the right to vote by the respondents, a point which we will return to later.

As for the attributes of democracy, according to the SDSA survey, the majority of South Asians view democracy in terms of 'freedom', with 31 per cent of the region holding this conception. In comparison, 27 per cent of Bangladeshis agree with this definition. This is followed by justice and welfare (23 per cent), elections (20 per cent). 26 per cent of the respondents did not agree with any of the six positive attributes of democracy. The response and regional average is as listed in Table 4.1.

A few things of interest are readily apparent from this data. On the one hand, as noted above, 'freedom' is a relatively low popular definition of

Table 4.1 Attributes of Democracy: Bangladesh and South Asia

	Freedom	Others	Justice & Welfare	Popular Rule	Election	Peace & Security	Rule of Law	Negative Meanings
Bangladesh	27 per cent	26 per cent	23 per cent	21 per cent	20 per cent	12 per cent	3 per cent	2 per cent
South Asia	40 per cent	13 per cent	29 per cent	23 per cent	12 per cent	11 per cent	2 per cent	5 per cent
Difference	−13 per cent	+13 per cent	−6 per cent	−2 per cent	+8 per cent	+1 per cent	+1 per cent	−3 per cent

Source: Suri et al., 2010, Table 1, p. 15.

democracy in Bangladesh compared to the rest of South Asia. Likewise, 'justice and welfare' was a considerably less popular definition of democracy in Bangladesh than the South Asian average. On the other hand, 20 per cent of Bangladeshis defined democracy in terms of 'elections', opposed to the South Asian average of 12 per cent. Bangladeshis, moreover, *double* the South Asian regional average of those defining democracy as 'others', 26 per cent to 13 per cent. These numbers suggest the prevalence of those responding 'others' and demonstrates that Bangladeshis have a fragmented view of democracy. More than any other nation – the second-highest 'others' respondent was Nepal (14 per cent) – Bangladesh offers a diverse view of the definition of democracy. The PRCGS show that Bangladeshis have identified three major attributes with democracy; they are: people can openly criticize the government (81 per cent); there are honest, two-party elections (71 per cent), and free press/the media can report without censorship (64 per cent).[27] In a survey conducted by the International Foundation for Election Systems (IFES)[28] in 2000, most Bangladeshis characterized the Bangladeshi political system as a democracy (65 per cent rural, 53 per cent urban). Few (2 per cent urban, 5 per cent rural) say it is not, a quarter or more described it as 'somewhat' of a democracy (24 per cent rural, 38 per cent urban).[29] We can glean the attributes respondents associate with democracy from a proxy question. Respondents were provided with a list of fundamental rights and were asked, 'How important is it to you that the following rights be respected in Bangladesh?' The list included the following eight options: (1) One can choose from several parties and candidates when voting; (2) Honest elections are held regularly; (3) The private property of individuals is protected by law; (4) Citizens have the right to form political parties; (5) The right to publicly criticize the government is protected; (6) All can freely practice the religion of one's choice; (7) All can form associations or unions without any government involvement; and (8) Women are given equal treatment under the law. Respondents were asked to rate them on a scale of 1–4 (very important, somewhat important, not very important, or not at all important). Choice of parties (political parties), is rated the highest among rural respondents (3.93), but is third in preference among urban respondents (3.91). Urban respondents rank honest elections first (3.93) in importance among the different rights.[30]

The appearance of elections as almost the central feature in the conceptualization of democracy warrants further explication. The IFES survey of 2000, the USAID survey of 2004, the SDSA survey of 2005 and the GBS 2010 survey have shown us that 'the public seemed to be almost fixated on elections and the right to vote'.[31] The SDSA survey of the region revealed that Bangladeshis value the power of voting more than the southern Asian average. Findings from the focus group of the USAID study 'also demonstrated that the public is hyper-focused on their right to vote, and perhaps less cognizant of their role beyond going to the polls every few years'.[32] A similar perception is found in the survey among the younger population. *Giving Youth a Voice*: Bangladesh Youth Survey[33] of 2011 (BYS) informs that 'when defining democracy, a wide majority stated that elections are a core parameter'. The report states:

> Our survey reflects that Bangladeshi youths' perceptions about democracy are mainly defined by having free and fair elections. When ranked, this was given first priority by an overwhelming majority of 65 per cent, in addition to 18 per cent who ranked it either second (8 per cent) or third (10 per cent). Among all other options, rule by consent and access to information have been top priorities, while free public debates got the highest percentage as the second most important factor. Again, access to information got the highest support as the third ranked option (38 per cent). Among all options, 'free public debate' as a core feature of democracy got the lowest ranked percentage (at 26 percentage points).

Two questions need to be asked; does this interest in elections translate into participation? If so, why do people vote in Bangladesh? The IFES survey, conducted before the 2001 elections, informs that the majority of respondents stated that they would participate in the election – 85 per cent certain, 10 per cent most likely; only 3 per cent respondents said that they are less likely/definitely not voting.[34] The Community Development Library survey of 2001 (CDL Survey 2001), conducted in July 2001, shows that there is a high rate of participation among the respondents.[35] 80 per cent of respondents of the USAID survey in 2004 stated that they were certain to vote in the next election.

The survey identified 69 per cent of the respondents as 'core voters', i.e., those who voted in the past election and will definitely vote in the next election.[36] According to the SDSA survey,[37] Bangladesh holds the second-highest index of political participation in South Asia, with 83 per cent of respondents claiming high (39 per cent) or moderate (44 per cent) levels of voter participation. Implicit within these numbers, 64 per cent of respondents claim to vote in every election, and 20 per cent claim to vote in most elections.

These claims are borne out by the data on voter participation in past elections. There is a noteworthy upward trend of participation in the elections held since independence. In 1973 the voter turnout was 54.91 per cent of registered voters; in 2008 the share went up to 85.26 per cent. The International Republican Institute (IRI) Opinion poll conducted between 17 and 22 April 2009 shows that 95 per cent of respondents indicated that they have voted.[38] The Bangladesh Youth Survey (BYS) of 2011 shows that among those aged 21 or older 89 per cent had voted in at least one national election. Overall, 28 per cent had voted in two (25 per cent) or even more (3 per cent) national elections.[39] The percentage of voter turnout has grown significantly particularly since 1991, when elections have been participated in by all parties and fair elections have taken place (Appendix 1).

Answers to the question as to why Bangladeshis vote with such enthusiasm can be found in some of the surveys previously mentioned, as well as other studies. According to the SDSA survey, 66 per cent of Bangladeshi voters think that their vote has an effect on 'the ways things are run in [their] country'. These numbers dwarf Western democracies by comparison.[40] Other evidence further underscores that Bangladeshi democrats and non-democrats alike both participate in politics at higher rates than their average South Asian counterparts, 58 per cent to 46 per cent for democrats and 49 per cent to 36 per cent non-democrats respectively.[41] The IFES survey has two different questions in this regard: first, a general question on the reasons of voting to all the respondents and second, to those who voted in 1996 as to why they had voted. Responses to both questions are instructive. Generally Bangladeshi citizens feel that election is the only way to influence government policy.

Seventy-one per cent of rural respondents and 65 per cent of urban respondents completely agree with the statement: 'Voting gives people like me a chance to influence decision-making in our country.' Another 19 per cent of rural respondents and 22 per cent of urban respondents somewhat agree with this statement. Very few respondents disagree with the statement.[42]

The leading reason for voting in the previous election given by these respondents was that it was the right of every citizen to vote (28 per cent).

A qualitative ethnographic study on the expectations of the poor from the government reveal that the poorer segment of the citizens see election as a form of empowerment:[43]

Our discussants were aware of the democratic political process. Most explained that government is formed 'from the people' or 'with the people' [*jonogon niey/diey shorkar*], that is, that governments are formed if people support them and vote them in. There was a strong sense of empowerment: 'without my vote there is no government', said one rickshaw-puller in Dhaka. The term *'public'* (a Bengali word, we were told whenever we asked), also conveys in its context a strong sense of an active, politicised, conscious electorate, widely used in preference to *lok* or people. It seems to connote a political population, as distinct from the moral social collective that is *jonogon*.

Overall, the finding of the study is worth mentioning:

Poor people in Bangladesh are remarkably confident about their ability to vote a poorly performing government out of power and are also confident that their votes matter. Their confidence is high enough for most groups to state that violent protests to overthrow government is undesirable – they will simply wait to vote the government out of power at the end of its tenure. Casting a negative vote against the incumbent is clearly a cheaper and much less riskier choice than participating in violent protests. This is also an option that Bangladeshis have exercised – voting out two governments since the transition to democracy in the 1990s. The important point, however, is that voting is perceived to be an alternative to protest. This suggests that poor Bangladeshis see the vote as a referendum on the incumbent government and their votes are based on their evaluation of the incumbent's performance rather than the challenger's leadership styles or policies.[44]

However, the overemphasis on election by the Bangladeshi population is somewhat troubling. The growing literature on democratization which has appeared in the last three and a half decades has shown that election is a necessary component of democracy but not alone sufficient. The use of election as the key indicator of democracy and the assumption that elections are a sufficient measure of democracy prevalent in studies on democracy in the 1980s gave rise to the concept of 'fallacy of electoralism'.[45] In the words of Larry Diamond, this fallacy

consists of privileging electoral contestation over other dimensions of democracy and ignoring the degree to which multiparty elections, even if genuinely competitive, may effectively deny significant sections of the population the opportunity to contest for power or advance and defend their interests, or may leave significant arenas of decision-making power beyond the reach or control of elected officials.[46]

In the words of Chris Adcock, 'the presence of a functioning electoral system does not automatically ensure the existence of true democracy or rule out the possibility of authoritarian structures and practices'.[47] In addition to the inability of election to encompass the various elements of democracy, it is now well known that elections can be manipulated through various ways, and that it is not a proof of participation in the process of making decisions.[48] This conceptualization of democracy has implications for the nature and quality of democracy in the country, as we will see later.

Despite the significance attached to democracy and election, and the presence of a wide variety of political parties, Bangladeshi citizens do not have a positive view about the political parties, a backbone of any democratic process, nor are they satisfied with the party processes. Active membership of political parties is very low according to the WVS 1996: 11 per cent, inactive members are about 8 per cent, the remainder of respondents said they are not members of any political parties. In 2002, when respondents were asked to identify whether he/she belongs to any political party, 23.5 per cent responded positively while 76.5 per cent did not answer. The confidence in political parties, a combination of 'a great deal' and 'quite a lot' was 71.8 per cent in 1996 and 79 per cent in 2002. But confidence seems to be in decline since 2002. In the USAID 2004 survey, on the 0–100 favourability scale, 'political parties' received a fairly lukewarm score of 44. It is well known that Bangladeshis are passionate about politics, yet only 2 per cent of the public said that someone being 'a member of the best political party' was one of the qualities they look for in a leader. Only 1 per cent said they look for a leader who comes from a family of political leaders, although Bangladeshi political parties are dominated by families – both at national and local levels. 'A majority of people (53 per cent) who are not formal members of political parties said that parties use violence to get their way.'[49]

The IFES 2000 survey found that most respondents had 'a great deal' or 'a fair amount' of confidence in a range of governmental and other institutions, but among these institutions political parties ranked fairly low. Only 64 per cent of the rural population and 59 per cent in urban areas had confidence in political parties. The percentage was far greater for the media or courts.[50]

As for interest in politics, in 1996, 51 per cent said they are either very interested or somewhat interested; but in 2002 interest in politics had declined: the total of very interested and somewhat interested came down to 40.70 per cent. In both years 11.60 per cent people responded saying they are very interested. The number is similar to the party membership response in 1996. Similar perceptions about political parties and interest in politics are found in two surveys conducted among the youth. The British Council survey, 'Bangladesh: The Next Generation', conducted in 2009[51] revealed that almost three-quarters of the youth (74 per cent) were not interested in politics, and that only one in four young people in Bangladesh would firmly agree with the statement, 'I am interested in politics.' The other three would express indifference and be unsure about their capacity to influence national decisions. Less than one-third of the youth did not expect to become involved in political activities. Another one-third, however, said they should be involved in politics. Only one-tenth of the surveyed youths said they are involved in political activities. The Bangladesh Youth Survey (BYS), a survey conducted by the Brac University in 2011, shows that only 2 per cent of youth are members of any political party.[52]

Interestingly, while the political parties have received a low ranking among national institutions, the military is held in high esteem. In the early 2000s, Bangladeshis held a high opinion of their military, and this positive inclination has increased over time. Among the respondents of WVS 1996, 56.80 per cent said that they have confidence in the military – 18.80 per cent said they have 'a great deal of confidence.' In 2002, 74.40 per cent held a positive view of the military of which 35.50 per cent (almost double of 1996) said they have 'a great deal of confidence'. The IFES survey records an 86 per cent approval rating of the army in rural areas and 88 per cent in urban areas.[53] Other surveys have shown a consistent trend in the military's popularity. According to a Pew Survey, in 2002, 60 per cent of Bangladeshis viewed the military in a positive light.[54] In 2004, approval rating was at 77 per cent, making the military the most popular political institution in Bangladesh, ahead of the National Parliament (62 per cent approval), Local government (61 per cent), political parties (44 per cent), and the police (33 per cent).[55] The approval of parliament was far greater in 1996 (84.40 per cent) and 2002 (88.70 per cent) according to the WVS.

The SDSA survey of 2004–05, furthermore, offers a host of interesting findings on the current view of the military in Bangladesh. It is important to note that democratic institutions in Bangladesh are generally rated higher within the nation than in the rest of South Asia; the national government, for example, holds an 81 per cent positive rating from its populace, compared to the 56 per cent regional popularity average.[56] That said the Bangladeshi military came in as *the most* popular national political institution, boasting an 87 per cent approval rating, opposed to the regional 72 per cent average.[57] This 15 per cent difference is very significant for understanding the motivations behind the internal workings of the political system of Bangladesh. The approval rating of the military further increased to 93 per cent of the population holding a positive view of the military as a political institution in 2007.[58] Overall, notwithstanding some variations, clearly the military's acceptability has increased over time.

Does the popularity of the military mean that Bangladeshis would like to see a broadening of its mandate to govern the country? Available surveys provide conflicting data on this issue. In WVS 1996, 93.20 per cent said that military rule is very bad or fairly bad. In 2002, the number was smaller – 80.90 per cent. But 59 per cent of respondents in the SDSA survey supported army rule. This number is second only to Pakistan in South Asia (where 60 per cent of respondents supported military rule), and 24 per cent higher than the third-most pro-military state, Nepal (35 per cent).[59] But on the other hand, according to the USAID survey,

> the public does not see the military as the answer to community problems – only two per cent of the respondents said that they turn to military personnel [to] solve problems and disputes in their communities. In fact, in the focus groups, participants expressed the worry that if the military stayed around in their communities, they would become just like the police force, which is not viewed in a positive light.[60]

In a similar vein, only 3 per cent of the respondents of the *Daily Star–Nielsen* survey in 2008, favoured martial law.[61]

However, the SDSA survey offers a telling exercise which clearly demonstrates the importance of the military in the Bangladeshi political structure. The study's 'funnel of democracy' test – a six-step test meant to determine if respondents favour all aspects of democracy and, if not, to see which points cause the most divergence – shows both the high initial support for democratic ideals, and the strong approval of military rule.

In the first step of the funnel, 97 per cent of respondents were in favour of a government ruled by elected leaders (4 per cent higher than the regional average of 93 per cent). In the second step of the funnel, after excluding those who prefer dictatorship sometimes or are indifferent between democracy and dictatorship, the number comes down to 78 per cent, far greater than the regional average of 67 per cent. In the third step in the process, those who support military rule are excluded and it comes down to 35 per cent. The difference between these two steps means that about 43 per cent respondents of the survey are not opposed to military rule. After excluding those who want monarchical rule and those who want a strong ruler without any democratic restraint, the percentage of democrats comes down to 14 per cent. In the final stage after excluding those who want rule by experts rather than politicians, the number stands at 8 per cent.[62] Data from WVS 1996 and WVS 2002 in regard to 'having experts make political decisions' are instructive: in

1996, 85 per cent felt it was very good or a good idea; in 2002, there was a slight increase – 86.50 per cent.

The precipitous drop – 43 per cent–between steps two and three in the democracy funnel test, demonstrating support for military rule, is the most severe divergence in any southern Asian country on any of the funnel of democracy's tested factors.[63]

The funnel test also reveals the Bangladeshi population's proclivity towards 'strong leaders without democratic restraints', or in other words, populist authoritarianism is not entirely an alien idea to Bangladeshi political leaders and citizens. This is not a unique trait of Bangladeshi politics and society, the regional survey showed us: 'Throughout the region there is a two-third approval of the rule of a "strong leader who does not have to bother about elections".'[64] The SDSA report reminded us, 'This should come as no surprise in a region that has a long tradition of strong leaders like Indira Gandhi, Zulfikar Ali Bhutto or Sheikh Mujibur Rahman who owed their power to their democratic popularity, but once safely entrenched, tended to bypass institutional norms of liberal democracy.'[65]

Assessing the Nature and Quality of Democracy

The preceding discussions have demonstrated that while there is a lack of clear understanding of democracy and its institutions, Bangladeshis aspire to democracy, view elections as a critical element of democracy and participate in them in large numbers. Since the first general elections in 1973, ten parliamentary and three presidential elections have been held up to 2015. Additionally three referenda have taken place; one of which was to ratify an amendment to the constitution (1991) while two others were to provide legitimacy to military rulers who usurped power through coups. The nation has been ruled by elected civilian regimes for more than 28 years and for the remainder either by direct military rule or a pseudo-civilian regime as a proxy of the military. On four occasions, transitional caretaker governments headed the country; of which all but one was of short duration – three months or less. The tenure of the governments varied, but since 2001 four parliaments have completed the full term of five years each as stipulated in the constitution (for duration of various governments, see Table 4.2).[66] Parliamentary elections between 1973 and 1990 have been marred by irregularities and vote rigging in favour of the incumbent parties and in many instances major opposition parties have boycotted the elections (Table 4.3); all elections held under caretaker governments were considered fair by local and international observers. The 2014 election, as mentioned before, was held under the incumbent government. The question then is what kind of democracy, in terms of nature and quality, have these elections and governance produced in Bangladesh?

Measuring democracy is a challenging task, despite a long tradition in political science of such endeavour since the mid-1950s. The publication of Samuel Huntington's seminal study in 1991 about the 'third wave of democracy' renewed the tradition; consequently the urgency and necessity to differentiate between democratic regimes and assess the qualities of democratic governance has gained salience. Huntington argued that globally democratic regimes have proliferated in three waves and reverse waves. According to him the first wave was between 1826 and 1926; this was followed by a reverse wave when many countries slid into autocracy. The second wave began after World War II, which was short-lived and ended by 1962. Then came the 'Third Wave' beginning in 1974 with the end of the Portuguese dictatorship and continued in force through the 1990s. The third wave, unlike the two previous waves, Larry Diamond claims, made democracy a 'global phenomenon'.[67] Although Huntington suggested at the time of writing that a reverse wave is looming, many scholars insist that it continued until the mid-1990s. Huntington's arguments have attracted criticisms both on conceptual and methodological grounds,[68] but overall the issue of democratization and its various dimensions continue to dominate both academic and policy discourses. The number of countries that have abandoned autocratic systems of governance and moved towards some form of electoral system since the mid-1970s bears out the central thrust of the argument. In 1973 slightly more than a quarter of countries could be categorized as democratic. In 1980 the share was about one-third, in 1992 about half and three-fifths by 2000.[69] The wave reached its peak in 2006 when about 64 per cent of all countries (123 out of 193) were described as democracies by the Freedom House, an international monitoring group.[70] The number and share have since slightly dropped.

As more studies on the proliferation of democratic regimes were conducted, several issues emerged. Firstly, these studies underscored that democratization is a process which has various stages and each of them

Table 4.2 Nature and Duration of the Different Forms of Government

Period	Nature of Regime	Duration
16 December 1971 to 10 January 1972	Interim Government, Presidential form, Multi-party Democracy under Nazrul Islam	Less than 1 month
10 January 1972 to 6 March 1973	Interim Government, Parliamentary form, Multi-party Democracy under Sheikh Mujibur Rahman	1 year 2 months
7 March 1973 to 27 December 1974	Parliamentary form, Multi-party Democracy under Sheikh Mujibur Rahman	1 year 9 months
28 December 1974 to 25 January 1975	Emergency rule, Parliamentary form, under Sheikh Mujibur Rahman	1 month
25 January 1975 to 15 August 1975	One-party rule, Presidential form, under Sheikh Mujibur Rahman	7 months
15 August 1975 to 7 November 1975	Military rule, Presidential form, under Khandaker Mushtaq Ahmed backed by a section of military	2 months +
7 November 1975 to 30 May 1981	Military rule, and military-dominated civilian regime, Presidential form under General Ziaur Rahman	6 years 6 months
30 May 1981 to 24 March 1982	Transitional regime, Presidential form, under Abdus Sattar (Vice President of Ziaur Rahman regime)	10 months
24 March 1982 to 6 December 1990	Military rule and military-dominated civilian regime, Presidential form, under General Hussain Mohammed Ershad	8 years 9 months
6 December 1990 to 27 February 1991	Caretaker administration, Presidential system, under Justice Shahabuddin Ahmed	2 months +

Period	Government	Duration
27 February 1991 to 24 November 1995	Bangladesh Nationalist Party (BNP) government headed by Khaleda Zia, Presidential form until 6 August 1991 and subsequently Parliamentary form, Multi-party Democracy	4 years 8 months +
24 November 1995 to 19 March 1996	Interim government headed by Khaleda Zia, Multi-party Democracy	2 months +
19 March 1996 to 30 March 1996	BNP government headed by Khaleda Zia	11 days
30 March 1996 to 23 June 1996	Caretaker administration, substantial power to the caretaker administration headed by Justice Habibur Rahman	2 months +
23 June 1996 to 15 July 2001	Awami League government headed by Sheikh Hasina, Parliamentary form, Multi-party Democracy	5 years
15 July 2001 to 9 October 2001	Caretaker administration, with substantial power to the head of the caretaker administration headed by Justice Latifur Rahman	2 months +
10 October 2001 to 28 October 2006	BNP-led four-party coalition government headed by Khaleda Zia, Parliamentary form, Multi-party Democracy	5 years
28 October 2006 to 11 January 2007	Caretaker administration, Presidential form, headed by President Iajuddin Ahmed	2 months +
12 January 2007 to 6 January 2009	Caretaker administration, headed by Fakhruddin Ahmed, backed by the military	1 year 11 months
6 January 2009 To current (2015)	AL-led 14-party alliance government headed by Sheikh Hasina, Parliamentary form, Multi-party Democracy	

Source: Compiled by the author.

Table 4.3   National Elections – Fairness Index

Year	Type	Per cent officially reported to have been secured by ruling party or the regime under which the poll was conducted	Features
1973	Parliamentary	97.6 per cent of seats	Moderately fair, with sporadic rigging
1977	Referendum	98.9 per cent of votes	Extensively rigged, boycotted by one or more important political parties
1978	Presidential	76.0 per cent of votes	Extensively rigged
1979	Parliamentary	69.6 per cent of seats	Extensively rigged
1981	Presidential	65.5 per cent of votes	Extensively rigged
1985	Referendum	94.0 per cent of votes	Extensively rigged, boycotted by one or more important political parties
1986	Parliamentary	51.05 per cent of seats	Extensively rigged, boycotted by one or more important political parties
1987	Parliamentary	83.7 per cent of seats	Extensively rigged, boycotted by one or more important political parties
1991	Parliamentary	*	Fair

1996 (Feb)	Parliamentary	84.3 per cent of seats	Extensively rigged, boycotted by one or more important political parties
1996 (June)	Parliamentary	*	Fair
2001	Parliamentary	*	Fair
2008	Parliamentary	*	Fair
2014	Parliamentary	78 per cent of seats	Extensively rigged, boycotted by one or more important political parties

* Caretaker government supervised election, no incumbent

Source: Compiled by the author based on the election results, newspapers reports, observations and personal interviews.

warrants closer attention. Hence, 'theories of democratic transition' emerged. The demise of the Soviet Union and the transition of the eastern European countries to democracy in the 1990s added to the impetus. The proponents of the transition thesis, often called transitologists, argue that the democratization process comprises four stages: decay of authoritarianism, transition, consolidation, and deepening.[71] Unwittingly, the researchers within this paradigm adopted a linear path- dependent model suggesting that once a country is on the path to democracy it will progress in one direction. Carothers notes, 'No small amount of democratic teleology is implicit in the transition paradigm, no matter how much its adherents have denied it.'[72] Over time, a few other limitations and weaknesses of the paradigm, especially its assumptions, became evident. Early studies of transition have been palpably dominated by an 'overly deterministic, pessimistic bent of structural explanation'.[73] The complete neglect of the international dimension is another significant flaw. Questions such as whether or not exogenous factors play any role, and if so, what role do they play, received almost no attention in the first generation transition literature. Interestingly, Huntington's study mentioned the significance of exogenous factors both directly and indirectly (as the snowball effect).

The second issue was whether to adopt a binary frame: a regime is either democratic or not; two schools of thoughts emerged – dichotomous and continuous. Sartori[74] favoured a binary model, as did Huntington, Alvarez et al.[75] and Linz.[76] On the other hand, Dahl,[77] in his classic study, adopted a gradational frame and other scholars, such as Bollen and Paxton[78] insisted on the merit of gradation. It is in this context that several taxonomies of regimes were devised. Based on the defining characteristics of democracy, a four-fold typology was devised to understand the regimes and conduct a meaningful comparison at international level. The regimes were categorized as liberal democracies, minimal democracies, authoritarian systems, and interrupted regimes:

> A liberal democracy is a regime in which there is meaningful and extensive competition, sufficiently inclusive suffrage in national elections, and a high level of civil and political liberties. Minimal democracies are those political regimes with competition and inclusive suffrage but without a high level of civil liberties. Authoritarian regimes are those political regimes that fail to meet

the first requirement of competition and/or the second requirement of inclusiveness. Finally, a country will be classified here as an interrupted regime if it is occupied by foreign powers during wartime, or if there is a complete collapse of central authority, or if it undergoes a period of transition during which new politics and institutions are planned.[79]

This framework categorizes various regimes and makes distinctions between democratic and non-democratic regimes on the one hand and between, what Schedler described as, new and old democracies.[80]

Notwithstanding the utility, this taxonomy did not address an emerging phenomenon: in some instances the transition process from an autocratic regime to a democratic regime was stalled before consolidation. The third issue, therefore, was the importance of the quality of democracy. By the beginning of the twenty-first century, the primary euphoria associated with the 'third wave' had subsided. A whole new set of studies and analyses expressed serious concerns that some democracies were rolling back. Although the essay entitled 'The Democratic Rollback: The Resurgence of the Predatory State' by Larry Diamond in *Foreign Affairs* in 2008 drew the most attention,[81] scholars had been making the argument since the early 2000s; the work of Carothers,[82] Ottaway,[83] and Nathan[84] are cases in point. Researchers since then have demonstrated that while a number of countries have progressed towards democratic systems, some have since regressed to authoritarianism, and others have remained stagnant either by choice or by default. It was a stark contrast to the predictions of the transition thesis. Thus, while a number of researchers became engaged in analysing the nature and quality of newly consolidated democracy, an array of political scientists have been concerned with the reverse wave.

O'Donnell and Schmitter warned in 1986 that transition from authoritarianism can result in a liberalized authoritarian regime (*dictablanda*) or a restrictive, illiberal democracy (*democradura*).[85] As time elapsed it became evident that some regimes had adopted constitutionalism and electoral processes to the extent that free, fair, competitive, multi-party elections were held at regular intervals and limited political rights and civil liberties granted, but the essence of democracy – to allow the voices of people in governance – remained unfulfilled. This deficiency has been blamed on the unwillingness of the political class, irrespective of ideological persuasion. At this point it became evident that the binary frame to understand the state of democracy was unhelpful; consequently the question metamorphosed into how to describe these democracies?

Various adjectives are being used to describe these regimes; for example, 'semidemocracy', 'virtual democracy', 'electoral democracy', 'pseudodemocracy', 'illiberal democracy', 'semi-authoritarianism', 'soft authoritarianism', 'electoral authoritarianism'.[86] Larry Diamond has broadly described them as 'hybrid regimes'.[87] Increasingly it has become accepted that hybrid regimes are neither a subtype of autocracy nor of democracy but a regime type on their own, encompassing those political systems that on plausible grounds cannot be classified as either autocracy or democracy.[88] Hybrid regimes are not to be confused with regimes in transition. Hybrid regimes are a particular type of regime whereas a regime in transition is precisely that, a regime changing from one type to another.[89]

These developments warranted a more nuanced taxonomy of various democracies. Freedom House began using a gradation list dividing democracies into four categories: full democracies, flawed democracies, hybrid regimes, and authoritarian regimes. Further refinement of these categories has been proposed by Moller and Skanning.[90] This typology divides democracies into four types and autocracies into two. Within their framework democracies are: minimalist democracy, electoral democracy, polyarchy, and liberal democracy:

> Minimalist democracy requires only that political competition for leadership take place via regular elections with uncertain outcomes. Electoral democracy goes beyond this by demanding higher levels of electoral integrity. The notion of polyarchy adds to this respect for the freedoms of speech and association. And liberal democracy adds the rule of law, understood as equality before and under the law.[91]

As for autocracies, the two categories are: closed autocracies and electoral autocracies.

The new phenomenon and consequent taxonomies based on a continuous concept of democracy required that ways for measuring regimes be devised and indices developed for meaningful evaluations and effective comparisons across countries and over time. There were already a number of datasets measuring established democracies; some of these are being enlarged to add the new democracies as various new datasets are gathered. These measurement indices include the Vanhanen Index (VI) developed by Tatu Vanhanen (also known as the Polyarchy Index) with the support of the Peace Research Institute Oslo (PRIO); Freedom House indices (the Political Rights, Civil Liberty, Nations in Transit, and Countries at the Crossroads indices); the Polity IV database (particularly the Polity2 variable); a binary measure of democracy and dictatorship ('DD') constructed by Adam Przeworski et al.; a binary measure constructed by Michael Bernhard, Timothy Nordstrom, and Christopher Reenock ('BNR'); a multi-dimensional index produced by the Economist Intelligence Unit ('EIU'); the Bertelsmann Transformation Index ('BTI') funded by the Bertelsmann Foundation and the Combined Index of Democracy (CID) by the University of Wurzberg under Hans-Joachim Lauth and Oliver Kauff.[92] Efforts to gather survey data through Democracy Barometers projects have also been made.[93] These indices have been criticized on methodological and conceptual grounds although many agree that they provide a significant service.[94] Some of these datasets utilize a binary framework and therefore are of limited utility in assessing the quality of democratic regimes in transition, while others have less relevant elements included in the indices.[95]

Given the limitations of the extant datasets, we decided not to use one particular set in assessing the nature and quality of democracy; instead we identified a set of features and gathered data from several datasets to evaluate the regimes since 1991. The selected indices are: competitive elections, corruption, democratic quality, press freedom, civil liberties, and the rule of law. The selection is based on two considerations: that almost all 'thick' definitions of democracy explicitly or implicitly underscore these as qualities of liberal democracy; and that these indices have been used in determining whether a regime should be classified as a 'hybrid regime'.[96] The brief political history of Bangladesh described in Chapters 2 and 3 not only demonstrates the fragility of democracy despite conducting several successive free and fair elections until 2014 but also reveals serious shortcomings of governance. Non-functioning of the parliament,[97] absence of the rule of law, and politicization of the judiciary has prompted observers to describe Bangladesh as an 'electoral democracy'. Overall, the Bangladeshi political system combines regular democratic elections with a number of democratic deficiencies, such as corruption, lack of press freedom, and poorly working systems of checks and balances between the executive and the legislative branches of government.

We use data from the European Intelligence Unit's *Democracy Index*, Freedom House's *Freedom in the World*, Transparency International's *Corruption Perceptions Index* (CPI), Reporters Without Borders' *World Press Freedom Index*, Amnesty International (AI) and the United States' State Department (USSD)'s Terror Scale in assessing the quality of democracy. Instead of using single year data we have used data over a decade, when available we have used data for two decades (1991–2011). These sources use a gradational system. However, drawing on their numerical gradations we will mark them in a binary based on thresholds for each category, i.e. competitive elections, corruption, democratic quality, press freedom, civil liberties, and the rule of law.

Competitive elections: The condition of having free and fair elections is considered a basic requirement for a democracy in all conceptualizations, but as discussed previously all elections are not equally consequential. Therefore, we will consider elections which 'make a potential difference'. Here, we have utilized the Economist Intelligence Unit (EIU) *Index of Democracy*'s 'electoral process and pluralism' score on a 0–10 scale, where 10 represents the top score. In order to make an assessment of the elections, the designers behind the Economist index have looked at a number of aspects. For example, are elections for the national legislature and head of government free and fair? Do opposition parties have a realistic prospect of achieving government positions? Available overall scores are: for 2006 – 6.11; for 2008 – 5.52; for 2010 – 5.87; for 2011, 2012 and 2013 – 5.86; for 2014 – 5.78; and for 2015 – 5.73.[98] Bangladesh scores relatively highly on the category 'electoral process' (6 and above) in the EIU index. The average is above 7 on a 10-point scale. Similar composite scores are reported in the Polity IV data where the country has been rated 6 between 1991 and 2006; −6 between 2007 and 2008; 5 between 2009 and 2012; 4 for 2013; and 1 for 2014. Both EIU and Polity IV data, and particularly the latter, show a decline.[99]

Levels of corruption: In order to assess the levels of corruption, we have utilized the country ranking provided by Transparency International's Corruption Perceptions Index (CPI). On the CPI 1–10 scale, where 10 represents no corruption and 1 high corruption, Bangladesh scored 1.2 in 2003; 1.3 in 2004; 1.5 in 2005; 1.7 in 2006; 2.0 in 2007 and 2008; 2.1 in 2009; 2.4 in 2010 and 2.7 in 2011. Bangladesh scored equivalent to 2.6 and 2.7 in 2012 and 2013 and equivalent to 2.5 in 2014 and 2015.[100] While there is a positive trend in terms of the corruption ranking, the average score between 2003 and 2015 is extremely poor.

Lack of democratic quality: By lack of democratic quality we mean the lack of checks and balances of government and government accountability. The EIU 'functioning of government' index uses a series of data to arrive at an aggregate score. These data are gathered through questions such as: Is there an effective system of checks and balances on the exercise of government authority? Are sufficient mechanisms and institutions in place for assuring government accountability to the electorate in between elections? Is the civil service willing and capable of implementing government policy? In addition to the questions the EIU takes into account the World Values Survey (WVS) data, where available. The scores for 2006 and 2008 are 5.07; for 2010–13 are 5.43; and for 2014, 5.07.[101] Using a slightly above the mid-point – 6 – as the threshold we find that the country average is below the threshold.

Press freedom: The state of press freedom in Bangladesh is derived from data in the *World Press Freedom Index* by Reporters Without Borders.[102] The index ranges from 0 to 110, where 0 signifies the top rating – i.e. no press freedom obstacles – and 110 the worst rating. Countries with scores above 20.00 are characterized as having a 'problematic press freedom situation'. Between 2002 and 2012 Bangladesh has scored above 60 twice (2004 and 2005); above 50 twice (2007 and 2011–12); above 40 eight times (2002, 2003, 2006, 2008, 2010, 2013, 2014 and 2015) and once above 30 (2009).

Civil liberties: We have utilized three sets of longitudinal data from the Freedom House's *Freedom in the World* index to arrive at our conclusion on the state of civil liberties in Bangladesh:

(a) 20 years (1994–2013) of ratings of Civil Liberties: Bangladesh's score has been consistently 4 in a scale of 0 to 7 (average is 4).[103]
(b) ten years of aggregate scores (2004 – 13, average 31.6 on 0–60 scale);[104]
(c) eight years' subcategories' data of civil rights (2006 and 2013) of which one subcategory passed the 60 per cent threshold (9 out of 15 points) (Table 4.4).

Evidently, the record here is somewhat mixed. Despite some years with serious deterioration, other years show a positive trend.

Table 4.4 Subcategories of Political Rights and Civil Liberties

Year	Political Rights			Civil Liberties			
	Electoral Process	Political Pluralism	Functioning of Government	Freedom of Expression	Associational and Organizational Rights	Rule of Law	Personal Autonomy and Individual Rights
2006	8	10	4	8	8	6	9
2007	8	10	4	8	8	6	9
2008	3	5	4	7	6	6	9
2009	9	9	4	8	8	5	9
2010	9	11	6	9	8	7	9
2011	9	11	6	9	9	7	9
2012	9	11	5	9	8	7	9
2013	9	11	5	9	7	6	9

Note: Scores – the ratings process is based on a checklist of 10 political rights questions and 15 civil liberties questions. Political Pluralism and Participation (4), and Functioning of Government (3). The civil liberties questions are grouped into four subcategories: Freedom of Expression and Belief (4 questions), Associational and Organizational Rights (3), Rule of Law (4), and Personal Autonomy and Individual Rights (4). Scores are awarded for each of these questions on a scale of 0 to 4, where a score of 0 represents the smallest degree and 4 the greatest degree of rights or liberties present. The highest score that can be awarded to the political rights checklist is 40 (or a total score of 4 for each of the 10 questions). The highest score that can be awarded to the civil liberties checklist is 60 (or a total score of 4 for each of the 15 questions).
Source: Freedom House, 'Freedom in the World: Aggregate and Subcategory Scores', various years, http://www.freedomhouse.org/report/freedom-world-aggregate-and-subcategory-scores.

Rule of law: Poor rule of law indicates that a regime selectively uses laws for its own benefit and persecutes potential opponents. It also undermines the independence of the judiciary. Extra judicial activities including extra judicial killings are indicative of the presence of a hybrid regime as opposed to a liberal democracy. Operations of vigilante groups are commonly sanctioned by the government in hybrid regimes. We have utilized three sources to determine the rule of law situation: (1) scores in the subcategory of 'rule of law' in the *Freedom in the World* (2006–13, average 6.2 on a 0–15 point scale, the higher the points, the better is the rule of law situation) (Table 4.4); (2) terror scale of Amnesty International (1991–2014, average 3.3 on a 1–7 scale where 7 is the worst); (3) terror scale of USDS (1991–2014, average 3.7 on a 1–7 scale where 7 is the worst).[105] Drawing on these three sources we have concluded that the rule of law situation in Bangladesh is a matter of serious concern.

When compiled, the disaggregated data on six key features of governance and the state of democracy, shows that four indicators have poor records while civil liberties has a mixed one. The only positive aspect is regular highly competitive elections.[106] As I have previously mentioned, these indices are used to determine whether a democracy can be categorized as a 'hybrid regime'. It is well to bear in mind that a hybrid regime, by definition has a system of competitive election and lacks almost all other aspects of political and civil rights and freedom. Therefore, we conclude that Bangladesh is not a regime in transition to a liberal democracy but a 'hybrid regime'.

Having categorized Bangladesh as a hybrid regime it is incumbent on us to tackle the question as to why a hybrid regime has emerged in Bangladesh. Equally important is to bring some specificity to the nature and quality of democracy in the country because a hybrid regime is an expansive category which allows various kinds of regime that are neither democratic nor autocratic.

Why Hybrid Regime?

The question then is why do hybrid regimes emerge in some but not in all countries that are transitioning from autocracy? The question is pertinent in the case of Bangladesh. We can point to two factors; the transition process and the lack of hegemony of the ruling class.

Often transition to democracy means building coalitions and negotiating pacts. In such situations, 'traditional rulers remain in control, even if pressured from below, and successfully use strategies of either compromise or force – or some mix of the two – to retain at least part of their power'.[107] Popular sectors are then significantly marginalized and their demands for transparency and accountability are pushed aside. The high degree of continuity (in terms of policy and personnel) between (previous) authoritarian and elected civilian regimes undermines the democratization process. In that sense the experience of Bangladesh in past decades is not qualitatively different from Venezuela's democratic transition in the 1950s which Terry Karl has described as the perpetuation of a corrosive system.[108]

It is quite obvious to any observer of Bangladeshi politics that despite the 'transition to democracy' the ruling elites connected to the previous military regimes have maintained significant prominence and returned to power within a short period of time. Not only has the BNP, a product of the military regime, emerged as the major party, but the Jatiya Party (JP), founded by military ruler General Ershad, has become the kingmaker. The AL has never admitted that the introduction of the one-party system in 1975 was a colossal mistake and that it paved the way for institutional authoritarianism in Bangladesh.

It is equally important to bear in mind that authoritarianism not only resides in political institutions and works through the mechanisms of governance but also remains present within social practices, which Pinheiro has described as 'socially-rooted authoritarianism' – that is 'profound authoritarian trends that pervade not only politics but society'.[109] These trends have not been addressed in the democratization process of Bangladesh, as is true for many other countries which underwent the transition. The inability or unwillingness to address these deep-seated tendencies embedded in the society makes the country a candidate for a hybrid regime. The democratic transition of the 1990s in Bangladesh which neither replaced the traditional rulers (i.e. the entrenched political class), nor addressed the social basis of authoritarianism, remained incomplete; resulting in a hybrid regime irrespective of which party is in power.

The situation has become worse because of the lack of hegemony of the ruling class. Hegemony, according to Gramsci, is

the 'spontaneous' consent given by the great masses of the
population to the general direction imposed on social life by the
dominant fundamental group; the consent is 'historically' caused
by the prestige (and consequent confidence) which the dominant
group enjoys because of its position and function in the world of
production.[110]

The question of hegemony, however, is not merely material, it is also a
politics of moral and intellectual leadership. To assert its hegemony, the
ruling class must be able to defend its own corporate interests by
universalizing them, by ensuring that these interests can at least
apparently 'become the interests of the [. . .] subordinate groups'. To this
extent, hegemony implies consent rather than domination, integration
rather than exclusion, and co-optation rather than suppression. From
this point of view, a ruling class is hegemonic when it establishes both
material dominance and intellectual and moral leadership over society
and when it succeeds in persuading subaltern classes that positions of
subordination and superordination are just, proper, and legitimate.

Political developments over the past three decades in Bangladesh
demonstrate that the Bangladeshi political elites have not been able to
offer an ideology that provides moral and intellectual leadership and
secures spontaneous consent. The ideologies of the major parties, such
as the AL and the BNP, do not provide any substantive solution to the
daily struggles of the people and uplift them for a common cause.
These parties' incessant squabbling over the role of their deceased
leaders, the rewriting of history in a narrow partisan manner and their
inability to provide a vision for the future of the country which has
more than 60 per cent of citizens below the age of 25 have not helped
them to become moral leaders.

Yet, it is well known that the leaders of these parties wield
enormous influence and exercise significant power over the citizens at
large and their respective parties. Not only have these two parties
together secured 80 per cent of popular votes in general elections, the
leaders have maintained their hold over these parties for three
decades. The effort by the military backed caretaker regime between
2007 and 2008 to dislodge both Sheikh Hasina and Khaleda Zia
from party leadership and exile them, known as the 'Minus Two
Formula', failed miserably (see Chapter 3).[111] An explanation of this

phenomenon is in order. I argue that the concept of 'tutelary power' is helpful in understanding why and how these leaders have retained their positions and how that phenomenon has impacted upon the nature and quality of democracy.

Tutelary Powers

Tutelary power refers to the extra-democratic, often extra-constitutional, power of individuals, groups or institutions. The presence of such powers undermines the authority of democratic politics and 'they (elected representatives) are subordinate to the whims and wishes of their unaccountable masters'.[112] According to Puhle,

> This type of defective democracy is characterized by the existence of reserved domains of undemocratic forces functioning as extra-democratic power centers and veto players, like the military or some traditional oligarchic factions and groups. Apart from the classical case of Atatürk's Turkey, this type has been more frequent in Latin America (down to its somewhat reduced form in contemporary Chile) and in Southeast Asia, than in other parts of the world.[113]

In new democracies this often means that power lies with the military (for example, Guatemala, El Salvador) or clerical leadership (for example, Iran). The concept has been used more frequently and its analytical value has been tested more vigorously in the context of Latin America.[114]

Tutelary power as practised in Bangladesh takes the form of party leaders who have unbridled power over the party with almost no accountability and without any effective checks and balances; often they have been elevated to leadership positions due to their family lineages or their claim to foundation of the party. Consequently they established 'dynastic rule' within parties. These unrestrained powers are exercised 'legitimately' as they are institutionalized in party constitutions and reaffirmed through regular practices (Chapter 5). The extent of the party leaders' power is summarized by a headline of a news report: 'Bosses bigger than parties'.[115]

The most palpable example of the concentration of power in the hands of a leader is the handing over of power to the party chief by the central committee on important issues.[116] On crucial matters the party central committee, the AL, the BNP and the JP, often leaves the final decision with the party leader delegating 'full authority'. Even when the party councils are held the chief is given the authority to appoint the committees, which are constitutionally required to be elected by the council members. In 2012, the AL council provided such power to Sheikh Hasina and in 2009, it was Khaleda Zia who secured the authority from the party councillors.[117]

Two examples suffice to illustrate the extent of tutelary powers of the leaders. On 2 September 2007, Khaleda Zia expelled the BNP Secretary General Abdul Mannan Bhuyian and Joint Secretary General Ashraf Hossain before she was arrested by the police without any consultation with the party committees. She also appointed an acting secretary general. These expulsions came in the wake of Bhuyian's unveiling of proposals for party reforms.[118] The second example pertains to the deliberations and decision making of the parliamentary committee on constitutional amendment in 2011. A 15-member constitution amendment parliamentary committee was appointed in July 2010, in which the main opposition BNP declined to participate. The proceedings of the committee show that it had unanimously concluded that the CTG system should be maintained and that a strict limit of 90 days be imposed on its tenure. In its 27 meetings between 21 July 2010 and 29 May 2011 the committee gathered opinions from three former chief justices, ten constitutional lawyers/experts, representatives from six political parties (including the AL, which was represented by the PM), 18 intellectuals, editors of 18 newspapers and media, and the leadership of the sector commanders forum (an organization of the commanders of the freedom fighters of 1971). Most of them urged the committee to look into the inadequacies of the caretaker system, only a few suggested a complete abolition of the system. Accordingly, the committee formulated its recommendation on 29 May 2011 which proposed only minor amendments to the caretaker provision. However, after meeting the PM, the committee decided to make a u-turn: Article 58, which is the basis of the CTG, will be scrapped altogether.[119]

These party constitutional provisos and practices establishe clientelistic relationships between party members and the leadership and ensures a patrimonial political culture on the one hand, while establishing a highly personalized, authoritarian style of leadership on the other. The patron–client relationship legitimizes hierarchy and the right or obligation of the superior to be superior and protect the lesser. Kochanek highlights this aspect, 'leaders are expected to be authoritarian and authority becomes highly personalized'.[120] This kind of leadership exercises extra-constitutional power within the party and with state power when elected to public office. The primary sources of their authority remain outside the constitutional realm and therefore it is natural that they emerge as the 'tutelary power' and inhibit democratic transformation.

The question then is how these powers are naturalized within the political process and acquiesced in by the citizens despite their democratic ideals? The entire political class, irrespective of their party affiliations, has adopted two strategies to that end: majoritarianism and coercion. The former is achieved through elections. In this regard the Bangladeshi political class has internalized the archetypal characteristics of what O'Donnell has called 'delegative democracy'.[121]

Delegative Democracy

In delegative democracy what is needed is to create a majority and establish a claim that the elected leader embodies the nation. The system is highly individualistic, yet it emphasizes the electoral process, because election is the way to create a majority. 'This majority must be created to support the myth of legitimate delegation.' And given the significance, 'elections are very emotional and high stakes events.' Ironically, the role of the election and electorates are limited: 'Candidates compete for a chance to rule virtually free of all constraints save those imposed by naked, non-institutionalized power relations. After the election, voters/delegators are expected to become a passive but cheering audience.' Typically the presidential system provides the opportunity, although it is easy to discern how that fits into the parliamentary system in Bangladesh where the prime minister has a presidential aura:

> Whoever wins election to the presidency is thereby entitled to govern as he or she sees fit, constrained only by the hard facts of existing power relations and by a constitutionally limited term of office. The president is taken to be the embodiment of the nation and the main custodian and definer of its interests.[122]

Gramsci further opined that consent and coercion co-exist in all societies. The coercive elements inherent in a hegemonic system are laid bare if, and when, the ability of the ruling classes to organize consent weakens. Under normal circumstances, the elements of coercion are kept latent, concealed. The ruling classes seek and, of course, prefer the active and voluntary consent of the subordinate masses. But when the masses 'do not "consent" actively or passively' or the consent is not sufficient to reproduce capitalist relations, the apparatus of state coercive power 'legally enforces discipline on those [...] who do not consent'.[123] That is why the ruling classes, in any society, attempt to impose a general direction on social life through their ideology and ensure social conformity to that ideology. If this fails, coercion becomes the principal tool to rule the masses. The enactment of laws inimical to human rights, either creating or continuing to make use of paramilitary force such as the RAB, and providing impunity to coercive forces by all elected civilian regimes in the past two decades reveal that the political class of Bangladesh has opted for coercion to make up for the absence of hegemony.

In the event of lack of hegemony and consequent dependence on coercion, the political class not only tramples on political rights and civil rights at will, but also resists any efforts to hold it accountable. In common understanding accountability is of two kinds: vertical and horizontal. There is an inherent contradiction in underscoring the importance of elections on the one hand while opposing the notion of accountability on the other. For the political class accountability has only one meaning – vertical accountability (making elected officials answerable to the ballot box); whereas, 'in institutionalized democracies, [...] accountability runs also horizontally, across a network of relatively autonomous powers (i.e., other institutions) that can call into question, and eventually punish, improper ways of discharging the responsibilities of a given official'.[124] Catalina Smulovitz and Enrique Peruzzotti have suggested a third kind of accountability – societal accountability:

> Societal accountability is a non-electoral, yet vertical mechanism of control that rests on the actions of a multiple array of citizens' associations and movements and on the media, actions that aim at exposing governmental wrongdoing, bringing new issues onto the

public agenda, or activating the operation of horizontal agencies. It employs both institutional and noninstitutional tools.[125]

In Bangladesh, not only does the political class oppose but actively frustrates any efforts to build institutions that will be the source of horizontal accountability. The long-standing struggle to create the National Human Rights Council (NHRC) in Bangladesh is illustrative in this regard. While the NHRC finally came into being in 2010, it has remained fragile and ineffective due to lack of resources and the government's unwillingness to provide it any power. Similar attitudes towards the Anti-Corruption Commission (ACC) corroborate the point. In 2013, the outgoing chief of the ACC described the commission as 'a toothless tiger'.[126] These institutions are considered by the political class, irrespective of their party affiliations, as unnecessary, burdensome and detrimental to the political mission.

Accountability has three main features: information, justification and punishment or compensation.[127]

The first element; information about a political act or series of acts by a politician or political body (the government, parliament and so on), is indispensable for attributing responsibility. The second; justification, refers to the reasons furnished by government leaders to justify their actions and decisions. The third; punishment or compensation, is the conclusion drawn by the elector or whatever other person or body, following an evaluation of the information, justifications and other aspects and interests behind the political act.[128]

Despite the passing of the *Right to Information (RTI) Act* in 2009, it is well known that individuals and organizations have little access to information. The NHRC chief has expressed his frustration that the home ministry has not provided information the commission requested in years.

One of the blatant ways to violate the rule of law is to allow groups of people to enjoy impunity when they have been or are engaged in extrajudicial killings or involved in enforced disappearances. Take for example 'Operation Clean Heart' by the BNP-led coalition government in 2002, which was officially described as an 'anti-crime' drive. The defence forces were given a free hand to deal with a deteriorating law and order situation. The operation continued for almost three months, between 16 October 2002 and 9 January 2003. Press reports recorded 57 deaths at the hands of the forces under suspicious conditions; the government admitted 12 deaths of 'heart attack' while the deceased were in custody. On 24 February 2003, the parliament passed the *Joint Drive Indemnity Act 2003*, providing indemnity to the defence personnel who took part in the special operation. Around 24,023 army and 339 navy personnel along with BDR, police and Ansar (auxiliary force) members were involved in the anti-crime drive. The joint force had arrested 11,245 people, including at least 2,482 listed criminals, and recovered 2,028 firearms and 29,754 bullets. The indemnity law stipulated that anyone harmed during the operation cannot seek justice. However, the *Indemnity Act* was annulled in 2015 by the High Court after a writ petition was filed by a lawyer in 2012. The High Court not only declared the indemnity act illegal but ruled it unconstitutional and *void ab initio* (dead from birth). The HC's observations while passing the verdict are important to note. It said that the *Joint Drive Indemnity Act 2003* was against the rule of law, that all citizens are equal before the law, that nobody, including members of law enforcement agencies, is above the law, and that the members of the joint force during the operation had taken the law in their own hands, and by doing so infringed the rule of law. These statements, in some measures, are fundamental points of democracy. Yet, what is ironic is that the HC underscored these points at a time when violation of the rule of law by members of the law enforcement agencies became widespread; moreover they continue to enjoy impunity.

Human rights groups insist that such violations have been on the increase since 2004, especially after the establishment of the elite force the RAB. According to human rights group Ain o Salish Kendra (ASK), the number of victims of extrajudicial killings was at least 210 in 2004, 377 in 2005, and 362 in 2006. The number declined under the caretaker government in 2007 and 2008, when the number of deaths were 180 and 175, respectively. In 2009, the number stood at 229. These extrajudicial killings are described by the authorities as 'crossfire' and 'encounters'. In 2010, 133 people were killed either in 'crossfire' incidents or while in custody. In 2012 the number declined to 91 but rose to 208 in 2013 and 146 in 2014.[129] According to the Odhikar, the total number of extrajudicial killings between 2004 and 2014, was 2260, of which 801 were allegedly killed by the Rapid Action Battalion (RAB).[130] *Ain o Salish Kendra* (ASK) reports that in 2015, a total of 183 people were killed by the law enforcement agencies.[131]

Abduction or enforced disappearance is another measure of the state of the rule of law. It has increased dramatically since 2010. Reports by relatives and friends of individuals having been abducted by plain-clothed members of law enforcing agencies, including the RAB and or supporters of the regime has become a normal phenomenon. Although the Government denies any involvement either on the part of the police or the RAB, it has not sought to investigate. According to another human rights organization, Odhikar, there were three incident of enforced disappearances in 2009, 18 in 2010, 30 in 2011, and 24 in 2012. According to ASK, 53 disappeared in 2013. It documented 229 enforced disappearances between 2010 and 2013. The number increased dramatically after the controversial election in 2014. In 2014, at least 88 people disappeared. According to the ASK, between January and March 2015, family members and relatives of the victims informed them that 25 people were picked up by members of law enforcement agencies. Odhikar, said that between January and June 2015, 38 persons had disappeared; of them, eight were found dead, 20 were produced before the court, and the whereabouts of ten others were unknown. According to information gathered by Odhikar, from January 2009 to May 2015, 206 persons disappeared; of them,

> 28 bodies have been found either floating in rivers or lying in ditches and farmlands across the country. A total of 80 persons have been found alive; of them 25 people have been later "shown arrested in criminal cases" between September 2014 and August 2015 and then detained in prison, and the others were either freed without a case being filed against them or are unaware about whether a case has been filed against them.[132]

But those allegedly involved in these kinds of human rights violations continue to enjoy indemnity. At times, especially at the height of the political crisis between January and March 2015, comments of ruling party leaders including the prime minister gave the impression that their actions are preemptively indemnified. For example, the attorney general, on 3 February 2015, said the law enforcers should instantly retaliate by shooting at those who will throw bombs at transport convoys.[133] High-ranking officials of law enforcement agencies have made highly provocative comments. The deputy inspector general (DIG) of the police of Dhaka range, on 7 February, referring to suspected arsonists said, 'Not only shall you fire at them but their family members too should be annihilated. I give you this order and the liability is mine.'[134] On 4 February the DIG of the police of Chittagong range said the police force has 'the capability to avenge one killing with two'.[135]

Discussions on the state of democracy in Bangladesh show that its citizens' commitments to democracy as an idea, and as the best possible system of government despite its inadequacies, are clear and palpable. But Bangladeshis credit elections with importance. Their confidence in the democratic institutions (e.g., political parties) is lukewarm and they are not averse to the idea of strong leadership – whether civilian or military – without some democratic restraints. Our discussions also showed that a hybrid regime, neither democratic in its content nor authoritarian like autocratic military rule, has emerged since the democratization process began in 1991. One can find some concurrence between the popular conceptual inadequacies and the nature of democracy in the country. Establishing a causal relationship, that is whether popular concepts are shaped by experience or vice versa, was neither intended nor attempted in this chapter. But the question looms large as a result of our discussions. There is also a strong concurrence between lack of accountability within major political parties, which is institutionalized and codified in party constitutions, and the nature of governance which is characterized by a hybrid regime. The presence of patriomonialism, a hierarchical relationship between the superior (patron) and the subordinate (client), is not conducive to an accountable political structure and is destined to create tutelary power centres outside the formal structures. In a system where horizontal accountability through election is the only visible mode of democracy and the popular perception of democracy is highly election-centric, it is not surprising that elections are viewed as emotional and high stake events in the zero-sum game of politics. Politicians view elections as their way to create a majoritarian coalition to rule for a constitutionally mandated period. The election results are seen as a 'licence to rule', not a 'mandate to govern'. Repetition of this pattern in the long history of the country, particularly since 1991, has been inimical to the institutionalization of democracy and a significant source of the pendulum-like swing between democracy and authoritarianism. Perhaps, Marium Bibi, mother of Noor Hossain has best captured the sentiment when she commented in 2010, 'I still don't see anything for which my son died.'[136] Not so implicit in this statement is that she sees no progress gained since Noor Hossain's death in 1987.

CHAPTER 5

POLITICAL PARTIES, ELECTIONS AND PARTY SYSTEM

Anyone who wants to draw the attention of a crowd in a public place in Bangladesh need only do one thing: say something about politics. Even an innocuous comment might create a crowd, a passionate debate is bound to ensue, and agreements and disagreements will follow. It seems to any observer of Bangladeshi society that everyone has an opinion on all things political. It is this public behaviour that has given rise to the adage that two Bangladeshis can establish four political parties. This well be a mathematical impossibility, but is intended to show the proclivity of Bangladeshis for creating political parties. There is a plethora of political parties in the country. This is, undoubtedly, one of the key indicators of the vibrancy of Bangladeshi politics.

Peter Bertocci, a long-time observer of Bangladeshi politics, opined, 'Bangladesh displays a bewildering array of "political parties" and leaders.'[1] Baxter et al. commented in the early 2000s that 'The factionalism of Bangladesh politics has led to a multiplicity of parties.'[2] Even a cursory look at Bangladeshi politics bears out these statements. Election Commission (EC) records show that the number of political parties contesting elections has grown significantly since 1973 when only 14 parties participated. In 1976, when the military regime of Ziaur Rahman required registration of political parties for participation in the political process, more than 50 parties registered with the government. In 1979, 29 parties participated in the election; the number reached 75 in 1991. Five years later the number had reached 81. In 2008, under the caretaker government, the EC again made registration a requirement for participation in the elections. A total of 117 parties submitted applications for registration of which 39 parties received the EC's approval. In August 2013, the EC further approved the application of nine parties from a pool of 43 applicants.[3] As of March 2016, 41 parties were registered with the EC.[4] These numbers only represent parties that have filed at least one candidate in the parliamentary elections and/or sought the approval of the EC. It is worth mentioning that there are a host of parties which did not take part in the election and operate without formal approval. Therefore, the total number of parties in Bangladesh is much higher than these records show.[5]

These political parties can be categorized into two groups based on their organizational strengths, efficacy and relevance. The parties with well-developed electioneering organizations, and well-articulated and long-standing grassroots extensions belong to the first group.[6] By this standard, and based on the results of the four elections held between 1991 and 2008, there are only a handful of political parties in Bangladesh. But, in a country where money and muscle power play a pivotal role in elections, caution must be exercised in judging the relevance of parties based solely on electioneering capabilities. The strengths of some parties may lie in their ability to articulate popular aspirations and their capacity to mobilize supporters and sympathizers at critical moments of political events, even if they do not do well in electoral politics. Therefore, the list of this group is bound to be different from the list of parties represented in the parliament.

The second group is comprised of parties with little or no support within the populace. These parties are often referred to as 'name-only' political parties.[7] 'A president, a general secretary, a tiny office, and a telephone seem to be all the requirements for forming a party.'[8] Some cannot even boast this basic setup – their existence is limited to their own letterheads.

Notwithstanding the variations in size, organization and influence, these parties represent a broad spectrum of ideologies: from radical left to radical right; from staunch secularists to hardcore Islamists, and all shades of political thoughts in between. Based on the party constitutions and election manifestos, the ideological orientations of major parties are listed below:

Table 5.1 Ideological Orientations of Political Parties

Name of the party	Ideological orientation
Bangladesh Awami League (BAL)	Centrist, believes in role of government in economy, considers limited role of religion in politics, espouses liberal social values, proponent of Bengali nationalism
Bangladesh Nationalist Party (BNP)	Centre-right, proponent of open market economy, views Islam as a central element of social and political life, espouses liberal social values, proponent of Bangladeshi nationalism
Jatiya Party (JP)	Centre-right, proponent of open market economy, believes in significant role of Islam in politics, espouses liberal social values, advocates Bangladeshi nationalism
Jamaat-e-Islami (JI)	Islamist, right wing, supporter of open market economy with certain restrictions due to religious factors, espouses conservative social values, supports Muslim nationalism
Communist Party of Bangladesh	Socialist, secularist, believes in command economy, highly liberal on social issues
Islami Oikya Jote	Orthodox Islamist, supporter of restricted market economy, espouses highly conservative social values, supports Bangladeshi nationalism
Bangladesh Islami Andolon	Orthodox Islamist, supporter of restricted market economy, espouses highly conservative social values, supports Bangladeshi nationalism
Jatiya Samajtantrik Dal (JSD)	Centre-left, secularist, believes in role of government in economy, espouses liberal social values, supports Bengali nationalism
Socialist Party of Bangladesh	Socialist, secularist, believes in command economy, highly liberal on social issues

Note: Three parties listed here have various factions; they are the JSD, the JP and the IOJ; however, ideologically, there are little variations among these factions. (Divisions of parties are discussed later.)

Elections, Parties and Party Systems[9]

Election data provide an idea of the reach and support of political parties in Bangladesh. Of the ten parliamentary elections held between 1972 and 2014, six were held under a parliamentary system of government, one parliament amended the constitution to introduce the presidential form of government in 1975, while another elected under a presidential system reversed it through an amendment 16 years later. The results of these elections demonstrate the strength and appeal of parties to the larger population and their impact on politics. In this context we can divide these elections into four broad timeframes: 1973, 1979–86, 1991–2008 and 2014. Elections in the second phase were conducted under military regimes and two parties were created under the direct patronage of the government. Although there are marked differences in political environment between the first two phases, as I will demonstrate later, from the party-system perspective, there is a strong resemblance. The third phase represents a period when elections (except the February 1996 election) were fairly conducted under non-partisan caretaker regimes between 1991 and 2008. The 2014 election marks the fourth phase.

The first election held under the newly framed constitution in 1973, within less than 15 months of independence, provided a landslide victory to the Awami League. The AL received 73 per cent of popular votes and 293 out of 300 seats (Appendix 2). Despite the growing resentments against the government, and the emerging viable opposition (for example, the Jatiya Samajtantrik Dal, JSD), the ruling AL was organizationally stronger than its opponents. Many have argued that the 1973 election results do not represent the extent of the popularity of the ruling party; however, for the sake of understanding the relative strength of the parties which participated in the election, it is necessary to underscore that the ruling AL was ahead of others.

The constitutional stipulation of an election allowing participation of various parties implies the presence of a multi-party system. But election results, especially allegations of manipulation of the ruling AL,[10] revealed the proclivity towards creation of a dominant party system. The crucial features of the dominant party system are that it ensures unbridled control of one party over state and politics, and turns the election into a formality to anoint the same party. In the words of Ware, in the dominant party system one major party has the ability to obtain, 'enough parliamentary seats to control a government on its own'.[11] Suttner argues that in this system, 'future defeat [of the dominant party] cannot be envisaged or is unlikely for the foreseeable future'.[12] The effort to create a dominant party system in 1973 in Bangladesh provided the momentum to create a one-party system in January 1975.

The military coup d'état in August 1975 and subsequent military rule between 1975 and 1990, brought back the multi-party system; but the tendency towards creating a dominant party system was palpable. The introduction of 'Kings' Party (that is to launch parties by the ruling military rulers using the state machinery), and manipulation of election results are testimonies in this regard. Results of elections held between 1979 and 1988 show that the parties in power have secured decisive victories. The BNP secured 207 seats (41.2 per cent of popular votes) in 1979, the JP secured 153 seats (42.3 per cent of popular votes in 1986, and 251 seats (68.4 per cent of popular votes in 1988 (Appendix 3). While in power, both the BNP (established in 1978) and the JP (established in 1986), sought to create a system which would ensure their victory in subsequent elections. In the dominant party system, the ruling party not only tries to manipulate elections and control the parliament, but also seeks to establish a monopoly over political agendas and public policy.[13] The introduction of the concept of Bangladeshi nationalism vis-à-vis Bengali nationalism, religion vis-à-vis secularism as state principles by the BNP, and the insertion of Islam as the state religion by the JP have shaped the public discourse and were intended to provide them with the much-needed monopoly over discourse to erect the edifice of the dominant party system. Evidently these efforts did not succeed.

The collapse of the General Ershad-led military government in 1990 marked the transition point. However, by then the party system had experienced three changes: intensification of division of parties or factionalism (especially after 1976); building alliances (particularly after 1982); and the reemergence of Islamist parties (after 1976). When an urban popular uprising unseated the regime in 1990 and a democratization process was expected to ensue, the Bangladeshi party system, both ideologically and organizationally, became more complex than ever before. Interestingly, despite fragmentation of major parties and the creation of various alliances (these issues are discussed later in the chapter), the 1991 election demonstrated that the country was entering into a *de facto* two-party system. Almost 61 per cent of popular votes were secured by two parties – popular votes were divided almost equally among the AL and the BNP (30.1 per cent and 30.8 per cent, respectively, Appendix 4).

The election also brought to the fore the fact that about one-third of the electorate had yet to lend support to either of these two parties. The question was whether a single party could capture these votes and pose a challenge to the emerging party system. Both the JP of General Ershad and the Islamist party hoped that it would be able to capture these votes unilaterally. But:

> The 1996 election confirmed a voting pattern that emerged in 1991. The major parties (except JI) not only retained their vote share, but also increased it. The increase was proportionate to the increased turnout, and in areas of their strength. The increase was at the cost of minor parties and individuals [i.e. independent candidates].[14]

The 1996 results also revealed that, 'while the BNP and AL have a vote base throughout the country, the JP and JI have particular areas of strength and are less broadly represented in other areas'.[15]

The 2001 election delivered a decisive victory to the BNP and its allies, yet the share of popular votes of the AL and the BNP was closer than what the number of parliamentary seats won by respective parties revealed. A distinctive change was noticed in the 2008 election; the AL made significant headway in terms of share in popular votes as it secured 49 per cent of votes. But the BNP's position as the second major political party remained unaffected with 33.2 per cent of votes (Appendix 5).

Notwithstanding the two-party system, two other parties – the JP and the JI – became visible and relevant in the electoral equation. By 2008 Bangladesh had a two-party system with two smaller significant parties – the JP (Ershad) and the JI – with a combined total share of at least 12 per cent of popular votes.

Unfortunately, these developments did not persuade the major political parties, particularly the ruling AL between 2009 and 2013, to abandon the 'dominant party system' mindset. The experience of alteration of power in the previous 22 years and the potential for losing the forthcoming election, in conjunction with the dominant party mindset, led to the annulment of the caretaker government proviso in 2010. It was evident that the AL was reluctant to have a formidable opposition in the election; the BNP on the other hand made several strategic mistakes leading to its boycott of the election held on 5 January 2014. The violence perpetrated by opposition activists prior to the election which lessened their popular appeal alongside the war crimes trials which had significant popular support helped the regime move ahead with an election. The election was participated in by only 12 out of 40 registered parties with about 22 per cent voter turnout.[16] The result was a forgone conclusion, particularly when 154 seats were uncontested (Appendix 6). The AL won more than three-quarters of seats with 79.14 per cent of votes cast. The JP won 34 seats with 11.31 of votes cast.

The AL, before and after the election, enticed or coerced the JP (Ershad), to act as the official opposition party for constitutional requirements and moral legitimacy. The recognition of the JP (Ershad) as the opposition party also stems from the necessity that a dominant party system requires an opposition but a party which does not pose an imminent threat to the ruling party; to reiterate Suttner it is a system where 'future defeat [of the dominant party] cannot be envisaged or is unlikely for the foreseeable future'.[17] By this account, the 2014 election, despite low voter turnout and being boycotted by major opposition parties, may turn out to be the most consequential election in the history of the nation. Fragile democracy, as practiced since 1991, may have taken a turn for the worse.

Therefore, as of March 2016, the party system in Bangladesh stands at a crossroads: there are four potential scenarios − first that the current endeavour to establish a dominant party system meets the fate of the previous attempts of 1975, 1978 and 1986 and the country returns to the business-as-usual situation with AL−BNP dominance; second that with the weakening/ dissipation of the BNP due to its strategic mistakes and state persecution[18] a dominant party system emerges with a weak party serving as a loyal (to regime) opposition; third, that utilizing the vacuum created by the regime to develop a new system a new party appears to replace the BNP; fourth, that one of two extant minor parties steps up to be the effective major opposition.

Ethos and Practices: Similarities Within Parties

Notwithstanding the differences in ideological orientation and origin, and an acrimonious relationship between the two major parties, most of the political parties in Bangladesh share some common characteristics and ethos. These features include the lack of internal democracy, concentration of power in the hands of the party chief, familial connection as the means of accession to and continuance in the party hierarchy, and predominance of 'dynastic succession'.

The issue of lack of internal democracy became a matter of public discourse during 2007 and 2008, particularly due to the tacit encouragement of the military-backed caretaker government, but it has been a major issue of concern among political analysts since the early 2000s. Barman et al., referring to the AL, the BNP and the JP, maintain that, 'all of these parties have an internal organizational structure that is hardly democratic, and the party activities such as policy-making, decision-making, and committee structuring are centered [on] the cult of the leader'.[19] Other analysts, for example Ahmed, concur with this contention: 'none of the major parties are democratic in composition'.[20] Khan remarks, 'All parties profess to adhere to democratic principles. But the reality is different.'[21]

Evidence of the lack of accountability of the party leadership includes the absence of regular party conventions/conferences, and the continuation of the same leaders in party leadership for more than three decades. The constitutions of the BNP and the AL call for holding national councils every two and three years, respectively. But throughout the 1990s, none of these parties held their councils. The national council of the AL was not held between 2002 and 2009. The national council of the BNP, held in December 2009, was the first for 16 years. The National Executive Committee of the BNP, supposed to sit every three months, did not meet between 1996 and 2006. The National Standing Committee, the highest decision-making body of the party, is required to meet once a month according to the party constitution. But no meeting was convened between 2002 and 2006, when the party was ruling the country. In the absence of functioning committees the decisions are made under constitutional and extra-constitutional powers of the party chief. Party members, even those who hold memberships in the decision-making forums, do not have the freedom to express their opinions, because dissenting views are regarded as disobedience and disobedient members are 'disciplined' without judging the merit of their opinion.[22] Ahmed aptly notes, 'Those who refuse to abide by the despotic decisions of the leadership risk suspension or expulsion and, in extreme cases, may lose their membership (in the parliament).'[23] As for the continuation of leadership, except for a handful of parties (for example the CPB, the JI), leaderships have been in the hands of the same individuals for the past three decades. Sheikh Hasina assumed the AL leadership in 1981, Khaleda Zia became the BNP chief in 1984, and General Ershad has been the chair of the JP since its founding in 1986. in 2009 General Ershad declared his intention to be the life-long president.[24]

The party secretary general positions of the AL and the BNP have also been in the hands of a small number of individuals. The AL had five individuals who were acting or full time in this position between 1982 and 2014. As for the BNP, since 1979, six leaders have occupied this position.[25] However, this phenomenon is not limited only to these large parties; Rashed Khan Menon has led the leftwing Workers Party since 1980, the year the party came into being. Hasanul Huq Inu of the JSD (Inu) became the party Secretary General in 1986, and party president in 2002. Both are in their positions as of late 2014 with very little prospect of either stepping down. The familiar faces for more than three decades in the party leadership of almost all parties in Bangladesh provide the impression that leadership is a matter of perpetuity and that the party structures are only there to provide a stamp of validation to the decisions of these leaders.

The party constitutions provide enormous powers to the leaders. The constitutions of three parties, the BNP, the AL and the JP, are cases in point.

The party constitution of the BNP provides the following authority to the chairperson:

(1) The chairman as the chief executive of party will control, monitor and coordinate all activities of the party and for this will have full authority over national council, national standing committee, national executive committee, subject committees and other committees nominated by the chairman and will control, monitor and coordinate their activities; (2) The chairman, if

necessary, can take punitive measures against the members of above committees; (3) The chairman as the president of the national executive committee will determine responsibilities, power and duties of officials of the committee; (4) The chairman, if necessary, can cancel national executive committee, national standing committee, subject committees and other committees nominated by the chairman; (5) The chairman will preside over the meetings of national council, national standing committee, national executive committee but if necessary he or she can hand over the responsibility to another member; (6) The chairman can fill up the vacancies in national standing committee and national executive committee.[26]

The chairperson can appoint up to 10 per cent members of the National Council and 10 per cent of the 351 member National Executive Committee.

Similarly, the AL constitution provides the party president the power to appoint 21 members in the 166-member National Committee (NC), and 26 members in the 73-member Executive Committee (EC). Interestingly, all EC members are ex-officio members of the NC; therefore, essentially 47 members of the NC are handpicked by the president of the party. Granting membership to the 41-member advisory committee is entirely at the discretion of the party president.[27]

However, these provisions pale in comparison to the power enjoyed by the president of the Jatiya Party (JP) headed by former military leader H. M. Ershad. The party constitution stipulates that the chairperson can suspend and/or dissolve any committees including the presidium and the central working committee elected at the party council by the council members. The 11-member parliamentary nomination board, which selects the nominee for elections, has two ex-officio members: the president and the secretary general; the remainder are appointed by the chairperson. If the board fails to reach to a consensus regarding any nominee, the chairperson's unilateral decision is to be considered final according to the constitution. If any dispute arises regarding the interpretation of the party constitution, the final authority rests with the party chairperson. As for the advisory committee, it is the sole discretion of the chair.[28]

Nepotism is rife in the Bangladesh political leadership. Jahan writes:

In AL and BNP many family members (near and extended) of
Sheikh Hasina and Khaleda Zia have already held important
political positions. Though Sheikh Hasina has recently defined her
family to include only her sister and their children, seven members
of Sheikh Hasina['s] extended family have been elected to the
tenth parliament. They include three cousins, three nephews and
the father-in-law of her daughter. Her son, Joy and her sister,
Rehana's son Redwan Siddique Boby have not yet been elected to
any political office, but both are involved in party and campaign
activities. Joy has also been named the technology advisor to the
Prime Minister. In the BNP too, in addition to her son Tareque
Rahman, Khaleda Zia's sister was a member of the eighth
parliament as well as a cabinet minister. Khaleda's brother was also
a member of the eighth parliament. Three of her nephews were
politically influential. In the Jatiya Party, Ershad's brother, sister
as well as his wives have been MPs and held various party
positions.[29]

This trend exists within other parties; Jahan points to the BJP whose
president Andaleev Rahman Partha is the son of the founder of the party
Naziur Rahman, and to Bikalpadhara whose party spokesperson Mahi B.
Chowhdury is the son of President Badruddoza Chowdhury and the
likely successor. While in the 1980s familial connection as a means to
accede to leadership was limited to the central leadership, it has now
proliferated to local levels.[30]

Succession to leadership positions is generally arranged to ensure it
will remain within the family. In short, heredity is the only means of
accession to power. The appointment of Tareq Rahman as the joint
secretary general in 2002 and senior vice president in 2009 of the BNP
sent a clear signal that he is the heir apparent. In the case of the AL,
'there is no clear dynastic successor to Sheikh Hasina, but speculation has
centered around several family members including her sister Sheikh
Rehana and son [Sajib] Wajed Joy'.[31] The latter has been appointed as an
advisor to the prime minister. Two factions within the JP vying to
succeed General Ershad are led by his wife Rowshan Ershad and his
brother G. M. Qauder.

These characteristics together reflect and reproduce the culture of patrimonialism. Kochanek, Ahmed, and Bertocci view this as the key element in understanding the behaviour of Bangladeshi elites.[32] In their view, the relationship between the party loyalist and the leaders is unmistakably a patron–client relationship. Kochanek insists, 'leadership is highly personalized, based on patrimonial authority and loyalty, and maintained through a complex, informal network of patron–client relations'.[33] Ahmed shares this opinion and explains, 'Party leaders tend to attract members, supporters and voters through patronage, rather than by developing a group of supporters genuinely dedicated to the party goals.'[34] The patron–client relationship legitimizes hierarchy and the right or obligation of the superior to be superior and protect the lesser. Kochanek highlights this aspect, 'leaders are expected to be authoritarian and authority becomes highly personalized'.[35]

Rightward Move of Parties

Throughout the first 42 years, on three counts, the Bangladeshi political landscape has gradually shifted towards the right: first, new conservative parties have emerged; secondly, left-leaning parties have weakened; and third, major parties have adopted more conservative positions on social and economic issues.

Between 1972 and 1975, in a continuum drawn from left to right, political parties which dominated mainstream politics were located either left of centre or left of the continuum. Four right-wing parties, including the JI and the Muslim League (ML) were banned through an executive order on 18 December 1971 for their active opposition to the independence war, followed by a constitutional bar on religion-based parties. There were no parties which represented the conservative ideology. The ruling AL was located closest to the centre with a clear left-of-centre political agenda. The Communist Party of Bangladesh (CPB) and the National Awami Party (Muzaffar, a pro-Soviet Union party) were allies of the AL although their programme included transformation of Bangladesh into a socialist state. The Jatiya Samajtantrik Dal (JSD) which emerged in 1972 when a group of young activists split from the AL, was located further left on the continuum. The National Awami Party (NAP) led by Maulana Bhashani, although not a typical leftist organization, represented positions which called for egalitarianism and social justice, and served as an umbrella for left-leaning activists, particularly those who opposed the AL. Its closest ally was the Communist Party of Bangladesh (Leninist) launched in 1972, renamed the United People's Party (UPP) in 1974, which became a stage for political activists who were commonly known as pro-Chinese leftists. In large measure this strand represented the pro-Chinese left who participated in the independence war. There were, of course, an array of clandestine left political parties, for example the Sarbahara Party (SP) led by Siraj Sikdar, which attracted attention through its militant activities. Some of the left parties operated underground and some declined to recognize independence and continued to carry East Pakistan in their names. The only party that can be placed on the right of the continuum, but only slightly, was the BJL led by Ataur Rahman Khan, a veteran former AL leader who launched the party in 1970. The presence of these left-of-centre and leftist parties infused the political discourse with expressions like socialism, equality, and justice for the downtrodden.

With the introduction of the multi-party system and the removal of the ban on the religion-based parties in 1976, the political landscape experienced a dramatic shift.

The BNP, which underscored the religious identity of the Bangladeshis and adopted an economic programme for capitalist development, paved the way for the emergence of centrist and right-of-centre parties. The repressive measures of the AL between 1974 and 1975 and of the military junta between 1975 and 1978 had already weakened the anti-AL parties, particularly those with left leanings. The emergence of the Democratic League (DL) under the leadership of Khondoker Mushtaq Ahmed, reemergence of Islamists, initially as the Islamic Democratic League (IDL) and later as the Jamaat-e-Islami (JI), and the Bangladesh Muslim League (BML) clearly extended the continuum to the right. Centrist parties, such as the Gano Azadi League (GAL) and the Jatiya Janata Party (JJP), populated the middle ground but implicitly contributed to the expansion of the continuum and pushing the right-wing parties further away from the centre. The left parties seemed to lose their appeal and moderated their positions. The JSD, for example, had revamped itself by 1978 after its flirtation with armed revolution and its failed attempt to capture state power in November 1975. The CPB, on the other hand, extended tacit support to the military ruler Ziaur Rahman and his agenda in 1977–78. A number of left-leaning parties and leaders, for example Kazi Zafar Ahmed of the UPP and Serajul Hossain Khan of the Jatiya Gonottantri Party (JGP), joined the BNP. Continued fragmentation of left parties, more than parties of centrist or right-of-centre persuasions, significantly weakened them. By 1984, when the then military ruler General Ershad launched the Jatiya Party (JP), economic liberalization had created a new social class who were not only apprehensive of economic equity but also conservative in their social outlook. The JP was hoping to represent this new class; it wanted to carve out a space away from the BNP; therefore its party platform incorporated a more conservative tone. The decision to declare Islam the state religion is a case in point.

By the early 1990s, both global and domestic political developments, accentuated the preeminence of conservative parties and infused the political arena with conservative discourses. Among the external developments were the demise of the Soviet Union and the domino effects in eastern Europe, the Chinese move towards an open economy, neoliberal interpretation of globalization, and the growing strength of political Islam represented by the success of the Iranian revolution and the victory of the Afghan Islamists. The collapse of the international socialist movement gave rise to the claim that liberal democracy and the free market had won the ideological battle, epitomized in the pronouncement of Francis Fukuyama that the world had reached the 'End of History'.[36] The influence of Reganomics and Thatcherism were making their mark in the economic arena. The domestic political changes included the acceptance of the JI as a legitimate political actor, and the proliferation of Islamist parties such as the Islami Oikya Jote (IOJ).

But the most dramatic shift came when the AL veered to the right. Between 1991 and 1996, two developments indicated a major shift in the ideological and organizational position of the AL. One was the increased use of Islamic rhetoric and symbols, and the other was its close relationship with the JI. The former became evident in the statements of party leaders and party publicity materials as well as in party chief Sheikh Hasina's dress. The AL was eagerly presenting itself as a good custodian of Islam in Bangladesh highlighting the 'achievements' of the Mujib regime including enhancing Islamic education in the country, establishing the Islamic Foundation and joining the OIC in 1973. These claims were accompanied by the carrying of prayer beads and the wearing of scarves by Sheikh Hasina. The latter is testified by the close cooperation between the AL and the JI during the 1991–94 period as parliamentary opposition parties (discussed later). The AL's decision to make these moves came after the 1991 election which it had hoped to win easily. The unexpected results led to some soul searching within the party as to whether it should move toward the right, vacating its centrist position, or strengthen its centrist conviction, which may be described as a 'liberal left' position. In the context of electoral politics the question for the AL was, could a centrist party hope to win, or even fare well, electorally? The AL leaders seemed to conclude in the negative, and therefore moved towards the right. The 1996 victory was interpreted by the AL leaders as a vindication of this position.

Overall, the period under review was characterized by the gradual departure of the term 'socialism' from political rhetoric and electoral promises, economic programmes adopted by parties more aligned with the global capitalist agenda, and religion became a political issue rather than a matter of private faith. Election manifestos of the AL, the JSD and the CPB, of 1996 and 2001 are illustrative of this change.

Islamist Parties: Variations and Influences

The prominence of religion in the political discourse is facilitated by the rise of Islamist parties. Islamist parties, in this context, refers to political parties that 'draw on Islamic referents – terms, symbols, and events taken from Islamic tradition – in order to articulate a distinct political agenda'[37] and whose overall political agenda includes Islamization of society or transformation of the Bangladeshi state into an Islamic state. It is well to bear in mind that in Bangladesh, as elsewhere, Islamists should be referred to in the plural as they are neither a monolithic force nor belong to one single party. Given that the Islamists have re-emerged from oblivion, carved out an influential space within the political landscape, emerged as kingmakers in electoral politics, and impacted on the political discourse, it is imperative that we take a close look at them.

Islamist political parties can be divided into five categories: pragmatists, idealists, *pir* (Preachers of Islam) and *mazar* (Shrines) – centric, urban elite-centric, and 'jihadists'. Of the five categories of

Islamist parties, those which fall within the first four operate within mainstream politics while those in the fifth category are clandestine and some have been proscribed since 2005. Table 5.2 looks at the support bases of the political parties included in each category.

The results of four elections participated in by the Islamist parties show that support for the JI dwindled over time – from 12.13 per cent in 1991 to 8.61 per cent in 1996 to 4.29 per cent in 2001, and stagnated at that level as it secured 4.48 per cent in 2008. The Islami Oikya Jote (IOJ) won one seat in both 1991 and 1996, but the percentage of votes it received in both elections was 0.79 per cent and 1.09 per cent respectively – a negligible rise of 0.33 per cent. In 2008 its share of the popular vote slumped to 0.16 per cent. The statistics compiled from the documents of the Election Commission reveal that the total share of the vote won by Islamist parties declined by 4 per cent between the 1991 and 1996 elections. In the 1991 election 17 Islamist parties secured 14.87 per cent of votes, compared to 10 per cent in June 1996. This took place against a 20 per cent rise in voter turnout.[38] In 2008, nine parties together garnered 6.27 per cent of popular votes.[39] (Appendix 7 and Appendix 8).

Fragmentation of Parties

One of the key characteristics of the party system in Bangladesh is the fragility of the parties; that is, parties tend to fragment. Almost all parties – big and small, parties with little popular support and parties with grassroots organization – have faced some kind of split in the past four decades. The tendency became significant after 1976, initially at the prodding of the military regime as it embarked on founding a political party; but the record is not significantly different during the civilian regimes, particularly after 1991.

The extent of the fragmentation tendency can be understood from close examination of selected political parties. It is well to bear in mind that not all splits follow the same pattern, neither are they equally damaging to the party. The AL, for example, has experienced seven splits since independence. In some instances, leaders have left the party with a small number of followers and founded their own parties. The founding of the JJP by retired General M. A. G. Osmani, the GAL by veteran leader Abdur Rashid Tarkabagish, and the Bangladesh

Table 5.2 Taxonomy of Islamist Political Parties

Distinguishable Traits	Support Base	Name(s) of the Organization(s)
Pragmatist/Opportunist Want to establish Islamic order in society through the state; participate in elections; believe in 'Islamic revolution'; committed to implementation of Shari'a; believe in primacy of political goals and propagate politicized interpretation of Islam	Support within various strata of the society; organizational structures are geographically spread around the country; growing support within educated middle class with very active front organizations for students, youth and women; have socio-cultural organizations	Bangladesh Jamaat-e-Islami (JI)
Idealist and Orthodox Want a 'pure' Shari'a-based Islamic state; View Islam as primarily 'a way of life'; despise the 'secular' nature of the constitution and the social life, view militancy as a justifiable means to capture state power	Closely tied to *quami madrassahs*, where leaders of the organizations come from; support base is largely within *quami madrassahs* and in rural areas; each organization has small pockets of support base in various parts of the country; support bases and organizations are weak	Jamiat-e-Ulema, Bangladesh Khilafat Andolon (Bangladesh Khilafat Movement), Bangladesh Khilafat Majlish, Nizam-e-Islam Party

Pir (preacher of Islam)-centric and _Mazar_ (Shrine)-based Aim to establish a state based on traditional Islam and shari'a; critical of the JI	Support is spread throughout the country as followers of the _pir_ or _mazar_, lacks organizational structure; party is organized around individuals	Zaker Party, Bangladesh Islami Andolon, Bangladesh Tariqat Federation
Urban Elite-Centric Emphasize ideological struggle against the secular polity and system; want to establish Khilafat; internationally connected; underscore the global struggle	Highly educated middle class leadership; young, educated support base, particularly among higher learning institutions (e.g. university); proficient in usage of technology to spread the message	Hizb ut-Tahrir Bangladesh
'Jihadists' Militant Islamists who aim to establish an Islamic state in Bangladesh through 'jihad'	Support base is small and sparsely spread around the country, especially in rural areas; leadership and activists are primarily from _qwami madrassah_ backgrounds	Harkat-ul-Jhad al-Islami Bangladesh (HuJIB), Jamaat-ul-Mujahideen Bangladesh (JMB), Hijbut Tawheed, Shahadat-e-Al Hikma

Source: Ali Riaz and Kh Ali Ar Raji, 'Who Are the Islamists?' in Ali Riaz and Christine C. Fair, _Political Islam and Governance in Bangladesh._ London: Routledge, 2011. p. 48.

Democratic League (BDL) by Khandaker Mushtaq Ahmed in 1976 all follow this pattern and had little impact on the AL; but the founding of the JSD in 1973 had a significant bearing on the party's organization. The most significant split took place in 1978 when the AL leaders Mizanur Rahman Chowdhury and Abdul Malek headed two separate factions bearing the same name. The involvement of key leaders with one or the other factions gave credence to the idea that the party was facing an existential crisis. The factions continued to exist for quite some time and participated in the 1979 election as the AL. This crisis was addressed by electing Sheikh Hasina, exiled daughter of Sheikh Mujibur Rahman, in 1981. One of the factions led by Mizan Chowdhury dissipated in 1984 when he joined the Janadal, a party founded by then military ruler H M Ershad. Two further major splits of the party took place after Hasina assumed the leadership: in 1983 under the leadership of Abdur Razzaq who revived the BKSAL and then 1993 under the leadership of Kamal Hossain who founded the Gono Forum (Figure 5.1). The party was on the brink of formal division in mid-2007 when four party stalwarts, Abdur Razzaq, Tofail Ahmed, Suranjit Sengupta and Amir Hossain Amu, proposed reforms to the structure of the party governance with the active encouragement of the military-backed caretaker government. The effort was rebuffed by Hasina and the reforms did not come to pass.

The BNP has faced several splits since its founding in 1978. In 1983, soon after the party was dislodged from power and the incumbent military ruler Ershad started the process of founding the JP, a number of senior leaders split from the party under the leadership of Shamsul Huda Chowdhury. The division came about after two separate groups of BNP leaders met Ershad. It was a public knowledge that intelligence agencies were engaged is lining up politicians for the new party; the agencies were either bribing or coercing leaders to join the new organization. This was akin to what these agencies did during the formation of the BNP in 1978. A smaller faction led by Shamsuzzaman Dudu and Shawkat Hossain Nilu also emerged. In 1983. The BNP (Huda) faction finally joined the Janadal of Ershad while the mainstream led by Abdus Sattar continued. Khaleda Zia assumed the party leadership in 1984. Soon after her assumption of the leadership Shah Azizur Rahman founded a faction under the name of the BNP. The faction did not last long. A number of prominent leaders opted to defect and join the JP. The party faced a

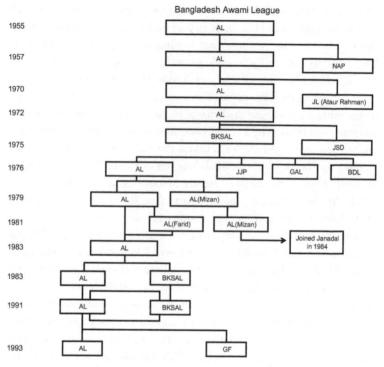

Figure 5.1   Bangladesh Awami League Fragmentation

small-scale division when K. M. Obaidur Rahman created his own faction of the BNP in 1988; his faction merged with the mainstream in 1996. The party managed to avoid any division until the military-backed caretaker government came to power in 2007 and started to push for reforms. In June 2007, while political activities were banned under the law, the BNP Secretary General Abdul Mannan Bhuyian announced a package of reform measures to 'democratize' the party. Ostensibly these measures were intended to oust Khaleda Zia from the party leadership as part of the so-called 'minus-two' formula of the government. This led to the expulsion of the secretary general by Khaleda Zia who appointed Delwar Hossain as the acting secretary general immediately before her arrest. But the machination continued and in October the division was formalized – Saifur Rahman, former finance minister, claimed that he had assumed the party leadership and replaced Khaleda Zia's appointed secretary general with another leader. BNP leaders loyal to Khaleda Zia claimed that a 'shady force' was responsible for the split.[40] While the BNP leaders were unable to publicly identify the 'shady force' at that time, cables from the US Embassy in Dhaka to the State Department in 2007 were very clear as to who was pulling the strings. According to a cable sent on 3 July 2007, the directorate general of forces intelligence (DGFI), the elite intelligence agency, was 'bullying some politicians and plotting behind the scene'.[41] While the party did split at that time, by mid-2008 as the caretaker government began its negotiation for the election two factions came together after some trepidation (Figure 5.2).

The JP's journey, in this regard, is not different from the AL and the BNP. Its first taste of division came in 1997 when former PM Kazi Zafar Ahmed led a breakaway faction. This was a result of intense infighting after Ershad was released on bail from jail in exchange for the JP's support to the AL-led government. Ershad, who was jailed after his downfall in 1990 and remained behind bars throughout the Khaleda Zia regime (1991–96) joined the AL-led coalition after the 1996 election. The JP Secretary General Anwar Hossain Manju joined the cabinet.

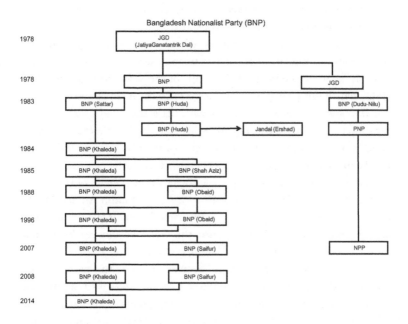

Figure 5.2   Bangladesh Nationalist Party Fragmentation

In 1997, Ershad was released on bail and a good number of JP leaders alleged that the party was becoming an extension of the AL. The Zafar faction joined the opposition BNP in August 1997. The second split appeared a year later when Anwar Hossain was asked to resign from the cabinet as the party decided to quit the coalition to join the opposition. Manju defied party instruction and claimed to represent the JP. Later in 1998 the JP (Ershad) became the founder member of the BNP-led four-party alliance. But the JP could not stay with the alliance too long as Ershad was arrested and tried for a number of corruption cases and the party faced the dilemma whether to risk Ershad's long incarceration or compromise with the government. It chose the latter which secured Ershad's bail, but at the cost of another split: a faction led by Naziur Rahman Manzur decided to stay with the BNP. The party was later renamed the Bangladesh Jaitiya Party (BJP). Thus until the Zafar group merged with the Ershad faction in 2002 four parties with JP or a similar name existed. However, angered by the party's decision to participate in the 5 January 2014 election, Kazi Zafar Ahmed split from Ershad in late 2013 and later joined the BNP-led alliance. Thus, as of October 2015, four different parties are in existence as JP of which three are registered with the Election Commission (Appendix 9).[42]

These are not the only parties which serve as examples of the continuous disintegration of parties; among the smaller left parties, the trend is far more pronounced. The split of the Jatiya Samjatantrik Dal (JSD), which until 1976 was considered to be the main opposition party but has now become a small party with little clout and organizational capability, is telling in this regard (Appendix 10). But there are striking exceptions to this trend; the Communist Party of Bangladesh (CPB) has faced a division only once since independence: in 1993, as a result of the demise of the Soviet Union and the changes in the policies of the Soviet Communist Party. The reformist group led by Saifuddin Ahmed Manik and Nurul Islam Nahid parted with the party, but their faction ceased to exist within a year as Manik joined the Gono Forum led by Kamal Hossain and Nahid joined the AL (Appendix 11).

The other party which stands out as an exception to this pattern is the Jamaat-e-Islami. The JI came close to a split in 1983–84 as a group of young activists raised concerns about party policies. Maulana Abdul Jabbar tried to launch a separate JI, and his supporters within the youth wing (Islami Jubo Shibir) led by Ahmed Abdul Kader (known as Abdul

Kader Bachhu) formed a new youth organization. However, within a short span of time they abandoned the effort and joined a new Islamist organization. This is not to say that Islamists are not prone to internal strife and division; instead closer observations of smaller Islamist parties show that they tread the same path as their secularist counterparts. The history of the IOJ is a case in point. The IOJ was founded as an alliance in 1990 with seven parties, but apparently became a single party within a few years; it has splintered into several organizations bearing the same name.[43]

These disintegrations and subsequent trajectories of the breakaway factions reveal some common features. First they originate in personality clashes rather than ideological differences within the party. Barring a few exceptions (e.g the emergence of BKSAL in 1983), these divisions of parties are intended to challenge the party leadership. This is borne out by the fact that after several years party leaders return to the party and under the same leadership which it once criticized. This is true of all parties. Second, these divisions are often prompted by external factors, such as machination of the ruling party to split the opposition. The ruling party has both resources at its disposal to entice opposition leaders and power to coerce them, if need be. Thirdly, intelligence agencies seem to act as the instrument for division of the parties, either to lure leaders to the new party or serve the interests of the regime. Although this phenomenon emerged during military rule post-1975, civilian regimes have not been reluctant to adopt this tactic. Fourthly, major parties tend to withstand splits. They tend to maintain a grip over their support base. Whether this is due to grassroots organization or because parties are associated with individual leaders and families is an open question. But our observations suggest that, to date, breakaway factions have failed to make a serious dent on the mainstream of the party.

Forging Alliances

Despite the dominance of two political parties in Bangladesh in recent decades and the extant fragmentation tendency, forging alliances has remained a significant feature of the party system of the country. In the past two decades we have witnessed a flurry of alliances. One political observer noted that, between 1992 and September 2014, 32 alliances emerged and that many of these perished within 30 days.[44] Alliances have taken two distinct forms: alliances of smaller parties and alliances centering on a large party. The former is often predicated by the necessity to gain strength and increase bargaining power, while the latter is mostly to dissuade parties to join the rival camp. These alliances are not always based on ideological affinities; however alliances of smaller parties are often ideology driven. In addition to the issue-based alliances, which emerged and disappeared within a short span of time, we have also witnessed the emergence of demand-based broader alliances, and electoral alliances turning into ruling coalitions.

Forging alliances is a pre-independence tradition of Bangladeshi politics. In several instances political parties of Pakistan came together to press their demands. The electoral alliance formed in late 1953, called the United Front, can be categorized as the first post-1947 successful example of alliance building. The Front was under the leadership of Maulana Bhashani, Huseyn Shaheed Suhrawardy and A. K. Fazlul Huq representing four parties, namely the Krishak Praja Party (KPP), the Awami League (AL), the Gonotontri Dal (GD), and the Nizam-e-Islam Party (NI). The alliance brought together major opposition parties in East Pakistan against the ruling Pakistan Muslim League (PML) demanding more power to the provincial government. The alliance secured a landslide victory in 1954 and acted as a ruling coalition for only 56 days as the cabinet was dissolved by the central government. In 1962, while Pakistan was still under military rule, nine prominent politicians called upon the citizens to coalesce demanding complete withdrawal of martial law and launch a movement. These leaders founded the National Democratic Front (NDF) on 4 October 1962 with the Awami League (AL), the Krishak Sramik Party (KSP), the Jamaat-e-Islami (JI), the Nezam-i-Islami (NI), National awami Party (NAP), and a faction of the Muslim League (ML, Council). The alliance did not succeed in making any headway due to differences among the partners. With the death of Husseyen Shahid Surwaradi in late 1963, the alliance dissipated.

On 21 July 1964, six opposition parties of Pakistan formed the Combined Opposition Party (COP) against the military dictatorship of Ayub Khan (1958–69). The members of the alliance were: the Pakistan Muslim League (Council) (led by Khwaja Nazimuddin and Mian Mumtaz Khan Daultana); the Awami League (led by Sheikh Mujibur Rahman); the National Awami Party (led by Maulana Bashani); the North West Frontier group of the National Awami Party (led by Wali

Khan); the Nizam-e-Islam Party (led by Chaudhry Mohammad Ali and Farid Ahmad); and the Jamaat-e-Islami (led by Maulana Maududi). The COP, a conglomeration of both leftist and rightist parties, nominated Fatemah Jinnah (sister of the founding father of Pakistan Muhammad Ali Jinnah) as a presidential candidate against the military ruler Ayub Khan in the indirect election held in January 1965. In 1966, as East Pakistan witnessed a mass upsurge in support of the Six Point Programme of the Awami League, the Pakistani government clamped down on the AL leaders and arrested Sheikh Mujib. A year later, on 30 April 1967, five right-wing and Islamist parties of Pakistan founded an alliance called Pakistan Democratic Movement (PDM) which was intended to steer popular support away from the AL.

In January 1969, eight political parties formed an alliance known as the Democratic Action Committee (DAC). The DAC brought together parties from both right and left of the spectrum such as the Nezam-e-Islam, the Jamaat-e-Islami, the AL and the National Awami Party (NAP, pro-Moscow). Among the major political parties, the NAP led by Maulana Bhashani and the Pakistan People Party (PPP) led by Zulfiqar Ali Bhutto remained outside the alliance.

In post-independence Bangladesh, the first alliance was put together by octogenarian leader Maulana Bhashani in late 1972. Seven parties, including the Bangladesh Jatiya League (BJL) led by Ataur Rahman Khan, joined hands on 29 December ahead of the first parliamentary election. But, the unity of the alliance collapsed before the election. Renewed efforts to bring these parties together led to the founding of the seven-party alliance in May 1973 with Maulana Bhashani at the helm. The surprise member of the alliance was the JSD, and it is alleged that the failure of the alliance to move forward is largely due to the JSD leadership's hesitations.

In 1973, an unusual move in regard to forging alliances came from the ruling AL. In June, Prime Minister Sheikh Mujibur Rahman called for the unity of all 'patriotic forces.' The call was immediately responded by the CPB and the NAP (led by Muzaffar Ahmed). Although these three parties had ideological affinities, the call for an alliance came at a time of strained relations: the CPB and the NAP had launched an anti-government movement early that year and faced significant persecution at the hands of the government and the ruling party. By October, a three-party alliance emerged. This was the first instance where the ruling party took the initiative to forge an alliance, especially soon after an election which delivered a thumping victory. Within less than two years, the alliance turned out to be the foundation of the only national party called the BKSAL (Bangladesh Krishak Sramik Awami League) and the one-party state.

Maulana Bhashani continued his efforts to bring the left parties under a broad alliance. He saw some success in April 1974: six parties forged the All Party United Front. The parties include the NAP, the Bangla Jatiya League, the Bangladesh Jatiya League, the Gonomukti Union, the Bangladesh Communist Party (Leninist), and the Bangladesh Krishak Samajbadi Dal. By the end of the year an emergency was proclaimed and a one-party system was introduced which sealed the fate of this alliance. The military regime of General Ziaur Rahman (1975–81) went one step further than the Mujib regime in regard to founding a party while in power; it set up the edifice of a new party called the Jagodal (Jatyitabadi Gonotantrik Dal, Nationalist Democratic Party) under the leadership of Vice President Abdus Sattar and then forged an alliance with five other parties in the wake of the presidential election in 1978. The 19-point programme announced by Zia in 1977 became the basis of the six-party Jatiyatabadi Front (Nationalist Front, NF), which comprised Jagodal, the Muslim League (ML), the United People's Party (UPP), the Bhashani faction of the NAP, the Bangladesh Labour Party (BLP) and the Bangladesh Scheduled Caste Federation (BSCF). The country, prior to independence, witnessed the division of an established political party by a military ruler using the state's power and purse to provide a civilian façade to the regime, thanks to General Ayub Khan who wooed a section of the ML in 1962. But the emergence of the Jagodal was unprecedented. Leaders and activists of various parties were enticed to join the party, primarily through dispensation of patronage, bribes and hand-outs. The NF was a mishmash of parties from the left to the right. It included a party which was banned until 1976 for its opposition to the independence war and its leaders' collaboration with the Pakistani regime during the war. Protagonists argued that this configuration is a reflection of the politics of consensus, and an attempt to transcend the ideological boundaries that divide the nation. But the leadership, rhetoric and composition of the party all pointed to the fact that it was a platform for those who opposed the Mujib regime. Among the Mujib opponents, the only party missing in this line up was the JSD.

It remained outside the alliance as it had already tried to unseat Zia through military coups. Within five months of launching the front, in October 1978, the constituent parties merged into a new party – the Bangladesh Nationalist Party (BNP).

The 1978 presidential election also engendered an opposition alliance: the Gono Oikya Jote (GOJ, People's Unity Alliance). Five political parties, namely the AL, the JJP, the NAP (Muzaffar), the BPL and the GAL, founded the alliance and nominated retired General M. A. G. Osmani, the commander-in-chief of the freedom fighters in 1971, as its candidate. The constituents of the alliance were ideologically closer compared to their counterpart. General Osmani was an AL leader until he resigned from the party protesting the introduction of the one-party state in 1975, and the GAL was led by a former AL leader, while the NAP (M) was one of the three parties which formed the three-party alliance in 1973. The nature of alliances is succinctly described by Khan and Zafarullah

> The JF (Jatiyatabadi Front) was a combination of people/groups with heterogeneous, conflicting and divergent interests and ideologies [. . .] It [is] also assembled together rightists, religious fanatics and die-hard conservatives as well as so-called leftists and progressives. The JF suffered from a dichotomy that was both political and ideological in nature and it was only Zia who could strike a balance and keep them together. The GOJ, on the contrary was, without doubt, a homogeneous group as its components who mattered (the Awami League, the National Awami Party, and the Communist Party) had already established rapport and worked in close alliance during the Bakasl rule (1972–75).[45]

Thus, it is not inaccurate to say that these two alliances represented two poles of the political spectrum: pro and anti-AL. This provided the first indication of an emerging two-party system in the country, and to date, this dichotomous polarization continues to be a defining feature of the Bangladeshi political landscape.

While various efforts to bring opposition parties together to launch a popular movement against the Zia regime had little success, a movement against the Ershad regime (1982–90) created alliances from the outset. Student organizations of various political persuasions joined hands in

1982 against the Ershad regime, yet the student wing of the BNP was left out of the 'All Party Student Action Committee'. This combination shaped the subsequent alliances of the political parties. For example, pressed by the student leaders 19 political parties issued a press statement on 14 January 1983, followed by another statement on 17 January signed by 15 parties. By April, these parties decided to form an alliance, popularly known as 'the 15-party' alliance. These parties were: the AL (Hasina), the JSD, the CPB, the Workers Party (WP), the Sramik Krishak Samajbadi Dal (SKSD), the AL (Mizan), the BSD, the AL (Farid), the Samyobadi Dal (SD, Toaha), the SD (Nagen), the NAP (Muzaffar), the NAP (Harun), the Ekata Party, the Gano Azadi League (GAL), and the Majdoor Party. In August 1983, the BNP formed an alliance of seven like-minded parties: the UPP, the Jatiya League, the Jatiya Gonotantraik Mukti Union, the National Awami Party, the Communist League, and the Krishak Sramik Party (KSP). In a similar vein the Democratic League (DL) under the leadership of Khondker Mushtaq Ahmed brought together 12 smaller parties and formed the National United Front (NUF). Among these alliances the 15-party combination was the most diverse in terms of ideological persuasion while the two other alliances were more cohesive. The only major party which remained outside any alliance was the Jamaat-e-Islami (JI), but it soon began to liaise with both seven-party and 15-party alliances in regard to agitation programmes. The ten-party NUF gradually fizzled out.

General Ershad, taking a leaf out of the playbook of Ziaur Rahman, formed his own party called the Janadal in November 1983, with defectors from various parties, followed by the formation of an alliance – the Jatiya Front (National Front) – in August 1985. The UPP and the Gantantrik Party (led by Anwar Zahid and Serajul Hossain Khan), and splinter groups from the BNP, the Muslim League, the BKSAL, the JSD, and the Jatiya League joined the alliance which was then turned into the Jatiya Party (JP) on 1 January 1986.

The 15-party alliance experienced a split in 1986 when the AL and seven parties decided to join the parliamentary election held in May reneging on their promise to boycott any election under the Ershad regime; the JI followed suit. But five left-leaning parties of the alliance (the JSD led by Hasanul Huq Inu, two factions of the BSD, the Workers Party and the Sramik Krishak Samajbadi Dal) formed a separate alliance and continued the movement along with the BNP-led seven-party alliance. Two years later, as another election approached due to the untimely demise of the third parliament (1986–88), both alliances (and the JI) decided to boycott, a faction of the JSD led by A. S. M. Rob, and stitched together an alliance of 76 parties called the Combined Opposition Parties (COP). Evidently the COP was created with the help of the ruling party, and most of its constituents were 'name only parties'. The fleeting existence of the COP demonstrated that it is not the number of parties that makes an alliance effective but the organizational strength of these parties, and the *raison d'être* which make an alliance appealing to the citizens. It also reaffirmed that the Bangladeshi political scene was becoming bi-partisan.

The urge to build alliances among the political parties subsided in the early years of the new democratic era (1991–2006). The election was seen by the major parties, namely the AL and the BNP, as their opportunity to return to state power; they seem to have concluded that in the electoral equation these smaller parties, with whom they had aligned for almost eight years, could contribute little. Thus, although the AL shared a few seats with its time-tested allies (the NAP, the CPB and the BKSAL), the BNP decided to participate alone. Within three years, some of the parliamentary opposition parties came together to press for the inclusion of a/the caretaker government proviso in the constitution. A four-month process culminated in a press conference on 27 June 1994 which marked the emergence of an alliance of the five parliamentary opposition parties, i.e., the AL, the JI, the JP, the NDP (led by Salahuddin Quader Chowdhury), and the Gonotontri Party (GP). The alliance drew attention to the fact that it was neither a ruling coalition nor an election alliance; but comprised only those who were already elected to the parliament. Other parties with members in the parliament, i.e, the WP, the JSD (Siraj), the Gono Forum and the Islami Oikyo Jote (IOJ) did not join the press conference and the alliance.[46] In subsequent months, these parties continued street agitations separately but maintaining close contacts.

As the parliamentary opposition parties assembled under the leadership of the AL, left-wing parties with no representation in parliament rallied to form their own alliance. In 1994, nine left parties including the BSD, formed an alliance called the Left Democratic Front. The alliance expanded and adopted a political platform in 1996 when it became 'the 11-party alliance'. The parties which joined the alliance were, the CPB, two factions of the BSD, the Gono Forum, the Gonotontri Party (GP), the Samyobadi Dal (Marxist-Leninist), the Sramik Krishak Samajbadi Dal (SKSD), the Communist Center, the Gano Azadi League (GAL) and the Ganatantric Majdoor Party (GMP). The alliance vowed to break the stranglehold of the two parties and create a 'third force' in politics. The alliance participated in two elections (1996 and 2001), but failed to secure any seats in the parliament. However, it managed to act as a pressure group.

After its defeat in the 1996 election, the BNP strived to mount street agitation against the AL regime. To strengthen its capacity to rattle the government it reached out to its allies and by 1998 it also created a schism within the regime. Accordingly, it lured a larger faction of the JP led by Ershad from the ruling coalition. In late 1998, a four-party alliance, comprised of the BNP, the JI, the JP (Ershad) and the IOJ, emerged. The alliance secured the victory in the 2001 election.

As for the left-leaning parties, they remained united as an alliance until 2005. The AL, on the other hand, with an eye on the scheduled election in 2006, began crafting a new alliance. With the JSD (Inu) and the NAP (Muzaffar) on board it approached the 11-party alliance. Seven of the 11 parties accepted the invitation while four parties (the CPB, two factions of the BSD and the SKSD) left the alliance. Yet it was portrayed as a new alliance – 11 parties joined three parties to form the 14-party alliance. Although a number of parties exited the alliance, it continued to be identified as 'the 14-party alliance'. It was further broadened in late 2006 as the street agitation gained momentum against the BNP regime ahead of the scheduled election. The JP (Ershad) left the BNP-led ruling coalition alliance, while one faction remained. Soon the AL put together what it described as the 'Grand Alliance.' It was a combination of 'the 14 parties,' the Bikalpa Dhara (BD) led by former President Badruddoza Chowdhury, the JP led by former President Ershad, and the newly founded Liberal Democratic Party (LDP) led by Oli Ahmed (who defected from the BNP in 2006). Other smaller parties jumped on the bandwagon, and the AL was not hesitant in embracing an Islamist party with a chequered past. Opposition to the BNP regime was the sole criterion for joining the alliance. Only a handful of parties such as the CPB and two factions of the BSD remained outside these alliances, and the Gono Forum left the alliance as it was opposed to the inclusion of the JP (Ershad).

During the two years of political hiatus between 2007 and 2008, the Grand Alliance metamorphosed: some parties exited, some were silently shown the door. When the 2008 election approached, although the AL led alliance still called itself the Grand Alliance, it was no longer as grand as in early 2007. In fact, it turned out to be an alliance of only nine parties, some of which were parties in name only. In the subsequent five years only two parties were represented in the cabinet. Ahead of the election in early 2014, after the elimination of the caretaker government proviso, the AL formed on 19 November 2013 what it described as an 'all-party government' with only five other parties It was, according to an analyst, 'all but an all-party government'.[47] In 2012, the BNP, on the other hand, expanded its alliance to a bloc of 18 parties which include the LDP (which was by then back to the BNP-fold), the ML and a number of other smaller parties. The alliance had picked up two more parties, one a breakaway faction of the JP (Ershad), by mid-2014.

Alliance making is not an exclusive preserve of the mainstream parties; smaller radical Islamist and left-leaning parties too have been engaged in this endeavour. The JI appeared on the political scene in 1976 through an alliance with the ML. The leaders and activists of the previously defunct resurfaced on the political scene under the umbrella of the Islamic Democratic League (IDL). In the 1979 parliamentary election the IDL formed an alliance with the ML. But the JI since then has created strategic alliances with the AL and the BNP, until it finally joined the four-party alliance in 1999.

Smaller Islamist parties attempted to emulate the JI, but with limited appeal and support base they had to come together first to secure a seat at the table of alliances. The first effort to build an alliance of the Islamists parties sans the JI, was initiated in 1981 to compete in the presidential election. The alliance called the Ulema Front nominated Maulana Muhammadullah, popularly known as Hafezzi Huzur. Surprisingly, he secured the third position behind Ziaur Rahman of the BNP and Kamal Hossain of the AL. His share of the popular vote was meagre, only 1.79 per cent, but more than retired General Ataul Gani Osmani's share of 1.39 per cent and the JSD nominee Major Jalil's share of 1.15 per cent. This result encouraged these parties, particularly Hafezzi Huzur, to venture into politics more robustly. Consequently, in

1984 Hafezzi Huzur brought 11 parties to establish the Sommilita Sangram Parishad (Combined Action Committee). These parties were Jamiat-e-Ulema-e-Islam, Khelfat-e-Rabbani Party, Islami Jubo Andolon, Khademul Islam Jamaat, Majlish-e-Tahaffuj-e-Khatm-e-Nabuat, Majlish-e-Dawat-ul-Haque, Islami Jubo Shibir, Jatiya Mukti Andolon, Khelfat Andolon, Nejam-e-Islami, and the IDL. The alliance members chose different paths in the wake of the 1986 parliamentary election in which Hafezzi Huzur decided to take part while all major parties boycotted. A year later another alliance,the Islamic Constitution Movement emerged under the leadership of Syed Fazlul Karim, popularly known as the *pir* of Char Monai. The alliance later transformed into one single party.

In the early 1990s, a group of smaller Islamist parties, that is the Khelafat-i-Majlish, Nezam-i-Islam, Faraizi Jamaat, Islami Morcha, the Ulama Committee, a splinter group of the NAP (Bhashani), and the Islamic Shashantantra Andolon formed the IOJ. The composition of the alliance changed over time and the alliance faced break up as some parties of the alliance moved to create their own alliance, with the same name.

There has been a number of instances where the Islamists founded issue-based alliances, for example to protest the Supreme Court verdict banning *fatwa* (religious edict) in 2001; to oppose the women's development policy in 2008 when the Khelafat Majlish and Islami Shasantantra Andolon (ISA) founded the 'Anti-Qu'ran Law Resistance Committee'[48] and the IOJ led another group named the Islamic Laws Implementation Committee; and to oppose the education policy in 2010. In a similar vein, a front named 'Islamic and like-minded 12 parties', came into being in early 2011. Parties comprised in the alliance were: Khelafat Majlish, Islamic Andolon Bangladesh, Ulema – Mashaekh Parishd, Bangladesh Khlefat Andolon, Sammilito Ulema – Mashaekh Parishd, National Democratic Party (NDP), Islami Oikya Andolon, Bangladesh Muslim League, Bangladesh NAP, NAP (Bhashani), Jatiya Ganatantrik Party (JAGPA), Islamic Party, Nezam-i-Islami Party. In late February 2013, with the Shahbagh movement at its peak, Islamists launched the 'Iman O Desh Rakhha Porishod', (Council for Protection of Faith and the Country). The organizers claimed that 'Nine religion based parties' and the *ulema* of *qwami madrassah*s founded this alliance in the face of on-going 'anti-Islamic activities' and to demand harsh punishments for those involved in demeaning God and the Prophet Muhammad. Some of these organizations were already members of other alliances such as the AL-led Grand Alliance or the BNP-led 18 party alliance, yet they formed another front which underscores their Islamist credentials. Despite variations of names, these Islamist alliances tend to include the same parties.

Radical left-wing parties, both clandestine and those which operated within mainstream politics, have also founded coalitions in the past decades. Among those, a few warrant mention, although most of these alliances have not succeeded in making any mark. In April 1973, the clandestine Sarbohara Party led by Siraj Sikdar, formed a ten-party alliance. During the Zia era, five parties formed an alliance called the Gonofront under the leadership of Muhammad Toaha in September 1979. One of these alliances in 2015 is the Democratic Revolutionary Front, comprised four parties: Jatiya Mukti Council, Jatiya Gono Front, Naya Gonotantraik Gono Morcha and Gonotantrik Gono Moncha.

This narrative shows that in the past four decades alliance building has become an integral part of the party system of Bangladesh. This neither indicates organizational weakening of major parties nor does it imply diminishing appeal of the major parties; instead it shows that both the AL and the BNP have felt that alliance provides an impression of consensual politics, i.e., these parties are trying to incorporate voices outside their traditional support base. Whether they are intended to mask the intra-party practices of consolidation of power is an open question, but what is beyond doubt is that the alliance building trend does not represent a qualitative change in politics. In large measure, they serve utilitarian purposes.

For the two larger parties, alliance building is beneficial on two counts. First, it weakens rivals. The incessant efforts of the AL and the BNP to bring the JP (Ershad) within its fold since 1991, and the JI until 1999 are testimonies to this intent. Secondly, it boosts the share of the popular votes. Three elections conducted between 1991 and 2001 revealed that the AL and the BNP each commands about 32 per cent of popular votes. Thus each would like to ensure that even the smallest share of the popular vote is drawn to their side (or at least taken away from the rival). The JP and the JI – combined – have about 12 per cent of popular support which has accorded them the kingmaker's position.

Smaller left-leaning parties' efforts to build alliances have been predicated by their desire to break the bipartisan control of politics – ideologically and organizationally. It is imperative for them in order to carve out a space. As the political landscape shifted rightward and left-leaning parties have faced fragmentation, alliance formation has become both an existential and strategic necessity. Notwithstanding the cleavages, smaller Islamist parties outside the JI's sphere, intend to influence the public sphere and political discourse, and shrink the liberal space. Despite fragmentation and realignment, they regroup based on issues, and consequently influence policies.

Despite a chequered history of democracy and faltering democratization, there has been no dearth of political parties in Bangladesh since its independence in 1971, as the preceding discussion has demonstrated. The number of parties has fluctuated over the past four decades.

Obviously, the presence of a large number of parties makes the political landscape vibrant; but it cannot mask the fact that parties lack democracy and leadership is highly skewed towards familial connections, both of which are inimical to a healthy democratic system and should raise serious concerns. Voting patterns show that the Bangladeshi electorate favours a competitive election, although their choices have created a *de facto* two-party system. At the same time the parties and the party system have experienced both changes and continuity. The changes include overall ideological shift of the political landscape, fragmentation of parties, and intensification of alliance building, while the prevalence of a patrimonial style of leadership has continued.

The presence of a large number of political parties of different ideological persuasions is a positive element of the system. This reveals Bangladeshis' aspiration for a pluralistic political culture. The history tells us that ruling elites have acted at various junctures to the contrary attempting to fashion a dominant party system. Over this period, Bangladesh has journeyed from a multi-party system to a one-party system to a dominant party system and returned to a multi-party system; but as of late-2015, the possibility of the emergence of *a de facto* dominant party system looms large.

CHAPTER 6

QUEST FOR A NATIONAL IDENTITY: MULTIPLE CONTESTATIONS

What began as a spontaneous protest gathering with a handful of people on the evening of 5 February 2013 at the Shahabagh square in Dhaka soon attracted millions. The first group of protesters came together to denounce the verdict against Abdul Quader Mollah by the International Crimes Tribunal. Mollah, a Bangladesh Jamaat-e-Islami leader given a life sentence for committing crimes against humanity during the war of independence in 1971. Following the verdict, as he was leaving the court, Mollah showed the victory sign. Many thought that the verdict was lenient, and that a surreptitious deal between the ruling Bangladesh Awami League and the BJI ahead of the scheduled national election at the end of the year might have taken place. The victory sign of Mollah was seen as an added provocation. The protestors demanded a harsher punishment, the highest penalty under the law of the land: the death sentence, for him and for the others who were being tried for crimes of similar magnitude. The rallying cry of the gathering became – *'fanshi chai'* ('we demand hanging'). Their demands soon escalated, including banning of the largest Islamist party, the BJI. The gathering, in the words of a journalist, resembled 'a liberal street festival with a morbid demand'.[1] From the first day of the gathering, various spontaneous slogans were chanted by the protestors. One among them was *'Ami ke? Tumi ke? Bangali Bangali'* ('Who Am I? Who Are You? Bengali, Bengali'). The essential point of the slogan was to underscore the secular credential of the movement, in opposition to the religious identity. As the movement was framed against the Islamists, the organizers might have felt it necessary to highlight their secular ethnic identity. Of course, the history of 1971, which was at the heart of the war crimes trial and demands for justice for the nation, provided the compelling impetus to use that slogan. The slogan was the defining feature of the gathering at various levels. But within days, the organizers faced scathing criticisms: they were told this slogan excludes non-Bengali nationalities such as Chakma, Marma, Tripura, Garo, Santals to name a few, with many youths from these communities were participating in the gathering. The issue was debated online, in person and in print; some felt that the slogan reveals the ethnic chauvinism and exclusionary nature of nationalism, while others deployed the argument of 'authenticity' – that this should be identical to 1971 to represent the spirit of the liberation war. One activist author summarized, 'Day and night we hear the slogans of "*Ami ke, tumi ke?*" ("Who are you, Who Am I?"), and thousands roar back "*Bangali Bangali.*" Those of us aware of the chauvinistic side of that concept in post-1971 Chittagong Hill Tracts cannot be at peace with such ethnically singular determinism.'[2] Many insisted that the protest has welcomed diverse groups despite their distinct identities and this particular slogan betrays that spirit, some argued that the slogan revealed that the Shahbagh movement is yet to be become as inclusive as it needs to be, others suspected the intention of those who are raising the question. As the debate continued, the activists added more identifiers, and the demonstration continued. Meanwhile the debate brought to the fore an issue the nation has yet to resolve: the issue of a national identity.

The establishment of Bangladesh and the preceding nationalist movements were based on identity politics. Yet, the issue of national identity has remained unresolved and debates about the subject continue to play a pivotal role in the politics of the country. Generally speaking, two contesting identities and their political articulations have dominated the political landscape for the past 45 years. These two identities are ethnic and religious, that is the Bengali and Muslim identities, respectively. The pendulum like swing between these identities has given rise to the notion that the country has a 'split personality'.[3] This dichotomous division is often portrayed as a contestation between secularism and Muslim identity. The binary framing of the debate conceals the complexity of national identity formation and identity politics. Equally important to consider are whether the notion of Muslim identity is fraught with schisms, and whether the debate among the secularists about an ideal disposition of a secular identity has remained incomplete.

However, the question remains why and how the nation continues to be fragmented on the question of the national identity The issue is particularly salient because the dominant historical narrative of the founding of the country insists that Bangladesh was established on the basis of ethnic nationalism and as a rejection of the religiously informed national identity of Pakistan.

The Historical Lineage

Historians and social scientists speak of a distinctly identifiable 'Muslim consciousness' in Bengal beginning in the late nineteenth century. Rafiuddin Ahmed, for example, suggests, 'Despite the cultural ambivalence that has characterized Bengal Muslim history since the medieval period, a self-conscious community defining itself primarily as Muslim did emerge over time by the early twentieth century.'[4] The trajectory of identity politics in Bengal needs to be contextualized within the broad trend of Muslim identity politics in undivided colonial India. The colonial state played a pivotal role both in the construction of the material basis and the politics of identity in Bengal.

The question of identity as a distinct issue appeared at the cusp of the nineteenth century in India as a sector of the Muslim community began to lament the disintegration of the Mughal Empire and to endeavour to locate their position within the changing political structure. Both Shah Waliullah (1703–62) and Syed Ahmed Barelvi (1786–1831) can be seen as representatives of that endeavour, though they approached the issue from different directions. For them, the question was simple: how to regain the 'lost glory of Islam'? This question privileged religion in general and particularly Islam as an identifier and social demarcator of identity. Such differentiation had, in fact, already found its place in the colonial ruler's approach towards the Indians.[5]

By the time Syed Ahmed Khan (1817–98), Altaf Hussain Hali (1837–1914) and Muhammad Iqbal (1878–1938) became engaged in this passionate quest for the causes of the moral decay and political decline of the Muslim community, the tone and tenor of the debate had shifted. So had the sociopolitical environment. By then the uprising of

1857 had ended in disarray, and north Indian Muslims had plunged into despondency. The 1858 proclamation of non-interference by the Queen was primarily a doctrine, but also in part a practice.[6] In any case, it was beneficial to Muslims. In subsequent years this favourable environment enabled Muslims to emphasize their distinctive religious identity. Within the Muslim community different intellectual strands emerged. They are commonly referred to as reformist, revivalist and modernist. Regional variations also appeared. Members of different social strata took distinctly different stances; for example, the *ashraf*, higher class, and *ailif l atraf*, lower class reacted in diametrically opposite ways to the British administration. Although there was a struggle for a Muslim nationhood, the discourse was not monolithic in any sense; there were tensions within the identity discourses and their contours and contents varied. The differences remained in subsequent years, even as late as 1940. Various drafts of the Lahore Resolution of 1940 reflected these differences.[7] The underlying assertion of difference was striving to find its place within the paradigm of 'inclusionary secular nationalist' politics articulated by the Indian Congress.

In the nineteenth century, for the colonial power the project was somewhat different. It had already discovered, legitimized and entrenched difference within the legal system (e.g., the 1772 Act); it was time to politicize it. The *Indian Councils Act of 1892*, which allowed 'communal' nomination to government councils, initiated the policy of 'separate representation'. The partition of Bengal in 1905 provided an impetus to the Muslim claim to separate political representation. But the Morley-Minto reforms of 1909, which allowed for separate electorates in representative bodies at all levels of the electoral system, further institutionalized the division. This was a watershed in the history of Indian Muslims. On the one hand, it 'gave birth to a sense of Muslims being a religio-political entity in the colonial image – of being unified, cohesive and segregated from Hindus';[8] while on the other hand, 'it effectively consigned [them] to being a perpetual minority in any scheme of constitutional reform'.[9]

Subsequent political developments, namely the Lucknow Pact of 1916, the Nehru report of 1928, the *Communal Act of 1932* and the *Government of India Act of 1935*, exposed the inherent contradictions of the politics of difference. The rising Hindu communalists did not spare the opportunity take advantage of it.[10] The political agenda of the

Indian Muslims at that point was two-fold: 'to defend their gains and privileges in areas where Muslims were strong and powerful, and to secure "safeguards" and concessions in provinces where they were weak in numbers and economically vulnerable'.[11]

By the mid-1930s, articulation of the distinctive Muslim identity lost its way in the corridors of power politics. The Indian Congress had by then begun moving away from the agenda of an inclusive secular nationalist politics. The policy of majoritarianism triumphed within the Congress because they perceived it as an antidote to the rising influence of Muslim identity politics. The Congress saw a tactical benefit in portraying Muslims as 'religious communalists', which in turn would establish the congress as the sole representative of 'secular nationalism.' This binary mode of identification was also intended to denigrate the quest of Muslims and rob their efforts of legitimacy.

In Bengal the phenomenon described as 'Muslim consciousness', or in other words, 'Muslim identity' began as a manifestation of a contradiction within a rural population. The roots of this manifestation can be traced back to the promulgation of the Permanent Settlement.[12] The Permanent Settlement of 1793 and the complementary juridico-legal measures[13] brought enormous changes to rural Bengal. A new landed class emerged, followed by massive sub-infeudation of land. The remnants of the classes engaged in non-agricultural activities were enticed to the land. Subsequently, English education was introduced making it possible for the emergence of an educated class subservient to the interests of the colonial state. Thus, in the nineteenth century broadly speaking, four classes became prominent in agrarian Bengal – the new *zamindars*, their intermediaries (including *Jotedars*), peasants, and sharecroppers. There was a religious differentiation between these new land owners and the peasants, the former being Hindus while the latter were Muslims. The new landed class became engaged in reckless expropriation of agricultural surplus, making the rent question a primary one, and the contradiction between the landed class (i.e. *zamindars* and their intermediaries) and the peasants became dominant.

In urban Bengal the new educated middle classes, solely dependent upon the largesse of the colonial state (for it was state patronage that made their existence possible) continued to grow. The intimate relationship between the new educated middle class and the colonial state is demonstrated in the social movement called the 'Bengal Renaissance'.

The members of this middle class, as noted previously (Chapter 1), came exclusively from the Hindu community.

Contrary to this development among urban Hindus, in the early nineteenth century, two Muslim revivalist movements, the Faraizi movement (c.1830–c.1857) and Tariqah-i-Muhammadiya (c.1820–c.1840), emerged and became popular in various parts of East Bengal. The Faraizi movement which 'spread with extraordinary rapidity in the rice swamp districts of eastern Bengal'[14] became popular among the Muslim peasants with messages of Muslim solidarity on the one hand and anti-British nationalism one the other. More indigenous than the Tariqah-i-Muhammadiya, the Faraizi movement propagated a message that provided a sense of Muslim identity which had until then been absent among the poorest segments of the Muslim peasants. The pan-Islamic transnational identity, which was at the heart of the Tariqah-i-Muhammadiya's campaign, also resonated because of its distinctiveness from the Hindus in rural Bengal. These movements, often violent, had combined personal religiosity, class consciousness and anti-colonial sentiment, and demonstrated that rural poor Muslims can act as a community. (This is what is referred to as a different imagination of nation in Chapter 1.)

In the late nineteenth century, the policies of the colonial state in favour of the commercialization of agriculture and cultivation of cash crops paved the way for the emergence of a class of small owner-cultivator. Taking advantage of high fertility of the soil of Eastern Bengal, the peasants, predominantly Muslim, began to cultivate rice and jute as cash crops, which again fortunately found a favourable international market. The small owner-cultivator class and surplus farmers benefited from this situation and gradually began to appear as the competitor of Hindu *zamindars*. The patronage of the state to the Muslims following the partition of Bengal (1905) gave this burgeoning class ample opportunity to take advantage of education and jobs, and flourish.

By the beginning of the twentieth century, the Muslim community began to reap benefits as the colonial rulers decided to utilize the division within their subjects. In eastern Bengal, state patronage, commercialization of agriculture, and vitality of agriculture brought changes in the structure of the predominant Muslim peasantry. Nonetheless, the principal contradiction remained the same; the landed class versus the peasants. As the landed classes were predominantly Hindus, Muslim identity became the principal marker of difference and religion a means of political mobilization.

The annulment of the Partition of Bengal (1912) made the Muslims of eastern Bengal in general and the landed class in particular hostile to the colonial state as they thought partition would bring more opportunities for them. Although the discontent of the peasants against the Hindu landed class and the money-lenders, did not disappear, the annulment gave the Muslim landed class and the burgeoning middle classes (those in the process of emerging from within the richer peasants) an opportunity to direct resentment against the colonial state. The opposition to the partition of Bengal by the Hindus in general, driven largely by economic interests, allowed the Muslim leadership to portray the annulment as an anti-Muslim political project of the Hindus.

In the twentieth century, two strands of Muslim political activism spread through the eastern part of Bengal; one was closely connected to the larger Indian political mobilizations, while the other had distinctive marks of local concerns. Take for example the Khilafat-Non Cooperation Movement between 1919 and 1924. The peasants of East Bengal not only joined the movement spontaneously but also brought about a sea change in the tactics and agenda of the movement. Agitation and mobilization of the peasantry outgrew and outlived the Khilafat movement. As noted by Tajul Islam Hashmi, 'the undercurrent of peasant politics flowing beneath the so-called constitutional politics of the urban bourgeoisie, also played an important role in arousing mass consciousness among peasants in the region'.[15] It is worth noting here that the participation of the middle class educated Muslims was very limited. One of the leaders of the movement, Maulana Islamabadi, noted that out of 20 Muslim lawyers in Chittagong none took part in the movement, in Dhaka not a single highly qualified Muslim joined the movement, and out of about 200 lawyers and graduates in the seven districts of Rajshahi division only one showed some interest.[16] The successful boycott of the elections for the Legislative Council in November 1920, the highest in comparison to all other parts of India, demonstrates that the peasantry in eastern Bengal was far more organized than it appeared at the beginning of the movement and that they had an agenda to pursue.

During the height of the movement in 1921, boycott of the government survey and settlement operations in various parts of East

Bengal including Bogra and Pabna districts by the peasants clearly show the strength of their resistance to the colonial state. Although the peasants of East Bengal 'might have been initiated to the doctrine of civil-disobedience by the leaders from above, they soon followed a totally different path, one which led to mob violence against agents of exploitation and withholding of all payments to landlords and moneylenders'.[17] Radicalization also brought about the demise of the movement in the sense that it sent a warning signal to the elite nationalist leaders of both Congress and Muslim League of an imminent 'danger' – an uncontrolled mass movement. The colonial state, the elite nationalist leaders and local vested groups such as landlords contained the threat in the later part of the 1920s. The sudden withdrawal of the Congress from the movement helped foster the perception that it was largely a 'Muslim' movement.

Over subsequent years, peasant politics in eastern Bengal underwent a major transformation: the centrally organized constitutional politics of the urban educated middle class subsumed the peasants' movement. This marked the beginning of the hegemony of the non-Bengali leadership and elite nationalist ideology. Thus in the 1940s when the ML pursued an identity politics the specificities of Bengal were subsumed under the politics of Muslimness. Religion – a marker of distinctiveness and difference – became important and was transformed into a 'political ideology'.

In the decades prior to the partition of 1947, a vigorous debate on issues pertaining to community identity took place as the Muslim middle class began organizing literary and social organizations and publishing journals and periodicals. *Anjumans* began to appear in the late nineteenth century. For example, Syed Ameer Ali established the Central National Mohammadan Association in 1877, and Bangiya Sahitya Bishayayani Mussalman Sabha came into existence in 1899. The number of such organizations proliferated in the early twentieth century.[18] The issue of language was at the centre of these debates and was a source of dilemma for the members of the Bengali-speaking Muslim community. While some argued that it was necessary to adopt Urdu or Arabic as the language of instruction and interactions as a mark of Muslim identity, others maintained that Bengali was the language of the Bengali Muslim community. This difference also reflected social differentiation within the Muslim society. Those who claimed an immigrant ancestry, and who were therefore assumed to belong to a higher class (*ashraf*) suggested Urdu/Arabic; while those who came from the middle class, often described as *atraf*, favored Bengali. Although not completely resolved, 'the linguistic choice of the Bengali Muslims during the start of the 20th century tilted towards Bengali' writes Dhurjati Prasad De. He adds, 'Although the spirit of separativeness [sic] was very much present, the majority of the Bengali Muslims decidedly were in favor of the vernacular, i.e. Bengali, and accepted it as the vehicle of their cultural consciousness.'[19] Tazeen Murshid writes, 'By the second and third decades of the twentieth century [...] more and more Bengali Muslims admitted that Bengali was their mother tongue.'[20] Anisuzzaman notes, 'Towards the end of the nineteenth century, the emerging Bengali Muslim middle class showed a different orientation. With their roots in the soil, they proclaimed that their mother tongue was Bengali and nothing else.'[21] Of the organizations which favoured Bengali, one deserves special mention. The Muslim Shahitya Samaj, established in Dhaka in 1926, made a mark on the identity debate. The association and its mouthpiece *Shikha* argued for a rationalist Muslim identity rooted in the Bengali cultural tradition. Works of the literati associated with the organization demonstrated that Muslim and Bengali identities were not mutually exclusive.

Therefore, the argument that in the 1940s, particularly in 1947, Bengalis of the eastern part of undivided Bengal rejected their Bengali identity and subscribed to a pan-Indian Islamic identity is erroneous. Interestingly, even the founder of Pakistan Muhammad Ali Jinnah did not subscribe to it. In April 1947, during a conversation with the last Viceroy of India Lord Mountbatten, he made the following remarks: 'Your Excellency does not understand. A man is Punjabi or a Bengali before he is Hindu or Moslem. They share a common history, language, culture and economy.'[22] The explanation of their support for the Pakistan movement as an act of 'Muslim unity in India' at the expense of regional distinctiveness is far from the truth. This line of interpretation makes an *a priori* judgment that Bengaliness and Muslimness are two distinctly different and irreconcilable categories. This judgment is rooted in a particular interpretation of the history of Islamization of Bengal and an uncritical acceptance of Islam as a transcendent idea.[23]

Therefore, it will be helpful to lay out a revisionist history of the arrival and expansion of Islam in Bengal. Islam has remained central to

the social milieu of what is now known as Bangladesh since the
beginning of Islam's expansion in the thirteenth century. 'An acute
multi-dimensional conflictual situation at the close of the Sena era
[c.1097–1225], with intense feeling raging between Brahmins and
Buddhists, Brahmins and non-Brahmins, upper class Aryans and non-
Aryans, produced the opportunity for a prophetic break in Bengal
society. The Muslim Sufis, with their charisma and adaptive skills and
occasional armed support from Muslim rulers, took full advantage of the
climacteric, and converted a major section of the Bengali population to
Islam.'[24] The egalitarian appeal of the religion was one, but not the only,
factor, for the mass conversion. The ongoing contestations between
various social classes/castes and alliance making between members of
non-Brahmin castes and Muslims and/or Buddhists played a significant
role too. Equally it is important to note 'the phenomenal proselytizing
success of the pioneer Sufis of the thirteenth century encouraged a larger
influx of saintly preachers from the West and Central Asian heartland of
Islam in the fourteenth century'.[25] For three centuries Sufis continued to
migrate to Bengal. By the eighteenth century, more efficient agricultural
technologies that were invented by Muslim rulers helped the peasants
clear forests and create more arable lands; these peasants continue to
embrace Islam.[26] The early history of the expansion and consolidation of
Islam in Bengal have left some indelible marks: first, the Islamic
tradition in Bengal has successfully adapted to Hindu and other local
religious traditions.[27] The adaptation and accommodation of various
religious and cultural traditions have enriched the experience of the
Muslim community. By allowing shared customs, traditions and
practices to be part of a universal faith, the adherents have learned that
monolithic Islam is non-existent. Richard Eaton, concluded that,
'It would be wrong [...] to view Islam as some monolithic agency that
simply 'expanded' across space, time and social class, in the process
assimilating great numbers of people into a single framework of piety.
Rather, the religion was itself continuously reinterpreted as different
social classes in different periods became its dominant carriers.'[28] Eaton
goes on to say, 'what made Islam in Bengal not only historically
successful but a continuing vital social reality has been its capacity to
adapt to the land and the culture of its people, even while transforming
both'.[29] Therefore, since the beginning of the expansion of Islam in
Bengal variations in interpretations of religion and rituals have become

embedded into the ethos of its adherents; this remains the mainstay of Islam in Bangladesh. Second, despite substantial differences with the dogmatic creeds of Islam the Sufi tradition remained strong for centuries. Examples of differences include the notion of *tawhid*, a fundamental issue of the faith, which is interpreted differently. While the commonly understood Islam stands for absolutely one transcendent and all-powerful God, the Sufis underscored the immanent unity of God. This is not to say that Sufi tradition was the dominant strand or subscribed to by a majority of the local inhabitants. Migrations from West and Central Asia, influence of ruling elites, and trade with the Islamic heartland brought a more orthodox version of Islam to Bengal as well. Thus, three trends – a local syncretic Islam, a Sufi variation, and an orthodox interpretation – endured in Bengal. Third, Islam became institutionalized; initially through the *khanqa*'s of the saints but later through educational institutions called *madrassahs*. The significance and strength of *madrassahs* in contemporary Bangladesh must be viewed against this historical background.

The preceding discussion has demonstrated that Muslimness in Bengal had a distinct local contour, and that a large number of Bengali Muslims in rural Bengal were mobilized by economic concerns and against the immediate power structure. As Ahmed Kamal has pointed out, 'Islam and the notion of egalitarianism inherent in Islam, became a very important force, especially when the oppressors were seen as belonging to the overtly hierarchical Hindu religion.'[30]

The presence of religious icons in these movements, use of religious idioms in political discourse, and evocation of religious texts in fashioning the messages do not of themselves constitute an unambiguous assertion of Muslim identity akin to north Indian Muslims. Tajul Islam Hashmi's contention that there are two distinct modes of the use of religion, *religion-as-aim* and *religion-as-reason*, is worth recalling here. In dealing with the peasant movements in East Bengal between 1920 and 1947, Hashmi contends:

> Sometimes peasants are mobilized in the name of restoring their faith, in movements with 'religion-as-aim', but often religion becomes the frame of revolt in movements with 'religion-as-reason.' The first category of movements involves peasants in a holy war (jihad or crusade) against the 'enemy of the faith.'

The 'enemy of peasants' is easily converted into the 'enemy of the faithful' when the peasants concerned suffered religious persecution in the hands of the same exploiting class(es).[31]

In the second instance, religion is utilized as a mobilizational ideology to establish justice sanctioned by religion.

Among the educated Bengali Muslim community, as the works of Muhammad Shahidullah, Qazi Abdul Wadud, Abul Hossain, Qazi Motahar Hossain, Abdul Quader demonstrate, the Bengali identity is present as robustly as their Muslim identity. The majority of *anjumans* and associations have dealt with the issue of language (Urdu versus Bengali) as a proxy to the identity debate and resolved the matter in favour of Bengali because the Muslim identity cannot preclude the ethno-linguistic identity. In a similar vein, within the political realm, Fazlul Huq's insistence to Muhammad Ali Jinnah that areas with a Muslim majority 'should be grouped to constitute independent states in which constituent units shall be autonomous and sovereign',[32] and the efforts of Hussain Shahid Suhrawardy supported by Abul Hashim and Fazlur Rahman in April 1946 for an independent Bengal are indicative that Bengali identity has long constituted a principal element of identity and imagination of the nation.

The presence of these two dimensions is important in understanding why the Bengalis of the newly founded Pakistan underscored the ethnic identity issue vis-à-vis the state-sponsored effort to create a Muslim national identity in Pakistan.

The precursor to the national identity debate emerged in post-partition East Bengal, later named East Pakistan, as the national language debate. The debate surfaced well before partition, but there seems to be a clear understanding among the Muslim Bengali intelligentsia that Bengali would have to be one of the state languages of Pakistan. As such one can say the Urdu versus Bengali debate was resolved within the Bengali Muslim community, especially within the educated class. But soon after partition, the Pakistani state reignited it when it proclaimed Urdu as the state language. The claim for Urdu as the lingua franca of Pakistan was a challenge to the distinctiveness of the Bengali-speaking community. But we must exercise caution to avoid the common misperception and grand narrative that the Bengali language movement was a clash of two identities – 'Muslim' and 'secular', represented by support for Urdu and support for Bengali, respectively. The popular support for the language movement was tied to an array of factors, especially the economic situation. Ahmed Kamal's perceptive study of the decline of the Muslim League between 1947 and 1954 is extremely helpful in understanding these grievances.[33] It provides ample documentary evidence that there was a growing discontent among the population of East Bengal and those grievances fuelled both the 1952 language movement and the rejection of the Muslim League in the elections of 1954. Yet, I call the language movement the precursor of the national identity debate as it laid bare the nature of the Pakistani state, and by extension offered the space for creating a counter-narrative of identity and nationalism. In the initial stage of this new nationalism, the Muslim identity was blended with egalitarianism. Kamal writes:

Islam was so important in the day to day politics that even secular demands were tinged by religious nationalism. The nascent Bengali linguistic nationalism of the 1950s also drew many of its metaphors and concepts from the idioms and institution of Islam. The earliest writings of the genre, while making a critique of the new state, still projected a vision of a just society as had been achieved under Omar, the second caliph: 'When shall we get an ideal ruler like Hazrat Omar, when the era of Four Caliphs will come back.'[34]

It is worth noting that the quotation Kamal uses to exemplify the point is from a pamphlet written by Sheikh Mujibur Rahman in 1948, who later became the champion of the Bengali nationalist movement.[35] In a similar vein, Murshid writes, 'The language movement was an act of two-fold self-assertion – cultural and political – in an essentially political power struggle. It implied no self-conscious denial of Islam.'[36] Therefore, the growing appeal of Bengali identity, from its inception, was not a disavowal of the religious identity.

Generally speaking, identity politics takes two contesting shapes: 'the politics of domination and the politics of resistance. The main motivation of the former is the quest for power for which identity is invoked as a means of mobilisation. The latter is the politics of rights in which identity serves as a cohesive force for achieving internal solidarity.'[37] In the post-partition context, as the Pakistani state elevated

Islam to the pedestal of 'national identity' and underscored Muslimness
as the basis of unity to emasculate the regional difference and cultural
identities, Bengali ethnic identity emerged as the politics of resistance.
The Bengali political leadership and educated class underscored the
ethnic identity. Thus, by the 1960s ethnic Bengali identity became the
central element of the movement for democratic rights and legitimate
claims on national resources (see Chapter 1). 'Given the cultural
disparity between the east and the west, the cultural neglect was felt as
cultural oppression by the intelligentsia. But whether it was the central
issue in the separation of Bangladesh is doubtful, even if culture
provided inspiration and legitimacy.'[38]

   This is not to say that there was not any trend within the East
Pakistani society that highlighted religious identity; instead a group of
the intelligentsia (e.g., Farrukh Ahmed, Golam Mostafa, Talim
Hossain), cultural organizations and various political parties (e.g. the
Muslim Leagues, the Jamaat-e-Islami, the Nezam-i-Islami etc.) tried to
underscore the Muslim identity vis-à-vis the Bengali identity. But they
were overpowered because by then the identity issue had become an
intrinsic part of the political movement for regional autonomy,
economic equity and political representation in the state apparatuses.
As such it was identified with support for the Pakistani state and its
policies of exploitation. Muslim League leaders' efforts to conflate Islam,
Pakistan and the party as one entity in opposition to the demands of the
Bengalis, be it about language or democratic share in power, backfired.
The Pakistani state's verbiage of 'Hindu conspiracy' to undermine the
integrity of the new nation did not resonate with the population of East
Pakistan; whether it was in the late 1940s by Jinnah and his successors,
or in the 1970s by Moududi and his ilk. A politicized religion was
rejected by the Bengalis, and so were its proponents such as the ML
and the JI dominated by the non-Bengali-speaking leaderships. Equally
important was the trend which was 'deeply influenced by humanist
thought, and which envisaged a liberal democratic society where culture
belonged to the secular arena'.[39] In some ways it was a continuation of
the intellectual tradition of the 1930s journal *Shikha*. However, it was
feeble and remained limited within a small, educated urban group. The
material basis for a communal divide and emphasis on Muslim identity
weakened due to the migration of the Hindus. The relative deprivation
of the people of East Pakistan could no longer be attributed to Hindu

landowners; but only to the state which was hell bent on identifying itself as the protector of Islam. This created the space for idioms, icons and symbols not associated with Islam but with the Bengali culture to occupy the central stage of public discourse.

Did the gradual decline of Islam in the public sphere – political and cultural, and the consequent salience of Bengali cultural symbols, icons and rituals mark a shift from a 'religious' to a 'secular' culture (or at least, a drift towards secular culture)? The dominant Bengali nationalist historiography insists so. But we can also view this as a return to the long standing 'eclectic local cultural roots'[40] – wherein the syncretic tradition of Islam is practised; wherein the personal religiosity, public display of faith and adherence to religious culture in social life are viewed as a separate domain from politics which is determined by other material concerns. The arguments of Partha Chatterjee, in regard to the role of religion in the anti-colonial movement in undivided India may be of some help here. Chatterjee argued that the modernist paradigm and the ideology of Enlight-enment have created a separation between religion and politics. But not all within society accepted this separation between religion and politics. Instead some framed them as two separate domains: outer and inner, materiality and spirituality. While such a dichotomous division, by itself, may have been shaped by the discourse of modernity, Indian elites tried to create a differentiation of their own in which religion remains within the inner domain. Am I then suggesting that there was no 'secular outlook' towards culture and identity during the period in question? The answer is negative. Indeed, there was a visible presence of a worldview that can neither be identified with the politicized Islam advanced by the Pakistani state nor can it be viewed as a representation of eclectic Islam which was a defining characteristic of rural Bengal. The rising urban educated middle class, as they became less connected to the cultural ethos of rural syncretic Islam, personal religiosity aside, propounded a world view akin to secular culture. With the expansion of the material basis of this class (Chapter 1), their numbers grew. Members of this class emerged as the leaders of the Bengali nationalist movement. Thus a connection between the nationalist movement and a secular outlook was assumed, whereas it could also be read as a disjuncture between the cultural ethos and worldview of the rural population and the nascent middle class.

Three surveys in the 1960s are instrumental in understanding that until the end of the decade the majority of East Pakistanis did not view any conflict between being a Bengali, a Muslim and a Pakistani. As the decade was coming to an end, the middle class was gradually moving away from religion as their principal marker of identity. A 1966 study by Howard Schuman showed that a large proportion (48 per cent) of the 1,001 respondents – urban factory workers, full-time rural cultivators, and of similar groups in East Pakistan – preferred to call themselves Pakistanis and a relatively small percentage of respondents (11 per cent) identified themselves as first and foremost Bengalis. Men were more than four times as likely to say Pakistani as to say Bengali,

> Not that there was necessarily any opposition to claims of being a Pakistani rather than being a Bengali. On the contrary, it seems likely that no conflict at all was perceived between the two; instead, one's Bengali identification was simply included in the more general and at least equally desirable identification as a Pakistani.

However it is noteworthy that another survey among 204 students of a college in Dhaka in March 1964 revealed that 24 per cent of the respondents identified themselves primarily as Bengali, a ratio of three-to-one. Schuman concluded, 'The emphasis on "Bengali" was thus somewhat greater among these students than among the common man, and this may well reflect the fact that Bengali nationalism was already beginning to rise in the student population.'[41] The 1966 study by Sayeed bin Khalid, among students of both East and West Pakistan showed a remarkable difference between their perceptions of the role of religion as the bond between the two wings. Among the East Pakistani students, 46.6 per cent felt that Islam is an effective bond while the number was 80.6 per cent among the West Pakistani students.[42]

Nasim A. Jawed's survey of *ulama* and professionals in both East and West Pakistan, shows a further move away from religious identity among professionals in East Pakistan.[43] In response to the question regarding national identity put to East Pakistani professionals, 40 per cent expressed some form of allegiance to Islam, while 60 per cent can be categorized as 'secular' – that is, those who 'either rejected Islam totally or, in most cases, saw it strictly as a matter of personal, not national, identity'.[44] Further disaggregation reveals that among those who saw Islam as an issue of national identity, 16 per cent were 'Islamic nationalists', that is those who 'solely or predominantly identifies with his Islamic faith and desires to see it as the only real collective bond among his Muslim countrymen'. And 24 per cent were 'Islamic-cum-patriotic', that is 'those who saw no disparity between Islam and nationalism'.[45] Among those categorized as secularists 16 per cent rejected all kinds of nationalisms, and 16 per cent were considered as regional secularists, that is a provincial identity had a significant element in their self-description. As for the desired basis of the nationhood of Pakistan, 56 per cent wanted secular culture to form the basis of Pakistani nationhood. 4 per cent of respondents stated that 'secular culture/class interest' should constitute nationhood, and 28 per cent of respondents cited 'provincial culture' (a mix of secular culture and Islam). Only 12 per cent of respondents stated that Islam alone should make up Pakistani nationhood (as opposed to 53.6 per cent of West Pakistani professionals).[46]

It is against this background that Bangladesh emerged as an independent state in 1971. It was no surprise that Bengali identity became the rallying cry of the Bengali nationalists through the nine-month long war against the Pakistani army, who tried to justify genocide in the name of 'national integrity' and 'saving Islam'. The abominable use of Islam by the military and their local supporters, especially political parties such as the ML, the JI and others during the war, in addition to the experience of the past quarter century made it imperative that the issue of religion and politics be addressed in earnest. The need for addressing the issues of nationalism in post-independence society and of the role of religion in the public sphere was interpreted by a large section of the AL leadership as a mandate for inserting a constitutional proviso regarding these. This mindset led to the inclusion of Bengali nationalism, and secularism in the four state principles in the constitution in 1972.

Bengali nationalism, as it emerged to become a hegemonic ideology through the course of history, did what all other nationalisms do: it effaced the differences within its ranks. The economic deprivation and regional disparity of the Pakistani state was targeted towards East Pakistan, not the Bengalis alone; therefore it hurt other nationalities within East Pakistan; the Pakistani state did not acknowledge ethnic and cultural diversity – of the Baluchis and the Chakmas as much as the Bengalis. But as the state-building process ensued the ruling AL seems to have disregarded this lesson of the Pakistani state.

This mindset was on display during the constitution-making process. The issue of national identity came up during the debate on the draft constitution at the Constituent Assembly (which comprised only the AL members who won the national and provincial elections in 1970. The only exception was an independent member from the Chittagong Hill Tracts.) The debates, particularly the reactions of the ruling party members, on 25 October and 31 October are pertinent. On 25 October, while discussing Article 14 of the proposed constitution, the question of ethnic minorities came to the fore. Article 14 provided that one of the fundamental responsibilities of the state would be to free the working population – peasants and labourers – and the 'backward sections' of the population from all kinds of exploitation. The article did not specify these 'sections'. Manabendra Narayan Larma, an independent member from the Chittagong Hill Tracts, the home of several ethnic groups, moved an amendment to the above article proposing that 'a) the lawful rights of the minority and backward nations (nationalities) should be preserved; b) in order to improve their educational, cultural and economic standards they should be given special rights; and c) full opportunities should be given to them by the state to enable them to be at par with the advanced nations (nationalities).' Larma also proposed that since the Chittagong Hill Tracts are a tribal area, in order to ensure that its political, economic, and religious rights are not infringed upon it should be an autonomous tribal region. Larma was dismayed by the attitude of the ruling regime and expressed his discontent: 'The framers of the constitution have forgotten my land, my people [...] We have been deprived of our rights, the country has become independent, but we continue to have a cursed life.'[47] Larma's amendments were rejected on procedural grounds but his comments infuriated the ruling party members. They portrayed these comments as a challenge to Bengali nationalism, the *raison d'être* of the new nation state. Some even described these comments as a conspiracy against the sovereignty of Bangladesh. A similar situation arose on 31 October. Abdur Razzaque Bhuiyan, a member of the ruling party, proposed an amendment to Article 6 of the proposed constitution. He proposed that the clause regarding citizenship should include that 'the citizens of Bangladesh will be known as

Bangalee'. Manabendra Narayan Larma objected to this amendment saying that inhabitants of Chittagong Hill Tracts have been living there for centuries and have never been asked to be Bangalee. 'I don't know why this constitution wants to make us Bangalee', he said. Larma continued, 'you cannot impose your national identities on others. I am a Chakma, not a Bengali. I am a citizen of Bangladesh, Bangladeshi. You are also Bangladeshi but your national identity is Bengali [...] [the hill people] can never become Bengali.'[48] Despite such pleas the amendment was passed, and Larma walked out in protest. Following Larma's walkout, Deputy Leader of the House Syed Nazrul Islam requested him to return to the session, saying 'I hope that he will accept this opportunity to identify himself and his people as Bengalis.'[49]

The question regarding national identity was a mark of the changed objective condition in post-colonial Bangladesh. The 'enemy' against whom nationalism was pitted had disappeared; postcolonial society necessitated the fashioning of a new social order. But the ruling party and the elites were neither willing nor understood that their hegemony was about to be ruptured. The inclusion of the Bengali identity by itself was neither a secular phenomenon nor a threat to the Muslim identity as our previous discussion has shown; but its combination with secularism as the state principle provided an opportunity to be interpreted as a disapproval of Muslim identity. The proscription of the religion-based parties (for their anti-liberation roles during the war) followed by the adoption of secularism and insistence on the Bengali identity created an environment within which it was presented by the detractors as a state-sponsored effort to undermine religion in public and private life and replace it with the 'secular Bengali identity'.

As for secularism, the constitution stipulated in Article 12 the following:

in order to achieve the ideals of secularism,

(a) all kinds of communalism
(b) patronization by the state of any particular religion
(c) exploitation (misuse) of religion for political purposes
(d) discrimination against, and persecution of, anyone following a
    particular religion will be ended.[50]

This proviso seemed to some to be a logical extrapolation of the non-communal politics put forward by the AL prior to independence; to some this was the culmination of the growing secular outlook among the urban educated elites in the late 1960s, but to others it was a surprise. For there was no prior reference to 'secularism' in the political commitment of the ruling party. Instead, Article 2 of the AL's election manifesto in 1970 stated that no law would be enacted against the dictums of the Qu'ran and the Sunnah. Evidently there was no clear understanding of the term secularism among the policy-makers and intelligentsia.[51]

What was meant by 'secularism' in the constitution? The context suggests that it was meant to be 'non-communalism' as the experience of the previous quarter century of the country showed that communal division of the populace leads to violence and fragmentation of social cohesion. Tazeen Murshid notes, '"Secular" came to be defined as the binary opposite of "communal" implying a tolerance of other religious communities.'[52] The constitution, which was originally written in Bengali, used the term *dharmanirapekshata*, which means religious neutrality. The translated version identifies this as secularism. As such the term 'secularism' was overly ambitious, if not misleading; for secularism has multiple meanings. Even in its simplest formulation, secularism can be divorced from the process of secularization. There are at least three dimensions of secularization: constitutional secularization (that is, 'whereby religious institutions cease to be given special constitutional recognition'), institutional secularization (that is, 'when religious structures lose their political saliency'), and ideological secularization (when 'the basic values and belief systems used to evaluate the political realm and to give it meaning cease to be couched in religious terms').[53] While the constitutional proviso may have fulfilled one of three dimensions, there was no clue in the behaviour of the political elites as to how to address the other two.

Secularism is also a matter of determining the relationship between the state and religious institutions. Three Western models were readily available to consider: the US model, the French model, and the English (or other European) model. The first suggests that the state will neither be guided by nor will it intervene in religious matters leaving individuals and society to practise their religions (including atheism) at will and limiting the role of the state to ensure the freedom to practice as such; the French model (*laïcité*) ensures that religions remain outside the public sphere and enables the state to exercise an overt control over religious institutions; and the English model which enshrines a distinction between the established Church of England, institutionally connected to the state, and a deeply secular society. These models have grown out of their own historical necessities, but also provide clues as to how the relationships between two influential institutions – state and church – can be fashioned.

If the idea of secularism was unclear, the actions of the regime accentuated this ambiguity. Sheikh Mujib categorically declared that he was proud to be Muslim and that his nation was the second largest Muslim state in the world. He not only frequently made use of Islamic expressions in his speeches but repeatedly insisted that his vision of 'secularism does not mean the absence of religion'.[54] Mujib also led the Munajaat (Islamic prayer) on 4 November 1972 during the session after the passage of the Constitution Bill.[55] The state-controlled media, especially radio and television, began to undercut the spirit of secularism when they adopted a policy of equal opportunity for all religions. Instructed by the government, they read extracts from the holy books of Islam, Hinduism, Buddhism, and Christianity. Their policy of distributive justice in terms of allocating time to the different religions, undermined the concept of secularism. The government not only extended indulgence to all religions but also subjected itself to religious pressure. It was under this kind of pressure that the government increased funding for religious education in 1973. The annual budgetary allocation for *madrassah* (Islamic educational institutions) was increased to Taka 7.2 million in 1973 from Taka. 2.5 million in 1971. Furthermore, in March 1975 the government revived the Islamic Academy which they had banned in 1972, and then elevated it to a foundation to help propagate the ideals of Islam. As Mujib joined the Islamic Summit held in Lahore in February 1974, it became evident that establishing any semblance of secularism was off the agenda. Two months later Bangladesh took the lead at the Islamic Foreign Ministers' Conference held in Jeddah in establishing the Islamic Development Bank.

Whether these steps marked a slow drift away from secularism or a recognition of the ubiquity of Islam in social life is a matter for debate; but they definitely demonstrated that the regime's moral leadership, or so to say ideological hegemony, was waning and religious rhetoric and gestures were adopted to compensate.[56] As for the issue of national identity, inclusion of Bengali nationalism and secularism in the constitution followed by lip-service of the ruling elite, did not resolve it for good. Instead, the half-hearted measures, symbolic vacillation and the absence of an honest discussion brought it to the fore.

With the demise of the Mujib regime in a violent coup and the rise of the military regime of Ziaur Rahman, the issue gained further salience because of constitutional changes and 'Islamization from above'. The constitutional changes such as proclaiming the identity of the citizens to be 'Bangladeshi' (as opposed to Bangalee), deletion of secularism, inclusion of a Qu'ranic verse as the preamble and absolute faith in Allah were meant to create a new ideological terrain to gain legitimacy. The identity of the nation was linked with the territorial limit in order to isolate it from the so-called 'Bangalee sub-culture' of India. Religion, territoriality of identity, and national security constituted the core of this new ideology. The new ideology presented the identity issue as if there is a contradiction between being Muslim and being Bengali. It was not the constitution alone that created the environment that promoted the saliency of Muslim identity, but also the actions of the regime. Domestic and foreign policies demonstrated the regime's preference for being identified as a Muslim country. The reemergence of Islamist parties, proliferation of *madrassahs*, reintroduction of Islamic studies in general education, state patronage of Islamic organizations, infusion of Islamic symbols in the public sphere and public culture were all making a contribution to highlight the Muslim identity. The government established a 'Ministry of Religious Affairs' to coordinate religious activities on behalf of the government. Soon '*id-i-milad-i-nabi*', the Prophet Muhammed's birthday, was declared a national holiday. State-controlled electronic media began broadcasting *Azan* (the call to prayers) five times a day and programmes on Islam's role in daily lives. These efforts were further accelerated during the era of the military dictator Hussain Muhammad Ershad with the declaration of Islam as the state religion.

If the Mujib regime's decision to include secularism can be criticized for being devoid of any societal discussions, the Zia regime's decision of Islamization can be described as dictatorial imposition. It reflected the faith of the majority of the population, but that does not mean that it was implemented with the consent of the people. Yet, the heightened

presence of Islam in public life and acquiescence of the majority served as
a reminder that historically religion has remained a part of the Bengali
Muslim population's perception of their identity.

The passing of the military regimes and the beginning of the
democratic transition in 1991 have neither reversed the tide back to the
days of ethnicity-based identity with state-sponsored 'secularism' nor has
the idea of an exclusively Muslim identity become hegemonic. Instead,
the contestation has become a part of the political upheaval. The two
major parties, the BAL and the BNP, represent the opposite end of
the spectrum when it comes to the Bengali–Bangladeshi dichotomy.
In making their cases, often supporters of both camps adopt a majoritarian
argument; that is the identity of the Bangladeshi citizens should be
Bengali as ethnic Bengalis constitute the majority of the population is
countered with the argument that the majority of Bangladeshis adhere to
Islam by faith. A majoritarian Bengali nationalist discourse by definition
marginalizes the identities of other ethnic groups (such as Chakma,
Marma, Hajong, Garo); it creates a national identity which has built-in
exclusionary characteristics contributing schisms within the society. The
Bangladeshi state since its founding pursued a majoritarian model of state
building which alienated the indigenous population. The argument for a
Muslim identity, in equal measure, creates an exclusionary environment as
it rejects the non-Muslim identity and makes them subservient to the
majority. However, in the past decades, we have witnessed a palpable
presence of religion in the public sphere, and perhaps a significant shift in
public perception in regard to identity has occurred as well.

But before we explore the nature and the extent of that shift, it is
necessary to investigate how a growing salience of Muslim identity in
the quest for a national identity in Bangladesh was influenced by global
and regional factors.

The Global Shadow

Discussion of the factors beyond the historical and geographical
boundaries of Bangladesh needs to begin with the recognition that the
return of religion to public life is a global phenomenon. In the 1960s, it
was predicted that most of humanity would soon be either atheists or
agnostics.[57] The classic and perhaps the most quoted example of the
claim is the cover story of the international news magazine *Time* on

8 April 1966 entitled, 'Is God Dead?' But by the 1980s, studies reporting the return of religion to the public sphere, began to draw attention. Jose Casanova, basing his analysis on empirical data, argued that religion has been 'deprivatized' in a number of countries around the world.[58] Similarly Jeffry Hadden, in 1987, challenged the basis of the claims that religion was supposed to lose ground and insisted that these claims are based on a doctrine rather than results of systematic inquiry.[59] In 1998, a researcher of religion and politics proclaimed, 'around the world, religion is leaving, or refusing to accept, its assigned place in the private sphere'.[60] Peter Berger argued passionately in 1999 that 'the assumption that we live in a secularized world is false'.[61] By then it had become well accepted within academic circles that the argument for the gradual decline of religion in public life as a result of modernization and consequent expansion of secularism was premature and perhaps, misplaced.[62] Berger further argued that:

> Certain religious institutions have lost power and influence in many societies, but both old and new religious beliefs and practices have nevertheless continued in the lives of individuals, sometimes taking new institutional forms and sometimes leading to great explosions of religious fervors. Conversely, religiously identified institutions can play social or political roles even when very few people believe or practice that the institutions represent.[63]

However, even in 1999, some hold on to the idea that religion has lost its public role and that the idea of God has run its course.[64] Yet, by the end of the century, many had to accept the 'mea culpa'.[65]

Religious rhetoric in public discourse has increasingly become naturalized. While in the 1970s many states, particularly in the developing world, were adopting policies to create a separation between religion and politics, public discourses which accepted religion's role within daily lives and naturalized the role through various social practices and institutions were on the rise. This is reflected in popular culture – 'the public space in which a society and its constituent individuals and communities imagine, represent, and recognize themselves through political discourse, commercial and cultural expressions, and representations of state and civic organizations'.[66] Once naturalized, various social groups adopt it as their own and engage in competition to represent it. In the Indian context, the consequences of the naturalization of a Hindutva ideology provide us with an excellent example. Thomas Blom Hansen's work on the naturalization of Hindutva ideology through popular culture in India over a long period of time even before the rise of the BJP as a formidable political force demonstrates this phenomenon convincingly. Consequently,

> Non-Hindutva politicians can [now] compete over who is a more authentic Hindu. School children can be taught a history where militant Hinduism is normalized and minority religions such as Islam (and as a corollary, Indian Muslims) are alienated. Government employees can join Hindutva organizations and the prime minister can pronounce, in a cavalier manner, that Muslims are a source of 'problems' everywhere in the world.[67]

The public discourses are then adopted by political parties of various creeds, whether or not these parties subscribe to religion as a political ideology. The reproduction of this rhetoric creates an environment within which individuals feel comfortable identifying with religious identity.

Thirdly, globalization has acted as an influential factor. The phenomenon called globalization has been discussed, dissected and debated in various ways. While its meanings and processes remain contentious, there seems to be a broad agreement among social scientists as to its impact. The most profound impact of globalization has been dislocation, both cognitively and spatiotemporally. The unsettling effects of globalization are true for individuals and nation-states alike. The pace and speed of globalization has destabilized the sense of certainty and security that individuals had enjoyed for decades. With the compression of time and space, individuals now face a new world where boundaries have disappeared and their identities are in flux. Anthony Giddens, in his sociological analysis of high modernity, insisted that modernity brings a fundamental change: it breaks down the protective framework offered by the community and tradition. In a situation like this, Giddens argues, 'The individual feels bereft and alone in a world in which she or he lacks the psychological support and the sense of security provided by more traditional settings.'[68] Giddens has explained this situation with two key theoretical formulations, 'ontological security' and 'existential anxiety'. Ontological security, according to Giddens, is the basic need of individuals for 'a sense of continuity and order in events, including those not directly within the perceptual environment of the individual'.[69] It refers to a 'person's fundamental sense of safety in the world and includes a basic trust of other people'.[70] 'To be ontologically secure is to possess, on the level of the unconscious and practical consciousness, "answers" to fundamental existential questions which all human life in some way addresses.'[71] The absence of these answers accentuates existential anxiety. Giddens further argued that the doubt and insecurity inherent in our time, favours a resurgence of religion.[72]

The framework provided by Giddens is immensely helpful in understanding the role of religion in various societies in recent decades. Catarina Kinnvall has aptly demonstrated how ontological insecurity has played a key role in the resurgence of 'religious nationalism' in India, both Hindu and Sikh.[73] Kinnvall argues that collective identities can help individuals who feel vulnerable and experience existential insecurity to reaffirm their threatened self-identity. She argues that facing ontological insecurity an individual seeks affirmation of his/her self-identity by drawing closer to any collective that is perceived as being able to reduce insecurity and existential anxiety. This collective could be religion, nationalism or ethnicity. She adds that, 'Religion, like nationalism, supplies existential answers to individual's quests for security by essentializing the product and providing a picture of totality, unity and wholeness. The fact that God has set the rules and made them difficult to contest relieves the individual psychologically from the responsibility of having to choose.'[74]

In the context of South Asia ontological insecurity has become an issue of great importance, because of the mode of its interactions with the global economy. Countries, and by extension their citizens, have remained perpetually at the receiving end of the global economy. The neo-liberal economic agenda and political and economic cosmopolitanism have furthered their marginalization. Thus a resistance to this process was called for. In the absence of a viable leftist critique of globalization and political forces to mount resistance to this process, increasingly religion became the only mode of resistance. It is not surprising that religious identities have assumed greater visibility and religio-political forces in South Asia have gained further ground after these countries adopted a neo-liberal economic agenda.

Fourthly, the failure of the state. Extant studies which have attempted to examine the causes of the return of religion to the public domain have underscored the failure of states as a significant factor. For example, Emile Sahliyeh insisted that two factors are key in this regard: social upheaval and economic dislocation connected to the processes of modernization.[75] Mark Juergensmeyer argued that, 'In many parts of the world [the] secular state has not lived up to its own promises of political freedom, economic prosperity, and social justice.'[76] William Miles's study reaffirmed these findings and added that the 'religious dimension to group identity and statist politics' are additional factors.[77] Over the past two decades social scientists have compiled a clearer picture. We can say that the lack of performance legitimacy of the ruling elites (that is, the inability of the secular elites to deliver common good); the brutal authoritarianism that results in an erosion of the civil society and hence leaves the religious centres (e.g., mosque, temple, church) as the only viable public space; uneven economic development including urbanization; rupture in the hegemony of secularist politics; and the politics of expediency of secular parties, are pivotal in the global rise of religio-political forces.[78] The importance of religious centres in the event of the absence of other avenues of political expression needs to be highlighted. These institutions not only offer physical and moral space, but can exercise moral authority and provide moral leadership and a logistical basis for mobilization. Importantly, these factors are not mutually exclusive, and their simultaneous occurrence is not necessary. Nowhere is this more evident than in the Muslim majority countries of the Middle East and North Africa (MENA).

Since the 1970s most of the countries in MENA were ruled by authoritarian regimes, which heavy-handedly dealt with all opposition parties. This led to a situation where the choice was left between Islamists and authoritarian rulers. As these countries faced changes in recent years, Islamist parties succeeded in garnering popular support. In many instances they have highlighted that the failure of the state is intrinsically connected to the ideology (that is secularism) these regimes subscribed to. As for South Asia, comprehending the abject poverty and the inability of states' to take care of the marginalized sections of the society require no statistics, anyone familiar with the political economy of these states understands this. The World Bank estimates that at least 406 million people live below the poverty line in South Asia, equivalent to 31 per cent of the population of the region.[79] Despite impressive economic growth in recent years, the region has the highest rates of malnutrition and the largest numbers of undernourished children in the world. India also has the largest number of school-age children who have either not attended or have dropped out of schools. An authoritarian system of governance has remained the defining feature of Pakistan since the 1950s, Bangladesh was under military rule for 15 years (1975–90), until recently the Nepalese monarch had the power to frustrate the democratic aspirations of the people at his will, and Sri Lanka's democracy lacks any substantive participation from the Tamils. These failures have delegitimized states and ruling blocs. As the ruling blocs no longer enjoy hegemony over the masses, conflicting tendencies have emerged within these societies. On the one hand, the ruling blocs resort to various means to maintain their hold over power; while religio-political forces attempt to demonstrate that failure is inherently connected to the secularist liberal ideology. In the absence of a hegemonic ideology, religion becomes a candidate to fill the vacuum. The public discourse is then filled with religious symbols and idioms and religious identity takes centre stage.

Finally, a series of global events contributed to the identification with religion, particularly with Islam. The year 1979 was a watershed moment in this regard. The Iranian Revolution, and the Soviet invasion of Afghanistan unleashed a series of events that not only brought Islamist forces to the fore but also created an environment within which Muslim identity as basis of political activism and Islamism as a political ideology flourished. The reactions of the West to the Iranian revolution and adoption of an unstated policy, with the support of Saudi Arabia, of creating a 'Sunni Wall'[80] around Iran (that is encircling Iran by hardening Sunni identity in various neighbouring countries), were pivotal. Equally important was US policy towards Afghanistan. First, 'the Reagan administration ideologized the war as a religious war against the evil empire',[81] therefore providing legitimacy to the identification with religion as a cause. Secondly, it 'privatized war in the course of recruiting, training and organizing a global network of Islamic fighters against the Soviet Union'.[82] This helped the organization of a global network based on Muslim identity. In the case of Afghanistan, the rise of the Taliban after the defeat of the Soviet Union made the situation worse.

The foreign policies of the West in general, particularly the United States and Britain, have created and reinforced the perception that Islam is under attack, that Muslim communities throughout the world are subject to repression and that the United States supports the perpetrators. The question is not the veracity of these allegations but the perception. The news and images of the Gulf War of 1991 and the plight of the Palestinian people has touched a chord with both the middle class and the disenfranchised in Bangladesh. These images are understood as vindicating/demonstrating/proving Muslim victimhood.[83] Arguably the images of Iraqis suffering under US-enforced sanctions, the violence against Muslims in Bosnia, Kosovo, Chechnya, and Kashmir foster a pan-Islamic message that appeals to the Muslimness of the audience and is reproduced in public discourses. This has happened elsewhere in the Muslim world, and it is my contention that Bangladesh is by no means an exception.[84] One can argue that this is a perception prevalent in the Muslim world rather than a justifiable reaction to deliberate policies of the Western governments. But as Charney and Yakatan have reminded us, 'perceptions matter'.[85] It is well to bear in mind that perceptions are not abstract constructions; they are rooted in the realities around individuals. Additionally, to the disgruntled, disenfranchised sections of society the religious element is easier to understand than the complex logic of global politics and/or imperialism.

Obviously one cannot draw a direct and causal relation between these sentiments and Muslim identity, but one cannot simply disregard it either. But these point us to the important understanding that the idea of a Muslim is now also shaped by transnational events and ideologies which are disseminated in Bangladesh, as elsewhere, via transnational organizations, interactions through travel and migration and by mainstream and social media.

What Do They Think?

The domestic historical narrative of identity construction and the global dimension of the relationship between religion and politics demonstrate that various factors have played roles in creating a conducive environment for a shift towards a religiously informed identity. But how much has the Bangladeshi population tilted towards underscoring their Muslim identity? What roles do they see and expect to see Islam play in their public and political lives? We can explore the answers to these questions through the data of a series of public opinion polls collected since 1969.

The pre-independence survey conducted by Jawed asked then East Pakistani professionals what was their personal professed ideology; a quarter of the respondents (25.4 per cent) reported Islam as their personal ideology, 18.6 per cent noted Islamic democracy, 18.6 per cent Islamic socialism, 13.6 per cent socialism, 10.2 per cent favoured democratic socialism, 6.8 per cent professed democracy, 3.4 per cent conveyed communism/Marxism, and 3.4 per cent stated that they did not subscribe to an ideology.[86] Thus, a majority did not view Islam as their personal ideology; instead more respondents subscribed to some form of democratic and/or distributive justice as their personal ideology.

Compared to Jawed's relatively secular findings, surveys in the 1990s and early-2000s such as the World Values Survey have documented a consistent move towards a greater role for religion.[87] Over the course of Bangladesh's two surveys – taking place in 1996 and 2002 – a clear tendency towards identifying with religion as marker of personal identity among its population is obvious. The indicators of this religiosity increased between the six-year period of these surveys. In response to the question of the importance of one's religion to life, 82.45 per cent of respondents said 'very important' in 1996, with that number increasing to 87.8 per cent in 2002. In 1996, in response to the question of how much confidence Bangladeshis have in religious institutions, 85.6 per cent of respondents said 'a great deal'. This number increased to 90 per cent in 2002. In regards to membership in religious organizations, 33.6 per cent of Bangladeshis reported membership in 1996, which increased to 43.3 per cent in 2002. Finally, that 96.6 per cent of Bangladeshis consider themselves a 'religious person' in 2002 demonstrates the country's pervasive religiosity. Of this population, 86 per cent identified as Muslim in 1996, while 92 per cent identified as Muslim in 2002.

The respondents of the 2002 survey were asked about their preference in regard to the relationship between the state and religion. The vast majority of Bangladeshis polled in 2002, for example, either agreed (34.8 per cent) or strongly agreed (59 per cent) that one of government's roles is to protect religion. A large majority, furthermore, agreed strongly (31.9 per cent) or agreed (39.1 per cent) that politicians who do not believe in God are unfit for public office. Only 21.1 per cent of respondents disagreed with this proposition.

These numbers are instructive in regard to the public perception of Islam's role in the public sphere. Despite personal religiosity and respect for religion as an institution to be protected by the state, in 2002, significant reservations were expressed about the role of religious leaders in public office. In response to the proposition that it was 'better if more people with strong religious beliefs in public office', only 5.2 per cent agreed strongly, and 18.6 per cent agreed. In contrast, 49.9 per cent disagreed. 22 per cent of respondents neither agreed nor disagreed with this notion. In a similar vein, the majority of respondents in 2002 felt that religious leaders should not influence government, with 17 per cent agreeing strongly and 53.5 per cent agreeing with this notion. Among the respondents 18.5 per cent agreed strongly and 56 per cent agreed with the proposition that 'religious leaders should not influence how people vote'. This conscious divide between religion and politics is also apparent in the choices of political parties. In 1996, 71.8 per cent of respondents said that the party they would never vote for was the most prominent Islamist political party, the Jamaat-e-Islami (JI); only 3.8 per cent said that the JI was their first choice political party. These numbers changed in 2002: complete rejection of the JI dropped to 47.7 per cent and its support increased to 5.3 per cent. It is well to recall that the JI was a part of the BNP-led ruling coalition when the second survey was conducted; less than a year ago Bangladeshi voters delivered a stunning two-thirds majority to the alliance. Yet, there was a clear majority who would not prefer a robust role for religiously informed public officials.

We may recall that the USAID's survey report published in 2004 established that following democracy 'government ruled by Islamic law, with respected religious figures as leaders' was the favoured option of the respondents: it captured 21 per cent of support.[88]

In subsequent years, personal religiosity among Bangladeshis has increased significantly as demonstrated in the Gallup tracking poll between 2006 and 2009. In response to the question – 'is religion an important part of your daily life?' – 96 per cent per cent responded positively in 2006, 99 per cent in 2007, 99 per cent in 2008 and 100 per cent in 2009.[89] These surveys also show an upward trend in confidence in the religious institutions.

Support for religion's role in public life seems to gain strength along with personal religiosity. The Pew Research Center's 'Global Opinion Trends 2002–2007' show that 62 per cent of Bangladeshi respondents felt that religious leaders had a positive impact on the running of Bangladesh.[90] When asked if religion should have an influence in political decisions in the Gallup Poll of 2012, entitled 'Insights South Asia: Bangladesh Survey 2012', 32 per cent of respondents said that religion should be the 'most influential' factor, 20 per cent said that it should have a major influence, and 16 per cent claimed that it should hold minor influence. A mere 17 per cent of the surveyed population responded that religion should have no influence over political decisions.[91] In the 2013 survey conducted by the Pew Research Center, almost 70 per cent of Bangladesh's respondents felt that religious leaders should have a role in politics (25 per cent stating that they should hold a 'large influence' and 44 per cent stating 'some influence'). Religion in party politics is also widely supported, as 41 per cent of Bangladeshi Muslims insisted that Islamist political parties are better than secular parties, 39 per cent held that they are equivalent, and only 16 per cent believed that Islamist parties are worse than their secular counterparts.[92]

These statistics drawn from an array of surveys conducted over more than four decades and compared with pre-independence data clearly reveals that there is a palpable support for a public role of Islam in Bangladesh, that the support has grown, and that the population has gradually moved towards providing more space to religiously informed public figures and accepting religion-informed political rhetoric. Of course, they also tell us that there are a significant number of people who are opposed to the presence of religion in the public sphere. In this sense, these data bear out the presence of contestation on the issue of religion. But is this a contestation between a 'secularist' understanding of religion's private role and a 'non-secularist' understanding of a public presence of Islam? Or, to return to the central question of the present chapter, a contestation between two notions of national identity?

Multiple Contestations?

No religion is monolithic, therefore the perception of Islam among the respondents to the surveys discussed in the previous section could well be different. When the respondents of these surveys are suggesting that religion in general and particularly Islam should play roles in public life, and use Islam as a demarcator of the identity of the individual and the nation, they might be talking about different perception of Islam. Religion, especially popular religion, in any society is an 'institutionalized bargain', a power contract at a given moment of time and a given place. In the region now called Bangladesh, Islam has grown as a local construct as the seminal works of Richard Eaton[93] and Asim Roy[94] have demonstrated. Simply stated, 'Islam did not descend upon a ready-made ancient agrarian civilization [...] On the contrary, it advanced hand in hand with a new agricultural civilization. It developed as in eastern Bengal as a vector not only of religious change, but of social and technological revolution.'[95]

While there have been changes within this strand of Islam, the essential elements of it – syncretism and adaptation – have remained in place and reflected in the practices of Sufism, *Pir* (Saint), *Mazars*, as well as the pietistic movement of Tabligh Jaamat. But over time these local traditions have faced challenges from transnational ideas and thoughts. Global interconnectedness has and is bringing new interpretation and meanings of Islam to the country as highlighted in our discussion earlier. The increased religiosity among the Bangladeshi population, palpable changes in dress, social behaviour, and increased sensitivity towards religious issues are indicative of the ongoing changes.

Transnational Islamic and Islamist organizations, both pietist and political, have made their presence known in Bangladesh.[96] There are literalist restrictive interpretations which have taken the shape of political Islam where Islam is considered as a political ideology by its adherents and therefore driven by the ideologues' rigid interpretations; on the other hand, there are efforts to find a compassionate, inclusive, egalitarian interpretation of Islam fit for the contemporary world and responsive to the needs of Muslims according to their societal contexts.

While discussions about the latter are few and far between in contemporary Bangladesh, the former has become a major strand within society and politics. The acrimonious political environment, desire for short-term gains, lack of true democratic space, and poor governance have contributed to the strengthening of this representation of Islam. Whereas the local traditions and hermeneutics of Islam,[97] examples of which are available in the history of the country, have not been explored.

Political expediency of major parties has helped the forces of textual Islam to thrive. But seldom have we asked what religiously-informed identity means to the citizens of Bangladesh.

The quest for identity, therefore, does not involve only a contestation between the 'secularists' and 'the Islamists', as the conventional wisdom and popular discourse suggest; but comprises multiple contestations. Variations within Islamic ideas and constructions of Muslimness are one part of it. The other remains within what is often described as the proponents of 'secularism'. As well as differences as to what secularism means, there are divisions as to where to begin. Some are of the opinion that the state should be a secular institution and that a top-down approach should be adopted. The state, in this instance, is viewed as both an instrument of authority and of hegemony. Whether this approach is viable and effective is an open question. The rise of the BJP and their 'Hindutva' thesis in India, point to the weaknesses of this notion. Others argue that secularization of society and polity is the prerequisite for building a secular state. But how can a deeply religious society, like Bangladesh be secularized? What would such secularization mean?

These unresolved questions are at the heart of the quest for a national identity in Bangladesh. To date, although the issue has dominated daily politics, the debate has not been waged robustly and openly. Until such time the half-hearted quest will continue to be a part of Bangladeshi politics.

CHAPTER 7

UNPACKING THE PARADOX OF DEVELOPMENT

The World Bank, on 1 July 2015, sent out a press release from its headquarters in Washington DC. The headline was 'WB Update Says 10 Countries Move Up in Income Bracket'. The apparently mundane, annual ritualistic press release delivered good news for Bangladesh. The press release said, 'The World Bank's latest estimates of Gross National Income per capita (GNI) continue to show improved economic performance in many low-income countries, with Bangladesh, Kenya, Myanmar, and Tajikistan now becoming lower-middle income countries, joining those with annual incomes of $1,046 to $4,125.'[1] The news surprised many, particularly those who had followed the events in Bangladesh during the previous months. Political upheaval, general strikes and violence crippled the country for three months. The World Bank estimated a loss of $2.2 bn, and major multilateral agencies revised its projection of the growth for the remainder of the fiscal year. Yet the country seems to have made progress, many observers noticed. The achievement was not made in a day, nor in a few months. Prime Minister Sheikh Hasina, told the media, 'I can assure you it won't take until 2021, before that time we would be able to establish ourselves as a middle-income country. Bangladesh doesn't want to stay at the lower ladder [. . .] it wants climb to the peak and we'll do whatever is necessary for that.'

Of course, achieving lower middle income status is not a leap forward, but indeed a glimmer of hope for a country whose political history over the past four decades is characterized by a volatile political environment, violence, and the breakdown of governing institutions. Frequently, these manmade disasters along with natural calamities draw the attention of the world's media to Bangladesh. The occasional exception to this pattern of media coverage is when the country is referred to in the context of conflicts in other parts of the world, as a corollary to the role of the United Nations in bringing peace; Bangladesh has been the largest contributor to the UN Peace Keeping Mission for decades. This positive contribution was and still is overlooked. There is also an untold narrative: it has produced a development success story since its inception, particularly since the 1990s. The World Bank's announcement underscored that it is important to take a close look at this paradox.

At its independence, some Western policy-makers dubbed Bangladesh 'the international basket case',[2] and analysts concluded that it would be a test case for development.[3] But in the past decade, those who have followed the country's trajectory and those who looked beyond the surface, have started to use phrases like 'paradox', 'puzzle', 'conundrum', 'surprise', and/or 'model' to describe the country. Initial pessimism regarding the viability of the country has disappeared; instead it is now described as 'the next Asian Tiger'. The phrase draws parallels with the economies of Hong Kong, South Korea, Singapore and Taiwan in the early 1970s. In 2007, Goldman Sachs included Bangladesh in the list of emerging economies called the Next 11.[4] In the same year, JP Morgan called it one of the frontier five markets.[5] The McKinsey report based on surveys of apparel buyers of the world in 2011 said that Bangladesh could be the world's largest exporter of ready-made garments and household textiles.[6] *The Economist* of London proclaimed in late 2012 that the country is, 'Out of the Basket'.[7] Before these laudatory assessments of private sector investors came statements from global multilateral institutions which described a situation called the 'Bangladesh conundrum'.[8] The World Bank president Robert Zoellick, on a trip to Dhaka in 2007, said that the country holds the potential to become a 'powerhouse' in the international market.[9] What prompted these comments and assessments? What are these statements referring to? There is much to be explained in regard to these assessments, but in short, they allude to significant and sustained economic growth combined with achievements in important social indicators.

The Context

Before proceeding to discuss these accomplishments, it is necessary to remember the contexts – both global and domestic. Environmental, political, and economic aspects should be considered too. As discussed in Chapters 2 and 3, Bangladesh's domestic political situation has remained unstable for almost all of its existence. Add to this unhappy situation, endemic corruption – the country was ranked the world's most corrupt for five years in a row. The extent of corruption can be understood from a 2005 report by Transparency International (TI) which stated that in two out of five instances, parents must bribe officials to enroll their children in state schools.

Not only does the country lack natural resources, apart from a recent discovery of a small amount of natural gas and oil off-shore, nature has never been kind to it. In 1974 it experienced a devastating flood, followed by a famine that took the lives of at least a million; flooding hit the country in 1987, 1988 and 1998 and affected 40–75 per cent of the total area in each instance. Since independence tropical cyclones have wrecked the country many times, some with deadly impact. For example, 138,000 people perished in 1991, another in 2009 caused irreparable damage to the Sunderban, the largest mangrove forest of the world located in the southern part of the country. The country endured a number of external economic shocks through the period too. These include the oil crisis in the 1970s (the increase of the price of petroleum in the global market by the petroleum producing countries); the debt crisis of the 1980s (large debt owed by the least developing countries to various banks); the Asian financial crisis in 1997 (a series of currency devaluations and other events that spread through many Asian markets causing stock market declines and reduced import revenues) and the global financial crisis in 2007–8 (downturns in the stock markets throughout the world and collapse of large financial institutions in Western countries).

Economic Achievements

The overall economic growth of the country was noted by the World Bank in 2006 when it highlighted Bangladesh as one of only 18 developing countries with an annual growth rate that has never fallen below 2 per cent.[10] This was remarkable considering that not too long ago Bangladesh was regarded as one of the poorest 33 countries with very few prospects due to lack of natural resources and skilled human resources and repeated natural disasters. Data related to the annual growth, reflected in the gross domestic product (GDP), show a consistent upward trajectory. In 1972, the year after its independence, annual GDP growth rate was negative/minus 13.97 per cent. It was no surprise given that the country had experienced a nine-month long war. Due to guerrilla war tactics adopted by the freedom fighters, the infrastructure was in shambles. Although the economy made some progress, the performance was very poor throughout the first decade (1972–79): the average annual growth rate was only 1.88 per cent. In the second decade (1980–89) the average growth rate increased to 3.22 per cent, and in the 1990s the rate was 4.8 per cent. The economy started to achieve a reasonably better rate of growth in the 1990s. It improved further in the 2000s. Between 2000 and 2012, with the single exception of 2002, the country achieved annual growth at the rate of more than 5.5 per cent.[11] Despite political upheaval the growth rate was 6.01 per cent in 2013–14 and 6. 12 per cent in 2014–15.[12]

Concurrent to the growth, the structure of the Bangladeshi economy experienced a shift from an agriculture-based economy to a service-based economy. The share of agriculture before independence was 55 per cent as opposed to 35 per cent for the service sector and 10 per cent for industry. By the end of the first decade the contribution of the service sector reached equality with agriculture at 45 per cent.[13] The agriculture sector's share in GDP has continued to slide in recent decades, contributing 17.68 per cent in 2012, while industry's contribution has grown to 28.47 per cent and services' contribution rose to almost 54 per cent.[14] Despite the shift, agriculture has remained the principal employment generating sector. In 2012, the share of agriculture in employment was 48 per cent.[15]

The third distinctive feature of economic change is the reduction in the incidence of poverty. In 1973–74, almost 74 per cent of the population was considered below the poverty line. The percentage stood at 56.6 per cent in 1992, 48.9 per cent in 2000 and 31.5 in 2010.[16] This has led some economists to describe the growth as 'pro-poor',[17] while some have argued that the growth, especially between

1992 and 2000, has benefited the rich more than the poor.[18] It is also argued that inequality has increased as the growth rate has improved. According to Rizwanul Islam:

> During the 1970s and the 1980s, the degree of inequality in income was not very high in Bangladesh, and there was no major increase either. Indeed, compared to other developing countries of Asia (e.g., Malaysia, Philippines, Thailand), Bangladesh was a country with [a] lower degree of inequality. That situation continued till 1991–92. But there was a sharp increase in inequality between 1991–92 and 1995–96. And there has been further increase during 1995–96 and 2005.[19]

The increase of income inequity is further documented in the 2010 Household Income and Expenditure Survey (HIES) conducted by the Bangladesh Bureau of Statistics (BBS). For example, income accruing to the top 5 per cent of households has increased to 24.61 in 2010 from 23.62 per cent in 1995, while it has decreased for the bottom 5 per cent of households from 0.88 per cent to 0.78 per cent.

Social Developments

The consistent growth in GDP is a major achievement, but it has been surpassed by accomplishments in the social development indicators. Mahmud noted the country 'has achieved rapid and spectacular improvements in many social development indicators during the last two decades or so'.[20] Most notable achievements have been in the health and education sectors. Needless to say, both have great significance for the future of the nation. As for the health sector, *Lancet*, the world's leading general medical journal, prefaced a series of six articles on Bangladesh's health sector saying the country's exceptional health achievement is 'one of the great mysteries of global health'.[21] Infant mortality, children under five mortality, maternal mortality, total fertility rate (TFR), and life expectancy at birth have all improved significantly. As for education, progress in providing educational opportunities to children, especially to girls, is remarkable.

At independence infant mortality per thousand live births was 147.3. In 1980, the number was 133; in 1990 the number stood at 99.5. There has been a sharp decline since then. In 2000 it came down to 64.2. In 2012, only 33.2 infant mortality per thousand was recorded.[22] In the decade between 2000 and 2010, children under five mortality declined from 87.7 per thousand live births to 47.2; in 2012, the number stood at 40.9. The decline achieved in maternal mortality – from 322 per 100,000 in 2001 to 194 in 2010 – is equally impressive.[23]

Although Bangladesh still remains one of the most densely populated countries of the world (1,174 persons per square kilometer of land area), its annual population growth rate has declined significantly in recent decades – from 2.48 in 1974 to 1.37 in 2011. This was made possible due to dramatic decline in the total fertility rate (TFR) (that is the average number of children that would be born to a woman over her lifetime) on the one hand and the increase in contraceptive prevalence rate (CPR), on the other. In 1971–75, the TFR was 6.3 births per woman; in 1987–89 it was reduced to 5.1; in 1995–97 the number was 3.3. According to the latest demographic survey in 2010 it stands at 2.3 births per woman. The use of contraceptives among women was 61.2 per cent in 2011 as opposed to only 7.7 per cent in 1975.[24] According to the 2013 Human Development Report of the UNDP, between 1980 and 2012, life expectancy at birth has increased 14 years – from about 55 years to about 69 years.

In the education sector, the success is two-fold: increasing opportunity for all children, and ensuring equitable access to girls. The net enrolment rate (NER) at primary level was 50.4 per cent in 1970, reaching 66.7 per cent in 1980, and climbing to 72.0 per cent in 1990. By 2011, according to official statistics, it reached 98.7 per cent. Concurrently, specific efforts were made to establish gender parity. At independence NER for girls was only 33.9 per cent. At the end of the first decade, in 1980, it increased to 54.2 per cent. Between 1990 and 2011 the share increased from 66.3 per cent to 99.4 per cent.[25]

Bangladesh has already achieved targets of a number of Millennium Development Goals (MDG), and is on track to achieve others by the stipulated year of 2015.[26] In fact Bangladesh is a leader among the least developed countries (LDCs) in attaining these goals.[27]

The Causes of and the Conditions for Success

The question as to how these achievements were made has stimulated discussion and debate among economists, political scientists, development experts and policy-makers alike. Many have asked what the magic ingredient is. There is no single factor that has enabled the country to progress, but a combination of economic and social factors have facilitated the process. This is a result of different actors working at times together and at times autonomously; they are the state, the non-governmental organizations, private entrepreneurs, and individual citizens. Consistency in economic policies across the regimes since the 1990s has played a critical role, but in some ways the credit is due to three segments of the society: women in the garments industry, migrant workers, and farmers. Gradual changes to social behaviour, norms and attitudes on the one hand facilitated the economic and social achievements while economic growth has allowed these social changes to take place.

Despite often violent political change, various regimes over time have followed a single trajectory in regard to macroeconomic policies, particularly since 1982. Sen et al. have argued that, based on policy measures, Bangladesh's development history can be divided into four phases: 1972/73–1981/82 ('reconstruction and recovery amidst political turbulence'); 1982/83–1988/89 ('slow economic growth with growing macroeconomic instability'); 1989/90–1992/93 ('crisis driven economic reforms') and 1993/94 – to date ('higher economic growth and faster social development').[28] What is significant is that as the country underwent various stages of growth, political commitment to social development remained consistent:

> In Bangladesh, policies integral to the welfare of the poor, including family planning, disaster management, access to drinking water, and expansion of primary education (especially for girls) have taken on the character of public goods. Successive governments, irrespective of their political leanings and degree of democracy, have shielded these policies from budgetary and political pressures.[29]

This policy consistency has been complemented by the changes in social norms, particularly regarding the role of women in the society and economy. The more visible, active and effective role of women in economy and society is a result of the availability and use of micro-credit by women in rural areas since the early 1980s. This movement gained pace as the Bangladeshi state became more integrated in the global economy and women's participation in development became imperative. An array of non-government organizations (NGOs), including the Nobel Prize winning Grameen Bank and the world's largest NGO the BRAC, through their microcredit programmes, have helped rural women challenge the extant social behaviour. While many have questioned whether micro-credit has empowered women,[30] it is beyond doubt that micro-credit created space for women outside the traditional sphere and encouraged female education which in turn contributed to other social changes including reducing the population growth rate.

The export oriented ready-made garments (RMG) sector, which was almost non-existent until the early 1980s, has become the second largest exporter of the world employing 4 million workers; more than 90 per cent of whom are women. The sector, which provided 79 per cent of total export earnings in 2012–13 is an illustration of how various actors have played roles in economic growth and how it benefited from social changes and contributed to social norms. In 1978, earnings from the sector totalled a negligible $0.04 million; but in 2012–13 the sector earned $27.01 billion. The rise of this industry is an example of private entrepreneurship on the one hand, while on the other hand it is an example how women's labour can transform the economy of a nation. Cheap labour, which still remains the backbone of the industry, is provided by young female workers who have migrated from rural areas with little educational background or skills. The industry has not provided a hospitable environment for the women; 'this is an industry where the workers are not just exploited and forced to work in an environment of harassment, violence and abuse, but where basic guarantees of safety have been thrown to the wind, where corners have been cut to the extent that a building can collapse on top of thousands of workers.'[31]

Migrant workers have played an astounding role in the economic progress of the country. The short-term migration of labour from Bangladesh began in the mid-1970s as a result of infrastructural developments in the oil-rich Gulf and Middle Eastern countries. Since the oil boom of 1974, countries in the Gulf region have attracted a large number of short-term migrants for contractual jobs from relatively poor countries. Since 1976, Bangladeshi unskilled, semi-skilled, and skilled labourers joined this labour market. In the 1980s, labour migration was expanded to newly industrialized southeast Asian countries such as Singapore, Malaysia and South Korea. Between 1976 and 2013, about 8.71 million people took unskilled, semi-skilled, and skilled labourer jobs in various countries.[32] Labour migration has impacted positively on the nation's economy in at least two ways: first, it has kept the unemployment rate low and, second, it has brought a flow of remittances, often in the face of dwindling exports. Increasingly remittances from these migrants has become the main source of the country's foreign revenue. In 2013–14, the total remittances received by the country were $14.46 billion according to the Central Bank. The impact of the remittances is manifold: 'in 2009, earning from the migrant remittances was 2 times higher than the net income of the garments sector and 9 times higher than foreign direct investment to the country'.[33] The contribution of migrant worker remittances to Bangladesh's GDP has risen from 0.19 per cent in 1976 to 2.32 per cent in 1985 to 5.9 per cent in 2002. Between 2003 and 2008, the share of remittances as a percentage of GDP remained well over 6 per cent.[34] In 2013, the remittance was 11 per cent of the total GDP of Bangladesh. In the period 1990 to 2010, Official Development Assistance (ODA) and Foreign Direct Investment (FDI) averaged around 3 per cent and 1.5 per cent, respectively. A number of studies have demonstrated that remittances have contributed to poverty reduction. Ratha and Mahapatra contend that poverty has fallen by 6 percentage points in Bangladesh.[35] These findings are supported by other studies, for example Raihan et al.,[36] Vargas-Silva et al.[37] The remittances have significant impacts on other aspects of life. Barai has demonstrated with empirical data that indicators like nutrition, living conditions and housing, education, health care, social security, and investment of the recipient households have been positively affected by remittances.[38]

But these workers face inhuman conditions and enjoy no rights in the host countries. A 2011 report of the International Trade Union Confederation about the plight of migrant workers in Qatar is equally true for other places where Bangladeshi migrants have found jobs. The report states:

> [T]hey inhabit overcrowded barrack-like housing, in sprawling, dust-clogged, male-only suburbs [...] Bussed home exhausted after long hours working in often blistering heat, the men are squeezed up to ten to a room in company accommodation. Food is basic, sanitation often rudimentary and air-conditioning when it exists is sometimes ineffectual when summer temperatures soar over 40°C. Many work at dangerous jobs with little or no health insurance. The migrant workers are nothing if not resistant. Many say they are willing to put up with the heat and harsh conditions for the chance to support their families with wages way beyond what they can earn at home. All too often however, salaries are paid months overdue. Conned by unscrupulous recruitment agents, workers arrive in the Gulf to discover they are paid considerably less than they were promised back in their homelands, leaving the traumatised migrants struggling to pay off the debts they ran up to fund their passage to the Gulf let alone provide for their struggling families.[39]

Yet these migrant workers receive very little support from the Bangladeshi government. The abject failure of the Bangladeshi state to protect the interests of the migrant labourers is palpable in the fact that when they end up in jail or have problems with laws, embassies show indifference and no support is rendered to them. Corrupt middlemen, flawed immigration policies, lack of a strong government response and disparities in labour laws often place hard-working men and women in the most difficult situations. According to a press report, between 2003 and 2013 more than 20,000 migrant workers died at a young age while working outside the country.[40]

As for agriculture, particularly in the production of rice, the country has demonstrated a significant success. Between 1971 and 2013, rice production has tripled – from 10 million metric tons to 35 million metric tons. Similarly, production of wheat, corn, potato, onion and all other agricultural products has almost doubled. This is achieved against a background of decline in cultivable land due to population growth, urbanization, and rural infrastructure development. According to one estimate cultivable land has decreased at least 20 per cent since independence. Increased production is credited to the introduction of high-yielding varieties of rice and the increase of lands under irrigation (four fold increase to 5.1 million hectares between 1990 and 2011). Economists have argued that market-based reforms such as reduction of subsidy and increasing the participation of the private sector in the procurement and distribution of inputs have helped the growth in food production.[41] But these steps have not ensured fair prices for farmers, instead they have become subject to the vagaries of the market. On the other hand prices of agricultural inputs such as fertilizers, seeds have increased manifold due to market manipulation by unscrupulous middlemen. Availability of agricultural loans to small and marginal farmers is limited although most of the farmlands are of small size. Despite such adversity, farmers have made critical contributions to food production, and in turn to the economic growth of the country.

Notwithstanding the debate on the lack of accountability of the NGOs and criticisms of their commercial ventures, there is evidence that the NGOs have played a significant role in the achievements in social development indicators. Take for example the education and health sectors. NGOs, particularly the BRAC, have made an immense contribution to the expansion of educational opportunities. Non-formal educational institutions offer primary and pre-primary education, particularly to children from disadvantaged backgrounds, which has helped the country meet the MDG target regarding access to education. According to an assessment report by the British Council, in 2011 over 500 NGOs were catering for about 1.4 million students studying in 53,000 centres and BRAC accounts for over half of this figure.[42] Multilateral donor agencies have also provided crucial support to the education sector. The Female Secondary School Assistance Programme (FSSAP), a government programme to improve access to secondary education for girls by providing tuition stipends, was launched in 1993 at the national level with the support of the International Development Association (IDA) and other donors. This came after successful implementation on a smaller scale.[43]

Like the education system, the health system of Bangladesh is known for its pluralistic character, which means that both public and private actors are engaged in delivering services. Outside the public sector, both for-profit and non-profit NGOs are present. The NGOs have been at the forefront of delivering clinical services, 'mostly aimed at maternal, newborn, and child health, and family planning, in cities and towns, and satellite clinics and front-line workers in communities'.[44] Of the total 160,000 community health workers who provide these services, 105,000 are from NGOs.

Returning to the question as to how Bangladesh has achieved great progress both in economic and social development arenas, our discussions have shown that it is not an achievement of any particular regime, neither is it an accomplishment of the public sector alone. Above all, these successes are the result of the hard work of the resilient ordinary Bangladeshis, particularly the poorer productive sections of the society – farmers and workers, and achieved through active participation of women in general. Yet, they all face inequality and insecurity under the current economic system and remain marginalized under the extant political structures. The question remains whether the present rate of economic growth and social change – the paradox – can be sustained without addressing the issue of inequality and ensuring substantive participation of the citizens through effective democratic governance.

CONCLUSION

LOOKING BACK,
LOOKING AHEAD

The history of Bangladeshi politics is characterized by weak governance, fractiousness of leaders, fragility of democratic institutions, and volatility of political process. But the history, paradoxically, also tells us of the resilience of the Bangladeshi citizens in the face of natural and political disasters, of their ingenuity in finding ways to overcome adverse situations, and of their undaunted hopes despite reasons to become despondent. Patience and optimism against all odds mark the character of the people. One cannot ignore the nation's repeated efforts to establish an inclusive and democratic system of governance and rejection of authoritarianism of all varieties. A state which was born through violence has witnessed too many further incidents of violence and death since its independence; yet it has survived and has committed itself to the path of prosperity. The success in economic growth and social indicators testify to these qualities of people. One can extrapolate the past and paint a pessimistic picture, or alternatively, highlight only the achievements to claim that the nation is on the right track. Such a partial picture will neither do justice to the history, nor will it help the nation to chart the right course for the future. The past of a nation was not preordained, it was made by people, their leaders, the institutions they build and the practices they adopt; so is the future: it is to be created by the people. The future does not follow a simple, linear trajectory.

Two issues have dominated the politics of past decades: democracy and identity. A third issue – the role of religion in the public sphere – has gained salience in part as a corollary to the issue of identity and in part as a test to the scope of democracy. While the people of Bangladesh never wavered on demanding democracy, the leadership have either failed or were unwilling to create institutions which will provide democracy with the anchor it needs. The political impasse – whether in 1996, 2006 or 2013 – is not only a reflection of irreconcilable differences between two parties or two leaders but a testimony to the absence of or the innate weaknesses of the institutions which are supposed to regulate politics and society. Politicians of all shades, irrespective of the party, have manipulated the constitution and electoral processes whenever they had the power to do so for immediate gains. Institutions such as the Election Commission have remained weak at best, at worst subservient to the ruling party. In the absence of institutions to hold the government accountable, abuse of power and corruption have permeated to every corner of society. It has created an environment wherein blatant disregard for fundamental rights has become a norm; a culture of impunity for the powerful has taken hold. These are the indicators of a system which is democracy by name only (Chapter 4). Despite these weaknesses, the increasing voter turnout between 1991 and 2008 demonstrates that Bangladeshi citizens made the best use possible of the electoral system to express their voices. Emergence of a two-party system by the mid-1990s and the alteration of power between two parties since then were also indicative of this mindset. Of course, these elections did not always deliver good governance: the ruling party and its leaders have often failed to differentiate between the 'mandate to govern' and the 'licence to rule'. Besides, in the clientelist political culture of Bangladesh the state has remained the principal source for dispensation of patronage. Political parties have used and abused resources in the past for personal gain, and in order to maintain the party machines and their hold over party activists. Notwithstanding the high level of corruption, the state also provides impunity to ruling party activists. Therefore, each election has become a 'zero-sum' game and all parties fight hard. The first-past-the-post system (FPTP) contributed to this culture. Additionally, ruling parties have used the state machinery for reprisals against the opposition. That made an election a matter of existential struggle. Corruption and abuse of power make each incumbent a legitimate candidate for prosecution, but often threats of prosecution and courts and laws have been used as instruments of harassment. No political party, its leaders and activists are willing to endure this suffering. Therefore, both incumbent and opposition view winning the election as their only safeguard against possible post-poll adverse situations. This can be described as the 'cost of defeat'. The situation has become worse as the nation has moved further away from a culture of tolerance.

In popular discourses and in political debates, the issue of national identity is framed within a binary frame – Bengali versus Muslim/ secularism versus Islamism/ethnic identity versus religious identity. This framing presupposes and implies that these identities are not only mutually exclusive but also must be seen as contesting ideas, instead of any possibility of accommodation between them. The intellectual history of the period between the 1920s and 1930s shows that the issue has been dealt with and that such dichotomization has very little utility value. Besides, none of these identities is monolithic. To date, identity discussions have remained oblivious to the contestations within each category. Those who underscore the salience of ethnic identity are not forthright in acknowledging that it has a serious blind spot when it comes to the indigenous people's rights and privileges. A dominant Bengali identity, as any identity politics does, bulldozes the cultural heterogeneity of the Bangladeshi society. In a similar vein, insistence on an exclusive Muslim identity, masks the fact that religion in any society is a 'socially constructed and constituted set of practices that embody changing and often contradictory interests'.[1] There have been various strands of Islam in Bangladesh, for example, modernist, orthodox and folk, to say the least. Therefore, an identity based on a particular reading of a religious text adhering to one of these strands cannot capture the variations and respect the individual's choice to combine various aspects. Unfortunately, these two identities have been presented as proxies of two divergent political ideologies. As the issue of identity has been instrumentalized, they have transformed into what Amin Maalouf has described as a 'deadly identity'[2] and Arjun Appadurai has described as 'predatory identities'.[3] The defining characteristics of the deadly identity are 'negative, antagonistic and chauvinistic'.

Religion's presence in the public sphere in Bangladesh is not new, but its transformation into a political ideology and a tool of mobilization are intrinsically connected to the legitimatizing efforts of the military regimes, namely Zia (1975–81) and Ershad (1982–90).

The ideal disposition of the relationship between the state and religion was never debated in Bangladesh, its articulation in the original constitution was fraught with various interpretations. Whether a secular state can be created without secularization of the society is an open question but what is beyond doubt is that Bangladeshi society has not embraced the debate with an open mind. State patronage since independence has created the environment for a heightened role of religion in politics; consequently Islamists have gained prominence after 1976. This can be described as 'Islamization from above'. The expedient politics of the secularists must be credited for expanding the space. Changes in global politics since 1979 were conducive to the religio-political forces too. Discursive practices in Bangladeshi politics have changed so much in the past three decades that use of religion cannot be exclusively associated with the Islamists anymore. The status of Islam as a state religion in the constitution is a case in point: JP introduced it, BNP maintained it, AL explicitly reinstated it through the fifteenth amendment. The presence of religion in the debate on national identity has contributed to the reemergence of religion in the political arena, although identity issue and the state–religion relationship should have remained separate. History aside, the democratic principles do not allow exclusion of particular ideological forces from the political scene. Therefore, as efforts to expand the democratic space were made and political pluralism was preferred, the presence of religio-political parties became justified.

The most disconcerting development in the recent past is the high degree of polarization, divisiveness and the emergence of an environment of intolerance. The three issues I mentioned – democracy, national identity and the role of religion in politics – have become wedge issues dividing the nation down the middle. Of course, these issues cannot be resolved for good; nations face these questions at different turns of history; but the democratic process should allow them to be debated rather than used as tools to fragment the nation. It is natural to have competing ideas, ideologies and tendencies in a society at any point of time. People engage in contestations, finds ways to accommodate and learn how to coexist. In the course of nation or state building an issue or some issues take precedence, some remain unsettled. As the nation matures citizens of the country and the state gradually address those unresolved issues.

One of the issues that has stoked tension and division within the society is the International Crimes Tribunal (ICT), which is meant to try those who had perpetrated crimes against humanity in 1971. This must be viewed as a quest for justice, therefore it is no different from efforts to hold war criminals accountable elsewhere, such as in Cambodia, Rwanda and the former Yugoslavia. Those who have committed war crimes must be brought to justice, for the sake of the rule of law and as a step towards ending the culture of impunity. Bangladesh needs emotional closure. While there were individual victims who lost their lives and dignity, the trials are needed for delivering justice to the nation as an entity. It should allow the country to move on from its bloody birth. The process demanded that it be above partisan interests. The opposition's endeavour to save particular individuals and party leaders from the process, engage in wanton violence to stop the trials, and the regime's efforts to capitalize on the popular demand for the trials for party interests have done a disservice to the spirit of the justice. The regime and its supporters have often conflated the discussions on inadequacies and shortcomings in the process and procedures of the trials with the opposition to the trial and its spirit, and often they speciously termed those criticisms as support for those who perpetrated the heinous crimes. These too have not helped the process to be perceived as fair, non-vindictive and just at home and abroad.

With the rise of the Hefazat-e-Islam (HI) in 2013, attacks on personal faith have become a new norm in contesting ideas and opinions of individuals. Islamists and orthodox Islamic leaders with the explicit support of the BNP branded the organizers of the Shahbagh movement and by extension those who support them atheists and apostates. Such characterization blurred the line between personal faith and political ideology of individuals. Since then the political discourse has often centred on the religious credentials of targeted individuals. On the other hand, activists of the Shahbagh movement have frequently questioned the patriotism of its critics by suggesting that they are opposed to the 'spirit of liberation struggle'. Cooptation of the movement by the ruling party and the use of similar verbiage by the party leaders and cabinet members contributed to an unwarranted schism within the society.

These kinds of brandings, particularly when faith and patriotism become suspect, generate a feeling of enmity. In the process, a valuable lesson was lost that disagreements with one do not make him/her an enemy. To view political differences as enmity and depriving the opponents of their fundamental rights or adopting violence to resolve those differences engender a culture of intolerance that is injurious to the nation. As various tendencies, ideas and ideologies came to a head, it appeared that proponents of both postions have taken the path of destruction – of the other and of themselves.

The question then is: what needs to be done to break away from the past and create a better future? It is evident that issues of democracy, governance, inequality, corruption, accountability, and the obligation to judiciously address war crimes remain the challenges in front of the nation. One cannot be achieved at the expense of the other. In the coming years and decades Bangladeshi citizens and their leaders have to chart a course which will create an inclusive political and economic system which upholds the spirit of the liberation war articulated in the proclamation of independence: equality, human dignity and justice. These are the *raisons d'être* of Bangladesh. Given the history of the past 45 years and the current state of politics, one can say this is a tall order. I am not suggesting that it is an easy task, nor can these be achieved overnight. But a country with a 30 per cent youth population (10–24 years) cannot simply continue with reactive politics for ever; it is imperative that a new form of politics emerges that connects the essence and ideals of the liberation war to the future through an inclusive political system with rule of law and provisions of both economic and social justice.

APPENDICES

Appendix 1

Voter Turnout: 1973–2008

Year	Population	Registered voters	Total votes cast	Voter turnout, percentage of registered voters
2008	151,289,991	81,130,973	69,172,649	85.26 per cent
2001	134,477,534	74,946,364	56,185,707	74.97 per cent
1996	122,978,000	56,716,935	42,880,564	75.60 per cent
1991	109,880,000	62,181,743	34,477,803	55.45 per cent
1988	104,532,000	49,863,829	25,832,858	51.81 per cent
1986	101,673,000	47,876,979	28,873,540	60.31 per cent
1979	86,643,000	38,363,858	19,676,124	51.29 per cent
1973	73,210,000	35,205,642	19,329,683	54.91 per cent

Source: International Institute for Democracy and Electoral Assistance (International IDEA), Stockholm, 'Voter Turnout Data for Bangladesh', available at: http://www.idea.int/vt/country_view.cfm?CountryCode=BD (accessed 22 December 2011).

Appendix 2

Election Results: 1973

Party	Votes	%	Seats
Bangladesh Awami League	13,798,717	73	293
National Awami Party NAP (Muzaffar)	1,569,299	8	0
Jatiyo Samajtantrik Dal (JSD)	1,229,110	7	5
National Awami Party (NAP, Bhashani)	1,002,771	5	0
Communist Party of Bangladesh (CPB)	989,884	4	1
Independents	199,673	1	1
Invalid/blank votes	477,875	–	–
Total	19,329,683	100	300

Source: Bangladesh Election Commission.

Appendix 3

Elections Results: 1979–88

Party	1979 Votes	%	Seats	1986 Votes	%	Seats	1988 Votes	%	Seats
Bangladesh Nationalist Party	7,934,236	41.2	207						
Bangladesh Awami League	4,734,277	24.5	54	7,462,157	26.2	76			
Bangladesh Muslim League	1,941,394	10.1	5	412,765	1.4	4			
Jatiyo Samajtantrik Dal	931,851	4.8	8						
Bangladesh Awami League (Mizan)	535,426	2.8	2						
National Awami Party (Muzaffar)	432,514	2.2	1	202,520	0.7	2			
Bangladesh Gono Front	115,622	0.6	2						
Bangladesh Samyabadi Dal (Marxist-Leninst)	74,771	0.4	1						
Bangladesh Jatiya League	69,319	0.4	2						
Jatiya Ekata Party	44,459	0.2	1						
Bangladesh Ganatantrik Andolan	34,259	0.2	1						
Communist Party of Bangladesh	930,581	4.8	8	259,728	0.9	5			
Jatiya Party				12,079,259	42.3	153	17,680,133	68.4	251
Jamaat-e-Islami Bangladesh				1,314,057	4.6	10			
National Awami Party (Muzaffar)				369,824	1.3	5			
Jatiyo Samajtantrik Dal (Siraj)				248,705	0.9	3	309,666	1.2	3

	Votes	%	Seats	Votes	%	Seats	Votes	%	Seats
Bangladesh Krishak Sramik Awami League				191,107	0.7	3			
Workers Party of Bangladesh				151,828	0.5	3			
Bangladesh Freedom Party							850,284	3.3	2
Combined Opposition Party							3,263,340	12.6	19
Bangladesh Khilafat Andolon							242,571	0.9	
Jatiya Samajtantrik Dal (Rab)				725,303	2.5	4			
Independents	1,963,345	10.2	11	4,619,025	16.3	32	3,487,457	16.3	7
Invalid/blank votes	402,524	–	–	377,209	–	–	335,620		
Total	19,676,124	100	300	28,903,859	100	300	26,169,071	100	300

Source: Bangladesh Election Commission.

Appendix 4

Bangladesh Election: 1991–2001

Party	1991			1996			2001		
	Votes	%	Seats	Votes	%	Seats	Votes	%	Seats
Bangladesh Nationalist Party	10,507,549	30.8	140	14,255,986	33.6	116	23,074,714	41.40	193
Bangladesh Awami League	10,259,866	30.1	88	15,882,792	37.4	146	22,310,276	40.02	62
Jamaat-e-Islami Bangladesh	4,136,461	12.1	18	3,653,013	8.6	3	2,385,361	4.28	17
Jatiya Party (Ershad)							4,023,962	7.22	14
Jatiya Party (Manju)							243,617	0.44	1
Jatiya Party (Naziur)							521,472	0.94	4
Jatiya Party	4,063,537	11.9	35	6,954,981	16.4	32			
Bangladesh Krishak Sramik Awami League	616,014	1.8	5						
Communist Party of Bangladesh	407,515	1.2	5						
Islami Oikkya Jote	269,434	0.8	1	461,517	1.1	1	312,868	0.56	2
National Awami Party (Muzaffar)	259,978	0.8	1						
Ganatantri Party	152,529	0.4	1						
National Democratic Party	121,918	0.4	1						
Jatiyo Samajtantrik Dal (Siraj)	84,276	0.2	1						
Jatiyo Samajtantrik Dal (Rab)				97,916	0.2	1			
Krishak Sramik Janata League							261,344	0.47	2

	Votes	%	Seats	Votes	%	Seats
Workers Party of Bangladesh	63,434	0.2	1			
74 other parties				662,451	1.6	0
Vacant						2
Non-partisan and others				2,262,045	4.06	6
63 other parties	1,663,834	4.9	0			
Independents	1,497,369	4.4	3	449,618	1.1	1
Rejected votes				441,871		
Total votes				56,169,233		
Registered voters				74,951,319		
Invalid/blank votes	374,026			462,302		

Source: Bangladesh Election Commission.

Appendix 5

Election Results: 2008

Party	Alliance	Votes	%	Seats
Bangladesh Awami League	Grand Alliance	33,887,451	49	230
Jatiya Party	Grand Alliance	4,867,377	7	27
Jatiyo Samajtantrik Dal	Grand Alliance	429,773	0.6	3
Workers Party of Bangladesh	Grand Alliance	214,440	0.3	2
Liberal Democratic Party	Grand Alliance	161,372	0.2	1
Bangladesh Nationalist Party	Four Party Alliance	22,963,836	33.2	30
Jamaat-e-Islami Bangladesh	Four Party Alliance	3,186,384	4.6	2
Bangladesh Jatiya Party (BJP)	Four Party Alliance	95,158	0.1	1
Islami Oikya Jote	Four Party Alliance			
Independent and others		3,366,858	4.9	4
Total		69,172,649	99.99	300

Appendix 6

Election Results: 2014

Party	Votes	%	Seats
Awami League	36,173,883	79.14	234
Jatiya Party	5,167,698	11.31	34
Workers Party	939,581	2.06	6
Jatiyo Samajtantrik Dal	798,644	1.75	5
Jatiya Party (Manju)		0.30	2
Bangladesh Tarikat Federation		0.30	2
Bangladesh Nationalist Front		0.30	1
Independents		4.70	15
Repoll ordered	–	–	1
Invalid/blank votes	1,551,585	–	–
Total	47,262,168	100.00	300
Registered voters/turnout	92,007,113	51.37	–

Source: Bangladesh Election Commission and IFES Election Guide.

Appendix 7

Islamists' Share of Votes: 1991–2001

Party	1991			1996			2001		
	Seats Won	Number of Votes	%	Seats Won	Number of Votes	%	Seats Won	Number of Votes	%
Jamaat	18	4,130,000	12.13	3	3,640,000	8.61	17	2,380,000	4.29
IOJ	1	260,000	0.79	1	460,000	1.09	2	370,000	0.68
Khelafat Andolan	0	93,049	0.27	–	–		–	–	
Zaker Party	0	417,737	1.22	–	–		–	–	

Appendix 8

Islamists' Share of Popular Votes: 2008

Name of The Party	No of Candidates	Votes Secured	Percentage of Cast Votes
Jammat-e-Islami Bangladesh	40	3,160,000	4.48
Islami Andolan Bangladesh (Bangladesh Islamic Movement, BIM)	166	733,969	1.05
Jamiat-e-Ulama-e-Islam Bangladesh	6	173,633	0.25
Zaker Party	36	129,289	0.19
Islami Oikya Jote	4	108,415	0.16
Bangladesh Islami Front	17	31,450	0.05
Bangladesh Khelafat Majlish	9	28,546	0.04
Bangladesh Tarikat Federation	31	19,750	0.03
Bangladesh Khelafat Andolan	30	13,759	0.02
Total			6.27

Source: '25 small parties get 2pc votes in total', *Daily Star*, 2 January 2009, p. 1, available at: http://www.thedailystar.net/story.php?nid=69670.

Appendix 9

Jatiya Party (JP) Fragmentation

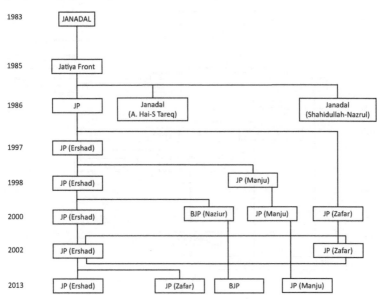

Appendix 10

Jaya Samajtantrik Dal (JSD) Fragmentation

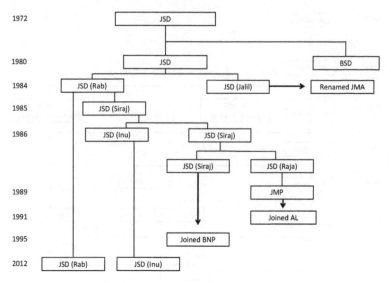

Appendix 11

Communist Party of Bangladesh (CPB) Fragmentation

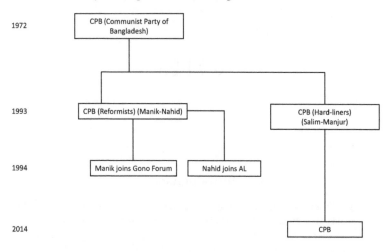

NOTES

Introduction

1. The estimates of deaths during the war vary; the Bangladeshi official number stands at 3 million, M. A. Hasan, a researcher on Bangladesh genocide and Convener of the War Crimes Facts Finding Committee, suggests 'nearly 1.8 million' people were killed (M. A. Hasan, 'Discovery of Numerous Mass Graves, Various Types of Torture on Women' and 'People's Attitude', paper presented at Keane University conference on Bangladesh Genocide, Bangladesh Genocide Study Group at Keane University, http://www.kean.edu/~bgsg/Conference09/Papers_and_Presentations/MA_Hasan_Paper_Discovery%20of%20numerous%20Mass%20Graves,%20Various%20types.pdf. Rudolph J. Rummel suggests the number of 1.5 million (Rudolph J. Rummel, *Statistics of Democide: Genocide and Mass Murder since 1900*, Munster: Lit Verlag, 1998, p. 155). Pakistani officials claim 26,000 civilian casualties. The number varies because of the methods used to calculate. In recent years, scholars have agreed that the number of deaths should not only include those who were killed by the perpetrators of the crime but also those who lost their lives due to the atrocities which forced them to relocate. In any genocide situation millions are displaced and die during their journey to safe havens, and in refugee camps. There is no accurate account of how many people died while fleeing Bangladesh and in the Indian refugee camps.
2. Archar K. Blood, *The Cruel Birth of Bangladesh – Memoirs of an American Diplomat* (Dhaka: University Press Limited, 2013).
3. Ibid.
4. World Bank, 'The Bangladesh Conundrum,' 2006 http://web.worldbank.org/WBSITE/EXTERNAL/EXTABOUTUS/EXTANNREP/EXTANNREP2K6/0,,contentMDK:21052781~pagePK:64168445~piPK:64168309~theSitePK:2838572,00.html.

5. Basharat Hossain, 'Poverty Reduction during 1971–2013 Periods: Success and its Recent Trends in Bangladesh', *Global Journal of Human-Social Science: E; Economics*; 14 (5), 2014, pp. 39–47.
6. World Bank, 'Bangladesh', 2014, http://data.worldbank.org/country/bangladesh.
7. Wahiduddin Mahmud, 'Social Development: Pathways, Surprises and Challenges', *Indian Journal of Human Development*, January–June, 2 (1): 79–92, 2008.
8. Moniruzzaman Uzzal, 'Bangladesh racing to achieve MDG on maternal mortality,' *Dhaka Tribune*, 28 May 2014, available at http://www.dhakatribune.com/development/2014/may/28/bangladesh-racing-achieve-mdg-maternal-mortality {accessed on 22 March 2016}.
9. Unicef, 'Bangladesh', available at http://www.unicef.org/infobycountry/bangladesh_bangladesh_statistics.html {accessed 22 March 2016}.
10. World Bank, 'Mortality Rate, infant, (per 1,000 live births)', available at http://data.worldbank.org/indicator/SP.DYN.IMRT.IN {accessed on 22 March 2016}.
11. Ernest Renan, 'What is a Nation?' in Geoff Eley and Ronald Grigor Suny, ed. *Becoming National: A Reader* (New York and Oxford: Oxford University Press, 1996), pp. 41–55.
12. Andrea Cassani, 'Hybrid what? The contemporary debate on hybrid regimes and the identity question', paper presented at 26th Congress of Italian Society of Political Science (SISP), 13–15 September 2012.

Chapter 1   Making of the Nation, Making of the State: Nationalism and Mobilization

1. Benedict Anderson, *Imagined Communities: Reflections on the Origin and Spread of Nationalism*. Revised Edition (London and New York: Verso, 1991), pp. 5–7.
2. Anthony Smith, *Ethnic Origins of Nations* (New York: Oxford University Press, 1986).
3. Fatma Muge Gocek, *Social Constructions of Nationalism in the Middle East* (New York: SUNY Press, 2002).
4. Elie Kedourie, *Nationalism* (London: Hutchinson, 1996); Gauri Viswanathan, *Masks of Conquest: Literary Studies and British Rule in India* (New York: Columbia University Press, 1989).
5. Partha Chatterjee, *Nationalist Thought and the Colonial World: The Derivative Discourse?* (London: Zed Books, 1986).
6. Pritish Acharya and Shri Krishan, 'An Experiment in Nationalist Education: Satyavadi School in Orissa (1909–26)', *Economic & Political Weekly* xlv/51 (2010), pp. 71–78.
7. Miroslav Hroch, 'From National Movement to the Fully-Formed Nation: The Nation-Building Process in Europe', *New Left Review* 198 (1993).
8. Homi Bhaba, 'Introduction: Narrating the Nation' in *Nation and Narration* (London: Routledge, 1990), pp. 1–7.
9. J. H. Broomfield, *Elite Conflict in a Plural Society: Twentieth-Century Bengal* (Berkeley & Los Angeles: University of California Press, 1968), p. 8.

10. Thomas Babington Macaulay, 'Minute on Education', in *Through Indian Eyes: The Living Tradition*, Donald J. Johnson, et al. (New York: CITE Books, 1992), p. 186.
11. Broomfield, *Elite Conflict in a Plural Society*, pp. 5–6.
12. Joya Chatterji, *Bengal Divided* (Cambridge: Cambridge University Press, 1994).
13. Government of Pakistan, Report of the Panel of Economists on the Fourth Five Year Plan, 1970–75, Islamabad; Planning Commission.
14. Khurrm Hossain, 'Why East & West Never Met', *Dawn*, 4 October 2012. http://beta.dawn.com/news/753999/why-east-west-never-met.
15. Constituent Assembly of Pakistan (CAP), *Debates*, 1 January, 1, 52, 1956.
16. Rounaq Jahan, *Bangladesh Politics: Problems and Issues* (Dhaka: University Press Limited, 1980).
17. For details of the economic deprivation and marginalization of the Bengali population from administrative and defense jobs, see Ali Riaz, *Unfolding State: The Transformation of Bangladesh* (Ontario, Canada: de Sitter Publications, 2005), pp. 43–49.
18. Nurul Islam, 'The Two Economies thesis: Road to the Six Points Programme'. *Daily Star*, 22 June 2014, p. 8, for details see Nurul Islam, *Bangladesh – Making of a Nation, An Economists Tale* (Dhaka: UPL, 2003). The ten authors of the report were:.
19. Anisuzzaman. 'Claiming and Disclaiming a Cultural Icon: Tagore in East Pakistan and Bangladesh'. *University of Toronto Quarterly* 77/4 (2008), pp. 1058–1069; http://muse.jhu.edu/ (accessed 21 September 2013).
20. Nurul Islam argues to the contrary: 'In popular perception and in a broad sense, the Six-Points Programme was a programme for autonomy of East Pakistan to allow a control over its foreign trade and exchange earnings, as well as over the government revenues and expenditures. The operational details and implications of its economic provisions, [...] were highly technical and were not and could not be so easily apparent/obvious to the non-experts that they meant in fact a very small step from independence' (Nurul Islam, Six-Points Programme or Independence? *Daily Star*, 26 March 2012. http://archive. thedailystar.net/newDesign/news-details.php?nid=227686.
21. Rehman Sobhan and Muzaffer Ahmad, *Public Enterprise in an Intermediate Regime, A Study in the Political Economy of Bangladesh* (Dhaka: Bangladesh Institute of Development Studies, 1980).
22. Stephan R. Lewis, *Pakistan, Industrialization and Trade Policies* (London: Oxford University Press, 1970).
23. Sobhan and Ahmad, *Public Enterprise in an Intermediate Regime, A Study in the Political Economy of Bangladesh*, pp. 61–62.
24. Long after the independence of Bangladesh, it was revealed that a 'conspiracy' to secede was hatched, although the conspirators had Sheikh Mujib's blessing but he was not directly involved (Shahida Begum, *Agartala Conspiracy Trial and Relevant Documents*, in Bengali, Dhaka: Bangla Academy, 2000). One of the

principal accused, Shawkat Ali, then an army captain who became the deputy speaker of the parliament in 2009, acknowledged this, saying, 'Until recently it was believed this case was a ploy to get rid of Sheikh Mujib, when in reality it was a case filed on very concrete and true accusations. We did conspire for secession of East Pakistan! The accusations were 100 per cent true' (in Conversation with Col (retd) Shawkat Ali, *Dhaka Courier*, 9 February 2012, http://www.dhakacourier.com.bd/?p=4749#sthash.QnrUhizU.dpuf).

25. *Time*, 'Pakistan: Prophet of Violence', *Time*, 18 April 1969.

26. Anthony D. Smith, 'Gastronomy or Geology? The Role of Nationalism in the Reconstruction of Nations', *Nations and Nationalism* 1/1 (1994), pp. 3–23.

27. Hossain, Kamal, 'Political Development in Bangladesh: Promise and Reality'. *Contributions to Asian Studies* XIV (1979), p. 103.

28. Bohanuddin Khan Jahangir, *Problematics of Nationalism in Bangladesh* (Dhaka; Center for Social Studies, 1986).

29. Mohammed Ayoob, 'Background and Developments', in *Bangladesh: A Struggle for Nationhood* (Delhi: Vikas Publications, 1971), p. 35.

30. *Guardian*, 'New order in Pakistan', 9 December 1970, p. 1, available at http://www.theguardian.com/theguardian/2010/dec/09/archive-karachi-bhutto-vote-1970.

31. Theda Skocpol, *States and Social Revolutions: A Comparative Analysis of France, Russia and China* (Cambridge: Cambridge University Press, 1979).

32. These conditions were: 1. The martial law has to be lifted; 2. The soldiers must return to the barracks; 3. A public enquiry into the incidents of massacre by the armed forces has to be conducted; 4. Power must be transferred to the elected representatives.

33. David Ludden, 'The Politics of Independence in Bangladesh', *Economic and Political Weekly*, XXXVI 35/27 (2011), pp. 79–85.

34. Ibid., p. 84.

35. US Department of State (USDS), *Foreign Relations of the United States, 1969–1976, Volume XI, South Asia Crisis, 1971*, Document 2, available at National Archives, Nixon Presidential Materials, NSC Files, Box 625, Country Files, Middle East, Pakistan, Vol. IV, 1 Mar 71–15 May 71.

36. Kamal Hossain, 'Interview' in *History of Bangladesh War of Independence: Documents*, Vol. 15 edited by Hasan Hafizur Rahman (Dhaka: Ministry of Information, Government of the People's Republic of Bangladesh), 1985, p. 278.

37. Siddiq Salik, *Witness to Surrender* (New York: Oxford University Press, 1997), pp. 39–40, 62, 228–234.

38. Government of Bangladesh (GOB), *History of Bangladesh War of Independence: Documents*, Vol. 3 edited by Hasan Hafizur Rahman, Dhaka: Ministry of Information, Government of the People's Republic of Bangladesh), 1985, p. 1.

39. Sharmin Ahmed, Tajuddin Ahmed: Neta O Pita (Tajuuddin Ahmed: Leader and Father, in Bengali), Dhaka: Oitijjho, 2014, p. 147.

40. A. K. Khondker, *Bhetore Bhaire 1971 [Inside and Outside, 1971]*, Dhaka: Prothoma, 2014);.

41. Simon Dring, 'Tanks Crush Revolt in Pakistan,' *Daily Telegraph*, 30 March 1971; Howard Whitten, 'When Tank Took Over the Talking', *The Age* (Melbourne), 29 March 1971.

42. Roberts Payne, *Massacre* (New York: McMillan, 1973), pp. 22–23.

43. Sydney H. Schanberg, 'He tells full story of arrest and detention,' *New York Times*, 18 January 2971, p. A1.

44. New York Times, 'Leader of rebels in east Pakistan reported seized', 27 March 1971, p. 1.

45. *The Age*, 'Pakistan Tragedy', 29 March 1971, p. 14.

46. Quoted in Mashuqur Rahman and Mahbubur Rahman Jalal, 'Swadhin Bangla Betar Kendro and Bangladesh's Declaration of Independence' *Forum*, March 2008, http://archive.thedailystar.net/forum/2008/march/declaration.htm.

47. A copy of the DIA report is available at: http://cbgr1971.org/files/Mar261971 DecOfIndep/DeclarationSMRcbgr02.pdf.

48. Interestingly, the claim that Ziaur Rahman should be credited for the declaration of the independence was not pushed until his death in 1980. Zia's reminiscences, published in 1972 didn't highlight this aspect. Instead he maintained that Sheikh Mujib's speech on 7 March 1971 was considered by him as the green signal for the liberation war.

49. Indian Ministry of Defence, Official history of the 1971 India-Pakistan War' New Delhi: History Division, Ministry of Defence, Government of India, 1992, p. 93. Available at http://www.bharat-rakshak.com/LAND-FORCES/ History/1971War/280-War-History-1971.html.

50. Jyoti Sen Gupta, *History of Freedom Movement in Bangladesh, 1943–1973, Some Involvement* (Calcutta: Naya Prakash), 1974, pp. 325–26.

51. Zahir Alam Khan, *The Way It Was: Inside the Pakistan Army*, Karachi: DYNAVIS Ltd., 1998). For an excerpt of the book, see: http://www. defencejournal.com/sept98/wayitwas1.htm.

52. Howard Whitten, 'Army Takeover', *Sydney Morning Herald*, 29 March 1971.

53. Tajuddin Ahmed, 'First On Air Speech (Broadcast By Swadhin Bangla Betar Kendra) Of Prime Minister Tajuddin Ahmad, Addressing The Nation, On Behalf Of The Government Of Bangladesh Headed By President Sheikh Mujibur Rahman.' 10 April 1971 (Bengali Text is available at http://www. tajuddinahmad.com/resources/speech1.pdf.

54. This contentious issue reached the Supreme Court via a writ petition in 2009 and the court opined that any document contrary to the claim that Mujib declared independence is untrue.

55. For details see Muyeedul Hasan, *Muldhara Ekattar [The Main Trends]* (1971, in Bengali) (Dhaka: University Press Limited, 1986); and Amirul Islam, 'Interview' in *History of Bangladesh War of Independence: Documents*, Vol. 15 edited by Hasan

NOTES TO PAGES 33-36

Hafizur Rahman (Dhaka: Ministry of Information, Government of the People's Republic of Bangladesh), 1985, 77–163. Hasan, *Muldhara Ekattar*, pp. 146–47, reports that a faction led by Sheikh Fazlul Hoq Moni, nephew of Sheikh Mujibur Rahman and a youth leader, attempted to assassinate Tajuddin Ahmed sometime in October 1971.

56. Sometime between August and October of 1971 the United States attempted to contact the Bangladesh government in exile through Harold Saunders of the National Security Council and George Griffin of the US consulate at Calcutta to bring an end to the conflict. A section of AL leaders under the leadership of Khandaker Mustaque Ahmad, foreign minister of the government-in-exile, favoured such negotiations and established contact, which was later foiled by the pro-independence leaders (for details see Ali Riaz, 'Beyond the 'Tilt': US Initiatives to Dissipate Bangladesh Movement in 1971', *History Compass*, 3, 2005; Muyeedul Hasan, *Muldhara Ekattar* ([*The Main Trends*] 1971, in Bengali) (Dhaka: University Press Limited, 1986), pp. 94–102; Rashid A. Chowdhury, 'United States Foreign Policy in South Asia: The Liberation Struggle in Bangladesh and the Indo-Pakistan War of 1971', unpublished PhD Dissertation, Department of History. University of Hawaii. 1989, 155–170; Henry Kissinger, *The White House Years* (Boston: Brown and Company, 1979), pp. 869–73.

57. The following description of the conflict within the AL during the liberation struggle is drawn from two sources, Hasan (1986) and Islam (1985). It is worth noting that both Hasan and Islam worked closely with the government in exile. Islam, an Awami Leaguer, was the person with whom Tajuddin Ahmed crossed the border. Later, Islam was appointed as the principal aide of the PM of the government in exile. Hasan, a close friend of Tajuddin Ahmed, joined him on 5 May and later became the principal emissary of the government in dealing with the Indian counterpart.

58. A. M. A. Muhith, *Emergence of a New Nation* (Dhaka: Bangladesh Books International, 1978).

59. The meeting was attended by a number of army officers including Colonel M. A. G. Osmany, Lieutanant Colonel Abdur Rab, Lieutenant Colonel Salehuddin Muhammed Reza, Major Kazi Nuruzzaman, Major Ziaur Rahman, Major Khaled Mosharraf, Major Shafiullah, Major Nurul Islam, Major Shafaat Jamil, and Major Mainul Hossain Chowdhury.

60. Abu Sayeed, *Bangladesher Swadhinata Judhyeir Arale Judhya* [*War Behind the Bangladesh Independence War*], in Bengali (Dhaka: Sarif Ahmed, 1989).

61. Hasan, *Muldhara Ekattar*, p. 61; Sayeed, *Bangladesher Swadhinata Judhyeir Arale Judhya*, p. 158.

62. Hasan, *Muldhara Ekattar*, p. 54.

63. Islam, 'Interview', p. 103.

64. According to the Hamoodur Rahman Commission, a Pakistani judicial commission appointed in 1972, 'to prepare a full and complete account of the circumstances surrounding the atrocities and 1971 war', about 90,368 were

made Prisoners of War (POWs), including 54,154 Army soldiers, 1,381 Navy personnel, 833 Air force staff, paramilitary including police personnel consisted 22,000, and 12,000 civilians government employees and their dependents from West Pakistan.

Chapter 2   The Rise and the Demise of Authoritarianism (1972–90)

1. World Bank, *Reconstructing the Economy of Bangladesh*, Vol. I and Vol. II (Washington DC: WB, 1972).
2. Muyeedul, Hasan, *Muldhara Ekattar [The Main Trends]* (1971, in Bengali) (Dhaka: University Press Limited, 1986), pp. 327–30.
3. Government of the People's Republic of Bangladesh, Memo No. 391(8)/Cab, dated 25 November 1971.
4. Government of the People's Republic of Bangladesh, Establishment Division, Memo No. Estbt. Dvn./3179(19), dated 16 December 1971.
5. In order to deal with the state of the bureaucracy in early 1972, we should describe, in brief, its structure during the Pakistan period. In Pakistan, Government services were classified under different categories: Class I, II, III, and IV. According to prestige and privileges, there were gazetted and non-gazetted officers. All the top administrative positions were filled by the Central Superior Servants who were selected by the Central Public Service Commission of the Government of Pakistan. The Central Superior Service was divided into several branches: 1. Civil Service; 2. Foreign Service; 3. Police Service; 4. Taxation Service; 5. Audit and Account Service; 6. Postal Service; 7. Controller of Exports and Imports. Among all these services, the officers belonging to the civil service occupied the most important administrative and executive positions. With enormous power in their hands they virtually controlled the entire administration. In addition, there was another provincial service known as EPCS (East Pakistan Civil Service) whose members occupied the subordinate and less important positions in the provincial administration.
6. A fourth group emerged in 1973 – officials who were stranded in Pakistan during the war. They were repatriated in August and subsequently the issue of the stranded Bengali bureaucrats became prominent.
7. A. K. Azad, 'The Saga of Bangladesh Army', *Weekly Holiday*, 1972.
8. United Nations, Ambassador Ema Sailor's Report of High-Level UN Consultants to Bangladesh. Vol. 1, March–April, Mimeograph (New York: United Nations, 1972).
9. Marcus Franda, *Bangladesh: The First Decade* (New Delhi: South Asian Publishers, 1982), p. 29.
10. Rehman Sobhan, *The Crisis of External Dependence, The Political Economy of Foreign Aid to Bangladesh* (Dhaka: University Press Limited, 1982), p. 7. According to the IBRD, in 1969/70, $320 million was disbursed in the then

East Pakistan: *Bangladesh: Development in Rural Economy*, Vol. 1, Washington DC: IBRD. 1974).

11. Kamal Hossain, *Bangladesh: Quest for Freedom and Justice* (Dhaka: University Press Limited, 2013), p. 125.

12. Private Pakistani citizens left 725 industrial enterprises with assets worth Tk. 2885.7 million. These companies controlled 47 per cent of Bangladesh's modern industrial assets and 71 per cent of its private industry. They relinquished six of the leading commercial banks which controlled 70 per cent of the deposits of the entire banking system in the region and also the insurance companies that constituted 90 per cent of the assets of insurance business.

13. Bangladesh Planning Commission (BPC), 'Policy Options and Recommendations for the Nationalization of the Industries', Mimeograph (Dhaka: Bangladesh Planning Commission, 1972).

14. Rehman Sobhan and Muzaffer Ahmad, *Public Enterprise in an Intermediate Regime, A Study in the Political Economy of Bangladesh* (Dhaka: Bangladesh Institute of Development Studies, 1980), p. 142. A total of 254 large industrial units (jute, textile, sugar, iron and steel, engineering and shipbuilding, fertilizer, pharmaceutical and chemical, oil, gas and mineral, paper and paper products, and forest industries combined) were nationalized. Additionally, 12 commercial banks with 1,175 branches all over the country and 12 insurance companies were brought into the public sector. About 80 per cent of trade was now concentrated in the hands of public sector trading corporations. Following nationalization, the economic picture reflected the state's central position: ten corporations had been set up to manage the nationalized industries; many commercial banks were organized into six nationalized banks; the insurance business was brought under the purview of two insurance companies; in order to meet the special needs of different sectors, such as agriculture, housing, and industry, four specialized financial institutions had been set up; and a trading corporation was established for controlling import business. Finally, three corporations were set up to steer the jute business. All of these together transformed the state into the largest economic enterprise by far.

15. These two lines of argument are not mutually exclusive and analysts do not cancel out one in favour of the other. For example, Sobhan and Ahmad (1980); Islam (Nurul Islam *Development Planning in Bangladesh, A Study in Political Economy* (London: C. Hurst and Company, 1977); and M. M. Akash, *Bangladesher Arthaniti O Rajniti, Sampratik Probonotasamuha*, Bangladesh Economy and Politics, Recent Trends, in Bengali (Dhaka: Jatiyo Shahittyo Prokashani, 1987, maintain that both circumstantial necessity and the ideological commitment of the AL were factors in the nationalization programme. Akash (1987), however, emphasized the ideological aspects, while Khan and Hossain (Azizur Rahman Khan and Mahbub Hossain, *The Strategy of Development of Bangladesh* (London: Macmillan, 1989)) find

nothing in the history of the AL to suggest that the party was implementing socialism and that nationalization was a step towards that end. A radical interpretation, advanced by Umar (Badruddin Umar, *Towards the Emergency* (Dhaka: Muktadhara. 1980)), suggests that nationalization was a sinister move of the AL to discredit socialism and pave the way for the development of a comprador bourgeoisie.

16. By 1972, there were 20 private industrial enterprises owned by foreign companies: 16 of them were pharmaceutical companies, while four others include the Bangladesh Tobacco Company, Lever Brothers, Bangladesh Oxygen and Pakistan Fibers. There were two branches of foreign-owned banks (which accounted for 8.41 per cent of deposits at the time of nationalization) and 33 tea estates were owned by the British. None of these were nationalized. Bengali private enterprise in the tea industry, though quite significant, was also spared from nationalization. According to Bangladesh Tea Board estimates, after March 1972, about 27.25 per cent of the acreage of tea estates was under the control of Bangladesh nationals, accounting for about 19.4 per cent of the output.

17. Swadesh Ranjan Bose, 'The Price Situation in Bangladesh', *The Bangladesh Economic Review* 1/3 (1974), p. 244.

18. Nurul Islam, *Development Strategy of Bangladesh* (London: C. Hurst & Company, 1978), p. 4.

19. Government of the People's Republic of Bangladesh (GPRB), *Memorandum for the Bangladesh Consortium, 1974–75* (Dhaka: Planning Commission, 1974), p. 9.

20. Kamal Hossain, a prominent AL leader and then minister of law and constitutional affairs, described the situation as follows: 'The radicals had urged that the freedom fighters, instead of being disbanded, should have formed the nucleus of 'the party of revolution' headed by Sheikh Mujib. The party could then have led a 'class struggle' within the framework of a one-party system, and thus taken society forward towards the goal of social revolution' (Hossain 1979:107; Kamal Hossain. 'Political Development in Bangladesh: Promise and Reality.' *Contributions to Asian Studies* Vol. XIV, 1979).

21. The ruling party envisaged that it could either pursue a politics of consensus or a politics of class conflict. Hossain (1979:107) recalls that: 'the alternative that had presented itself to the politics of 'class struggle' was the politics of 'consensus'. This policy would seek to accommodate all contending groups within the framework of the system. It was envisaged that the AL could continue to be a *de facto* one party, a coalition of contending factions, representing different tendencies, ranging from militant social revolutionaries on the left to conservative 'status quoists' on the right.

22. Sheikh Mujib's televised speech to the nation, 15 December 1974.

23. Ali Riaz, *Unfolding State: The Transformation of Bangladesh* (Ontario, Canada: de Sitter Publication, 2005), pp. 170–74.

24. The *Jatiyo Rakkhi Bahini Order, 1972* (President's Order no. 21 of 1972) was promulgated on 7 March 1972 with a retroactive effect from 1 February 1972.

25. Hossain, *Bangladesh: Quest for Freedom and Justice*, p. 127.
26. Moudud Ahmed, *Bangladesh: Era of Sheikh Mujibur Rahman* (Weisbadan: Franz Steiner Verlag, 1984), p. 56.
27. *The Jatiya Rakkhi Bahini (Amendment) Ordinance, 1973*, 30 October 1973, the changes were effective retroactively from the date of the establishment of the JRB.
28. *Mohsin Sharif vs the State*, 27 DLR, 1975 HC, p. 186, popularly known as the *Shahjahan Case* argued by Moudud Ahmed on behalf of the plaintiff in May 1974.
29. Ibid.
30. Tushar Kanti Barua, *Political Elite in Bangladesh* (Bern: Peter Lang, 1978), p. 168.
31. Quoted in Barua, *Political Elite*, p. 170.
32. *Gherao* is a political action of encirclement of a person or office to realize a demand.
33. Government of the People's Republic of Bangladesh (GPRB), *Economic Review 1974–75* (Dhaka: Planning Commission, 1975), p. 6.
34. Minister of Parliamentary Affairs, Jatiya Sangsad Debate (Parliamentary Debate), 3(4), 209 (Parliamentary Debate 1974, 209).
35. Betsy Hartman and James Boyce, 'Bangladesh: Aid to the Needy', *International Policy Report*, 4/1 (1978), p. 4.
36. The composition and function of the District Administrative Council was delineated in the *District Administration Act*, Act No. VI of 1975 and was approved by the parliament on 9 July 1975 (*The Bangladesh Gazette Extraordinary*, 10 July 1975). Subsequently 61 district governors were appointed by the president.
37. Ayesha Jalal, 'Constructing a State: The Interplay of Domestic, Regional and International Factors in Post-Colonial Pakistan', Colloquium Paper, Asia Program, Woodrow Wilson International Center for Scholars, Washington DC, 16 April 1986, p. 85.
38. Some of them subsequently denied their involvement.
39. Major Sarful Islam Dalim, for example, was discharged from the army on disciplinary grounds. It is alleged that his dismissal was a result of an untoward incident involving an Awami League leader. The story goes that Major Dalim's wife was insulted and intimidated by two sons of a close associate of Mujib, Gazi Golam Mostafa, in a social gathering. Following the incident, the Chief of Army Staff Major General Safiullah went to Mujib and placed the matter before him requesting action against those involved. Mujib, however, expressed his annoyance and later in August 1974 dismissed Dalim from the service.
40. Confidential Telegram from US Embassy, Dhaka to Department of State/ Secretary of State, 02158, 15 May 1974. Available at http://www.wikileaks.org/plusd/cables/1974DACCA02158_b.html.
41. Resignation Letter, Col. Abu Taher, Col Taher Organization, available at: http://www.col-taher.org/en/%e0%a6%94%e0%a6%aa%e0%a6%a8%e0%

a6%bf%e0%a6%ac%e0%a7%87%e0%a6%b6%e0%a6%bf%e0%a6%95-%
e0%a6%b8%e0%a7%87%e0%a6%a8%e0%a6%be%e0%a6%ac%e0%a6%
be%e0%a6%b9%e0%a6%bf%e0%a6%a8%e0%a7%80/%e0%a6%aa%e0%
a6%a6%e0%a6%a4%e0%a7%8d%e0%a6%af%e0%a6%be%e0%a6%97/.

42. Confidential Telegram from US Embassy, Dhaka to Department of State/ Secretary of State, 1973DACCA03156_ available at: http://www.wikileaks. org/plusd/cables/1973DACCA03156_b.html.

43. Confidential Telegram from US Embassy, Dhaka to Department of State/ Secretary of State, 02158, 15 May 1974. Available at http://www.wikileaks. org/plusd/cables/1974DACCA02158_b.html.

44. Office of Historian, Department of State, 'The Secretary's 8:00 a.m. Staff Meeting Friday, August 15, 1975', *Foreign Relations, 1969–1976, Volume E-8, Documents on South Asia, 1973–1976*, http://2001–2009.state.gov/docum ents/organization/97243.pdf.

45. Interview of coup makers Rashid and Farook with British journalist Anthony Mascarenhas on ITV, quoted in Inam Ahmed, 'Conspiracy hatched for the dark night', *Daily Star*, 19 November 2009. For details, also see Colonel Rashid, Colonel Farook. *The Road to Freedom* (Dhaka: Syed Ataur Rahman, 2008).

46. Another army officer, who later participated in the 3 November coup, revealed that he was approached by Farook in mid-March 1975 to help him move tanks to stage a coup. He declined and informed his superior officer (Major Nasir Uddin, *Gonotontrer Biponnodharay Bangladesher Shoshosro Bahini*. Dhaka: Agamee Prakashani. 1997, p. 59. Maj. Gen. Shafiullah, then Chief of Army Staff came to the conclusion that Zia was aware of the coup based on Ziaur Rahman's reaction on the morning of 15 August. For Safiullah's comment see his interview with *Weekly Jonomot*, published from London, 28 August and 3 September 1987. Safiullah was serving as the Bangladesh High Commissioner in UK during the time of this interview. In a personal interview in June 2000, Shafiullah maintained his position. However, Shafiullah's comment should be taken with great caution due to personal rivalry between them. For Shafiullah's version of the events of 15 August Coup see his interview with the *Daily Star*, 31 January 2010, http://archive. thedailystar.net/newDesign/news-details.php?nid=124155.

47. The involvement of this 'dubious trio', as they were called by their colleagues during the war of liberation, deserves special mention. During the liberation war while Mushtaq was serving as the Foreign Minister of the government in exile, Taheruddin Thakur was his special assistant and Chasi was the Foreign Secretary. All of them were seriously discontented with the leadership and were allegedly involved with the US move in mid-1971 to bring an end to the war. After independence Chasi was appointed vice chairman of the Bangladesh Academy of Rural Development (BARD), Mustaque and Thakur found positions in cabinet. Whether this 'trio' maintained their close connection with US intelligence and acted in 1975 as per their instruction remains a

mystery to date. If we take into account the presence of another character of this drama, in both places and at both times (i.e. in India in 1971 and in Bangladesh in 1975), the plausibility of a US role in the coup cannot be discounted altogether. The person is Philip Cherry, a senior CIA staff member. Cherry was in charge of the CIA station in New Delhi from June 1971 and took charge of the Dhaka station of the CIA in August 1974. There is however no hard evidence of US involvement.

48. Except Zia and Osmani, none of the new appointees had been involved in the liberation war. In fact, most of them had been associated with the Pakistan administration in different capacities. As more reshuffling in the administration took place, it became further evident that the once-ostracized pro-Pakistani bureaucrats were back in the driver's seat.

49. *The Indemnity Ordinance 1975* (Ordinance No. XLX of 1975) was promulgated 'to restrict the taking of any legal or other proceedings in respect of certain acts or things done in connection with, or in preparation or execution of any plan for, or steps necessitating, the historical change and the Proclamation of Martial Law on the morning of the 15th August, 1975' (*The Bangladesh Gazette Extraordinary*, 26 September 1975). The law remained in place until the AL came to power in 1996. On 12 November 1996, the parliament repealed the ordinance. This paved the way for the trial of those accused of killing Sheikh Mujibur Rahman.

50. Some analysts, for example Zillur Rahman Khan (1984), characterized this coup as a pro-Mujib coup. This interpretation is very common in Bangladesh. Some concurrent events and massive propaganda between November 4 and 7 against Khaled had helped to characterize the coup as such. The presence of Khaled's mother and a brother in a pro-Mujib demonstration on 4 November is one of the reasons why people believed it to be a pro-Mujib move. But I have found very little evidence to support this notion despite the fact that some Mujib loyalists were involved in the coup. Khaled himself was concerned with restoration of the chain of command in army.

51. Emajuddin Ahamed, *Military Rule and Myths of Democracy* (Dhaka: University Press Limited, 1988), p. 79.

52. A leaflet distributed by the Sangstha on 5 November contained a 12-point demand of the sepoys which included a call for changing the structure as well as functions of the army; abolition of colonial practices such as the Batman system; recognition of the Revolutionary Sainik Sangstha as the central policy-making body of the army and entrusting the supreme authority to this organization; immediate release of all political prisoners; confiscation of properties of all corrupt officials and individuals; ending discrimination between officers and sepoys in the armed forces; and increasing the salaries of sepoys.

53. The conflict between the soldiers and their officers spread to some other cantonments in subsequent days resulting in indiscriminate killings. In Rangpur cantonment more than 15 officers were killed on 8 November. Later it spread to

naval bases as well. It is reported that in an uprising in the Navy between 13 and 15 November, seven officials and 40 others were killed in Chittagong.

54. This is how the JSD later described Zia and justified their decision to bring Zia in the forefront (see *Sammyabad*, the underground party newsletter of the JSD, No. 4, 23 February 1976).

55. On 19 November 1976 the post of CMLA was handed over to Zia by Sayem in the 'national interest' through a Presidential Proclamation. Later on 21 April 1977 Sayem relinquished the office of president because of 'failing health' and Zia became president as well.

56. Karl Marx, 'Eighteenth Brumaire of Louis Bonaparte', in D Fernbach (ed.), *Karl Marx: Surveys From Exile, Political Writings*, Vol. 2 (Harmondsworth: Penguin, 1974), p. 236.

57. Ibid., p. 151.

58. G. H. Peiris, 'Political Conflict in Bangladesh', *Ethnic Studies Report* 16/1 (1998), p. 51.

59. Syed Serajul Islam, *Bangladesh: State and Economic Strategy* (Dhaka: University Press Limited, 1988), p. 121.

60. Franklin Vivekananda, 'Why Aid Does Not Work?' In Franklin Vivekananda (ed.), *Bangladesh Economy: Some Selected Issues* (Stockholm: Bethany Books, 1986), p. 324.

61. SIPRI. *SIPRI Yearbook 1981* (Oxford: Oxford University Press, 1981).

62. Talukdar Maniruzzaman, *Group Interests and Political Changes, Studies of Pakistan and Bangladesh* (New Delhi: South Asia Publishers, 1982), p. 203.

63. The terms 'disinvestment' and 'denationalization' are used here to refer to policy measures taken by the government towards what is commonly known as privatization. In the context of Bangladesh, in the industrial sector 'disinvestment refers to the process of selling off abandoned units through public tenders, while denationalization refers to the return of the units to their Bangladeshi former owners on administratively determined ground' (Sobhan and Ahmed, 1980:7).

64. A. M. A. Rahim, 'A Review of Industrial Investment Policy in Bangladesh, 1971–1977', *Asian Survey*, 18 (11), November 1978, p. 1185.

65. *New York Times*, 20 October 1977 quoted in Jérémie Codron, 'Putting Factions "Back in" the Civil-Military Relations Equation: Genesis, Maturation and Distortion of the Bangladeshi Army', *South Asia Multidisciplinary Academic Journal*, September 2007, http://samaj.revues.org/document230.html.

66. Douglas C. Makeig, 'National Security', in James Heitzman and Robert Worden, *Bangladesh: A Country Study* (Washington DC: Library of Congress, 1989), p. 241.

67. *New York Times*, 'Revolution Brings Bangladesh Hope', *New York Times*, 9 December 1990, p. A4.

68. Ibid.

69. *Le Monde* (Paris), 'Le président Ershad annonce une série de concessions', 5 December 1990.

Chapter 3   From Optimism to Retreat of Democracy (1991–2015)

1. Stanley Kochanek, 'Bangladesh in 1996: the 25th Year of Independence', *Asian Survey* 37 (2) (1997), pp. 136–42.
2. Harun-ur-Rashid, 'The Caretaker Conundrum', *Daily Star*, 28 June 2006, p. 6. For a contrasting argument see: Gyasuddin Molla, 'Democratic Institution Building Process in Bangladesh: South Asian Experience of a New Model of "Care-Taker Government" in a Parliamentary Framework', *Heidelberg Papers in South Asian and Comparative Politics*, Working Paper no 3 (Heidelberg: South Asia Institute, University of Heidelberg, 2000).
3. At the time of the 'failed coup' I was a broadcast journalist of the BBC World Radio Bengali service stationed in London which allowed me to gather information and follow the events closely. Subsequently I have interviewed a number of sources inside and outside the Bangladesh Army to piece together the series of events. Two books by General Nasim and by General Abdul Matin – have documented these events from conflicting perspectives as these officers were principal actors on opposing sides during this period. See, Abu Saleh Muhammad Nasim, *Ami Nasim Bolchi [I am Nasim Speaking]* (in Bengali) (Dhaka: Columbia Prokashani, 2001); Abdul Matin, *Amar Dekha Barthya Sena Abhuythan [The Abortive Coup of 1996, As I Saw it]* (Dhaka: Gyan Bitoroni, 2001).
4. Howard B. Schaffer, 'Back and Forth in Bangladesh', *Journal of Democracy* 13/1 (2002), pp. 76–83.
5. Ali Riaz, *God Willing: The Politics of Islamism in Bangladesh* (Lanham, MD: Rowman and Littlefield, 2004).
6. A cable from the US Embassy in Dhaka to the State Department on 10 January 2007 states, 'We have declined to be drawn into a discussion of the constitutionality of holding or postponing the election, emphasizing instead that the problem is political in nature and can only be solved if the two parties agree. We stress to both sides the damage done to Bangladesh's economic status and democracy by the parties' refusal to compromise' (Cable 07DHAKA53, http://www.cablegatesearch.net/cable.php?id=07DHAKA53).
7. Somini Sengupta, 'Bangladesh Leader Declares Emergency', *New York Times*, 11 January 2007, http://www.nytimes.com/2007/01/11/world/asia/11cnd-bengla.html?_r=2&scp = 1&sq = &; Faiz Ahmed Chowdhury, 'Geo-politics, Democratization and External Influence: The Bangladesh Case', IGS Working Paper Series No: 05/2013, Published by the Institute of Governance Studies, BRAC University, March 2013; Nurul Islam, 'The Army, UN Peacekeeping Mission and Democracy in Bangladesh', *Economic and Political Weekly* XLV/29 (2010).
8. UNDP, *Elections in Bangladesh 2006–2009: Transforming Failure into Success* (Dhaka: UNDP, 2010).

9. Jalal Alamgir, 'Bangladesh's Fresh Start', *Journal of Democracy*, 20(3), July 2009, p. 48.

10. *Economist*, 'No Going Back', 19 April 2007, http://www.economist.com/node/9052421.

11. *Economist*, 'Not Uniformly Bad', 8 February 2007, http://www.economist.com/node/8668962.

12. Alamgir, 'Bangladesh's Fresh Start,' p. 51.

13. Farid Ahmed, '152 soldiers sentenced to die for mutiny in Bangladesh', CNN, 5 November 2013, http://www.cnn.com/2013/11/05/world/asia/bangladesh-soldiers-death-sentence/index.html.

14. *Financial Times* (Dhaka), '5th Amendment of Constitution: SC upholds HC verdict with certain modifications', 29 July 2010, http://www.thefinancialexpress-bd.com/more.php?news_id=107484&date = 2010-07-29. For full text of the verdict, see: http://www.dwatch-bd.org/5th%20Amendment.pdf.

15. For the full text of the verdict see: http://www.supremecourt.gov.bd/scweb/documents/563864_CA48.pdf.

16. *Daily Star*, 'Taher trial illegal', 23 March 2011, p. 1.

17. The caretaker system was first challenged in 1996 (Writ Petition No. 1729 of 1996) in the High Court Division. The High Court rejected the petition. In January 2000 a Supreme Court lawyer challenged the thirteenth amendment again in the High Court in a writ petition saying the change distorts the principle that the republic will be governed by an elected government. The High Court rejected the petition in 2004 (57 DLR 171). However, after the petitioner died, another Supreme Court lawyer filed an appeal in June 2005 against the High Court ruling in the Supreme Court. In 2011, the Supreme Court heard the appeal beginning 1 March. For ten days opinions and arguments from eight amici curiae, and the counsels for both sides of the appeal were heard before the verdict was reached.

18. For the full verdict of the Supreme Court, see: Civil Appeal no. 139 pf 2005 with Civil Petition for Leave to Appeal No. 596 of 2005 at http://www.supremecourt.gov.bd/resources/documents/526214_13thAmet.pdf. Note that the full verdict was issued on 16 September 2012; the short order was issued on 10 May 2011. Reporters and legal experts have identified discrepancies between the short order and the complete verdict (Shawkat Liton, 'Full Judgment vs Short Order,' *Daily Star*, 19 September 2012, p. 1.

19. Among the POWs there were 56,998 armed force regulars, 18,287 paramilitary persons and 17,376 civilians including 4,616 police and 1,628 civilian government servants, 3,963 others including over 6,000 women and children.

20. *New York Times*, 'Bangladesh Will Try 1,100 Pakistanis', 30 March 1972, p. 3.

21. *New York Times*, 'Bhutto Threatens to Try Bengalis Held in Pakistan', 29 May 1973, p. 3.

22. Srinath Raghavan, *1971: A Global History of the Creation of Bangladesh* (Harvard, MA: Harvard University Press, 2013), p. 270.

23. Time, 'UNITED NATIONS: China's First Veto,' 4 September. 1972; this was the first veto by China since its entry to the United Nations Security Council as a permanent member. By then 85 nations had already recognized Bangladesh.

24. *Chicago Tribune*, 'China Vetoes Bangladesh UN Entry,' 26 August 1972, Section 1, p. 19.

25. 'Tripartite Agreement between India, Bangladesh and Pakistan for normalisation of relations in the subcontinent', 9 April 1974, http://statelesspeoplei nbangladesh.net/tripartite_agreement.php.

26. Raghavan, *1971: A Global History*, p. 270.

27. Islamic Summit Conference is the earlier name of the Organization of Islamic Cooperation (OIC).

28. Ghulam Mustafa and Qasim Shahzad Gill, 'The Issue of Prisoners of War (POWS), 1971 and Recognition of Bangladesh', *International Journal of Business and Social Research*, 4(3), March 2014, pp. 114–18.

29. Kamal Hossain, *Bangladesh: Quest for Freedom and Justice* (Dhaka: University Press Limited), 2013, p. 243.

30. The *Bangladesh Collaborators (Special Tribunals) (Repeal) Ordinance, 1975* (Ordinance No. LXIII of 1975), 31 December 1975, http://bdlaws.minlaw. gov.bd/print_sections_all.php?id=510.

31. bdnews24, 'Country has no war criminals, Jamaat claims', bdnews24, 25 October 2007, http://bdnews24.com/bangladesh/2007/10/25/country-has-no-war-criminal-jamaat-claims.

32. Various opinion polls have demonstrated the overwhelming support for the war crime trials. For example, in an opinion poll conducted by the AC Nielsen in April 2013, '86 per cent of voters [stated] that they personally wanted the trials to proceed' (David Bergman, 'Majority support war crimes trials but oppose Shahbagh protests' *New Age*, 11 September 2013, http://www.newagebd.com/detail.php?date=2013-09-11&nid = 64812#. QdWUqH8gtko). A similar level of support was found in another opinion poll conducted by the ORG-Quest for the leading Bengali daily newspaper Prothom Alo in September 2013, where 90 per cent supported the trial, see: http://www.eprothomalo.com/images/Opinion-%20Survey-Sep-13.pdf. Both showed that almost 50 per cent of population have reservations about the process.

33. In surveys commissioned by *Prothom Alo* and conducted by Org-Quest Research (with a sample of 5,000 respondents each time), the percentages favouring CTG were 73 (2011), 76 (2012), 90 (April 2013), and 82 (October 2013). Surveys done by the *Daily Samakal* in late 2011 and late 2012, respectively, showed 55 and 62 per cent of respondents agreeing that without a CTG, no fair election could be held. Similar polling by AC Nielsen (for the *Dhaka Daily Star*), by the *Daily Star* and the Asia Foundation, by Democracy

International, and by the US and British international-development agencies shows overwhelming support for the CTG.

34. AFP, 'Fear stalks Bangladesh as vote 'farce' begins', *The Australian*, 5 January 2014, http://www.theaustralian.com.au/news/world/fear-stalks-bangladesh-as-vote-farce-begins/story-e6frg6so-1226795273808.

35. Suhasini Haider, 'Backing Bangladesh', *The Hindu*, 11 January 2014, http://www.thehindu.com/opinion/lead/backing-bangladesh/article5563231.ece.

36. Salil Triphati, 'Bangladesh Inquisitions', *Himal* Vol. 28, no 3, 2015, available at. http://himalmag.com/bangladeshi-inquisitions-bloggers-death/.

37. *Deutsche Welle*, 'Atheist bloggers flee Bangladesh', 11 September 2015, http://www.dw.com/en/atheist-bloggers-flee-bangladesh/a-18708933.

38. Mukul Devichand, 'Nowhere is safe': Behind the Bangladesh blogger murders,' *BBC Trending*, 7 August 2015, http://www.bbc.com/news/blogs-trending-33822674.

39. While the list is generally attributed to the HI, the organization has denied that it provided any such list. Records show that the original list was provided by an organization called Al Bayneat. *Daily Amar Desh*, 'Hefazat Didn't Provide Bloggers List: Shafi', 24 May 2015, http://www.amardeshonline.com/pages/details/2015/05/24/285591#.Vhw3l2BdGM8.

40. For developments until 1 April 2013 see: 'Bangladesh Authorities Go After Bloggers, Claim They are "Anti-Islamic", *Global Voices Advocacy*, 1 April, 2013; https://advox.globalvoices.org/2013/04/01/bangladesh-authorities-go-after-anti-muslim-bloggers/ for an update in 2015, see: 'Bloggers are Killed following a List', *Prothom Alo*, 15 May 2015, http://m.prothom-alo.com/bangladesh/article/528262/%E0%A6%A4%E0%A6%BE%E0%A6%B2%E0%A6%BF%E0%A6%95%E0%A6%BE-%E0%A6%A7%E0%A6%B0%E0%A7%87-% E0%A6%AC%E0%A7%8D%E0%A6%B2%E0%A6%97%E0%A6%BE%E0%A6%B0-%E0%A6%96%E0%A7%81%E0%A6%A8..

41. The Prime Minister visited his family and vowed that his killers would be brought to justice. Although generally the ruling party activists were supportive of Rajib Haider, some were critical of his writings. For example, the state minister for law publicly commented that even 'kafirs' (infidels) would not use the language used by Rajib Haider; he said, 'this is the language of Satan' (IslamicNews24.com. 27 February 2013, http://islamicnews24.net/%E0%A6%AC%E0%A7%8D%E0%A6%B2%E0%A6%97%E0%A6%BE%E0%A6%B0-%E0%A6%B0%E0%A6%BE%E0%A6%9C%E0%A7%80%E0%A6%AC%E0%A7%87%E0%A6%B0-%E0%A6%AD%E0%A6%BE%E0%A6%B7%E0%A6%BE-%E0%A6%95%E0%A7%8B%E0%A6%A8%E0%A7%8B/?lang=en.

42. *Dhaka Tribune*, 'Joy: Situation was too volatile to comment on Avijit murder', 11 May 2015, http://www.dhakatribune.com/bangladesh/2015/may/11/situation-too-volatile-comment-avijit-murder#sthash.UVfE8Gpu.dpuf.

43. *Bdnews24*, 'IGP suggests Bangladesh bloggers to not "cross the line", not write blogs that may hurt religious sensitivities', 9 August 2015, http://bdnews24.com/bangladesh/2015/08/09/igp-suggests-bangladesh-bloggers-to-not-cross-the-line-not-write-blogs-that-may-hurt-religious-sensitivities.

44. *Bdnews24*, 'Home Minister Kamal warns against writing anything that hurts religious sentiment,' 11 August 2015, http://bdnews24.com/bangladesh/2015/08/11/home-minister-kamal-warns-against-writing-anything-that-hurts-religious-sentiment.

45. *Daily Star*, 'Bangladesh PM says govt won't allow anybody to hurt religious sentiments', 4 September 2015, http://www.thedailystar.net/frontpage/hurting-religious-sentiments-wont-be-tolerated-pm-137617.

46. *Prothom Alo*, 'Awami Ulema League in communal politics', 10 August 2015. http://en.prothom-alo.com/bangladesh/news/74927/Awami-Ulema-League-in-communal-politics.

47. *VOA*, 'Bangladesh Bloggers Fear Threat from State', 11 September 2015, http://www.voanews.com/content/bangladesh-bloggers-fear-threat-from-the-state/2960088.html.

48. *Daily Star*, 'Bangladesh's editors demand repeal of section 57 of ICT Act', 24 August 2015, p. 1.

49. David Bergman, 'Free Speech Under Fire in Bangladesh,' *Aljazeera.com*, 17 April 2015, http://america.aljazeera.com/articles/2015/4/17/bangladesh-press-freedom.html.

Chapter 4   Democracy: Aspiration, Nature and Quality

1. Sen, Amartya, 'Democracy as a Universal Value, *Journal of Democracy* 10/3 (1999), pp. 3–17.

2. Joseph Schumpeter, *Capitalism, Socialism, and Democracy* (New York: Harper, 1975), pp. 242, 269.

3. Samuel P. Huntington, *The Third Wave: Democratization in the Late Twentieth Century* (Norman: University of Oklahoma Press, 1991), p. 7.

4. Adam Przeworski, M. Alvarez, J. A. Cheibub, and F Limongi, 'What Makes Democracies Endure?' *Journal of Democracy* 7/1 (1996), pp. 39–55.

5. Guillermo A. O'Donnell, 'Democratic Theory and Comparative Politics', *Studies in Comparative International Development* 36/1 (2001).

6. Robert Dahl, *Polyarchy: Participation and Opposition* (New Haven: Yale University Press, 1971).

7. Ibid.

8. Max Weber, 'Politics as Vocation', in John Dreijmanis (ed.), *Max Weber's Complete Writings on Academic and Political Vocation* (New York: Algora Publications, 2008), pp. 155–208.

9. Seymour Martin Lipset, 'The Indispensability of Political Parties', *Journal of Democracy*, 11/1 (2000), pp. 48–55.

10. T Maliyamkono, and F. Kanyangolo (eds), *When Political Parties Clash* (Dar-es-Salaam: Tema Publishers, 2003), p. 41.

11. Data were drawn from World Values Surveys 1996 and 2002; International Foundation for Election Systems Survey 2000; Community Development Center Survey 2001; USAID Democracy and Governance Survey 2004; State of Democracy in South Asia Survey 2004–05; Pew Global Attitudes Survey 2008 and 2013; Daily Star-Nielsen Survey 2008, International Republican Institute Opinion Poll Surveys 2009; Governance Barometer Survey 2010; and Bangladesh Youth Survey 2011.

12. World Values Surveys (WVS) is a series of surveys conduct by the World Values Survey Association (WVSA), a non-profit association based in Stockholm, Sweden. Building on the European Values Surveys first carried out in 1981 five waves of surveys were conducted between 1981 and 2008. The sixth round is ongoing since 2010. Altogether 97 countries have been surveyed since 2007. Bangladesh was included in two waves (1994–98 and 1999–2004). Two rounds of surveys were conducted. In each round about 1,500 respondents were selected through stratified sampling. The WVS Association affirmed that 'the surveys in each country are directed by participants from the given society, in order to ensure that the design and fieldwork are carried out with an inside understanding of the society being investigated' (World Values Surveys Association (WVSA), Values Change the World, Stockholm: WVSA, nd (2013), available at: http://www.worldvaluessurvey.org/wvs/articles/folder_published/article_base_110/files/WVSbrochure6–2008_11.pdf, p. 3.). These data are available at http://www.worldvaluessurvey.org/.

13. USAID, *Bangladesh: Knowledge, Attitudes and Practices, National Survey Covering Democracy and Governing Issues* (Dhaka: USAID, April 2004). The survey consisted of one-on-one interviews with 3,140 individuals in six divisions conducted between 17 November and 31 December 2003. The study consisted of two parts, a statistically designed nationwide quantitative survey of adults aged 18 and older, and 12 qualitative focus group sessions.

14. 0 = unfavourable, 50 = neutral, and 100 = favourable.

15. USAID, *Bangladesh: Knowledge, Attitudes and Practices*, p. iii.

16. 3 per cent responded 'do not know' or refused to respond.

17. *Daily Star*, 'The Daily Star-Nielsen Election Opinion Poll 2008', 21 November 2008. The survey was conducted between 4 and 12 November 2008 with a sample size of 5040 adults throughout the country. Available at http://archive.thedailystar.net/suppliments/2008/opinion percent20poll/o_poll.htm.

18. SDSA Team, *State of Democracy in South Asia. A Report* (New Delhi: Oxford University Press, 2008), see summary of the project in: http://www.democracy-asia.org/. A total of 19,409 sampled respondents were interviewed with the help of structured schedules using probability sampling. The survey was carried out between August 2004 and February 2005.

19. K. C. Suri, Peter R. deSouza, Suhas Palshikar, Yogendra Yadav, 'Support for Democracy in South Asia', Paper presented at Global Barometer Surveys Conference on 'How People View and value Democracy', Institute of Political Science of Academia Sinica, Taipei 15–16 October 2010, Table 5. The paper draws on a cross-sectional survey conducted in Bangladesh, India, Nepal, Pakistan and Sri Lanka. The total number of Bangladeshi respondents was 2,504.

20. Peter R. deSouza, Suhas Palshikar, and Yogendra Yadav, 'Surveying South Asia', *Journal of Democracy* 19/1 (2008), pp. 84–96. http://www.journalofdem ocracy.org/sites/default/files/YadavGraphics-19–1.pdf.

21. Pew Research Center, 'The World's Muslims: Religion, Politics and Society', Chapter 2: Religion and Politics, The surveys that are the basis for this report were conducted across multiple years, Bangladesh was surveyed in 2011–12, Total sample size was 2,196 of which 1,918 were Muslims. Available at http://www.pewforum.org/2013/04/30/the-worlds-muslims-religion-politics-society-overview/.

22. deSouza, et al., 'Surveying South Asia', pp. 84–96.

23. Pew Research Center, 'Views of the Changing World June 2003' (Washington, DC: The Pew Research Center For The People & The Press, 2003), p. 7, http://www.people-press.org/files/legacy-pdf/185.pdf; as for the Muslim population, 57 per cent responded positively (Pew Research Center, The Pew Global Attitudes Project, 'Iraqi Vote Mirrors Desire for Democracy in Muslim World', 3 February 2005, http://www.pewglobal.org/2005/02/03/ iraqi-vote-mirrors-desire-for-democracy-in-muslim-world/.

24. Suri, et al., 'Support for Democracy in South Asia', p. 16, Table 7.

25. Syeda Salina Aziz and Elvir Graner, *Governance Barometer Survey Bangladesh 2010* (Dhaka: Institute of Governance Studies, Brac University 2010), pp. 51–53. The Survey was based on a total of 4,002 households and interviews were carried out during February 2010.

26. Aziz and Graner, 2010.

27. Pew Research Center, The Pew Global Attitudes Project, 'Iraqi Vote Mirrors Desire for Democracy in Muslim World', 3 February 2005, http://www. pewglobal.org/2005/02/03/iraqi-vote-mirrors-desire-for-democracy-in-muslim-world/.

28. Thomas Carson, 'Issues and Priorities for Bangladesh: The 2000 IFES National Survey' (Washington DC: IFES, November 2001). The survey was conducted between 18 November and 15 December 2000. A nationally representative sample of 2,000 adults, 18 years of age and above, were interviewed by the IFES. This number was evenly divided by design between the rural and urban areas in Bangladesh. The sample was weighted and percentages for the national population presented in this report are representative of the adult population by age, sex and region.

29. Carson, 'Issues and Priorities for Bangladesh: The 2000 IFES National Survey'.

30. Ibid., p. 38, Fig. 31.

31. USAID, *Bangladesh: Knowledge, Attitudes and Practices*, p. iii.
32. Ibid., p. 13.
33. Elvira Graner, Fatema Samina Yasmin and Syeda Salina Aziz, *Giving Youth a Voice: Bangladesh Youth Survey* (Dhaka: Institute of Governance Studies, BRAC University, 2012), p. 58. The nationwide survey, with a sample size of 6,575 was conducted in December 2011. The gender proportion was nearly half and half (3,296 men and 3,279 women) and a rural–urban proportion was 70 to 30.
34. Thomas Carson, 'Issues and Priorities for Bangladesh: The 2000 IFES National Survey' (Washington DC: IFES, 2001), p. 25.
35. Community Development Library, *Voice Through Ballot: Election and People's Perception* (Dhaka: CDL, 2001). The survey was conducted in July 2001, the sample size was 1,557, with 40 per cent women and 60 per cent men.
36. USAID, *Bangladesh: Knowledge, Attitudes and Practices*, pp. 13, 29.
37. Sandeep Shastri, *Citizen Participation in the Democratic Process across South Asia*, unpublished paper, *Table* 4; paper based on the SDSA survey data.
38. International Republican Institute (IRI), 'Survey of the Bangladeshi Opinion' (Dhaka: IRI, 2009). The survey was conducted in conjunction with USAID. Additional information compiled from a series of nationwide polls conducted between May and December 2008 was also used. The sample size was 1,530 in all surveys with the exception of the May 2008 survey which used a sample size of 5,400. All respondents were older than the age of 18. Available at http://www.iri.org/news-events-press-center/news/iri-releases-survey-bangladesh-public-opinion.
39. Graner, et al., *Giving Youth a Voice: Bangladesh Youth Survey*, p. 53.
40. Sandeep Shastri, *Citizen Participation in the Democratic Process across South Asia*, Unpublished paper. Table 1; paper based on the SDSA survey data.
41. Suri, et al., 'Support for Democracy in South Asia'.
42. Thomas Carson, 'Issues and Priorities for Bangladesh: The 2000 IFES National Survey' (Washington DC: IFES, 2001), p. 25.
43. Tariq Ali and Naomi Hossain, 'Popular Expectations of Government: Findings from Three Areas in Bangladesh', PRCPB Working Paper No. 13, Dhaka: Programme for Research on Chronic Poverty in Bangladesh (PRCPB), Bangladesh Institute of Development Studies (BIDS); and Chronic Poverty Research Centre (CPRC), Institute for Development Policy and Management (IDPM), University of Manchester, February 2006, p. 12. This paper presents findings from research into expectations of government, based on focus group discussion sessions with over 100 poor and very poor people in rural and urban Bangladesh. Available at http://www.prcpb-bids.org/documents/workingpaper/wp13fulltext.pdf.
44. Ibid., p. 22.
45. Terry Karl, 'Electoralism', in R. Rose (ed.), *International Encyclopedia of Elections* (London: Macmillan, 2000).

46. Larry Diamond, 'Is the Third Wave Over?' *Journal of Democracy* 7/3 (1996), pp. 20–37.
47. Chris Adcock, 'Violent Obstacles to Democratic Consolidation in Three Countries: Guatemala, Colombia, and Algeria', ProQuest, http://www.csa.com/discoveryguides/demo/overview.php.
48. Kenneth Bollen citing early 1970s data has noted that a number of countries such as Albania, North Korea, the Soviet Union, Romania and Bulgaria were among the countries which recorded the highest levels of voter participation (Kenneth A. Bollen, 'Issues in the Comparative Measurement of Political Democracy', *American Sociological Review* 45/3 (1980), pp. 370–90. In a similar vein, Saddam Hussain's regime in Iraq received overwhelming 'approval' through periodic elections.
49. USAID, *Bangladesh: Knowledge, Attitudes and Practices*, p. vi.
50. Carson, 'Issues and Priorities for Bangladesh: The 2000 IFES National Survey', p. 20.
51. The survey, 'Bangladesh: The Next Generation', interviewed 2,166 young people between the age of 15 and 30 at their work, educational institutes and homes in 2009. British Council, Bangladesh Next Generation', Dhaka: British Council 2010. Available at http://issuu.com/nextgeneration/docs/next_generation_report.
52. Graner, et al., *Giving Youth a Voice: Bangladesh Youth Survey.*
53. Carson, 'Issues and Priorities for Bangladesh: The 2000 IFES National Survey', p. 20.
54. Pew Research Center, *Global Opinion Trends 2002–07: A Rising Tide Lifts Mood In The Developing World* (2007), www.pewglobal.org/files/pdf/257.pdf.
55. USAID, *Bangladesh: Knowledge, Attitudes and Practices*, p. 16.
56. Suri, et al., '*Support for Democracy in South Asia*', Table 11.
57. Ibid., Table 12.
58. *Global Opinion Trends 2002–07: A Rising Tide Lifts Mood In The Developing World.*
59. SDSA Team, *State of Democracy in South Asia. A Report* (New Delhi: Oxford University Press, 2008), p. 13.
60. USAID, *Bangladesh: Knowledge, Attitudes and Practices*, p. 20.
61. 'The Daily Star-Nielsen Election Opinion Poll 2008'.
62. SDSA Team, *State of Democracy in South Asia. A Report* (New Delhi: Oxford University Press, 2008), p. 13.
63. Ibid.
64. Ibid., p. 14.
65. Ibid.
66. According to the Bangladesh constitution, 'unless sooner dissolved by the President, Parliament stands dissolved on the expiration of a period of five years from the date of its first meeting. In the extra-ordinary situation of the country being engaged in a war, this period of five years may be extended by an

Act of Parliament by not more than one year at a time. The period cannot, however, be extended beyond six months after the termination of the war' (Bangladesh Election Commission, 'Tenure of All Parliaments', 2012, available at: http://www.parliament.gov.bd/index.php/en/about-parliament/tenure-of-parliament.

67. Larry Diamond, 'Democracy's Third Wave Today', *Current History* 110/739 (2011), p. 299.
68. For example, Renskee Doorenspleet, 'Reassessing the Three Waves of Democratization', *World Politics* 52 (2000), pp. 384–406; Adam Przeworski, Michael E. Alvarez, José Antonio Cheibub, and Fernando Limongi, *Democracy and Development: Political Institutions and Well-Being in the World, 1950–1990* (New York: Cambridge University Press, 2000); and Philippe C Schmitter, 'Waves of Democratization', in Seymor Martin Lipset et al. (eds), *Encyclopedia of Democracy*, vol. 2 (London: Routledge), pp. 346–50.
69. Diamond, 'Democracy's Third Wave Today'.
70. Freedom House, *Freedom In The World 2013: Democratic Breakthroughs In The Balance* (Washington DC: Freedom House), p. 29.
71. Some scholars have suggested that there are three stages: opening, breakthrough and consolidation (Thomas Carothers, 'The End of the Transition Paradigm', *Journal of Democracy* 13/1 (2002), pp. 5–12.
72. Carothers, 'The End of the Transition Paradigm', p. 7.
73. Amichai Magen, 'Evaluating External Influence on Democratic Development: Transition', CDDRL Working Paper 111, November 2009, p. 8.
74. Giovanni Sartori, *The Theory of Democracy Revisited* (London: Chatam House Publications, 1987).
75. Mike Alvarez, Jose Antonio Cheibub, Fernando Limogni, and Adam Przeworski, 'Classifying Political Regimes', *Studies in Comparative International Development* 31/2 (1996), pp. 3–36.
76. Juan Linz, *Totalitarian and Authoritarian Regimes*, in Fred Greenstein and Nelson Polsby (eds), *Handbook of Political Science* (1975), pp. 184–85.
77. Dahl, *Polyarchy: Participation and Opposition*.
78. Kenneth Bollen and Pamela Paxton, 'Subjective Measures of Liberal Democracy', *Comparative Political Studies* 33/1 (2000), pp. 58–86.
79. Renskee Doorenspleet, 'Reassessing the Three Waves of Democratization', *World Politics* 52 (2000), p. 389.
80. Andreas Schedler, 'The Menu of Manipulation', *Journal of Democracy* 13/2 (2002), pp. 36–50.
81. Larry Diamond, 'The Democratic Rollback: The Resurgence of the Predatory State', *Foreign Affairs* (2008).
82. Carothers, 'The End of the Transition Paradigm', pp. 5–12.
83. Marina Ottaway. 'Promoting Democracy after Conflict: The Difficult Choices', *International Studies Perspectives* 4/3 (2003), pp. 314–22.
84. Andrew J. Nathan, 'Authoritarian Resilience', *Journal of Democracy* 14/1 (2003), pp. 6–17.

85. Guillermo O'Donnel and Philippe Schmitter, *Transitions from Authoritarian Rule: Tentative Conclusions about Uncertain Democracies* (Baltimore: Johns Hopkins University Press, 1986), p. 9.
86. Steven Levitsky and Lucan Way, 'The Rise of Competitive Authoritarianism', *Journal of Democracy* 13/2 (2002), pp. 51–65.
87. Diamond, 'Thinking about Hybrid Regimes'.
88. Lauth 'Die empirische messung demokratischer Grauzonen'.
89. Diamond. 'Thinking About Hybrid Regimes'.
90. Jørgen Møller and Svend-Erik Skaaning, 'Regime Types and Democratic Sequencing', *Journal of Democracy* 24/1 (2013), pp. 142–55; Jørgen Møller and Svend-Erik Skaaning, *Requisites of Democracy: Conceptualization, Measurement, and Explanation* (London: Routledge, 2011); Jørgen Møller and Svend-Erik Skaaning, 'The Third Wave: Inside the Numbers', *Journal of Democracy* 24/4 (2013), pp. 97–109.
91. Møller and Skaaning, 'The Third Wave', 2013, p. 98.
92. There are other datasets, for example, Contestation and Inclusiveness indices; the Political Regime Change (PRC) dataset; the Democratization Dataset: Unified Democracy Scores, to name a few.
93. See for example, Asian Barometer, http://www.asianbarometer.org/.
94. For an extensive criticism of the extant indices and a proposal for a new approach, see *Michael Coppedge and John Gerring*', Conceptualizing and Measuring Democracy: A New Approach, *Perspectives on Politics* 9/2 (2011), pp. 247–67.
95. A brief idea about these datasets can be gleaned from the description provided by Coppedge and Gerring; Freedom House employs two indices, 'Political Rights' and 'Civil Liberties' (sometimes they are employed in tandem, sometimes singly) each of which extends back to 1972 and covers most sovereign and semi-sovereign nations (see www.freedomhouse.org). Polity IV also provides two aggregate indices, 'Democracy' and 'Autocracy', usually used in tandem (by subtracting one from the other), which provides the Polity2 variable. Coverage extends back to 1800 for most sovereign countries with populations greater than 500,000 (www.cidcm.umd.edu/inscr/polity). DD codes countries dichotomously (democracy/dictatorship), including most sovereign countries from 1946 to the present. BNR (2001) construct a binary measure that extends (for all sovereign nations) from 1919 to the present. The EIU index is composed of five core dimensions and 60 sub-components, which are combined into a single index of democracy. Coverage extends to 167 sovereign or semi-sovereign nations for 2006, 2008, and 2010 (Coppedge and Gerring, 'Conceptualizing and Measuring Democracy', *Perspectives on Politics* (2011), fn 4, p. 261.
96. Joakim Ekman, 'Political Participation and Regime Stability: A Framework for Analyzing Hybrid Regimes', *International Political Science Review* 30/1 (2009), pp. 7–21.
97. While the parliamentary sessions were held as per constitutional requirements and various laws were passed, opposition members, irrespective of parties,

remained absent. The percentage of boycott of sessions by opposition members was 34 in the fifth parliament (1991–1996), 43 in the seventh parliament (1996–2001), and 60 in the eighth parliament (2001–2006). The main opposition BNP attended only 54 days out of 337 days of sessions in the ninth parliament held until the end of 2012.

98. European Intelligence Unit, Economist, *Index of Democracy*, Various Years. Available at http://www.eiu.com.

99. Monty G. Marshall, 'Polity IV Project: Political Regime Characteristics and Transitions, 1800–2012', INSCR Data Page, available at: http://www.systemi cpeace.org/inscr/inscr.htm.

100. Transparency International, *Corruption Perception Index Report*, Various Years, http://www.transparency.org/research/cpi/overview.

101. European Intelligence Unit, Economist.

102. Reporters Without Borders, *World Press Freedom Index*, Various Years, http://en.rsf.org/press-freedom-index-2011–2012,1043.html.

103. Freedom House, *Freedom in the World*, Various Years, http://www.freedomhous e.org/reports.

104. Freedom House, *Freedom in the World*, 'Freedom in the World: Aggregate and Subcategory Scores', various years, http://www.freedomhouse.org/report/ freedom-world-aggregate-and-subcategory-scores.

105. Political Terror Scale (PTS), http://www.politicalterrorscale.org/countries. php?region=Eurasia&country = Bangladesh.

106. The 2014 election, although held on time, was marked by the boycott of the opposition parties and a high degree of irregularities.

107. Terry Lynn Karl, 'Dilemmas of Democratization in Latin America', *Comparative Politics*, 23/9 (1990).

108. Terry Karl, 'Petroleum and Political Pacts: The Transition to Democracy in Venezuela', in Guillermo O'Donnell, Philippe Schmitter, Laurence Whitehead (eds), *Transitions from Authoritarian Rule: Latin America* (Baltimore: The Johns Hopkins University Press, 1986).

109. Paulo Sergio Pinheiro, 'Democracy Without Citizenship: Democratization And Human Rights', http://www.nevusp.org/downloads/seminarios/france96/ 5-2-Paul.pdf accessed 20 November 2011.

110. Antonio Gramsci, *Selections from Prison Notebooks* (New York: International General, 1971), p. 12.

111. Economist, 'Bangladesh: the Minus Two', 6 September 2007, http://www. economist.com/node/9769010; see also, Secuirty-Risk.com, Bangladesh: Minus Two Politics Backfires? 30 April 2008, http://www.security-risks. com/security-trends-south-asia/bangladesh/bangladesh-:minus-two-politics-229.html.

112. Schedler, 'The Menu of Manipulation', p. 47.

113. Hans-Jürgen Puhle, 'Democratic Consolidation and "Defective Democracies"', Madrid: Universidad Autónoma de Madrid, Working Papers Online Series Working Paper 47/2005; http://portal.uam.es/portal/page/

portal/UAM_ORGANIZATIVO/Departamentos/CienciaPoliticaRelaciones Internacionales/publicaciones percent20en percent20red/working_papers/ archivos/47_2005.pdf (accessed 21 November 2011).

114. For a critique of the concept and its usage in the Latin American context, see Rhoda Rabkin, 'The Aylwin Government and 'Tutelary' Democracy: A Concept in Search of a Case?', *Journal of Interamerican Studies and World Affairs* 34/4 (1992–92), pp. 119–94.

115. Shawkat Liton, 'Bosses Bigger than Parties', *Daily Star*, 26 June 2014, p. 1, http://www.thedailystar.net/bosses-bigger-than-parties-30421.

116. IDEA/Center for Alternatives, *Bangladesh: Country Report*, p. 6.

117. Shakhawat Liton and Hasan Jahid Tusher, 'Same old formula', *Daily Star*, 30 December 2012, p. 1.

118. *bdnews24*, 'Mannan Bhuiyan, Ashraf Hossain expelled from BNP' bdnews24. com 3 September 2007, http://bdnews24.com/bangladesh/2007/09/03/mannan-bhuiyan-ashraf-hossain-expelled-from-bnp.

119. Badiul Alam Majumdar, 'Which Constitution? Whose Constitution?' *Prothom Alo*, 28 October 2013, p. 8.

120. Stanley A. Kochanek, 'Governance, Patronage Politics and Democratic Transition in Bangladesh', *Asian Survey* 40/3 (2000), p. 548.

121. Guillermo A. O'Donnell, 'Delegative Democracy', *Journal of Democracy* 5/1 (1994), pp. 55–69.

122. O'Donnell, 'Delegative Democracy', p. 60.

123. Gramsci, *Selections from Prison Notebooks*, p. 12.

124. O'Donnell, 'Delegative Democracy', pp. 61–2.

125. Catalina Smulovitz and Enrique. Peruzzotti, 'Societal Accountability in Latin America', *Journal of Democracy* 11/4 (2000), pp. 147–58.

126. *Dhaka Tribune*, 'ACC is a 'toothless tiger': Ghulam Rahman', 19 June 2013, http://www.dhakatribune.com/bangladesh/2013/jun/19/acc-%E2%80%98 toothless-tiger%E2%80%99-ghulam-rahman.

127. Andreas Schedler, 'Conceptualizing Accountability', in Andreas Schedler, Larry Diamond and Marc F. Plattner (eds), *The Self Restraining State: Power And Accountability In New Democracies* (Boulder, Co: Lynne Rienner, 1999), pp. 13–28.

128. Larry Jay Diamond and Leonardo Morlino, 'An Overview', *Journal of Democracy* 15/4 (2004), pp. 20–31.

129. *Dhaka Tribune*, '"Disappeartances" become a horror in 2014', 1 January 2015. http://www.dhakatribune.com/bangladesh/2015/jan/01/%E2%80%98 disappearance%E2%80%99-became-horror-2014.

130. Odhikar, 'Total Extra-Judicial Killings from 2001–2015.' Dhaka: Odhikar. http://1dgy051vgyxh41o8cj16kk7s19f2.wpengine.netdna-cdn.com/wp-content/uploads/2013/01/Statistics_EJK_2001-2015.pdf.

131. '183 Extra-judicial Killings in 2015', BBC Bangla, 1 January 2016, available at http://www.bbc.com/bengali/news/2016/01/151231_bd_human_rights_ask.

132. Asian Legal Resource Centre. 'BANGLADESH: Public justice system incapable of addressing relentless enforced disappearance', 31 August 2015, http://alrc.asia/alrc-cws-003-2015/.

133. *New Age*, 'AG urges law enforcers to shoot at arsonists', 4 February 2015, http://newagebd.net/92335/ag-urges-law-enforcers-to-shoot-at-arsonists/#s thash.i4bZ5MjG.0JJ3BqDK.dpuf.

134. *The Daily Observer*, 'Eliminate saboteurs, families: DIG Mahfuz', 8 February 2015, http://www.observerbd.com/2015/02/08/71390.php.

135. *The Daily Observer*, 'DIG says police can avenge one killing with two', 4 February 2015, http://www.observerbd.com/2015/02/04/70614.php.

136. Priyo.com, 'No democracy in Bangladesh yet: Noor Hossain's mother', 23 November 2011, http://news.priyo.com/story/2010/nov/23/12230-no-democracy-bangladesh-yet-noor-hossain%E2%80%99s-mother.

Chapter 5   Political Parties, Elections and Party System

1. Peter J Bertocci, 'Bangladesh in the Early-1980s: Praetorian Politics in an Intermediate Regime', *Asian Survey* 22/10 (1982), p. 993.

2. Craig Baxter, Yogender K Malik, Charles H. Kennedy, and Robert C. Oberst, *Government and Politics in South Asia* (Boulder, CO: Westview, 2002), p. 295.

3. *Bangladesh Chronicle*, 'EC Prepares Report on BNF Registration', 18 August 2013, http://www.bangladeshchronicle.net/index.php/2013/08/ec-prepares-report-on-bnf-registration/.

4. Bangladesh Election Commission, 'List of Registered Political Parties', http://www.ecs.gov.bd/English/RegisteredPoliticalPartyEng.php (accessed 11 October 2015). The number of parties does not include the Bangladesh Jamaat-e-Islami which lost its registration due to a court verdict on 31 August 2014.

5. In 1988, the estimated number of political parties was 108 according to the Library of Congress Country Study (A Country Study: Bangladesh, Library of Congress, http://memory.loc.gov/frd/cs/bdtoc.html#bd0118, accessed 24 November 2006.

6. Bertocci, 'Bangladesh in the Early-1980s', p. 993.

7. IDEA/Center for Alternatives, *Bangladesh: Country Report*, Dhaka: Center for Alternatives, published in conjunction with the International Institute of Democracy and Electoral Assistance (IDEA), 2004, p. 8.

8. Baxter et al., *Government and Politics*, p. 295.

9. For discussion on various party systems, see Giovanni Sartori, *Parties and Party Systems: A Framework for Analysis* (New York: Cambridge University Press, 1976).

10. Tushar Kanti Barua, *Political Elite in Bangladesh* (Bern: Peter Lang, 1978), p. 168.

11. Alan Ware, *Political Parties and Party Systems* (Oxford: Oxford University Press), 1996, p. 159.

12. Raymond Suttner, 'Party dominance "theory": Of what value?', *Politikon* 33 (3), 2006, pp. 277–97.

13. T J Pempel (ed.), *Uncommon Democracies: The One-Party Dominant Regimes* (Ithaca, NY: Cornell University Press), 1990, pp. 3–4.

14. Nazim Kamran Choudhury, 'Jatiya Sangsad Elections: Past and Future', *Daily Star*, 13 April 2001.

15. Nazim Kamran Choudhury, 'Jatiya Sangsad Elections: Past and Future', *Daily Star*, 13 April 2001.

16. Ellen Barry, 'Low Turnout in Bangladesh Elections Amid Boycott and Violence', *New York Times*, 6 January 2014, Asia-Pacific, A 14.

17. Raymond Suttner, 'Party dominance "theory": Of what value?', *Politikon* 33 (3), 2006, pp. 277–97.

18. Riyadul Karim, 'Burden of Cases on BNP's Shoulder' (in Bengali), *Prothom Alo*, 29 October 2014, p. 1; Wakil Ahmed Hiron and Reza Mahmud, 'BNP leaders are stuck in cases', *Samakal*, 19 March 2014, p. 1.

19. Dalem Ch Barman, M. Golam Rahman and Tasneem Siddiqui, 'Democracy Report for Bangladesh', International Institute for Democracy and Electoral Assistance (IDEA) (2001), p. 44, http://www.idea.int/publications/sod/upload/Bangladesh.pdf (3 July 2005).

20. Nizam Ahmed, 'From Monopoly to Competition: Party Politics in the Bangladesh Parliament', *Pacific Affairs* 76/1 (2003), p. 61.

21. Mohammad Mohabbat Khan, 'State of Governance in Bangladesh', *Round Table*, 370 (2003), p. 395.

22. IDEA/Center for Alternatives, *Bangladesh: Country Report*, Dhaka: Center for Alternatives, published in conjunction with the International Institute of Democracy and Electoral Assistance (IDEA), 2004, p. 6.

23. Nizam Ahmed, 'From Monopoly to Competition', p. 72.

24. Moloy Saha, 'Ershad wishes to hold JP rudder until death', *SNNBD*, 26 July 2009, http://www.snnbd.com/newsdetails.php?cat_id=0.02&id = 13886#.UnVA7OrD_WN.

25. Rounaq Jahan, *Political Parties in Bangladesh*. CPD-CMI Working Paper series, no 8, Dhaka: Centre for Policy Dialogue, 2014, pp. 30–31.

26. Bangladesh Nationalist Party (BNP), 'Constitution (Amended up to 8 December 2009)', http://bangladeshnationalistparty-bnp.org/content.aspx?tablename=webitem2&id=8&child=null&parentid=null (accessed 2 November 2013).

27. Bangladesh Awami League, 'Constitution', http://www.albd.org/index.php/en/party/constitution (accessed 2 November 2013).

28. Jatiya Party, 'Constitution', http://shujanbd.files.wordpress.com/2013/04/constitution_jp.pdf (accessed 2 November 2013). While I have highlighted these practices within the three main political parties, they are not limited to these parties only. The familiar faces for almost three decades in the party leadership of almost all parties in Bangladesh provide the impression that the leadership is a matter of perpetuity and that the party structures are only to provide a stamp of validation to the decisions of these leaders.

29. Jahan, *Political Parties in Bangladesh*, p. 31.

30. For examples of familial connections of the party leadership at local level, see Ali Riaz, 'Dynastic Politics and the Political Culture of Bangladesh', *Journal of International Relations* 8/II (2010), pp. 1–16.

31. Jahan, *Political Parties in Bangladesh*, p. 31.

32. Stanley A. Kochanek, 'Governance, patronage politics and democratic transition in Bangladesh', *Asian Survey* 40(3) (2000): 530–50; Peter J. Bertocci, 'Bangladesh in the early 1980s: Praetorian politics in an intermediate regime', *Asian Survey* 22 (10) (1982): 988–1008.

33. Kochanek, 'Governance, patronage politics', p. 530.

34. Nizam Ahmed, p. 72.

35. Kochanek, 'Governance, patronage politics', p. 548.

36. Francis Fukuyama, 'The End of History?' *National interest*, Summer 1989, later the book titled *The End of History and the Last Man* (New York: Free Press, 1992). by 1992 the question mark had disappeared, providing a definitive tone to the claim.

37. Guilain Denoeux, 'The Forgotten Swamp: Navigating Political Islam', *Journal of Middle East Policy* 9, 2 (2002): 56–81.

38. Ali Riaz and Kh Ali Ar-Raji, 'Who are the Islamists?' in Ali Riaz and C. Christine Fair, *Political Islam and Governance in Bangladesh* (London/ New York: Routledge, 2010), pp. 60–63.

39. *Daily Star*, '25 small parties get 2pc votes in total, 2 January 2009, p. 1.

40. *bdnews24*, '"Shady force" responsible for BNP split: Gayeshwar', 2 December 2007. http://bdnews24.com/politics/2007/12/02/shady-force-responsible-for-bnp-split-gayeshwar.

41. US Embassy cable, 08Dhaka721, 3 July 2007, http://wikileaks.org/cable/2008/07/08DHAKA721.html; also see US Embassy cable, 07Dhaka1061, 28 June 2007, http://wikileaks.org/cable/2007/06/07DHAKA1061.html.

42. Kazi Zafar passed away on 27 August 2015.

43. For details of the disintegration between 1990 and 2007, see Ali Riaz, *Islamist Militancy in Bangladesh: A Complex Web*, London: Routledge, pp. 42–43.

44. Syed Abul Maksud, 'Rajniti Chelekhela O Fazlamo Noy' ['Politics is not a Child's Play'], *Prothom Alo*, 30 September 2014, p. 10.

45. Mohammad Mohabbat Khan and Habib M Zafarullah, 'The 1978 President Elections: A Review' in S. R. Chakravarty and Virendra Narain (eds), *Bangladesh: Domestic Politics* (New Delji: South Asia Publishers), p. 102.

46. Dainik Bangla, 'Press Briefing of Awami League, JP, Jamaat: The Outline of the Caretaker Government Announced', *Dainik Bangla*, 28 June 1994, p. 1.

47. M. Abdul Latif Mondal, 'All but an all-party government?', *Dhaka Tribune*, 27 November 2013.

48. *Daily Star*, 'Bigots Fight Fiercely With Cops To Protest Women Policy', 11 April 2008, p. 1.

Chapter 6   Quest for a National Identity: Multiple Contestations

1. Joseph Allchin, 'Explaining Bangladesh's Month of Massive Street Protests and Violence', *Vice*, 3 March 2013, http://www.vice.com/read/explaining-Bangladeshs-month-of-massive-street-protests-and-violence.

2. Naeem Mohaimen, 'Shahbagh: The Forest of symbols', Alal-O-Dulal, 22 February 2013, http://alalodulal.org/2013/02/22/shahbagh-symbols/.

3. Lailufar Yasmin, 'Religion and After: Bangladeshi Identity Since 1971', *Open Democracy*, 19 April 2013, http://www.opendemocracy.net/opensecurity/lailufar-yasmin/religion-and-after-bangladeshi-identity-since-1971.

4. Rafiuddin Ahmed, 'Introduction: The Emergence of Bengal Muslims' in Rafiuddin Ahmed (ed.), *Understanding the Bengal Muslims: Interpretative Essays* (Delhi: Oxford University Press, 2001), pp. 4–5.

5. For example, in 1772, Warren Hastings and William Jones, decided to apply 'the laws of Koran with respect to Mohammedans and that of the Shaster with respect to Hindus' (Proceedings of the Committee of Circiut at Kasimbazaar, 15 August 1772, quoted in Bharatiya Vidya Bhaven, *History and Culture of the Indian People* 8/361). This was initially known as the Bengal Regulation Law 1772. In 1793, it was amended to Mohammedan Law and Hindu Law.

6. The changes in Muslim education initiated by May and continued by Northbrook in 1871 demonstrate that the Raj was trying to reach out to Muslims. On 23 October 1882, the secretary of state told the viceroy, 'if there be any real special grievances which affect the Muslim population which can be fairly removed by all means let it be done'.

7. Syed Sharfuddin Pirzada, *Evolution of Pakistan* (Karachi: Royal Book Co, 1995).

8. Mushirul Hasan, *Legacy of a Divided Nation: India's Muslim Since Independence* (London: Hurst & Company, 1997), p. 35.

9. Ayesha Jalal, 'Exploding Communalism: The Politics of Muslim Identity in South Asia', in Suagata Basu and Ayesha Jalal (eds), *Nationalism, Democracy and Development: State and Politics in India* (Delhi: Oxford University Press, 1999).

10. Ibid.

11. Mushirul Hasan, 'Minority Identity and Its Discontents, Ayodhya and Its Aftermath', *South Asia Bulletin* 14/2 (1994), p. 26.

12. Significant aspects of the Act were: (a) proprietary rights over land were established; (b) land was transformed into a commodity; (c) a secure and tractable revenue base for the Company was established: (d) attempt to transform the *zamindars* into a purely economic force was made. Contrary to the prevailing situation wherein it was unclear who owns land, the Act concentrated propriety rights in the hands of the state revenue collectors. Hence, *zamindars* become the new legal owners of land in Bengal. Furthermore, the old customary law requiring prior permission of the

Government for transferring land was abolished and thus, *zamindars* were made free to alienate lands by sale or gift. If a *zamindar* defaulted in paying the revenue, his land was to be sold in liquidation of arrears. The land was, therefore, made a marketable commodity, and paved the way for the infiltration of new capital and enterprise in agrarian Bengal. The permanent tax agreement between the *zamindars* and the government made it easier for the company rulers to be sure of a continuous flow of taxes without being involved in assessment every year. The Act took away the judicial and police powers which the *zamindars* had been enjoying till then. To encourage the free flow of trade and commerce *zamindars* were deprived of their right to levy *sairs* on merchandise passing through their territories.

13. Here I am referring to three legal measures enacted between 1793 and 1799. The government reserved the right to enact, whenever necessary, regulations for protecting the rights of ryots and dependent talukdars. By regulation VIII of 1793, the *zamindars* were directed to prepare *patta* (a lease, deed or document recording the terms by which a cultivator or under-tenant holds his land) by consolidating all the *abwabs* (regular exactions of different kinds) and rents heretoafter levied into *jumma* (total sum demandable) and deliver them to their *ryots* so that *ryots* could know the exact sum payable by them. No fresh *abwabs* over and above the *jumma* could be imposed. The situation, however, changed in subsequent years. The *zamindars* began to press the government for judicial and police powers, especially to distrain the *ryots*, in order to realize their rents. In 1795, government yielded to the pressure of the zamindars and they were given some restricted power of enforcing law. In 1799 the notorious Regulation VII (Qanun Haftam) enabled proprietors and farmers of land to realize their rents with greater punctuality. The regulation gave the landlords practically unrestricted right of distrain.

14. Rafiuddin Ahmed, *The Bengal Muslims 1871–1906, A Quest for Identity* (Delhi: Oxford University Press, 1981), p. 40.

15. Tajul I Hashmi, *Peasant Utopia; The Communalization of Class Politics in East Bengal, 1920–1947* (Dhaka: University Press Limited, 1994), p. 52.

16. Ibid., p. 56.

17. Ibid., p. 75.

18. For extensive discussion of these organizations, see Dhurjati Prasad De, *Bengal Muslims in Search of Social Identity 1905–47* (Dhaka: University Press Limited, 1998).

19. Ibid., p. 97.

20. Tazeen M. Murshid, *The Sacred and the Secular, Bengali Muslim Discourses, 1871–1977* (Calcutta: Oxford University Press, 1995), p. 139.

21. Anisuzzaman, 'The Identity Question and the Politics' in Rounaq Jahan (ed.), *Bangladesh – Promise and Performance* (London: Zed Books Ltd and Dhaka: University Press Limited, 2001), p. 52.

22. Larry Collins and Dominique Lapierre, *Freedom at Midnight* (New Delhi: Vikas Publishing House Pvt. Ltd., 1976), p. 104.

23. Barbara Daly Metcalf, 'Preface', *Moral Conduct and Authority, The Place of Adab in South Asian Islam* (Berkeley: California University Press, 1984), p. viii.

24. U. A. B. Razia Aktar Banu, *Islam in Bangladesh* (Leiden: E. J. Brill, 1992), p. 27.

25. Banu, *Islam in Bangladesh*, p. 12.

26. Richard M. Eaton, *The Rise of Islam and the Bengal Frontier (1204–1760)* (Berkeley: University of California Press, 1993 (pb 1996)).

27. Asim Roy, *The Islamic Syncretistic Tradition in Bengal* (New Jersey: Princeton University Press, 1984); Rafiuddin Ahmed, *The Bengal Muslims 1871–1906: A Quest for Identity* (New Delhi: OUP. 2nd edn, 1996); Sufia M. Uddin, *Constructing Bangladesh: Religion, ethnicity, and language in an Islamic nation* (Chapel Hill; The University of North Carolina Press, 2006, Banu, Islam in Bangladesh).

28. Richard M. Eaton, *The Rise of Islam and the Bengal Frontier (1204–1760)* (Berkeley: University of California Press, 1993 (pb 1996)), p. 305.

29. Eaton, *The Rise of Islam*, p. 315.

30. Ahmed Kamal, *State Against the Nation: The Decline of the Muslim League in Pre-independence Bangladesh, 1947–54* (Dhaka: University Press Limited, 2009), p. 34.

31. Tajul Islam Hashmi, *Peasant Utopia*, p. 13.

32. Quoted in Sharifuddin Pirzada (ed.), *Foundations of Pakistan 1923–1947* (Karachi: National Publishing House, 1970), p. 341.

33. Ahmed Kamal, *State Against the Nation: The Decline of the Muslim League in Pre-independence Bangladesh, 1947–54* (Dhaka: University Press Limited, 2009).

34. Ibid.

35. Sheikh Mujibur Rahman and Naimuddin Ahmed, *Purbo Pakistaner Durbhagha Jonoshadharan {The Unfortunate People of East Pakistan}* (Dhaka, 1948).

36. Tazeen M. Murshid, *The Sacred and the Secular, Bengali Muslim Discourses, 1871–1977* (Calcutta: Oxford University Press, 1995), p. 299.

37. K. N. Panikkar, 'Identity & Politics', *Frontline* 28/10 (2011).

38. Ibid.

39. Tazeen M. Murshid, *The Sacred and the Secular, Bengali Muslim Discourses, 1871–1977* (Calcutta: Oxford University Press, 1995), p. 288.

40. Ibid., p. 286.

41. Howard Schuman, 'A Note on the Rapid Rise of Mass Bengali Nationalism in East Pakistan', *American Journal of Sociology* 78/2 (1972), pp. 290–8. The study was conducted as part of a large cross-national project, interviews were conducted between December 1963 and April 1964. All respondents were Bengali Muslim males, born in East Pakistan, and all were within the age range of 18–32 years.

42. Khalid Bin Sayeed, 'Islam and National integration in Pakistan' in D. E. Smith (ed.), *South Asian Religion and Politics* (Princeton: Princeton University Press, 1966), p. 408. Quoted in Murshid, *Sacred and Secular* (1995), p. 336.

43. Nasim A. Jawed, *Islam's Political Culture, Religion and Politics in Predivided Pakistan* (Austin: University of Texas Press, 1999). A total of 163 persons were surveyed from East and West Pakistan in July 1969. These individuals were broken down into two categories: 'professionals', consisting of lawyers, university teachers, and journalists from the modern educated middle class, and *ulama*, defined by Jawed as 'those scholars of Islam who have received a mainly traditional Islamic education in traditional Islamic schools [. . .] and who are either teaching in such schools or hold positions in *imams* in mosques.' Of these 29 were *ulama* (12 from East Pakistan) and 134 professionals (60 from East Pakistan).

44. Ibid., p. 17, Table 2.2, p. 18; Table 2.4, p. 28.

45. Ibid., pp. 14, 19.

46. Ibid., Table C.5, p. 223.

47. Government of Bangladesh, *Bangladesh Gonoporishder Bitarka* [*Debates in the Bangladesh Constituent Assembly*], Vol. II, No. 9, 1972, pp. 292–95.

48. Ibid., p. 452.

49. Ibid., p. 461.

50. Government of Bangladesh, *The Constitution of the People's Republic of Bangladesh* (Ministry of Law, Dhaka: Government of Bangladesh, 1972), p. 5. The constitution further stipulated in Article 38, section 2: 'No persons shall have the right to form or be a member or otherwise take part in the activities of, any communal or other association or union which in the name of or on the basis of any religion has for its object, or pursues a political purpose', p. 13.

51. The latter was reflected in a three-day symposium held at the Rajshahi University on 19–21 August 1972 (See Ali Anwar (ed.), *Dhromo Niropekshota* [*Secularism*] (in Bengali) (Dhaka: Bangla Academy, 1973)).

52. Murshid, *The Sacred and the Secular* (2001), p. 286.

53. G. Moyser, 'Politics and Religion in the Modern World: An Overview', in *Politics and Religion in the Modern World*, edited by G Moyser, 1–27 (London: Routledge, 1991), p. 14.

54. Government of the People's Republic of Bangladesh, *Speech of Sheikh Mujibur Rahman*, 18 January 1974 (Dhaka: Department of Publications, Ministry of Information), p. 3.

55. *The Bangladesh Observer*, 5 November 1972, p. 1.

56. Ali Riaz, *God Willing: The Politics of Islamism in Bangladesh* (Lanham, MA: Rowman and Littlefield, 2004).

57. Harvey Cox, *The Secular City* (New York: Macmillan, 1965).

58. Jose Casanova, *Public Religions in the Modern World* (Chicago: University of Chicago Press, 1994), p. 211.

59. Jeffrey K Hadden, 'Toward Desacralizing Secularization Theory', *Social Forces* 65/3 (1987), pp. 587–611.

60. Jeff Haynes, 'Introduction', *Religion in Global Politics* (London: Longman. 1998).

61. Peter Berger, 'The Desecularization of the World: A Global Overview', in Peter Berger (ed.), *The Desecularization of the World: Resurgent Religion and World Politics* (Grand Rapids, MI: William B. Eerdmans Publishing Co. 1999),

pp. 1–18. It is important to note that Peter Berger, in the 1960s, was the most well-known proponent of the argument that religion will have very little, if any, role in public life.

62. Emile Sahliyeh, 'Religious Resurgence and Political Modernization', in Emile Sahliyeh (ed.), *Religious Resurgence and Politics in the Contemporary World* (New York: State University of New York Press. 1990), p. 3.

63. Peter Berger, 'The Desecularization of the World', p. 2.

64. Economist, 'Obituary: God', *Economist*, Millennium Issue, 29 December 1999, http://www.economist.com/obituary/displaystory.cfm?story_id=347578.

65. In 2007 *The Economist* argued that God is back; see Economist, 'In the Name of God', *The Economist*, 1 November 2007.

66. Thomas Blom Hansen, *The Saffron Wave*, p. 4.

67. Dibyesh Anand, 'The Violence of Security: Hindu Nationalism and the Politics of Representing "the Muslim" as a Danger', *The Round Table*, 94/379 (2005), pp. 205, 203–15.

68. Anthony Giddens, *Modernity and Self-Identity: Self and the Society in the Late-Modern Age* (Cambridge: Polity, 1991), p. 33.

69. Ibid., p. 243.

70. Ibid., p. 38.

71. Ibid., p. 47.

72. Ibid., p. 185.

73. Catarina Kinnvall, *Globalization and Religious Nationalism in India, The Search for Ontological Security* (London: Routledge, 2006), pp. 741–67.

74. Ibid., p. 759.

75. Sahliyeh, 'Religious Resurgence', p. 15.

76. Mark Juergensmeyer, *The New Cold War? Religious Nationalism Confronts the Secular State* (University of California Press, 1994), p. 23.

77. William F. S. Miles, 'Political Para-theology Rethinking Religion, Politics and Democracy', *Third World Quarterly*, 17 (1996), pp. 525, 525–536.

78. Ali Riaz, *God Willing*; Ismail, *Rethinking Islamist Politics Culture, the State and Islamism* (London: I.B.Tauris, 2006); Francois Burgat, *Face to Face with Political Islam* (London: I.B.Tauris, 2003); Bobby S. Sayyid, *A Fundamental Fear: Eurocentrism and the Emergence of Islamism* (London: Zed Books, 1997).

79. World Bank, Poverty and Equity, http://povertydata.worldbank.org/poverty/region/SAS.

80. Vali Reza Nasr, Seyyed, 'Islam, the State and the Rise of Sectarian Militancy in Pakistan' in Christophe Jaffrelot (ed.), *Pakistan: Nationalism without a Nation?* (New Delhi: Monohar, 2002), p. 92, 85–114.

81. Mahmood Mamdani, 'Inventing Political Violence', *Global Agenda* 2005, http://www.globalagendamagazine.com/2005/mahmoodmamdani.asp (20 October 2005).

82. Ibid.

83. The term victimhood implies three elements: first, a victim is someone's target; second, victimhood readily suggests being the undeserved target of

another's actions; and third and the corollary of these elements of real victimhood is that the victimizer becomes an intentional inflicter of harm on the innocent. Michael Ovey, 'Victim Chic? The Rhetoric of Victimhood', Cambridge Papers published by the Jubilee Center, 15/1, March 2006.

84. It is worth noting that, the consequences of US policies on the Muslim world – both real and perceived – have received more attention after 9/11 than before, but often these discussions have emphasized the Arab world or the Middle East leaving the majority of the global Muslim population out of the equation.

85. Craig Charney and Nicole Yakatan, *A New Beginning: Strategies for a More Fruitful Dialogue with the Muslim World* (Washington DC: Council on Foreign Relations, 2005), p. 5.

86. Jawed, *Islam's Political Culture*, Table C.31, p. 249.

87. World Values Survey 1996, 2002.

88. USAID, *Bangladesh: Knowledge, Attitudes and Practices, National Survey Covering Democracy and Governing Issues* (Dhaka: USAID, 2004).

89. Nicole Naurath, 'Religion, Secularism Working in Tandem in Bangladesh', Gallup World, 29 July 2009, http://www.gallup.com/poll/121937/religion-secularism-working-tandem-bangladesh.aspx. Results are based on face-to-face interviews with at least 1,000 adults, aged 15 and older, conducted in May 2006, May 2007, June 2008, and May 2009 in Bangladesh.

90. Pew Research Center, 'Global Opinion Trends 2002–2007: 47-Nation Pew Global Attitudes Survey', Washington, DC: Pew Research Center, 24 July 2007, http://pewglobal.org/files/pdf/257.pdf.

91. Gallup, Insights South Asia – Bangladesh Survey 2012 Results, http://www.gallup.com/strategicconsulting/158156/insights-south-asia-bangladesh-survey-2012-results.aspx. Gallup, 2012, A total of 1,000 face-to-face interviews in all parts of Bangladesh were conducted in May 2012.

92. Pew Research Center, 'Religion and Politics', *The World's Muslim: Religion Politics, and Society*, Washington, DC: Pew Research Center, April 2013; http://www.pewforum.org/files/2013/04/worlds-muslims-religion-politics-society-full-report.pdf.

93. Richard M. Eaton, *The Rise of Islam and the Bengal Frontier 1204–1760* (Berkeley: University of California Press, 1993).

94. Asim Roy, *The Islamic Syncretistic Tradition in Bengal* (Princeton: Princeton University Press, 1984).

95. Joya Chatterjee, 'The Bengali Muslim: A Contradiction in Terms? An Overview of the Debate on Bengali Muslim Identity', *Comparative Studies of South Asia, Africa and the Middle East* XVI/ 2 (1996), pp. 21, 16–24.

96. Ali Riaz, 'Interactions of "Transnational" and "Local" Islam in Bangladesh', *Transnational Islam in South and Southeast Asia: Movements, Networks, and Conflict Dynamics* (Seattle, WA: National Bureau of Asian Research, 2009).

97. For a recent exposition, see, Samia Huq, 'Defining Self and Other: Bangladesh's Secular Aspirations and Its Writing of Islam', *Economic and Political Weekly* XLVIII/50 (2013), pp. 51–61.

Chapter 7   Unpacking the Paradox of Development

1. World Bank, 'WB Update Says 10 Countries Move Up in Income Bracket', 1 July 2015, http://www.worldbank.org/en/news/press-release/2015/07/01/ new-world-bank-update-shows-bangladesh-kenya-myanmar-and-tajikistan-as -middle-income-while-south-sudan-falls-back-to-low-income.

2. The term was first used in a meeting on South Asia of the interdepartmental Washington Special Actions Group (WSAG, USA) on 6 December 1971. In that meeting Maurice J Williams, then the deputy administrator of the US Agency for International Development (USAID) and also chairman of the Interdepartmental Working Group on East Pakistan Disaster Relief, in projecting a famine, said, 'They'll be an international basket case.' Henry Kissinger, then US's national security advisor, quipped 'But not necessarily our basket case' (Document 235, Vol. XI of the *Foreign Relations of the United States* series for 1969–1976 titled *'South Asia Crisis, 1971'*). The quote is often inaccurately attributed to Henry Kissinger.

3. Just Faaland and John Richard Parkinson, *Bangladesh: The Test Case for Development* (London: C Hurst and Co., 1976).

4. Jim O'Neill, 'Beyond the BRICS: A Look at the "Next 11"', *BRICs and Beyond* (New York: Goldman Sachs, 2007), http://www.goldmansachs.com/our-thi nking/archive/BRICs-and-Beyond.html.

5. J. P. Morgan, 'Ho Chi Minh Trail to Mexico', *Emerging Market Equity Research* (New York: JP Morgan, 2007).

6. McKinsey and Company, *Bangladesh's Ready-Made Garments Landscape The Challenge Of Growth* (Frankfurt: McKinsey and Company, November 2011), http://www.mckinsey.de/sites/mck_files/files/2011_McKinsey_Bangladesh. pdf.

7. *Economist*, 'Bangladesh: Out of the basket', 3 November 2012, http://www. economist.com/news/leaders/21565627-lessons-achievements%E2%80% 94yes-really-achievements%E2%80%94-bangladesh-out-basket.

8. World Bank, 'The Bangladesh Conundrum', 2006, http://web.worldbank.org/ WBSITE/EXTERNAL/EXTABOUTUS/EXTANNREP/EXTANNREP2K6/ 0,,contentMDK:21052781~pagePK:64168445~piPK:64168309~theSite PK:2838572,00.html.

9. Shvoong, 'Bangladesh Will Be a 'Powerhouse' in International Market: The World Bank President', 5 November 2007, http://www.shvoong.com/law-and- politics/political-economy/1700108-bangladesh-powerhouse-international- market-world/#ixzz2vzijYnte.

10. 'The Bangladesh Conundrum'.

11. US Department of Agriculture, Economic Research Service, 2013.

12. 'GDP growth calculated at 6.51%', *Dhaka Tribune*, 14 May 2015, http://www. dhakatribune.com/bangladesh/2015/may/14/gdp-growth-calculated-651.

13. Dhaka: Bangladesh Bureau of Statistics, *Annual Yearbook*; various years.

14. Quandal, 'Bangladesh,' http://www.quandl.com/bangladesh/bangladesh- economy-data.

15. David Cheong, Marion Jansen, and Ralf Peters (eds), *Shared Harvest: Agriculture, Trade and Employment*, Geneva: International Labour Organization (ILO) and UNCTAD, 2013, Table 1, p. 3.

16. United Nations, UNdata, http://data.un.org/Data.aspx?d=MDG&f=series RowID%3A581, 2014.

17. Binayak Sen, Mustafa K. Mujeri, and Quazi Shahabuddin, 'Explaining Pro-Poor Growth in Bangladesh: Puzzles, Evidence, and Implications', in Timothy Besley and Louise J Cord (eds), *Delivering on The Promise of Pro-Poor Growth: Insights and Lessons from Country Experiences* (Washington, DC: World Bank and Palgrave Macmillan, 2007), pp. 79–118.

18. Stephan Klasen, 'Determinants of Pro-Poor Growth', *2020 Focus Brief on the World's Poor and Hungry People* (Washington DC: International Food Policy Research Institute, 2007).

19. Rizwanul Islam, 'Addressing the challenge of economic inequality', *Daily Star*, 19 March 2013, http://archive.thedailystar.net/beta2/news/addressing-the-challenge-of-economic-inequality/.

20. Wahiduddin Mahmud, 'Social Development: Pathways, Surprises and Challenges', *Indian Journal of Human Development* 2/1 (2008), pp. 79–92.

21. Lancet, 'Bangladesh: Innovation for Universal Health Coverage', 21 November 2013, http://www.thelancet.com/series/bangladesh.

22. Unicef ChildInfo, 'Child Survival and Health: Trends in Infant Mortality Rates, 1960–2012', http://www.childinfo.org/mortality_imrcountrydata.php.

23. USAID, 'Bangladesh: Maternal Deaths Decline by 40 Percent in Less Than 10 Years', 11 March 2011, http://blog.usaid.gov/2011/03/bangladesh-maternal-deaths-decline-by-40-per cent-in-less-than-10-years/.

24. National Institute of Population Research and Training (NIPORT), *Bangladesh Demographic and Health Survey 2011* (Dhaka: NIPORT, 2012).

25. Data gathered from United Nations Educational, Scientific, and Cultural Organization (UNESCO) Institute for Statistics; and Bangladesh Directorate of Primary Education.

26. Bangladesh is likely to meet targets relating to 1.9: Proportion of population below minimum level of dietary energy consumption; 2.1: Net enrolment ratio in primary education; 3.1: Ratios of girls to boys in primary education; 4.1: Under-five mortality rate; 4.2: Infant mortality rate; 4.3: Proportion of one-year old children immunized against measles; 5.1: Maternal mortality ratio; and 6.1: HIV prevalence among population aged 15–24 years. The four other areas where Bangladesh has made substantial progress are – 1.1: Proportion of population below poverty line; 2.3: Literacy rate of 15–24-year-olds, women and men; 7.8: Proportion of population using an improved drinking water source; and 7.9: Proportion of population using an improved sanitation facility.

27. Debapriya Bhattacharya, Towfiqul Islam Khan, Umme Salma and Gazi Joki Uddin, 'Attaining the MDGs: How Successful are the LDCs?' Paper presented

at a dialogue organized by Centre for Policy Dialogue (CPD) and Friedrich Ebert Stiftung (FES), Dhaka 21 September 2013.

28. Sen, et al., 'Explaining Pro-Poor Growth in Bangladesh: Puzzles, Evidence, and Implications', pp. 79–118.

29. Ibid., p. 88.

30. For example, Lamia Karim, *Microfinance and Its Discontents: Women in Debt in Bangladesh* (Minneapolis: University of Minnesota Press, 2011); Annaya Roy, *Poverty Capital: Microfinance and the Making of Development* (New York: Routledge, 2011).

31. *Guardian*, 'Bangladesh's garment workers face exploitation, but is it slavery?', 16 May 2013, http://www.theguardian.com/global-development/poverty-matters/2013/may/16/bangladesh-garment-workers-exploitation-slavery.

32. Bureau of Manpower Employment and Training (BMET), 'Overseas Employment and Remittances, 1976–2013', Dhaka: BMET, http://www.bmet.org.bd/BMET/viewStatReport.action?reportnumber=31.

33. Institute of Informatics and Development, 'Facing the Challenges of Labour Migration from Bangladesh', Policy Brief 4 (December 2011). Dhaka: IID.

34. Munim K. Barai, 'Development Dynamics of Remittances in Bangladesh', *Sage Open*. Published online 23 February 2012. DOI: 10.1177/2158244 012439073.

35. Dilip Ratha, and Sanket Mohapatra. 'Increasing the Macroeconomic Impact of Remittances on Development', Note prepared for the G8 Outreach Event on Remittances, Berlin, 28–30 November 2007.

36. Selim Raihan, Bazlul H. Khondker, Guntur Sugiyarto, and Shikha Jha, 'Remittances and Household Welfare: A Case Study of Bangladesh', *ADB Economics Working Paper Series*, no. 189. Philippines: Asian Development Bank, 2009.

37. Carlos Vargas-Silva, Shikha Jha, and Guntur Sugiyarto, 'Remittances in Asia: Implications for the Fight against Poverty and the Pursuit of Economic Growth', *ADB Economics Working Paper Series*, no. 182. Philippines: Asian Development Bank, 2009.

38. Barai, 'Development Dynamics of Remittances in Bangladesh', 2012.

39. ITUC, 'Hidden faces of the Gulf miracle', *Union View* 12, Brussels, May 2011. http://www.ituc-csi.org/hidden-faces-of-the-gulf-miracle,9144?lang=en.

40. Shariful Hasan, 'Deaths Like These Cannot be Accepted' (in Bengali), *Prothom Alo*, 10 February 2014, p. 1.

41. 'Bangladesh undertook two waves of agricultural reforms between the late 1970s and early 1990s. In the first, the markets for agricultural inputs – above all fertiliser and irrigation equipment were liberalized. This led to falling prices, greater availability, and increased use of these inputs. Tubewells and pumps, in particular, allowed a major expansion of winter ("boro") rice production that saw increases in domestic supply of rice outstrip population growth and thereby drove down the price of rice. This in turn made it easier to implement the second round of reforms where the markets for food grains were

liberalised and some large-scale programmes of food subsidies were ended'
(Lidia Cabral, Colin Poulton, Steve Wiggins, and Linxiu Zhang, 'Reforming
Agricultural Policy: Lessons from four countries', *Future Agricultures Working
Paper* (Brighton, UK: Institute of Development Studies, 2006), p. 6.
42. Hilary Thornton and Paul Thornton, 'Institutional Assessment of Education
in Bangladesh', Dhaka: British Council, March 2012. http://schoolsonline.bri
tishcouncil.org/sites/default/files/files/Institutional%20Assessment%20of%
20Education%20in%20Bangladesh.pdf.
43. 'The female secondary school stipend programme began as an experiment in
1982 by a local NGO in a single upazila [sub-district] with USAID financial
assistance under the supervision of the Asia Foundation. A second upazila was
included in 1984 and several more subsequently, totaling seven by 1992, when
NORAD took over support for the programme. The stipend programme
continued in the name of FESP from July 1992 to December 1996 as a sub-
project under the umbrella of the General Education Project of NORAD.
The experience of this pilot project has been described as highly successful
since the actual number of stipends provided far exceeded the projected
number at the time of inception and the number of awardee schools increased
by 12 per cent in four years of project life. Largely on the basis of the above
'success' the Bangladesh government launched in January 1994 a nation-wide
stipend programme for girls in secondary school (grades 6–10) in all 460
upazilas (sub districts) of the country with support from the World Bank, the
Asian Development Bank and the Norwegian Agency for Development
Cooperation, known as the Female Stipend Programme' (Simeen Mahmud,
'Female secondary school stipend programme in Bangladesh: A critical
assessment', Mimeo, Dhaka: Bangladesh Institute of Development Studies,
First Draft 28 May 2003; revised 2 July 2003).
44. A Mushtaque R. Chowdhury, Abbas Bhuiya, Mahbub Elahi Chowdhury,
Sabrina Rasheed, Zakir Hussain, and Lincoln C. Chen, 'The Bangladesh
paradox: exceptional health achievement despite economic poverty',
Bangladesh: Innovation for Universal Health Coverage 1, *Lancet*, vol. 382,
23 November 2013, p. 1737.

Conclusion: Looking Back, Looking Ahead

1. Shelley Feldman, 'Gender and Islam in Bangladesh: Metaphor and Myth', in
Understanding the Bengal Muslims: Interpretative Essays, Rafiuddin Ahmed (ed.)
(New Delhi: Oxford University Press, 2000), pp. 231–5.
2. Amin Maalouf, *In the Name of Identity: Violence and the Need to Belong* (New
York: Penguin, 2000).
3. Arjun Appadurai, *Fear of Small Numbers, An Essay on the Geography of Anger*
(Durham, NC: Duke University Press, 2006).

BIBLIOGRAPHY

Acharya, Pritish and Shri Krishan. 'An Experiment in Nationalist Education: Satyavadi School in Orissa (1909–26)'. *Economic & Political Weekly* xlv/51 (2010), pp. 71–78.

Adams, Alayne M., Tanvir Ahmed, Shams El Arifeen, Timothy G. Evans, Tanvir Huda, Laura Reichenbach. 'Bangladesh: Innovation for Universal Health Coverage'. *The Lancet*, 21 November 2013, http://www.thelancet.com/series/bangladesh.

Adcock, Chris. 'Violent Obstacles to Democratic Consolidation in Three Countries: Guatemala, Colombia, and Algeria'. ProQuest, http://www.csa.com/discovery guides/demo/overview.php.

Ahamed, Emajuddin. *Military Rule and Myths of Democracy* (Dhaka: University Press Limited, 1988), p. 79.

Ahmed, Moudud. *Bangladesh: Era of Sheikh Mujibur Rahman* (Weisbadan: Franz Steiner Verlag, 1984), p. 56.

Ahmed, Nizam. 'From Monopoly to Competition: Party Politics in the Bangladesh Parliament'. *Pacific Affairs* 76/1 (2003), p. 61.

Ahmed, Rafiuddin. *The Bengal Muslims 1871–1906, A Quest for Identity* (Delhi: Oxford University Press, 1981), p. 40.

———. 'Introduction: The Emergence of Bengal Muslims', in Rafiuddin Ahmed (ed.). *Understanding the Bengal Muslims: Interpretative Essays* (Delhi: Oxford University Press, 2001), pp. 4–5.

Akash, M. M. *Bangladesher Arthaniti O Rajniti, Sampratik Probonotasamuha.* Bangladesh Economy and Politics, Recent Trends, in Bengali (Dhaka: Jatiyo Shahittyo Prokashani, 1987).

Ali, Tariq and Naomi Hossain. 'Popular Expectations of Government: Findings from Three Areas in Bangladesh'. PRCPB Working Paper No. 13, Dhaka: Programme for Research on Chronic Poverty in Bangladesh (PRCPB), Bangladesh Institute of Development Studies (BIDS); and Chronic Poverty Research Centre (CPRC), Institute for Development Policy and Management (IDPM), University of Manchester, February 2006, p. 12, http://www.prcpb-bids.org/documents/workingpaper/wp13fulltext.pdf.

Allchin, Joseph. 'Explaining Bangladesh's Month of Massive Street Protests and Violence', *Vice*, 3 March 2013, http://www.vice.com/read/explaining-Bangladeshs-month-of-massive-street-protests-and-violence.

Alvarez, Mike, Jose Antonio Cheibub, Fernando Limogni, and Adam Przeworski. 'Classifying Political Regimes'. *Studies in Comparative International Development* 31/2 (1996), pp. 3–36.

Amartya, Sen. 'Democracy as a Universal Value'. *Journal of Democracy* 10/3 (1999), pp. 3–17.

Anand, Dibyesh. 'The Violence of Security: Hindu Nationalism and the Politics of Representing "the Muslim" as a Danger'. *The Round Table* 94/379 (2005), pp. 205, 203–215.

Anderson, Benedict. *Imagined Communities: Reflections on the Origin and Spread of Nationalism*. Revised Edition (London and New York: Verso, 1991), pp. 5–7.

Anisuzzaman. 'The Identity Question and the Politics', in Rounaq Jahan (ed.). *Bangladesh – Promise and Performance* (London: Zed Books Ltd and Dhaka: University Press Limited, 2001), p. 52.

———. 'Claiming and Disclaiming a Cultural Icon: Tagore in East Pakistan and Bangladesh'. *University of Toronto Quarterly* 77/4 (2008), pp. 1058–1069, http://muse.jhu.edu/.

Anwar, Ali (ed.). *Dhromo Niropekshota [Secularism, in Bengali]* (Dhaka: Bangla Academy, 1973).

Appadurai, Arjun. *Fear of Small Numbers, An Essay on the Geography of Anger*. Durham, NC: Duke University Press, 2006.

Asian Legal Resource Centre. 'BANGLADESH: Public justice system incapable of addressing relentless enforced disappearance', http://alrc.asia/alrc-cws-003-2015/.

Ayoob, Mohammed. 'Background and Developments'. In *Bangladesh: A Struggle for Nationhood* (Delhi: Vikas Publications, 1971), p. 35.

Azad, A. K. 'The Saga of Bangladesh Army'. *Weekly Holiday* (1972).

Aziz, Syeda Salina and Elvir Graner. *Governance Barometer Survey Bangladesh 2010* (Dhaka: Institute of Governance Studies, Brac University 2010), pp. 51–53.

'Bangladesh Authorities Go After Bloggers, Claim They are "Anti-Islamic"' *Global Voices Advocacy*, 1 April 2013, https://advox.globalvoices.org/2013/04/01/bangladesh-authorities-go-after-anti-muslim-bloggers/ 1.

Bangladesh Awami League. 'Constitution', http://www.albd.org/index.php/en/party/constitution.

Bangladesh Bureau of Statistics, Annual Yearbook, various years, Dhaka: BBS.

Bangladesh Chronicle. 'EC Prepares Report on BNF Registration'. 18 August 2013, http://www.bangladeshchronicle.net/index.php/2013/08/ec-prepares-report-on-bnf-registration/.

Bangladesh Election Commission. 'Tenure of All Parliaments', http://www.parliament.gov.bd/index.php/en/about-parliament/tenure-of-parliament.

Bangladesh Nationalist Party (BNP). 'Constitution (Amended up to 8 December 2009)', http://bangladeshnationalistparty-bnp.org/content.aspx?tablename=webitem2&id=8&child=null&parentid=null (accessed 2 November 2013).

Bangladesh Planning Commission (BPC). 'Policy Options and Recommendations for the Nationalization of the Industries'. Mimeograph (Dhaka: Bangladesh Planning Commission, 1972).

'Bangladesh Will Be a "Powerhouse" in International Market: The World Bank President'. Shvoong. 5 November 2007, http://www.shvoong.com/law-and-politics/political-economy/1700108-bangladesh-powerhouse-international-market-world/#ixzz2vzijYnte.

Banu, U. A. B. Razia Aktar. *Islam in Bangladesh*. Leiden: E. J. Brill, 1992, p. 27.

Barai, Munim K. 'Development Dynamics of Remittances in Bangladesh'. *Sage Open*. Published online 23 February 2012. DOI: 10.1177/2158244012439073.

Barman, Dalem Ch, M. Golam Rahman and Tasneem Siddiqui. 'Democracy Report for Bangladesh'. International Institute for Democracy and Electoral Assistance (IDEA) (2001), p. 44, http://www.idea.int/publications/sod/upload/Bangladesh.pdf.

Barua, Tushar Kanti. *Political Elite in Bangladesh* (Bern: Peter Lang, 1978), p. 168.

Baxter, Craig, Yogender K. Malik, Charles H. Kennedy, and Robert C. Oberst. *Government and Politics in South Asia* (Boulder, CO: Westview, 2002), p. 295.

Bdnews24. 'Home Minister Kamal warns against writing anything that hurts religious sentiment,' bdnews24, 11 August 2015, http://bdnews24.com/bangladesh/2015/08/11/home-minister-kamal-warns-against-writing-anything-that-hurts-religious-sentiment.

———. 'IGP suggests Bangladesh bloggers to not "cross the line", not write blogs that may hurt religious sensitivities', *bdnews24*, 9 August 2015, http://bdnews24.com/bangladesh/2015/08/09/igp-suggests-bangladesh-bloggers-to-not-cross-the-line-not-write-blogs-that-may-hurt-religious-sensitivities.

Berger, Peter. 'The Desecularization of the World: A Global Overview', in Peter Berger (ed.). *The Desecularization of the World: Resurgent Religion and World Politics* (Grand Rapids, MI: William B. Eerdmans Publishing Co. 1999), pp. 1–18.

Bergman, David. 'Free Speech Under Fire in Bangladesh,' *Aljazeera.com*, 17 April 2015, http://america.aljazeera.com/articles/2015/4/17/bangladesh-press-freedom.html.

Bertocci, Peter J. 'Bangladesh in the Early-1980s: Praetorian Politics in an Intermediate Regime'. *Asian Survey* 22/10 (1982), p. 993.

Bhaba, Homi. 'Introduction: Narrating the Nation'. In *Nation and Narration* (London: Routledge, 1990), pp. 1–7.

Bhattacharya, Debapriya, Towfiqul Islam Khan, Umme Salma and Gazi Joki Uddin. 'Attaining the MDGs: How Successful are the LDCs?' Paper presented at a dialogue organized by Centre for Policy Dialogue (CPD) and Friedrich Ebert Stiftung (FES). Dhaka 21 September 2013.

'Bloggers are Killed following a List', *Prothom Alo*, 15 May 2015, http://m.prothom-alo.com/bangladesh/article/528262/%E0%A6%A4%E0%A6%BE%E0%A6%B2%E0%A6%BF%E0%A6%95%E0%A6%BE-%E0%A6%A7%E0%A6%B0%E0%A7%87-%E0%A6%AC%E0%A7%8D%E0%A6%B2%E0%A6%97%E0%A6%BE%E0%A6%B0-%E0%A6%96%E0%A7%81%E0%A6%A8.

Blood, Archar K. The Cruel Birth of Bangladesh – Memoirs of an American Diplomat (Dhaka: University Press Limited, 2013).

Bollen, Kenneth and Pamela Paxton. 'Subjective Measures of Liberal Democracy'. *Comparative Political Studies* 33/1 (2000), pp. 58–86.

Bose, Swadesh Ranjan. 'The Price Situation in Bangladesh'. *The Bangladesh Economic Review* 1/3 (1974), p. 244.

Bureau of Manpower Employment and Training (BMET). 'Overseas Employment and Remittances, 1976–2013'. Dhaka: BMET, http://www.bmet.org.bd/BMET/viewStatReport.action?reportnumber=31.

Burgat, Francois. *Face to Face with Political Islam* (London: I.B.Tauris, 2003).

Cabral, Lidia, Colin Poulton, Steve Wiggins, and Linxiu Zhang. 'Reforming Agricultural Policy: Lessons from Four Countries'. *Future Agricultures Working Paper* (Brighton, UK: Institute of Development Studies, 2006), p. 6.

Carothers, Thomas. 'The End of the Transition Paradigm'. *Journal of Democracy* 13/1 (2002), pp. 5–12.

Carson, Thomas. 'Issues and Priorities for Bangladesh: The 2000 IFES National Survey' (Washington DC: IFES. November 2001).

Casanova, Jose. *Public Religions in the Modern World* (Chicago: University of Chicago Press, 1994), p. 211.

Cassani, Andrea. 'Hybrid what? The contemporary debate on hybrid regimes and the identity question', paper presented at 26th Congress of Italian Society of Political Science (SISP), 13–15 September 2012.

Charney, Craig and Nicole Yakatan. *A New Beginning: Strategies for a More Fruitful Dialogue with the Muslim World* (Washington DC: Council on Foreign Relations, 2005), p. 5.

Chatterjee, Joya. 'The Bengali Muslim: A Contradiction in Terms? An Overview of the Debate on Bengali Muslim Identity'. *Comparative Studies of South Asia, Africa and the Middle East* XVI/ 2 (1996), pp. 21, 16–24.

————. *Bengal Divided* (Cambridge: Cambridge University Press, 1994).

Chatterjee, Partha. Nationalist Thought and the Colonial World: The Derivative Discourse? (London: Zed Books, 1986).

Cheong, David, Marion Jansen, and Ralf Peters (eds). *Shared Harvest: Agriculture, Trade and Employment*. Geneva: International Labour Organization (ILO) and UNCTAD, 2013. Table 1, p. 3.

Chowdhury, Faiz Ahmed. 'Geo-politics, Democratization and External Influence: The Bangladesh Case'. IGS Working Paper Series No: 05/2013. Published by the Institute of Governance Studies, BRAC University, March 2013.

Chowdhury, Rashid A. 'United States Foreign Policy in South Asia: The Liberation Struggle in Bangladesh and the Indo-Pakistan War of 1971'. Unpublished PhD Dissertation. Department of History. University of Hawaii. 1989, pp. 155–170.

Collins, Larry and Dominique Lapierre. *Freedom at Midnight* (New Delhi: Vikas Publishing House Pvt. Ltd., 1976), p. 104.

Colonel Rashid and Colonel Farook. *The Road to Freedom* (Dhaka: Syed Ataur Rahman, 2008).

Community Development Library. Voice Through Ballot: Election and People's Perception (Dhaka: CDL, 2001).

Confidential Telegram from US Embassy. Dhaka to Department of State/Secretary of State. 02158, 15 May 1974, http://www.wikileaks.org/plusd/cables/1974DAC-CA02158_b.html.

Confidential Telegram from US Embassy. Dhaka to Department of State/Secretary of State, http://www.wikileaks.org/plusd/cables/1973DACCA03156_b.html.

Constituent Assembly of Pakistan (CAP). *Debates*, 1 January, 1, 52, 1956.

Coppedge, Michael and John Gerring. 'Conceptualizing and Measuring Democracy: A New Approach. *Perspectives on Politics* 9/2 (2011), pp. 247–267.

Cox, Harvey. *The Secular City* (New York: Macmillan, 1965).
Dahl, Robert. *Polyarchy: Participation and Opposition* (New Haven: Yale University Press, 1971).
Daily Amar Desh. 'Hefazat Didn't Provide Bloggers List: Shafi', 24 May 2015, http://www.amardeshonline.com/pages/details/2015/05/24/285591#.Vhw3l2BdGM8.
Daily Observer. 'DIG says police can avenge one killing with two', 4 February 2015 http://www.observerbd.com/2015/02/04/70614.php.
————. 'Eliminate saboteurs, families: DIG Mahfuz' , *The Daily Observer*, 8 February 2015, http://www.observerbd.com/2015/02/08/71390.php.
Daily Star. 'The Daily Star-Nielsen Election Opinion Poll 2008'. 21 November 2008, http://archive.thedailystar.net/suppliments/2008/opinion percent20poll/o_poll.htm.
————. 'In eyes of Gen Shafiullah.' 31 January 2010, http://archive.thedailystar.net/newDesign/news-details.php?nid=124155.
————. 'Taher Trial Illegal'. 23 March 2011, http://archive.thedailystar.net/newDesign/news-details.php?nid=178777.
————. 'Bangladesh's editors demand repeal of section 57 of ICT Act', *Daily Star*, 24 August 2015, p. 1.
————. 'Bangladesh PM says govt won't allow anybody to hurt religious sentiments', *Daily Star*, 4 September 2015, http://www.thedailystar.net/frontpage/hurting-religious-sentiments-wont-be-tolerated-pm-137617.
De, Dhurjati Prasad. *Bengal Muslims in Search of Social Identity 1905–47* (Dhaka: University Press Limited, 1998).
DeSouza, Peter R., Suhas Palshikar, and Yogendra Yadav. 'Surveying South Asia'. *Journal of Democracy* 19/1 (2008), pp. 84–96, http://www.journalofdemocracy.org/sites/default/files/YadavGraphics-19–1.pdf.
Deutsche Welle. 'Atheist bloggers flee Bangladesh'. 11 September 2015, http://www.dw.com/en/atheist-bloggers-flee-bangladesh/a-18708933. .
Devichand, Mukul. 'Nowhere is safe': Behind the Bangladesh blogger murders,' *BBC Trending*, 7 August 2015, http://www.bbc.com/news/blogs-trending-33822674.
Dhaka Tribune. 'ACC is a "toothless tiger": Ghulam Rahman'. 19 June 2013, http://www.dhakatribune.com/bangladesh/2013/jun/19/acc-%E2%80%98toothless-tiger%E2%80%99-ghulam-rahman.
————. 'Death penalty for Quader Molla', *Dhaka Tribune*, 18 September 2013, http://www.dhakatribune.com/law-amp-rights/2013/sep/17/quader-mollah-walk-gallows .
————. 'Disappearances' become a horror in 2014', *Dhaka Tribune*, 1 January 2015, http://www.dhakatribune.com/bangladesh/2015/jan/01/%E2%80%8098disappearance%E2%80%8099-became-horror-2014.
————. 'Joy: Situation was too volatile to comment on Avijit murder', *Dhaka Tribune*, 11 May 2015, http://www.dhakatribune.com/bangladesh/2015/may/11/situation-too-volatile-comment-avijit-murder#sthash.UVfE8Gpu.dpuf.
Diamond, Larry. 'Is the Third Wave Over?' *Journal of Democracy* 7/3 (1996), pp. 20–37.
————. 'The Democratic Rollback: The Resurgence of the Predatory State'. *Foreign Affairs* (2008).
————. 'Democracy's Third Wave Today'. *Current History* 110/739 (2011), p. 299.

Diamond, Larry Jay and Leonardo Morlino. 'An Overview'. *Journal of Democracy* 15/4 (2004), pp. 20–31.

Doorenspleet, Renske. 'Reassessing the Three Waves of Democratization'. *World Politics* 52 (2000), p. 389.

Eaton, Richard M. *The Rise of Islam and the Bengal Frontier (1204–1760)*, Berkeley: University of California Press, 1993 (pb 1996).

Economist. 'Obituary: God'. *Economist*, Millennium Issue. 29 December 1999, http://www.economist.com/obituary/displaystory.cfm?story_id=347578.

———. 'Not Uniformly Bad'. *Economist*, 8 February 2007, http://www.economist.com/node/8668962.

———. 'No Going Back'. *Economist*, 19 April 2007, http://www.economist.com/node/9052421.

———. 'Bangladesh: the Minus Two'. *Economist*, 6 September 2007, http://www.economist.com/node/9769010; see also, Secuirty-Risk.com.

———. 'Bangladesh: Out of the Basket'. *Economist*, 3 November 2012, http://www.economist.com/news/leaders/21565627-lessons-achievements%E2%80%94yes-really-achievements%E2%80%94-bangladesh-out-basket.

———. 'Bangladesh's Volatile Politics: The Battling Begums'. *Economist*, 10 August 2013, http://www.economist.com/news/asia/21583297-pendulum-swings-away-sheikh-hasina-and-her-government-battling-begums.

Ekman, Joakim. 'Political Participation and Regime Stability: A Framework for Analyzing Hybrid Regimes'. *International Political Science Review* 30/1 (2009), pp. 7–21.

European Intelligence Unit. Economist. *Index of Democracy*. Various Years, http://www.eiu.com.

Faaland, Just and John Richard Parkinson. *Bangladesh: The Test Case for Development* (London: C Hurst and Co., 1976).

Feldman, Shelley. 'Gender and Islam in Bangladesh: Metaphor and Myth' in Rafiuddin Ahmed (ed.), *Understanding the Bengal Muslims: Interpretative Essays* (New Delhi: Oxford University Press, 2000), p. 231n5.

Financial Times (Dhaka). '5th Amendment of Constitution: SC Upholds HC Verdict with Certain Modifications'. 29 July 2010, http://www.thefinancialexpress-bd.com/more.php?news_id=107484&date=2010-07-29.

Franda, Marcus. *Bangladesh: The First Decade* (New Delhi: South Asian Publishers, 1982), p. 29.

Freedom House. *Freedom In The World 2013: Democratic Breakthroughs In The Balance* (Washington D.C: Freedom House), p. 29.

———. *Freedom in the World*. 'Freedom in the World: Aggregate and Subcategory Scores'. Various years, http://www.freedomhouse.org/report/freedom-world-aggregate-and-subcategory-scores.

———. *Freedom in the World*. Various Years., http://www.freedomhouse.org/reports.

Gallup. Insights South Asia – Bangladesh Survey 2012 Results, http://www.gallup.com/strategicconsulting/158156/insights-south-asia-bangladesh-survey-2012-results.aspx.

Giddens, Anthony. Modernity and Self-Identity: Self and the Society in the Late-Modern Age (Cambridge: Polity, 1991), p. 33.

Gocek, Fatma Muge. Social Constructions of Nationalism in the Middle East (New York: SUNY Press, 2002).

Government of Bangladesh. *Bangladesh Gonoporishder Bitarka* [*Debates in the Bangladesh Constituent Assembly*], Vol. II, No. 9, 1972, pp. 292–95.
Government of Bangladesh. The Constitution of the People's Republic of Bangladesh. Ministry of Law (Dhaka: Government of Bangladesh, 1972), p. 5.
Government of the People's Republic of Bangladesh. Memo No. 391(8)/Cab, Dated Nov 25, 1971.
———. Establishment Division. Memo No. Estbt. Dvn./3179 (19), dated 16 December 1971.
———. *Speech of Sheikh Mujibur Rahman.* 18 January 1974 (Dhaka: Department of Publications, Ministry of Information), p. 3.
———. *Memorandum for the Bangladesh Consortium, 1974–75* (Dhaka: Planning Commission, 1974), p. 9.
———. *Economic Review 1974–75* (Dhaka: Planning Commission, 1975), p. 6.
Gramsci, Antonio. *Selections from Prison Notebooks* (New York: International General, 1971), p. 12.
Graner, Elvira, Fatema Samina Yasmin and Syeda Salina Aziz. *Giving Youth a Voice: Bangladesh Youth Survey* (Dhaka: Institute of Governance Studies, BRAC University, 2012), p. 58.
Hadden, Jeffrey K. 'Toward Desacralizing Secularization Theory'. *Social Forces* 65/3 (1987), pp. 587–611.
Hansen, Thomas Blom. *The Saffron Wave.* p. 4.
Hartman, Betsy and James Boyce. 'Bangladesh: Aid to the Needy'. *International Policy Report* 4/1 (1978), p. 4.
Hasan, Mushirul. 'Minority Identity and Its Discontents, Ayodhya and Its Aftermath'. *South Asia Bulletin* 14/2 (1994), p. 26.
———. *Legacy of a Divided Nation: India's Muslim Since Independence* (London: Hurst & Company, 1997), p. 35.
Hasan, Shariful. 'Deaths Like These Cannot be Accepted' (in Bengali), *Prothom Alo.* 10 February 2014, p. 1.
Hasan, Muyeedul. *Muldhara Ekattar* ([*The Main Trends*] 1971, in Bengali) (Dhaka: University Press Limited, 1986).
Hashmi, Tajul I. *Peasant Utopia; The Communalization of Class Politics in East Bengal, 1920–1947* (Dhaka: University Press Limited, 1994), p. 52.
Haynes, Jeff. 'Introduction'. *Religion in Global Politics* (London: Longman, 1998).
Hossain, Basharat. 'Poverty Reduction during 1971–2013 Periods: Success and its Recent Trends in Bangladesh'. *Global Journal of Human-Social Science: E; Economics*; 14 (5), 2014, pp. 39–47.
Hossain, Kamal. 'Political Development in Bangladesh: Promise and Reality'. *Contributions to Asian Studies* XIV (1979).
———. *Bangladesh: Quest for Freedom and Justice* (Dhaka: University Press Limited, 2013), p. 125.
Hossain, Khurrm. 'Why East & West Never Met'. *Dawn*, 4 October 2012, http://beta.dawn.com/news/753999/why-east-west-never-met.
Hroch, Miroslav. 'From National Movement to the Fully-Formed Nation: The Nation-Building Process in Europe'. *New Left Review* 198 (1993).
Huntington, Samuel P. *The Third Wave: Democratization in the Late Twentieth Century* (Norman: University of Oklahoma Press, 1991), p. 7.
Huq, Samia. 'Defining Self and Other: Bangladesh's Secular Aspirations and Its Writing of Islam'. *Economic and Political Weekly* XLVIII/50 (2013), pp. 51–61.

IDEA/Center for Alternatives. *Bangladesh: Country Report* (Dhaka: Center for Alternatives, published in conjunction with International Institute of Democracy and Electoral Assistance IDEA, 2004), p. 6.

Institute of Informatics and Development. 'Facing the Challenges of Labour Migration from Bangladesh'. Policy Brief 4 (2011). Dhaka: IID.

International Bank for Reconstruction and Development. *Bangladesh: Development in Rural Economy*, Vol. 1 (Washington D.C: IBRD, 1974).

International Republican Institute (IRI). 'Survey of the Bangladeshi Opinion' (Dhaka: IRI, 2009), http://www.iri.org/news-events-press-center/news/iri-releases-survey-bangladesh-public-opinion.

Islam, Amirul. 'Interview', in Hasan Hafizur Rahman (ed.). *History of Bangladesh War of Independence: Documents*, Vol. 15 (Dhaka: Ministry of Information, Government of the People's Republic of Bangladesh, 1985), pp. 77–163. .

Islam, Nurul. Development Planning in Bangladesh, A Study in Political Economy (London: C. Hurst and Company, 1977).

―――. *Development Strategy of Bangladesh* (London: C. Hurst & Company, 1978), p. 4.

―――. 'The Army, UN Peacekeeping Mission and Democracy in Bangladesh'. *Economic and Political Weekly* XLV/29 (2010).

―――. 'Six-Points Programme or Independence?' *Daily Star*, 26 March 2012, http://archive.thedailystar.net/newDesign/news-details.php?nid=227686.

Islam, Rizwanul. 'Addressing the Challenge of Economic Inequality'. *Daily Star*. 19 March 2013, http://archive.thedailystar.net/beta2/news/addressing-the-challenge-of-economic-inequality/.

Islam, Syed Serajul. *Bangladesh: State and Economic Strategy* (Dhaka: University Press Limited, 1988), p. 121.

IslamicNews24.com. 27 February 2013, http://islamicnews24.net/%E0%A6%AC %E0%A7%8D%E0%A6%B2%E0%A6%97%E0%A6%BE%E0%A6%B0-% E0%A6%B0%E0%A6%BE%E0%A6%9C%E0%A7%80%E0%A6%AC% E0%A7%87%E0%A6%B0-%E0%A6%AD%E0%A6%BE%E0%A6%B7% E0%A6%BE-%E0%A6%95%E0%A7%8B%E0%A6%A8%E0%A7%8B/? lang=en.

ITUC. 'Hidden Faces of the Gulf Miracle'. *Union View* 12. Brussels, May 2011, http://www.ituc-csi.org/hidden-faces-of-the-gulf-miracle,9144?lang=en.

J. P. Morgan. 'Ho Chi Minh Trail to Mexico'. *Emerging Market Equity Research* (New York: JP Morgan, 2007).

Jahan, Rounaq. *Bangladesh Politics: Problems and Issues* (Dhaka: University Press Limited, 1980).

Jahangir, Bohanuddin Khan. *Problematics of Nationalism in Bangladesh* (Dhaka; Center for Social Studies, 1986).

Jalal, Ayesha. 'Constructing a State: The Interplay of Domestic, Regional and International Factors in Post-Colonial Pakistan' (Colloquium Paper, Asia Program, Woodrow Wilson International Center for Scholars, Washington DC 1986), p. 85.

―――. 'Exploding Communalism: The Politics of Muslim Identity in South Asia', in Suagata Basu and Ayesha Jalal (eds). *Nationalism, Democracy and Development: State and Politics in India* (Delhi: Oxford University Press, 1999).

Jatiya Party. 'Constitution', http://shujanbd.files.wordpress.com/2013/04/constitution_jp.pdf.

Jawed, Nasim A. *Islam's Political Culture, Religion and Politics in Predivided Pakistan* (Austin: University of Texas Press, 1999).

Juergensmeyer, Mark. *The New Cold War? Religious Nationalism Confronts the Secular State* (University of California Press, 1994), p. 23.

Kamal, Ahmed. *State Against the Nation: The Decline of the Muslim League in Pre-independence Bangladesh, 1947–54* (Dhaka: University Press Limited, 2009), p. 34.

Karim, Lamia. *Microfinance and Its Discontents: Women in Debt in Bangladesh* (Minneapolis: University of Minnesota Press, 2011).

Karl, Terry Lynn. 'Dilemmas of Democratization in Latin America'. *Comparative Politics* 23/9 (1990).

————. 'Petroleum and Political Pacts: The Transition to Democracy in Venezuela', in Guillermo O'Donnell, Philippe Schmitter, Laurence Whitehead (eds). *Transitions from Authoritarian Rule: Latin America* (Baltimore: The Johns Hopkins University Press, 1986).

————. 'Electoralism', in R. Rose (ed.). *International Encyclopedia of Elections* (London: Macmillan, 2000).

Kedourie, Elie. *Nationalism* (London: Hutchinson, 1996).

Kelly, Annie. 'Bangladesh's Garment Workers Face Exploitation, but is it Slavery?' 16 May 2013, http://www.theguardian.com/global-development/poverty-matters/2013/may/16/bangladesh-garment-workers-exploitation-slavery.

Khan, Azizur Rahman and Mahbub Hossain. *The Strategy of Development of Bangladesh* (London: Macmillan, 1989).

Khan, Mohammad Mohabbat. 'State of Governance in Bangladesh'. *Round Table* 370 (2003), p. 395.

Khan, Mohammad Mohabbat and Habib M Zafarullah. 'The 1978 President Elections: A Review' in S R Chakravarty and Virendra Narain (eds). *Bangladesh: Domestic Politics* (New Delhi: South Asia Publishers), p. 102.

Kinnvall, Catarina. *Globalization and Religious Nationalism in India, The Search for Ontological Security* (London: Routledge, 2006), pp. 741–767.

Kissinger, Henry. *The White House Years* (Boston: Brown and Company, 1979), pp. 869–73.

Klasen, Stephan. 'Determinants of Pro-Poor Growth'. *2020 Focus Brief on the World's Poor and Hungry People* (Washington D.C: International Food Policy Research Institute, 2007).

Kochanek, Stanley. 'Bangladesh in 1996: the 25th Year of Independence'. *Asian Survey* 37/2 (1997), pp. 136–142.

————. 'Governance, Patronage Politics and Democratic Transition in Bangladesh'. *Asian Survey* 40/3 (2000), p. 548.

Le Monde [Paris]. 'Le président Ershad annonce une série de concessions'. 5 December 1990.

Levitsky, Steven and Lucan Way. 'The Rise of Competitive Authoritarianism'. *Journal of Democracy* 13/2 (2002), pp. 51–65.

Lewis, Stephan R. *Pakistan, Industrialization and Trade Policies* (London: Oxford University Press, 1970).

Linz, Juan. *Totalitarian and Authoritarian Regimes*. In Fred Greenstein and Nelson Polsby (eds). *Handbook of Political Science* (1975), pp. 184–185.

Lipset, Seymour Martin. 'The Indispensability of Political Parties'. *Journal of Democracy*, 11/1 (2000), pp. 48–55.

Liton, Shakhawat and Hasan Jahid Tusher. 'Same Old Formula'. *Daily Star*, 30 December 2012, p. 1.

Ludden, David. 'The Politics of Independence in Bangladesh'. *Economic and Political Weekly* XXLVI 35/27 (2011), pp. 79–85.

Maalouf, Amin. *In the Name of Identity: Violence and the Need to Belong* (New York: Penguin, 2000). .

Magen, Amichai. 'Evaluating External Influence on Democratic Development: Transition'. CDDRL Working Paper 111, November 2009, p. 8.

Mahmud, Simeen. 'Female Secondary School Stipend Programme in Bangladesh: A Critical Assessment'. Mimeo, Dhaka: Bangladesh Institute of Development Studies. First Draft 28 May 2003; Revised 2 July 2003.

Mahmud, Wahiduddin.'Social Development: Pathways, Surprises and Challenges'. *Indian Journal of Human Development* 2/1 (2008), pp. 79–92.

Makeig, Douglas C. 'National Security', in James Heitzman and Robert Worden (eds). *Bangladesh: A Country Study* (Washington DC: Library of Congress, 1989), p. 241.

Maliyamkono, T. and F. Kanyangolo (eds). *When Political Parties Clash* (Dar-es-Salaam: Tema Publishers, 2003), p. 41.

Mamdani, Mahmood. 'Inventing Political Violence'. *Global Agenda* 2005, http:// www.globalagendamagazine.com/2005/mahmoodmamdani.asp (20 October 2005).

Maniruzzaman, Talukdar. *Group Interests and Political Changes, Studies of Pakistan and Bangladesh* (New Delhi: South Asia Publishers, 1982), p. 203.

Marshall, Monty G. 'Polity IV Project: Political Regime Characteristics and Transitions, 1800–2012'. INSCR Data Page, http://www.systemicpeace.org/inscr/inscr.htm.

Marx, Karl. 'Eighteenth Brumaire of Louis Bonaparte', in D. Fernbach (ed.). *Karl Marx: Surveys From Exile, Political Writings*, Vol. 2 (Harmondsworth: Penguin, 1974), p. 236.

McKinsey and Company. *Bangladesh's Ready-Made Garments Landscape The Challenge Of Growth* (Frankfurt: McKinsey and Company, November 2011), http://www. mckinsey.de/sites/mck_files/files/2011_McKinsey_Bangladesh.pdf.

Metcalf, Barbara Daly. 'Preface'. *Moral Conduct and Authority, The Place of Adab in South Asian Islam* (Berkeley: California University Press, 1984), p. viii.

Miles, William F. S. 'Political Para-theology Rethinking Religion, Politics and Democracy'. *Third World Quarterly* 17 (1996), pp. 525, 525–536.

Minister of Parliamentary Affairs. *Jatiya Sangsad Debate [Parliamentary Debate]*, 3(4), p. 209.

Mohaimen, Naeem. 'Shahbagh: The Forest of symbols', *Alal-O-Dulal*, 22 February 2013, http://alalodulal.org/2013/02/22/shahbagh-symbols/.

Molla, Gyasuddin. 'Democratic Institution Building Process in Bangladesh: South Asian Experience of a New Model of "Care-Taker Government" in a Parliamentary Framework'. *Heidelberg Papers in South Asian and Comparative Politics*. Working Paper no 3 (Heidelberg: South Asia Institute, University of Heidelberg, 2000).

Møller, Jørgen and Svend-Erik Skaaning. *Requisites of Democracy: Conceptualization, Measurement, and Explanation* (London: Routledge, 2011).

———. 'Regime Types and Democratic Sequencing'. *Journal of Democracy* 24/1 (2013), pp. 142–55.

———. 'The Third Wave: Inside the Numbers'. *Journal of Democracy* 24/4 (2013), pp. 97–109.

Moyser, G. 'Politics and Religion in the Modern World: An Overview', in G. Moyser (ed.). *Politics and Religion in the Modern World* (London: Routledge, 1991), p. 14.

Muhith, A. M. A. *Emergence of a New Nation* (Dhaka: Bangladesh Books International, 1978).

Murshid, Tazeen M. *The Sacred and the Secular, Bengali Muslim Discourses, 1871–1977* (Calcutta: Oxford University Press, 1995), p. 139.

Mushtaque, A. R. Chowdhury, Abbas Bhuiya, Mahbub Elahi Chowdhury, Sabrina Rasheed, Zakir Hussain, and Lincoln C Chen. 'The Bangladesh Paradox: Exceptional Health Achievement Despite Economic Poverty'. Bangladesh: Innovation for Universal Health Coverage 1. *Lancet*, Vol. 382, 23 November 2013, p. 1737.

Nasr, Seyyed Vali Reza, 'Islam, the State and the Rise of Sectarian Militancy in Pakistan' in Christophe Jaffrelot (ed.), *Pakistan: Nationalism without a Nation?* (New Delhi: Monohar, 2002), pp. 85–114.

Nathan, Andrew J. 'Authoritarian Resilience'. *Journal of Democracy* 14/1 (2003), pp. 6–17.

National Institute of Population Research and Training (NIPORT). *Bangladesh Demographic and Health Survey 2011* (Dhaka: NIPORT, 2012).

Naurath, Nicole. 'Religion, Secularism Working in Tandem in Bangladesh'. Gallup World, 29 July 2009, http://www.gallup.com/poll/121937/religion-secularism-working-tandem-bangladesh.aspx.

New Age. 'AG urges law enforcers to shoot at arsonists', 4 February 2015, http://newagebd.net/92335/ag-urges-law-enforcers-to-shoot-at-arsonists/#sthash.i4bZ5MjG.0JJ3BqDK.dpuf.

New York Times. 'Revolution Brings Bangladesh Hope', 9 December 1990, p. A4.

O'Donnell, Guillermo A. 'Delegative Democracy'. *Journal of Democracy* 5/1 (1994), pp. 55–69.

———. 'Democratic Theory and Comparative Politics'. *Studies in Comparative International Development* 36/1 (2001).

O'Donnell, Guillermo and Philippe Schmitter. *Transitions from Authoritarian Rule: Tentative Conclusions about Uncertain Democracies* (Baltimore: Johns Hopkins University Press, 1986), p. 9.

O'Neill, Jim. 'Beyond the BRICS: A Look at the "Next 11"'. *BRICs and Beyond* (New York: Goldman Sachs, 2007), http://www.goldmansachs.com/our-thinking/archive/BRICs-and-Beyond.html.

Odhikar. 'Total Extra Judicial Killings from 2001–2015'. Dhaka: Odhikar, http://1dgy051vgyxh41o8cj16kk7s19f2.wpengine.netdna-cdn.com/wp-content/uploads/2013/01/Statistics_EJK_2001–2015.pdf.

Ottaway. Marina. 'Promoting Democracy after Conflict: The Difficult Choices'. *International Studies Perspectives* 4/3 (2003), pp. 314–322.

Ovey, Michael. 'Victim Chic? The Rhetoric of Victimhood'. Cambridge Papers published by the Jubilee Center. 15/1 2006.

Panikkar, K. N. 'Identity & Politics'. *Frontline* 28/10 (2011).

Peiris, G. H. 'Political Conflict in Bangladesh'. *Ethnic Studies Report* 16/1 (1998), pp. 1–63.

Pew Global Attitudes Project. 'Iraqi Vote Mirrors Desire for Democracy in Muslim World'. 3 February 2005, http://www.pewglobal.org/2005/02/03/iraqi-vote-mirrors-desire-for-democracy-in-muslim-world/.

Pew Research Center. 'Views of the Changing World June 2003' (Washington, DC: The Pew Research Center For The People & The Press, 2003), pp. 7, http://www.people-press.org/files/legacy-pdf/185.pdf.

——. The Pew Global Attitudes Project. 'Iraqi Vote Mirrors Desire for Democracy in Muslim World'. 3 February 2005, http://www.pewglobal.org/2005/02/03/iraqi-vote-mirrors-desire-for-democracy-in-muslim-world/.

——. *Global Opinion Trends 2002–07:A Rising Tide Lifts Mood In The Developing World* (2007) Available at: www.pewglobal.org/files/pdf/257.pdf.

——. 'Global Opinion Trends 2002–2007: 47-Nation Pew Global Attitudes Survey'. Washington, DC: Pew Research Center, 24 July 2007, http://pewglobal.org/files/pdf/257.pdf.

——. 'Religion and Politics'. *The World's Muslim: Religion Politics, and Society.* Washington, DC: Pew Research Center, April 2013, http://www.pewforum.org/files/2013/04/worlds-muslims-religion-politics-society-full-report.pdf.

Pinheiro, Paulo Sergio. 'Democracy Without Citizenship: Democratization And Human Rights', http://www.nevusp.org/downloads/seminarios/france96/5–2-Paul.pdf accessed 20 November 2011.

Pirzada, Syed Sharfuddin. *Evolution of Pakistan* (Karachi: Royal Book Co, 1995).

Political Terror Scale (PTS), http://www.politicalterrorscale.org/countries.php?region=Eurasia&country=Bangladesh.

Preston, Peter. 'New order in Pakistan'. *Guardian*, 9 December 1970, p. 1, http://www.theguardian.com/theguardian/2010/dec/09/archive-karachi-bhutto-vote-1970.

Priyo.com. 'No democracy in Bangladesh yet: Noor Hossain's mother', 23 November 2011, http://news.priyo.com/story/2010/nov/23/12230-no-democracy-bangladesh-yet-noor-hossain%E2%80%99s-mother.

Prothim Alo. '"Crossfires" kill 64 in last three months', *Prothom Alo*, 31 March 2015, http://www.en.prothom-alo.com/bangladesh/news/62651/Crossfires-kill-64-in-last-three-months.

——. 'Awami Ulema League in communal politics', *Prothom Alo*, 10 August 2015, http://en.prothom-alo.com/bangladesh/news/74927/Awami-Ulema-League-in-communal-politics.

Przeworski, Adam M., Alvarez, Jose Antonio Cheibub, and Fernando Limongi. 'What Makes Democracies Endure?' *Journal of Democracy* 7/1 (1996), pp. 39–55.

Przeworski, Adam, Michael E. Alvarez, José Antonio Cheibub, and Fernando Limongi. *Democracy and Development: Political Institutions and Well-Being in the World, 1950–1990* (New York: Cambridge University Press, 2000).

Puhle, Hans-Jürgen. 'Democratic Consolidation and 'Defective Democracies'. Madrid: Universidad Autónoma de Madrid. Working Papers Online Series Working Paper 47/2005, http://portal.uam.es/portal/page/portal/UAM_ORGANIZATIVO/Departamentos/CienciaPoliticaRelacionesInternacionales/publicaciones percent20en percent20red/working_papers/archivos/47_2005.pdf.

Quandal. 'Bangladesh', http://www.quandl.com/bangladesh/bangladesh-economy-data.

Rabkin, Rhoda. 'The Aylwin Government and "Tutelary" Democracy: A Concept in Search of a Case?'. *Journal of Interamerican Studies and World Affairs* 34/4 (1992–92), pp. 119–194.

Rahim, A. M. A. 'A Review of Industrial Investment Policy in Bangladesh, 1971–1977', *Asian Survey*, 18/11 (1978), pp. 1181–1190.

Rahman, Sheikh Mujibur and Naimuddin Ahmed. *Purbo Pakistaner Durbhagha Jonoshadharan [The Unfortunate People of East Pakistan]* (Dhaka, 1948).

Raihan, Selim, Bazlul H. Khondker, Guntur Sugiyarto, and Shikha Jha. 'Remittances and Household Welfare: A Case Study of Bangladesh'. *ADB Economics Working Paper Series*, no. 189. Philippines: Asian Development Bank, 2009.

Rashid, Harun-ur. 'The Caretaker Conundrum'. *Daily Star*, 28 June 2006, p. 6.

Ratha, Dilip and Sanket Mohapatra. 'Increasing the Macroeconomic Impact of Remittances on Development'. Note prepared for the G8 Outreach Event on Remittances, Berlin. 28–30 November 2007.

Renan, Ernest. 'What is a Nation?' in Geoff Eley and Ronald Grigor Suny (eds). *Becoming National: A Reader* (New York and Oxford: Oxford University Press, 1996), pp. 41–55.

Reporters Without Borders. *World Press Freedom Index*. Various Years, http://en.rsf.org/press-freedom-index-2011–2012,1043.html.

Riaz, Ali. *God Willing: The Politics of Islamism in Bangladesh* (Lanham, MD: Rowman and Littlefield, 2004).

———. 'Beyond the 'Tilt': US Initiatives to Dissipate Bangladesh Movement in 1971'. *History Compass* 3 (2005).

———. *Unfolding State: The Transformation of Bangladesh* (Ontario, Canada: de Sitter Publication, 2005), pp. 170–74.

———. 'Interactions of "Transnational" and "Local" Islam in Bangladesh'. *Transnational Islam in South and Southeast Asia: Movements, Networks, and Conflict Dynamics* (Seattle, WA: National Bureau of Asian Research, 2009).

———. 'Dynastic Politics and the Political Culture of Bangladesh'. *Journal of International Relations* 8/II (2010), pp. 1–16.

———. 'Unpacking the Islamists Agenda'. *Forum*, April 2013, http://www.thedailystar.net/beta2/news/unpacking-the-islamist-agenda/.

Roy, Annaya. *Poverty Capital: Microfinance and the Making of Development* (New York: Routledge, 2011).

Roy, Asim. *The Islamic Syncretistic Tradition in Bengal* (Princeton: Princeton University Press, 1984).

Saha, Moloy. 'Ershad Wishes to Hold JP Rudder Until Death'. 26 July 2009, http://www.snnbd.com/newsdetails.php?cat_id=0.02&id=13886#.UnVA70rD_WN.

Sahliyeh, Emile. 'Religious Resurgence and Political Modernization', in Emile Sahliyeh (ed.). *Religious Resurgence and Politics in the Contemporary World* (New York: State University of New York Press. 1990), p. 3.

Salik, Siddiq. *Witness to Surrender* (New York: Oxford University Press, 1997).

Sammyabad (The underground party newsletter of the JSD), No.4. 23 February 1976.

Sartori, Giovanni. *Parties and Party Systems: A Framework for Analysis* (New York: Cambridge University Press, 1976).

———. *The Theory of Democracy Revisited* (London: Chatam House Publications, 1987).

Sayeed, Abu. *Bangladesher Swadhinata Judhyeir Arale Judhya [War Behind the Bangladesh Independence War]* (Dhaka: Sarif Ahmed, 1989).

Sayeed, Khalid Bin. 'Islam and National Integration in Pakistan', in D. E. Smith (ed.). *South Asian Religion and Politics* (Princeton: Princeton University Press, 1966), p. 408. Quoted in Murshid. *Sacred and Secular* (1995), p. 336.

Sayyid, Bobby S. *A Fundamental Fear: Eurocentrism and the Emergence of Islamism* (London: Zed Books, 1997).

Schaffer, Howard B. 'Back and Forth in Bangladesh'. *Journal of Democracy* 13/1 (2002), pp. 76–83.

Schedler, Andreas. 'Conceptualizing Accountability', in Andreas Schedler, Larry Diamond and Marc F. Plattner (eds). *The Self Restraining State: Power And Accountability In New Democracies* (Boulder, Co: Lynne Rienner, 1999), pp. 13–28.

———. 'The Menu of Manipulation'. *Journal of Democracy* 13/2 (2002), pp. 36–50.

Schmitter, Philippe C. 'Waves of Democratization', in Seymor Martin Lipset et al. (eds). *Encyclopedia of Democracy*, vol. 2 (London: Routledge), pp. 346–350.

Schuman, Howard. 'A Note on the Rapid Rise of Mass Bengali Nationalism in East Pakistan'. *American Journal of Sociology* 78/2 (1972), pp. 290–29.

Schumpeter, Joseph. *Capitalism, Socialism, and Democracy* (New York: Harper, 1975), pp. 242, 269.

SDSA Team. *State of Democracy in South Asia. A Report* (New Delhi: Oxford University Press, 2008).

Sen, Binayak, Mustafa K. Mujeri, and Quazi Shahabuddin. 'Explaining Pro-Poor Growth in Bangladesh: Puzzles, Evidence, and Implications', in Timothy Besley and Louise J. Cord (eds). *Delivering on The Promise of Pro-Poor Growth: Insights and Lessons from Country Experiences* (Washington, DC: World Bank and Palgrave Macmillan, 2007), pp. 79–118.

Sengupta, Somini. 'Bangladesh Leader Declares Emergency'. *New York Times*, 11 January 2007, http://www.nytimes.com/2007/01/11/world/asia/11cnd-bengla.html?_r=2&scp=1&sq=&.

Shastri, Sandeep. *Citizen Participation in the Democratic Process across South Asia.* Unpublished paper. Table 4. Paper based on the SDSA survey data.

SIPRI. *SIPRI Yearbook 1981* (Oxford: Oxford University Press, 1981).

Skocpol, Theda. *States and Social Revolutions: A Comparative Analysis of France, Russia and China* (Cambridge: Cambridge University Press, 1979).

Smith, Anthony. *Ethnic Origins of Nations* (New York: Oxford University Press, 1986).

———. 'Gastronomy or Geology? The Role of Nationalism in the Reconstruction of Nations'. *Nations and Nationalism* 1/1 (1994), pp. 3–23.

Smulovitz, Catalina and Enrique Peruzzotti. 'Societal Accountability in Latin America'. *Journal of Democracy* 11/4 (2000), pp. 147–158.

Sobhan, Rehman. *The Crisis of External Dependence, The Political Economy of Foreign Aid to Bangladesh* (Dhaka: University Press Limited, 1982), p. 7.

——— and Muzaffer Ahmad. *Public Enterprise in an Intermediate Regime, A Study in the Political Economy of Bangladesh* (Dhaka: Bangladesh Institute of Development Studies, 1980).

Suri, K. C., Peter R deSouza, Suhas Palshikar, and Yogendra Yadav 'Support for Democracy in South Asia'. Paper presented at Global Barometer Surveys Conference on 'How People View and value Democracy'. Institute of Political Science of Academia Sinica, Taipei 15–16 October 2010, Table 5.

Thornton, Hilary and Paul Thornton. 'Institutional Assessment of Education in Bangladesh'. Dhaka: British Council, March 2012, http://schoolsonline.britishcouncil.org/sites/default/files/files/Institutional%20Assessment%20of%20Education%20in%20Bangladesh.pdf.

Time. 'Pakistan: Prophet of Violence', 18 April 1969.

Transparency International. *Corruption Perception Index Report*. Various Years, http://www.transparency.org/research/cpi/overview.

Triphati, Salil. 'Bangladeshi Inquisitions'. *Himal*, Vol. 28, no. 3, 2015.

Uddin, Major Nasir. *Gonotontrer Biponnodharay Bangladesher Shoshosro Bahini* (Dhaka: Agamee Prakashani. 1997), p. 59.

Uddin, Sufia M. *Constructing Bangladesh: Religion, ethnicity, and language in an Islamic nation* (Chapel Hill; The University of North Carolina Press, 2006, Banu, Islam in Bangladesh).

Umar, Badruddin. *Towards the Emergency* (Dhaka: Muktadhara, 1980).

UNDP. *Elections in Bangladesh 2006–2009: Transforming Failure into Success* (Dhaka: UNDP, 2010).

Unicef ChildInfo. 'Child Survival and Health: Trends in Infant Mortality Rates, 1960–2012', http://www.childinfo.org/mortality_imrcountrydata.php.

Unicef. 'Bangladesh', 2013, http://www.unicef.org/infobycountry/bangladesh_bangladesh_statistics.html.

United Nations data, http://data.un.org/Data.aspx?d=MDG&f=seriesRowID%3A581, 2014.

United Nations. Ambassador Ema Sailor's Report of High-Level UN Consultants to Bangladesh, Vol. 1. March–April. Mimeograph (New York: United Nations, 1972).

USAID. Bangladesh: Knowledge, Attitudes and Practices, National Survey Covering Democracy and Governing Issues (Dhaka: USAID, 2004).

——— Global Health Bureau. 'Bangladesh Maternal Death Decline by 40 Percent in Less than 10 Years', 2011 http://blog.usaid.gov/2011/03/bangladesh-maternal-deaths-decline-by-40-percent-in-less-than-10-years/.

———. 'Bangladesh: Maternal Deaths Decline by 40 Percent in Less Than 10 Years'. 11 March 2011, http://blog.usaid.gov/2011/03/bangladesh-maternal-deaths-decline-by-40-per cent-in-less-than-10-years/.

US Department of Agriculture. Economic Research Service. 2013.

US Department of State (USDS). Foreign Relations of the United States, 1969–1976. Vol. XI, South Asia Crisis, 1971, Document 2. Available at National Archives, Nixon Presidential Materials, NSC Files, Box 625, Country Files, Middle East, Pakistan, Vol. IV, 1 Mar 71–15 May 71.

Vargas-Silva, Carlos, Shikha Jha, and Guntur Sugiyarto. 'Remittances in Asia: Implications for the Fight Against Poverty and the Pursuit of Economic Growth'. *ADB Economics Working Paper Series*, no. 182. Philippines: Asian Development Bank, 2009.

Viswanathan, Gauri. *Masks of Conquest: Literary Studies and British Rule in India* (New York: Columbia University Press, 1989).

Vivekananda, Franklin. 'Why Aid Does Not Work?' In Franklin Vivekananda (ed.). *Bangladesh Economy: Some Selected Issues* (Stockholm: Bethany Books, 1986), p. 324.

VOA. 'Bangladesh Bloggers Fear Threat from State', *VOA*, 11 September 2015, http://www.voanews.com/content/bangladesh-bloggers-fear-threat-from-the-state/2960088.html.

Weber, Max. 'Politics as Vocation', in John Dreijmanis (ed.). *Max Weber's Complete Writings on Academic and Political Vocation* (New York: Algora Publications, 2008), pp. 155–208.

World Bank. *Reconstructing the Economy of Bangladesh*. Vol. I and Vol. II (Washington DC: WB, 1972).

————. 'The Bangladesh Conundrum'. 2006, http://web.worldbank.org/WBSITE/ EXTERNAL/EXTABOUTUS/EXTANNREP/EXTANNREP2K6/0,,content MDK:21052781 ~ pagePK:64168445 ~ piPK:64168309 ~ theSitePK:28385 72,00.html.

————. *Bangladesh: Strategy for Sustained Growth*, Bangladesh Development Series, Paper no 18 (Dhaka and Washington: World Bank, 2007), p. 125, fn 145.

————. 'Bangladesh', 2014, http://data.worldbank.org/country/bangladesh.

————. 'South Asia'. *Global Economic Prospects 2014*, http://www.worldbank.org/en/ publication/global-economic-prospects/regional-outlooks/sar January 2014.

————. 'WB Update Says 10 Countries Move Up in Income Bracket', July 1, 2015, http://www.worldbank.org/en/news/press-release/2015/07/01/new-world-bank-update-shows-bangladesh-kenya-myanmar-and-tajikistan-as-middle-income-while-south-sudan-falls-back-to-low-income.

————. *Poverty and Equity*, http://povertydata.worldbank.org/poverty/region/SAS.

World Values Surveys Association (WVSA). *Values Change the World*. Stockholm: WVSA (2013), pp. 3, http://www.worldvaluessurvey.org/wvs/articles/folder_published/article_base_110/files/WVSbrochure6–2008_11.pdf.

Yasmin, Lailufar. 'Religion and After: Bangladeshi Identity Since 1971'. *Open Democracy*. 19 April 2013, http://www.opendemocracy.net/opensecurity/lailufar-yasmin/religion-and-after-bangladeshi-identity-since-1971.

INDEX

abduction/enforced disappearance, 148
ABT (Ansarullah Bangla Team), 103,
   105, 146
ACC (Anti-Corruption Commission),
   86, 87, 146
accountability, 145–6, 236
   lack of, 140, 142, 149, 158, 229
Adcock, Chris, 122
Afghanistan, 81, 164, 212
agriculture and farmers, 225, 228,
   229–30
Ahmad, Muzaffer, 20, 45
Ahmed, Iajuddin, 83–4, 129
Ahmed, Muzaffar, 48, 52, 162, 175,
   177, 178, 180
Ahmed, Rafiuddin, 187
Ahmed, Shahabuddin, 39, 77
Ahmed, Tajuddin, 29, 32, 33–5, 64, 65
Ahmed, Tofail, 34, 64, 169
AL (Awami League), 15, 16, 19, 105,
   107, 141, 153, 160, 207, 234
   1970 election, 24, 26
   1973 election, 52, 154
   1975 military dictatorship, 63
   1991 election, 76–7, 156
   2014 election, 101, 157
   alliances, 88, 102, 175–6, 177, 179,
      180–1, 183
   ban of, 28

BNP/AL rivalry, 78, 80, 82, 180
   fragmentation, 33–4, 41, 43–4,
      47, 166, 169, 170
   ideological orientation, 153, 162,
      164–5
   nationalism, 23–4
   radicals, liberals and conservatives,
      33–4, 43–4, 47
   'Six Point Demand', 16–17, 18,
      20–1, 22, 24, 25, 175
   success, 22
   working class, 21, 22
Alamgir, Jalal, 85, 86–7
All Party United Front, 176
Alvarez, Mike, 132
Anderson, Benedict, 10, 11
Anisuzzaman, 193
anjumans, 192, 196
APAC (All-Party Action Committee), 48
Appadurai, Arjun, 233
Arefin Dipon, Faisal, 105
ASK (Ain o Salish Kendra), 100,
   147, 148
atheism, 97, 105, 204, 207, 235
atheist bloggers, 104–8
   killing of, 97, 104–5, 106
   see also freedom of speech
authoritarianism, 4, 75, 132–3, 211, 212
   liberalized authoritarian regime, 133

socially-rooted authoritarianism, 140
  see also autocracy; military
  dictatorship; populist
  authoritarianism; regime
autocracy, 6, 38, 127, 133, 134,
  139, 149
  see also authoritarianism
Ayub Khan, Muhammed, 15, 19, 22,
  24, 174, 176
  'Decade of Development', 16
  removal of, 23
Azad, A. K., 41
Azad, Humayun, 105

BAL (Bangladesh Awami League),
  see AL
Ban Ki-moon, 84–5, 100
Bangladeshi state, 25–37
  formation of, 3, 4, 27–33, 37
  four state principles, 5, 49, 50, 55,
    71, 201
  see also Bengali nation
Barelvi, Syed Ahmed, 187
Baxter, Craig, 151
BDR (Bangladesh Rifles), 42, 50,
  88–9
Bengal Renaissance, 12, 189–90
Bengali (language), 12, 192–3, 196
  language movement: 15, 19,
    196–7
Bengali nation, 11–24, 190
  Bengali nationhood, 4, 10, 11, 12,
    14, 17
  class issues, 4, 12–14, 19–21, 23
  cultural heritage, 19, 198
  ethnicity, 15
  Hindu-majority West Bengal vs
    Muslim-majority East Bengal, 14
  nation-making process, 4, 10–11,
    12, 17, 23–4
  a political entity, 3
  religious issues, 4, 14, 15–16
  see also Bangladeshi state; national
    identity; partition of Bengal

Bengali nationalism, 10, 15, 23–4,
  155, 187, 197, 199–200,
  201, 207
  AL, 23–4
  bhadrolok nationalism, 12–13
  middle class, 19, 21, 24, 189–90,
    193, 198, 199, 200
  subordinate class's strand of
    nationalism, 13–14
Berger, Peter, 208
Bertocci, Peter J., 151, 162
BGB (Border Guard Bangladesh), 98,
  103
Bhaba, Homi, 12
bhadrolok (gentlemen), 12–13
Bhashani, Abdul Hamid Khan,
  Maulana, 15, 16, 23, 48, 162, 174,
  175, 176
Bhutto, Zulfiqar Ali, 25, 26, 27–8, 92,
  126, 175
Bijoy Das, Ananta, 105
BJI (Bangladesh Jamaat-e-Islami), *see* JI
BJL (Bangladesh Jatiya League), 163,
  175, 176
BJP (Bangladesh Jaitiya Party),
  161, 172
BJP (Bharatiya Janata Party), 209, 218
BKSAL (Bangladesh Krishak Sramik
  Awami League), 56, 57, 58, 63,
  169, 170, 173, 176, 178, 179
BLF (Bangladesh Liberation Force, later
  renamed Mujib Bahini), 26, 34
BLP (Bangladesh Labour Party), 176
BNP (Bangladesh Nationalist Party),
  72, 97, 140, 141, 155, 159–60,
  177, 234
  1979 election, 72
  1991 election, 76–7, 78, 156
  alliances, 80–3, 102, 146–7, 172,
    179, 180, 183, 215
  BNP/AL rivalry, 78, 80, 82, 180
  fragmentation, 169–71
  ideological orientation, 153, 163
  street violence, 99, 102–3

Bollen, Kenneth, 132
BPL (Bangladesh People's League), 177
BRAC (Bangladesh Rural Advancement Committee), 225–6, 229
Broomfield, John Hindle, 13
BSCF (Bangladesh Scheduled Caste Federation), 176
BSS (Biplobi Sainik Sangstha), 65–6, 69, 70

capitalism, 75, 163, 165
Carothers, Thomas, 132, 133
Casanova, Jose, 208
Charney, Craig, 213
Chasi, Mahbubul Alam, 63, 64, 66
Chatterjee, Niloy, 105
Chatterjee, Partha, 11, 199
Chatterji, Joya, 13
China, 21, 92, 164
Chowdhury, Badruddoza, 161, 180
Chowdhury, Salahuddin Quader, 99, 179
civil liberties, 7, 132, 133, 135, 136, 137–8, 139
civil society, 12, 77, 83, 84, 90, 100, 103, 211
    war crimes trials, 94
    see also NGO
civilian regime, 32–3, 40, 173
    elected civilian regime, 1, 2, 73, 77, 126, 140
Communist Party, Pakistan, 15, 21
Constitution, 232
    1972 Constitution, 2, 5, 49–50, 202
    1973 Part IXA, 52–3
    1975 Fourth Amendment, 54–6, 63, 76
    1977 Second Proclamation Order no. 1, 71–2
    1979 Fifth Amendment, 89
    1991 Eleventh Amendment, 77
    1996 Thirteenth Amendment, 78–9, 90–1
    2011 Fifteenth Amendment, 90–1, 234

CTG, 79, 90–1
    four state principles, 5, 49, 50, 55, 71, 201
    Islam, 2, 71–2, 73, 234
    secularism, 49, 71, 201, 203–204, 234
COP (Combined Opposition Parties), 179
COP (Combined Opposition Party), 174–5
corruption, 1, 221, 228–9, 232–3, 236
    campaign against, 86
    an indicator of the nature of democracy, 6, 135, 136–7
CPB (Communist Party of Bangladesh), 48, 98, 153, 162, 163–4, 172, 176–7
CSP (Civil Service of Pakistan), 41
CTG (Caretaker Government), 1, 39, 74, 76, 78–9, 80, 126, 128, 129
    2007 election, 84–5
    annulment of, 90–1, 96, 143, 157
    Constitution, 79, 90–1
    military-backed CTG, 85–7, 141

DAC (Democratic Action Committee), 175
Dahl, Robert, 111, 132
De, Dhurjati Prasad, 193
death penalty, 88, 91, 96, 98, 99, 107, 185
democracy, 3, 5–6, 232, 236
    an aspiration only, 1, 2, 108, 232
    definition, 6, 110–12, 115–16
    delegative democracy, 144
    democratic/autocratic hybrid regime, 6, 7, 149–50
    democratic quality, lack of, 6–7, 135, 137
    election, 6, 110, 117, 118, 119–22, 126
    essential attributes of, 110–11, 116–18

intra-party democracy, lack of, 7, 87,
    158, 184
nature of, 6–7, 126–39
in non-Western cultures, 115;
one of the four state principles, 5, 49,
    50, 55
political party, 112
quality of, 133–9
'third wave of democracy', 127, 133
wide support for, 6, 113–15,
    126, 149
see also the entries below for democracy;
    election; hybrid regime; political
    party
democracy, categories of, 134
    electoral democracy, 134, 135–6
    formal democracy, 111
    illiberal democracy, 133, 134
    inclusive democracy, 5, 39, 108, 231
    liberal democracy, 132, 134, 135,
        139, 164
    minimal democracy, 132
    minimalist democracy, 134
    polyarchy, 134
    substantive democracy, 111–12
democracy, indices on, 135, 136
    Amnesty International, 136, 139
    BNR, 135
    BTI, 135
    CID, 135
    CPI, 136–7
    Democracy Barometers projects, 135
    EIU, 135, 136, 137
    Freedom House, 135, 136, 139
    Polity IV database, 135, 136
    Reporters Without Borders,
        136, 137
    Vanhanen Index, 135
democracy, surveys on, 6, 113–26, 214
    British Council survey, 123
    BYS, 119, 120, 123
    CDL Survey, 119
    Daily Star–Nielsen survey, 125
    GBS 2010, 115–16

IFES, 118, 119, 120–1, 123, 124
IRI Opinion Poll, 120
PRCGS, 114, 115, 118, 124
SDSA, 114, 115, 116, 119, 120, 124,
    125, 126
USAID, 113, 114, 115, 116, 119,
    123, 125
WVS, 113, 114–15, 122, 124,
    125–6, 137
democratization, 6, 122, 127, 155
    binary/gradational model, 132, 134
    democratic transition, 88, 132, 133
    hybrid regime, 139–40
    regime in transition, 134
    stages of, 132
detention, 52, 86, 95, 106
    1974 Special Powers Act, 53
development, 3, 8, 219–30
    'Bangladesh Conundrum', 2, 220
    'Bangladesh Paradox', 2–3, 8, 220,
        230, 231
    context, 221
    'Development Puzzle', 2, 220
    economic growth, 2, 8, 219, 220,
        221–3, 231
    farmers, 225, 228, 229–30
    migrant workers, 225, 226–8,
        229–30
    NGO, 8, 225–6, 229
    social development, 8, 220, 223–4,
        225, 229, 231
    state, policy consistency of, 225
    success, 224–30
    women, 8, 225–6, 230
DGFI (Directorate General of Forces
    Intelligence), 79–80, 171
Diamond, Larry, 122, 127, 133, 134
DL (Democratic League), 163, 169,
    178, 181

Eaton, Richard, 194, 217
EBR (East Bengal Regiment), 31, 35
EC (Election Commission), 82–3, 84,
    87, 101, 104, 232

political parties registered, 112,
151–2
see also election
education, 2, 104, 223, 224, 229
FSSAP, 229
Islamic education/*madrassah*, 164,
182, 195, 205, 206
Western education and nationhood,
11–12
egalitarianism, 5, 58, 163, 194, 195,
197, 198, 217
election, 126–7, 154–6
1970, 4, 24, 25, 26
1973, 52, 154
1979, 72
1991, 76–7, 78, 155, 156
1995, 78
1996, 80, 156
2001, 156
2007, 84–5
2008, 88, 156
2014, 5, 7, 100–1, 127, 157
2015 city corporations election, 104
boycott, 74, 127, 130, 157
democracy, 6, 110, 117, 118,
119–22, 126
election as a form of empowerment,
121–2, 233
electoral democracy, 134, 135–6
electoralism, 122
fraud and rigging, 52, 101, 127, 130,
131, 232
free and fair election, 6, 77, 88, 110,
111, 127, 130–1, 135, 136, 139
majoritarianism, 144, 149–50, 189
referendum, 25, 72, 73, 77, 126, 130
voter participation, 6, 88, 109,
119–21, 126, 232
voters list, 82–3, 87
see also democracy; EC
EPCS (East Pakistan Civil Service), 41
EPIDC (East Pakistan Industrial
Development Corporation), 20
EPR (East Pakistan Rifles), 29, 35

equality, 2, 6, 12, 33, 111, 134, 163,
236
Ershad, Hussain Muhammad, 64, 84,
101–2, 159, 165, 171–2, 233
military dictatorship, 59, 73–5, 155
resignation, 39
Ershad, Rowshan, 101, 102, 161
EU (European Union), 85
Faraizi movement, 14, 190
Farook Rahman, Syed, 59, 61, 62, 64,
69–70
Fazlul Huq, Abul Kasem, 14–15,
174, 196
Fernandez-Taranco, Oscar, 100
FPTP (first-past-the-post) system, 232
Freedom House, 127, 134, 135,
136, 137
freedom of speech, 25, 104, 105,
107, 110, 116
Information and Communication Act,
104, 106, 107–108
see also atheist bloggers
Fukuyama, Francis, 164
GAL (Gano Azadi League), 163, 166,
177, 178, 180
Gandhi, Indira, 126
GD (Gonotontri Dal), 15, 16, 174
Giddens, Anthony, 209–10
globalization, 164, 209–10
GMP (Ganatantric Majdoor Party), 180
GOJ (Gono Oikya Jote), 177
Goldman Sachs, 220
governance, 1–2, 236
see also parliament; presidential
system
government
government-in-exile, 4, 32–4, 36,
37, 40, 64
governments since 1971, 128–9
policy consistency and development,
225
GP (Gonotontri Party), 179, 180

Grameen Bank, 225–6
Gramsci, Antonio, 140–1, 145
Grand Alliance, 84, 180–1, 183
guerrilla, 9, 36, 222

Hadden, Jeffry, 208
Haider, Ahmed Rajib, 104–5, 106
Hali, Altaf Hussain, 187
Hasan, Khondokar Mahmud, 82, 83
Hashmi, Tajul Islam, 191, 195–6
Hasina, Sheikh, 77, 80, 81, 96, 101,
    164–5, 169, 219
  'minus-two' formula, 87, 141
  nepotism, 161
  tutelary power, 141–2, 143, 159
health-related issues, 2, 223–4, 229
hegemony, 48, 192, 203, 206, 211,
    212, 218
  coercion, 145
  definition, 140–1
  lack of hegemony of the ruling class,
    139, 140–1, 145
HI (Hefazat-e-Islam), 97–9, 100, 105,
    106, 235
Hinduism, 194, 195, 205, 209, 210
Hossain, Kamal, 43–4, 93–4,
    169, 181
Hossain, Noor, 109, 150
Hroch, Mirolav, 12, 17, 35
HRW (Human Rights Watch),
    89, 95
HUJIB (Harkat-ul-Jihad al-Islami
    Bangladesh), 81, 82, 168
human dignity, 2, 33, 236
Huntington, Samuel 110, 111,
    127, 132
Huq, Nizamul, 95–6
Huzur, Hafezzi, 181–2
hybrid regime, 134, 139
  democratic/autocratic hybrid regime,
    6, 7, 149–50
  lack of hegemony of the ruling class,
    139, 140–1, 145
  transition process, 139–40

ICT (International Crimes Tribunal),
    91, 95–6, 97, 99, 185, 235
ICT Act, 91, 92, 94, 95, 97
  see also Liberation War (1971);
    war crimes
IDA (International Development
    Association), 229
IDBP (Industrial Development Bank of
    Pakistan), 20
IDL (Islamic Democratic League), 72,
    163, 181, 182
impunity, 64, 87, 148–9, 232
  Joint Drive Indemnity Act (2003),
    147
  violation of rule of law, 146–7, 235
independence, 1, 27–8
  declaration of, 28–32
  India, 9–10
  Mujibur Rahman, Sheikh, 27,
    28–30
  principles of an independent
    Bangladesh, 25–6
  proclamation of, 2, 32–3, 236
  Ziaur Rahman, 30–2
  see also Liberation War (1971)
India, 65, 209, 210, 218
  Bangladesh's independence, 9–10
  India–Pakistan War (1971), 9–10,
    30–1, 36–7
  tripartite agreement between
    Bangladesh, Pakistan and India,
    92, 93
inequality, 8, 223, 230, 236
intolerance, 234, 236
Inu, Hasanul Huq, 159, 178, 180
IOJ (Islami Oikya Jote), 80–1, 153,
    164, 166, 173, 179, 180, 182
Iqbal, Muhammad, 187
Iranian Revolution, 164, 212
Islam, 233
  arrival and expansion in Bengal,
    193–5, 217
  in the Constitution, 2, 71–2,
    73, 234

global/regional factors supporting
  Muslim identity salience, 207–13
Islamic education/*madrassah*, 164,
  182, 195, 205, 206
Muslim identity, 7–8, 186–7,
  189–93, 195–6, 203, 206,
  213, 233
Muslim nationhood, 188
Pakistan, 15–16, 198
personal religiosity, 190, 199, 214,
  215, 216, 235
political ideology, 2, 72, 75, 192,
  217, 233, 235
in the public sphere, 2, 164–5,
  205–206, 215–16, 217
religion-as-aim/religion-as-reason,
  195–6
state religion, 2, 63, 73, 155, 164,
  206, 234
see also Islamism; religion
Islamic Constitution Movement, 182
Islamic Development Bank, 205
Islamism, 2, 5, 86, 212
anti-blasphemy law, 98, 104, 107,
  108
attacks/killings by Islamists, 81–2,
  97, 99–100, 105–6, 235
Bangladesh as Islamic state, 63, 81,
  165, 167, 168
Islamist parties, 81, 153, 155,
  165–6, 167–8, 172–3, 181,
  184, 216
Islamization, 71–2, 165, 193, 205,
  206, 234
issue-based alliances, 182–3
rise of, 78, 81, 163, 164, 211, 234

JAGPA (Jatiya Ganatantrik Party), 182
Janadal, 169, 178
Jawed, Nasim A., 200, 214
JF (Jatiyatabadi Front), 177
JI (Jamaat-e-Islami), 42, 72, 73, 78, 81,
  88, 101, 103, 106, 156
alliances, 181

election, 165
fragmentation, 172–3
ideological orientation, 153, 162
war crimes, 91, 92, 94–7, 99–100,
  185
Jinnah, Fatemah, 175
Jinnah, Muhammad Ali, 175, 193,
  196, 198
JJP (Jatiya Janata Party), 164, 166, 177
JMB (Jamaat-ul-Mujahideen
  Bangladesh), 81, 82, 168
JMJB (Jagrata Muslim Janata
  Bangladesh), 81
JP (Jatiya Party), 74, 80, 98, 101–2,
  140, 156, 160, 178, 234
fragmentation, 171–2
ideological orientation, 153, 165
JP Morgan, 220
JRB (Jatiya Rakkhi Bahini), 50–2, 63
JSD (Jatiyo Samajtantrik Dal), 47–8,
  66, 67, 70, 153, 162, 169, 172
Gonobahini, 54, 70

Kamal, Ahmed, 195, 195
Kamruzzaman, 35, 64, 99
Kant, Emmanuel, 11
Karl, Terry, 140
Khan, Ataur Rahman, 163, 175
Khan, Syed Ahmed, 187
Khondoker, Abdur Rashid, 59, 61,
  62, 64
Khilafat-Non Cooperation Movement,
  191
killing:
  atheist bloggers, killing of, 97,
    104–105, 106
  attacks/killings by Islamists, 81–2,
    97, 99–100, 105–6, 235
  extrajudicial killing, 100, 103, 139,
    146–8
  political killing, 49, 65, 103
  Special Powers Act (1974), 53
Kinnvall, Catarina, 210
Kissinger, Henry, 27, 61–2

Kochanek, Stanley, 144, 162
KPP (Krishak Praja Party), 14–15, 174
KSP (Krishak Sramik Party), 174, 178

Larma, Manabendra Narayan, 202, 203
Latin America, 142
LDP (Liberal Democratic Party), 84, 180, 181
leadership, 123, 141, 232
  concentration of power in political leader, 158, 159–60
  'dynastic' succession of party leadership, 7, 142, 158, 159, 161, 184
  patrimonialism, 143–4, 149, 162, 232
  tutelary power, 142–4
  without democratic restraints, 6, 125–6, 149
Left Democratic Front, 179–80
Liberation War (1971), 9–10, 30–1, 35–7, 40
  India, 9–10, 30–1, 36–7
  loss caused by, 42
  reconstruction after, 42–3
  tripartite agreement between Bangladesh, Pakistan and India, 92, 93
  see also independence; war crimes
Linz, Juan, 132
Lipset, Seymour, 112

Maalouf, Amin, 233
Macaulay, Thomas Babington, 13
Mahapatra, Sanket, 227
Mahmud, Wahiduddin, 223
mass uprisings
  1966, 22, 26, 175
  1969, 22–3, 26
  1990, 38–9, 74–5
  2006, 83–4
MDG (Millennium Development Goals), 224, 229

media, 95–6
  Amar Desh, 95–6, 97, 98, 105, 107
  Newspapers Ordinance (1975), 56, 63
  Printing Presses and Publication Ordinance (1973), 53
  state-controlled media, 19, 49, 52, 56
MENA (Middle East and North Africa), 211
migrant workers, 225, 226–8, 229–30
  remittances, 227
Miles, William, 211
military, 41, 68
  factionalism and rivalries, 35–6, 41–2, 60, 64
  military-backed CTG, 85–7, 141
  Operation Searchlight, 28, 35
  positive view of, 124
  resentments within, 59–60, 88
  see also military dictatorship
military dictatorship, 5, 16, 58, 59–75, 126, 128, 140, 155, 212
  changes in military bureaucracy, 64
  coup (1975), 59–67
  Islam as state religion, 59, 63, 71–2, 73, 75
  manipulation of constitutional processes, 59, 63, 71, 72, 73
  mutiny and execution, 66–7, 69–71
  views on military rule, 114, 124–6
  see also Ayub Khan, Muhammed; Ershad, Hussain Muhammad; military; Ziaur Rahman
ML (Muslim League), 15, 16, 162, 192, 197, 198
  war crimes, 91, 92
Mollah, Abdul Quader, 96, 99, 100, 185
Moni, Sheikh, 34, 35
Mujibur Rahman, Sheikh, 19, 24, 37, 126, 197, 205
  Agartala Conspiracy Case, 22, 23
  arrest, 31, 175
  death, 58, 61–2, 63, 64

independence of Bangladesh, 27, 28–30
'Mujibism', 47
non-cooperation movement, 10, 26
a populist leader, 39, 52
President of Bangladesh, 32–3, 55, 56–8
war crimes trials, 91, 93–4
see also AL; populist authoritarianism
Mukti Bahini (The Liberation Force), 35, 41
Murshid, Tazeen M., 193, 197, 204
Musharraf, Khaled, 35–6, 60, 64, 65, 66
Mushtaq Ahmed, Khondoker, 34–5, 62, 163, 169, 178
President, 63, 64–5, 66, 89
Muslim Shahitya Samaj, 193

NAP (National Awami Party), 16, 21, 48, 52, 162–3, 174–5, 176–7
Nasim, Abu Saleh Muhammad, 79–80
Nathan, Andrew J., 133
nation:
making of the nation, 11–12
'political entity/cultural entity' debate, 11
see also Bengali nation; national identity; nationalism
national identity, 17, 186, 187, 218, 233
Bangladeshi/Bengali dichotomy, 206, 207
Bengali ethnic identity, 3, 8, 10, 11, 186, 193, 196, 198–9, 202–3, 207, 233
contestation between secular/Muslim identity, 7–8, 186, 196–7, 218, 233
'deadly identities'/'predatory identities', 233
ethnic minorities, 21, 202–3, 207
historical lineage, 187–207, 233

identity politics, 186, 187, 189, 192, 197, 233
Muslim/Bengali combined identities, 193, 196, 198, 200
Muslim identity, 7–8, 186–7, 189–93, 195–6, 203, 206, 213, 233;
Pakistan, 15–16, 187, 196, 198, 201
religious identity, 163, 186, 188, 197, 198, 200–1, 209, 212, 213, 233, 234
secularism, 199, 200, 201, 203–4, 218, 233
see also Bengali nationalism; identity
nationalism, 11, 23–4
religious nationalism, 197, 210
see also Bengali nationalism
nationalization, 22, 39, 44–6
denationalization, 68–9
natural disaster, 8, 54, 220, 221, 222, 231
Nazrul Islam, Syed, 33, 64, 65, 128, 203
NDF (National Democratic Front), 174
NDI (National Democratic Institute, US), 83
NF (Nationalist Front), 176
NGO (non-government organization), 8, 225–6, 229
see also civil society
NHRC (National Human Rights Council), 146
NI (Nizam-e-Islam Party), 15, 167, 174, 175
Nirmul Committee, 94
Nixon, Richard, 27, 37
non-cooperation movement, 4, 10, 26, 78
NUF (National United Front), 178
Nurul Islam, 18–19

O'Donnell, Guillermo, 111, 133, 144
ODA (Official Development Assistance), 227

Odhikar, 107, 147–8

OIC (Organization of Islamic Cooperation), 165

Osmani, Muhammad Ataul Gani, 33, 35, 36, 64, 66, 166, 177, 181

Ottaway, Marina, 133

Pakistan, 3, 193
  Constitution (1956), 16
  East/West Pakistan disparity, 17–18, 20
  Islam, 15–16, 198
  national identity, 15–16, 187, 196, 198, 201
  Pakistani nationhood, 201
  tripartite agreement between Bangladesh, Pakistan and India, 92, 93
  united Pakistan, 4, 20
  Urdu, 12, 192, 193, 196, 197

paramilitary force, 17, 42, 48, 50, 57, 68, 88, 91, 145

parliament, 1, 54–5, 113, 124, 126
  dissolution of, 78
  parliamentary election, 126–7, 130–1, 154
  parliamentary system, 1, 76–7, 128, 129, 144, 154
  sovereignty of, 55
  Westminster-type parliamentary system, 1, 49–50, 91

partition of Bengal:
  1905, 13–14, 188, 190, 191
  1947, 15, 192, 196
  see also Bengali nation

party system, 7, 154–7
  alliances, 7, 155, 173–84
  changes, 7, 155, 184
  dominant party system, 7, 154–5, 156–7, 184
  fragmentation and factionalism, 7, 151, 155, 165, 166, 168–73, 184
  multi-party system, 128, 129, 133, 154, 155, 163, 184

one-party system, 56, 128, 140, 155, 176, 177, 184
  potential scenarios, 157
  two-party system, 156, 177, 179, 184, 232
  see also political party

Payne, Robert, 29

PDM (Pakistan Democratic Movement), 175

PICIC (Pakistan Industrial Credit and Investment Corporation), 20

Pinheiro, Paulo Sergio, 140

PML (Pakistan Muslim League), 174

polarization, 4, 5, 7, 177, 234–6

political dissidence, repression of, 49, 51, 107, 232

political party, 7, 112, 232–3
  centrist parties, 163
  common characteristics and ethos, 158–62
  'dynastic' succession of party leadership, 7, 142, 158, 159, 161, 184
  ideological orientation, 153, 174
  interest in politics, 123, 151
  intra-party democracy, lack of, 7, 87, 158, 184
  Islamist parties, 81, 153, 155, 165–6, 167–8, 172–3, 181, 184, 216
  leadership and concentration of power, 158, 159–60
  left-leaning parties, 162–3, 164–5, 172, 176, 179, 183, 184
  negative view of, 122–3
  nepotism, 158, 161, 184
  overabundance of, 112–13, 151–2, 184
  patrimonialism, 143–4, 149, 162, 232
  religion-based parties, 72, 163, 165, 216, 234

rightwing/conservative parties, 7, 162–5
see also party system
political violence,
2013, 98–100
2015, 102–4, 149, 219
population, 1, 224, 236
populist authoritarianism, 5, 39–58, 126
challenges faced by, 39–43, 50
coercive measures, 50–3, 54–5,
economic and political crises, 46–7, 50, 54
law and order deterioration, 49
nationalization, 39, 44–6
political dissidence, 49, 51, 52, 56
'Second Revolution', 56–7, 58
see also authoritarianism; Mujibur Rahman, Sheikh
PPP (Pakistan People's Party), 25, 27, 175
PPR (Political Parties Regulations), 72
presidential system, 1, 76, 128, 129, 154
press freedom, 7, 135, 136, 137
privatization, 68–9
Przeworski, Adam, 110, 135
pseudo-military regime, 1, 75, 126
Puhle, Hans-Jürgen, 142

RAB (Rapid Action Battalion), 98, 102, 103, 145, 148
Raghavan, Srinath, 93
Rahman Babu, Washiqur, 105
Rahman, Naziur, 161, 172
Rahman, Tareq, 82, 87, 103, 161
Raihan, Selim, 227
RAW (Research and Analysis Wing), 34
refugee, 1, 37, 39, 43
regime, 3, 128–9
four-fold typology of, 132–3
see also authoritarianism; civilian regime; democracy; hybrid regime

religion, 234
causes of the return of religion to the public domain, 207–13
popular religion, 217
religion-based parties, 72, 163, 165, 216, 234
religious identity, 163, 186, 188, 197, 198, 200–1, 209, 212, 213, 233, 234
religious nationalism, 197, 210
surveys on, 214–16
see also Hinduism; Islam; Islamism
Renan, Ernest, 3–4
RMG (ready-made garments), 226
Roy, Asim, 217
Roy, Avijit, 105, 106
rule of law, 110, 111, 117, 134, 236
impunity as violation of, 146–7, 235
as indicator of the nature of democracy, 7, 135, 136, 138, 139

Sahliyeh, Emile, 211
Sartori, Giovanni, 132
Sattar, Abdus, 73, 169, 176
Sayeed, Khalid Bin, 200
Sayeedi, Delwar Hossain, 95, 99, 170
Sayem, Abu Sadat Mohammad, 65, 66, 67–8, 89
SCF (Sector Commanders Forum), 94
Schanberg, Sydney 29
Schedler, Andreas, 133
Schmitter, Philippe C., 133
Schuman, Howard, 200
Schumpeter, Joseph, 110, 111
secularism, 23–4, 75, 185–6, 211
in the Constitution, 49, 71, 201, 203–4, 234
contestation between secular/ Muslim identity, 7–8, 186, 196–7, 218
drift towards secular culture, 199
middle class, 199, 200

national identity and, 199, 200, 201, 203–204, 218, 233
secular state, 2, 5, 211, 218, 234
secularization, 204, 218, 234
Western models of, 204
Sen Gupta, Jyoti, 31
Shafiullah, Kazi Mohammad, 35–6, 59–60
Shahbagh movement, 96, 97–8, 99, 104, 182, 186, 235
Sikdar, Siraj, 48, 163, 183
SKSD (Sramik Krishak Samajbadi Dal), 178, 180
Smith, Anthony, 11, 23
Sobhan, Rehman, 20, 23, 45
social justice, 33, 163, 211, 236
socialism, 26, 44, 45–6, 47–8, 49, 163, 165, 214
Sommilita Sangram Parishad (Combined Action Committee), 182
Soviet Union, 37, 132, 162, 164, 172, 212
SP (Sarbahara Party), 48, 163, 183
student activistm/organizations, 22–3, 25, 38, 47, 48, 74, 177–8
Sufism, 194, 195, 217
Suhrawardy, Huseyn Shaheed, 15, 16, 174, 196
Supreme Court, 56, 65, 75, 82, 97, 99, 182
annulling Constitution's amendments, 89–91
Suttner, Raymond, 155, 157
Swaraj Party, 14

Tagore, Rabindranath, 19, 26
Taher, Abu, 36, 60–1, 65–6, 67, 69, 70, 90
the Taliban, 81, 212
Tariqah-i-Muhammadiya, 14, 190
Tarkabagish, Abdur Rashid, 166
Thakur, Taheruddin, 63
TI (Transparency International), 136, 221

TIB (Transparency International Bangladesh), 100

Ulema Front, 181
UN (United Nations), 84–5
Bangladesh and UN Peace Keeping Missions, 220
UNDP (UN Development Program), 2, 224
United Front, 15, 16, 174
UNROB (UN Relief Organization in Bangladesh), 42, 43
UPP (United People's Party), 163, 164, 176, 178
US (United States), 37, 61, 212–13

Vanhanen, Tatu
Vanhanen Index, 135
Vargas-Silva, Carlos, 227
Venezuela, 140
Von Herder, Johann Gottfried, 11

Waliullah, Shah, 187
war crimes, 91–7, 235, 236
genocide, 1, 4, 9, 91, 92, 201
trials, 92–4, 95–7, 99, 157, 185, 186, 235
see also Liberation War (1971); ICT
Ware, Alan, 154–5
weapons, 39, 42–3, 50, 51, 61, 66, 67, 70, 147
Weber, Max, 112
Whitten, Howard, 29, 30, 31–2
women, 1, 49, 98
role in development, 8, 225–6, 230
World Bank, 39–40, 43, 212, 219, 220, 221
WP (Workers Party), 159, 178, 179
WVS (World Values Survey), 113, 114–15, 122, 124, 125, 137, 214

Yahya Khan, Agha Muhammad, 23, 24, 25, 27, 28
Yakatan, Nicole, 213

Zafar, Kazi, 164, 171, 172
Zafarullah, Habib M., 177
Zia, Khaleda, 77, 78, 98, 101, 103,
    169
  'minus-two' formula, 87, 141, 170
  nepotism, 161
  tutelary power, 141–2, 143, 159
Ziauddin, Ahmed, 95, 96
Ziauddin, Colonel, 36

Ziaur Rahman, 65, 66, 176, 233
  Liberation War (1971), 35–6
  death, 73
  declaration of independence, 30–2
  military dictatorship, 59, 62,
    67–71, 75
  opposition against, 70–1, 72–3;
    see also military dictatorship
Zoellick, Robert, 220